"The English tung is of smaii reach, stretching no further than this island of ours, nay not there over all; yet I do not think that anie language, be it whatsoever, is better able to utter all arguments, either with more pith or greater planesse, than our English tung is ... It is our accident which restrains our tung and not the tung itself, which will strain with the strongest and stretch to the furthest, for either government if we were conquerers, or for cunning if we were treasurers, not any whit behind either the subtile Greeke for couching close, or the statelle Latin for spreding fair."

—Roger Mulcaster
Elementarie, 1582

"You know I say nothing to him, for hee understands not me, nor I him: hee hath neither Latine, French, nor Italian ... and I have a poore pennieworth in the English ... Hee is a proper man's picture, but alas, who can converse with a dumbe show?"

—Merchant of Venice
1, 2, 72

"To sum up: The English language is a methodical, energetic business-like and sober language, that does not care much for finery and elegance, but does care for logical consistency and is opposed to any attempt to narrow-in life by police regulation and strict rules either of grammar or lexicon. As the language is, so also is the nation ... One need not be a great prophet to predict that in the near future the number of English-speaking people will increase considerably. It must be a source of gratification to mankind that the tongue spoken by two of the greatest powers of the world is so noble, so rich, so pliant, so expressive and so interesting."

—Otto Jespersen
Growth and Structure of
the English Language, 1905

The Spread of English

THE SOCIOLOGY OF ENGLISH AS AN ADDITIONAL LANGUAGE

The Spread of English

THE SOCIOLOGY OF ENGLISH AS AN ADDITIONAL LANGUAGE

Joshua A. Fishman
Robert L. Cooper
Andrew W. Conrad

NEWBURY HOUSE PUBLISHERS, INC. / ROWLEY / MASS.

Library of Congress Cataloging in Publication Data

Main entry under title

The Spread of English

    1. English language--Study and teaching--
Foreign students.   2. English language--
Social aspects.
I. Fishman, Joshua A. II. Cooper, Robert
Leon, 1931-   . III. Conrad, Andrew W.

PE1128.A2S68   401   77-110-68
ISBN 0-88377-087-3

Cover design by *VINCA*; acknowledgment to *Computer Graphics*,
     Melvin L. Pruett. New York: Dover. 1975.

NEWBURY HOUSE PUBLISHERS, Inc.

Language Science
Language Teaching
Language Learning

ROWLEY, MASSACHUSETTS 01969

Printed in the U.S.A.   First printing: September 1977
                    5   4   3   2   1

To those speech-and-writing-communities utilizing "small languages" that have already learned to live creatively in the company of "the mighty," and, even more, to those still learning how to do so.

Contents

Preface and Acknowledgments

This volume brings together many features and emphases which are more usually accorded separate treatment. While addressed to a matter of great practical importance, the role of English in the non-English mother-tongue world, it nevertheless moves ahead two topics of great theoretical significance for the sociology of language (and, perhaps, for the language sciences as a whole): the study of language maintenance—language shift and the study of language attitudes. While necessarily international in scope it recognizes the need to confirm and refine worldwide processes via local studies. While topically focused, this volume not only is methodologically diversified (employing experimental, field and documentary analyses in order to escape from that artifactual reliability of findings that stems from methodological monism) but methodologically innovative in some respects as well. Finally, this volume is interdisciplinary in nature in that it derives its talents, its hypotheses and its methods from an array of language sciences. The multifaceted nature of this volume will make it more valuable for the great variety of students, teachers, researchers, administrators and policy makers throughout the world who are concerned with the role of English on the one hand, and with the language sciences on the other.

For their help in literally making this volume possible Robert Cooper, Andrew Conrad and I wish to thank Mel Fox, Elinor Barber and Margorie Martus of the Ford Foundation; our various associates and assistants; the School of

Education of the Hebrew University in Jerusalem for ample computer time; and the Institute for Advanced Study in Princeton for handsomely typing the final manuscript.

The many, lovely months of quiet, hard work that I devoted to this volume during my 1975-76 stay at the Institute were rendered especially enjoyable and productive by the encouragement of Clifford Geertz, Albert Hirschman and Carl Kaysen, on the one hand, and by the cheerful assistance of Amy Jackson, Catharine Rhubart and Rebecca Szurovy, on the other hand. To all of them, my heartfelt thanks.

Finally, to the International Division of the Ford Foundation, which has supported a good bit of worldwide sociolinguistic research during the past dozen years, I want to express my hope that it will not only find this study to be of merit but that it will continue to advance the language sciences for the benefit of mankind.

Joshua A. Fishman

Institute for Advanced Study
Princeton, New Jersey
June 1976

The
Spread of
English

THE
SOCIOLOGY
OF
ENGLISH
AS
AN
ADDITIONAL
LANGUAGE

PART ONE

*International Perspective
on English*

Chapter 1

English as a World Language: The Evidence

Andrew W. Conrad
and
Joshua A. Fishman

OUTLINE

1.0   Introduction

2.0   English as an Official Language

1.2.1*   Non-English mother-tongue countries having English designated as an official language
1.2.2   Non-English mother-tongue countries in which there is some official status for English, but in which English is not designated as official

3.0   English in Education

3.1   Primary and Secondary Education

1.3.1   Percentage of school age population attending school (at any level), 1960 and 1970, by age and by area of the world
1.3.2   Number of students in primary and secondary English classes, with percentage of total enrollment, by area of the world

---

Table number: chap. 1, sec. 2, no. 1.

1.0 INTRODUCTION

The traveler returning to the United States from a vacation trip in Africa, Europe or Asia is often heard to comment that nearly everyone he met seemed to be able to speak at least some English. To such impressionistic accounts of the ubiquity of English as a world language, one might also add the clearly partisan evaluations of its importance as a lingua franca offered by the promoters of English. We are concerned here rather to present whatever evidence there may be as to the extent of English in non-English mother-tongue countries by discussing (a) its role as a diplomatic and official language, (b) its place in primary and secondary education, (c) the proportion of tertiary level foreign students studying in English mother-tongue countries from non-English mother-tongue countries, (d) the English-language press, and (e) the publication of books in English. Thus, this chapter represents an attempt to go beyond the *impression* that "English is everywhere" to some of the *evidence* which can either substantiate or modify that claim. Where is English promoted by governmental policy and where is its use discouraged? How do the majority of people in non-English mother-tongue countries learn English? How widespread is the English-language press? In which non-English mother-tongue countries are English-language books published? How large a part of total book publishing does this number represent? What proportion of tertiary level foreign students from non-English mother-tongue countries study in English mother-tongue countries? The evidence is addressed to these questions; it may also provide some tentative answers to broader questions about second-language use. Where our evidence does not carry us far enough to provide answers, it will at least point to the kinds of data that make the questions answerable in the future.

English is known by some persons in virtually every country in the world. Samarin has noted, "English . . . already meets many of the requirements of a true world *lingua franca*." (Samarin 1962, p. 73) It is *the* language of diplomacy,[1] the predominant language in which mail is written,[2] the principal language of aviation[3] and of radio broadcasting,[4] the first language of nearly 300 million people, and an additional language of perhaps that many more.[5]

The information collected here represents a compilation, collation, and refinement of data primarily from published sources on English in countries where no significant portion of the population speaks English natively. We have therefore excluded English mother-tongue countries from consideration as thoroughly as possible.[6] In comparing English with another language of wider communication, French, we have excluded, as well, the French mother-tongue countries from the French figures. (See Section 4.2 on book production)

In many countries not included in our list of English mother-tongue countries, there are communities of predominantly English-speaking persons, especially in former British colonies where an English "presence" has been long established (e.g., Rhodesia, South Africa, and India). These communities include third and fourth generation first-language speakers of English who are now developing a self-consciously distinct linguistic identity from other parts of the

English-speaking world. This linguistic self-consciousness has been associated with the growth of indigenous literatures. Some groups concerned with the promotion of English in the world have viewed this development with a certain degree of alarm; others have welcomed it as a sign that English, as a language of wider communication, manifests in this development just the sort of adaptability which makes it the primary candidate for a universal international language role. Whatever the interpretation, there is a growing literature in new varieties of a language that already has several long-recognized literary varieties. India, which has over 18 million "English-knowing bilinguals" (Kachru 1975a) reveals striking evidence of what has been termed "Indian English."[7] Charles Larson of American University lists numerous volumes of poetry and other general literary works written in non-English mother-tongue countries in Africa and reflecting local varieties of English (*English Around the World* 9:4ff., Nov. 1973). Ramchand (1970) presents a full discussion of the West Indian novel, written in still another variety of English. Mother-tongue dialect varieties of English are of course numerous; the development of several of these distinctive varieties for literary use is yet another indication of the continued functional and structural growth of the language.[8]

This effort to bring together exhaustive library and archival information regarding the place of English in non-English mother-tongue countries has both confirmed and refined earlier claims that English is the major language of wider communication and the primary natural language candidate for an international language in the world today. It has discovered widespread growth in the learning and diverse use of English coupled with a growth in the development of indigenous languages and literatures. English is to be found "at home," if you will, in diverse cultural settings, functioning peacefully alongside local languages as well as many other languages of wider communication. While the continued growth in public education in local languages may be producing a decline in the use of English-medium schooling at the lower educational levels, English is still growing as a subject of instruction and as a major vehicle of higher education and of publication on a worldwide basis.

The likelihood is that these trends will continue at least into the foreseeable future so that when and if this kind of study is updated in the future, as it should be, the picture may well be different in some specifics (the numbers will, no doubt, be larger overall), but the general picture will probably remain the same for quite a while.

2.0 ENGLISH AS AN OFFICIAL LANGUAGE

While the 152 nations of the world listed by Banks (1975) share among them-selves at least 75 official languages,[9] English, French, Spanish, and Arabic alone account for about 95 countries. In all, as of January 1, 1975, English was the sole "designated" official language[10] of some 21 countries, and the designated co-official language of some 16 more. (These totals include the 12 English mother-tongue countries listed in note 6. Table 1.2.1 excludes them and therefore lists only 25 countries.) Of the 16 countries recognizing more than one official language, 11 recognize a local language or languages alongside English, 2 recognize another language of wider communication alongside English (Canada and Cameroon, in both cases French), 2 recognize both another language of wider communication and a local language alongside English (Namibia and Philippines), and 1 (Tanzania) recognizes English and Swahili, which, though a local language in some sense, is now also becoming more than that in its spread in Africa.

There are a number of problems in any discussion of English as an official language. First is the question of criteria. What indeed constitutes "official"? Banks (1975) does not say what his criteria are. One might wonder why he does not include Kenya, for example, or Malaysia. In July, 1974, Kenya committed herself to a policy of implementing Swahili as the official language of government, legislative and administrative (Scotton, 1975*a*, p. 6). However, the problems of replacing English jurisprudential terms, or of replacing English administrative records, are enormous, and in fact the actual *practice* of the government has not yet changed significantly. If "official language" is taken to refer primarily to national policy, Kenya, indeed, has a policy of implementing Swahili as the official language and ought not be included among those countries where English is an official language. In practice, however, English continues to fulfill many official functions. Following Fisherman and Fishman (1975, pp. 497-498) we will use "official language" also to mean "one which is used by the government for its own internal operations and promoted through the power of the state." Kenya, then, as well as Malaysia, is listed in Table 1.2.2 among those countries in which English is an official language, since our definition includes both policy (those listed in Table 1.2.1) and practice (those listed in Table 1.2.2).

This broad definition includes the variety of different uses to which particular countries may put their "official" languages, whether the recording of laws, the conduct of parliamentary debate, administrative record keeping, or the operation of the courts. The particular meaning of the word "official" will vary from country to country, and it is these meanings we have attempted to indicate in Tables 1.2.1 and 1.2.2.

Table 1.2.1 includes, first of all, those countries listed by Banks (1975) as having English as one of the official languages (excluding here the twelve English mother-tongue countries listed in note 6), apparently on the single criterion of national *policy*. Following this list, which is marked "designated" in our table, we have listed several other countries whose policy does not designate English as official but in which English plays "official" roles in ways which fit our *practice* definition. (Table 1.2.2)

Listed among those countries which do not actually designate English as an official language are those which, through their constitutions, make mention of English as a *permitted* language in certain aspects of their official life. The Sudanese constitution, for example, declares that parliamentary proceedings "shall be conducted in Arabic without prejudice to such use of the English language as may be convenient." (Peaslee 1965, Vol. 1, p. 846) Further, "English has been designated the 'principal language' in the three southern provinces." (Banks 1975, p. 310) The language policies of Pakistan and of Burma also include such recognition of the special role of English in their internal affairs. Article 216 of the Burmese constitution reads, "The official language of the Union shall be Burmese provided that the use of the English language may be permitted." (Peaslee 1965, Vol. 2, p. 110) Further, Article 217 requires that "Two copies of the Constitution shall be made, one in the Burmese language and the other in the English language." (Peaslee 1965, Vol. 2, p. 110) The Pakistan constitution contains a similar proviso. "The national languages are Bengali[11] and Urdu but other languages, in particular English, may be used." (Peaslee 1965, Vol. 2, p. 982) Article 215 of that same document establishes a 1972 commission to examine and to report on the question of the replacement of English for official purposes. (Peaslee 1965, Vol. 2, p. 1049)

Although we have omitted the English mother-tongue countries from Tables 1.2.1 and 1.2.2, there are nonetheless, some interesting mentions of English in the constitutions of some of these countries. The Irish constitution, for example, includes the following provisions:

> 1. *The Irish language as the national language is the first official language.*
> 2. *The English language is recognized as a second official language.*
> 3. *Provision may, however, be made by law for the exclusive use of either of the said languages for any one or more official purposes, either throughout the State or any part thereof.*
>
> *(Peaslee 1965, Vol. 3, p. 464)*

Article 133 of the constitution of Canada reads as follows:

> *Either the English or the French language maybe used by any person in the debates of the Houses of the Parliament of Canada and of the Houses of the legislature of Quebec; and both those languages shall be used in the respective records and journals of those houses; and either of those languages may be used by any person or in any pleading or process in or issuing from any court of Canada established under this Act, and in or from all or any of the courts of Quebec. The acts of the Parliament of Canada and of the legislature of Quebec shall be printed and published in both those languages.*
>
> *(Peaslee 1965, Vol. 4, p. 233)*

However, in July 1974, the Official Language Act (Bill No. 22) "was enacted by the National Assembly of the Province of Quebec . . . By virtue of this act, French has been designated as the *sole official language of the province.*" (G. Richard Tucker, "French Becomes Official Language of Quebec," *Linguistic Reporter* 8:4, 3, Dec. 1975.)

Tables 1.2.1 and 1.2.2 are attempts to summarize the information we have discussed on English as an official language. Beside each country name (column 1) are several other columns. Column 2 includes either "S" or "C," indicating whether English is the sole designated official language or one of two

Table 1.2.1 Non—English mother-tongue countries having English designated as an official language

Country	Sole (S) co-official (C)	Constitutional mention	Relation	Function	Form Anglop power
Botswana	S	0			B
Cameroon	C	9/1/61	−		B
Fiji	S	0			B
Gambia	S	0			B
Ghana	S	1/31/64			B
India	C	10/5/63	−	3	B
Lesotho	C	0	0		B
Liberia	S	5/55			A
Malawi	C	7/6/64	+	1	B
Malta	C	10/29/65	=		B
Mauritius	S	0			B
Namibia	C	0	0		B
Nauru	C	0	0		B
Nigeria	S	10/1/63		1	B
Philippines	C	9/18/46	0		A
Rhodesia	S	0			B
Sierra Leone	S	4/27/61		1	B
Singapore	C	9/16/63	0	4	B
South Africa	C	4/25/61	=		B
Swaziland	C	0	0		B
Tanzania	C	12/9/62	−		B
Tonga	C	0	0		B
Uganda	S	9/30/63			B
Western Samoa	C	10/28/60	=	4	B
Zambia	S	10/24/64		1	B

Note: See text (pp. 9, 11, 13) for an explanation of the symbols used in these columns. Also see the following notes for more details about many of the countries.

Cameroon: Article 33: ". . . official languages are French and English . . ." Article 34n: "The text is bilingual—French and English." Article 59: "The revised Constitution shall be published in French and in English, French text being authentic." (Peaslee 1965, Vol. 1, p. 46).

Ghana: ". . . the working language is English . . ." (Peaslee 1965, Vol. 1, p. 212)

India: Article 120–1: ". . . business in Parliament shall be transacted in Hindi or in English." Article 120–2: "omit 'or in English' in 15 years." (Peaslee 1965, Vol. 2, p. 343f)

Liberia: "English is the official language." (Peaslee 1965, Vol. 1, p. 421)

Malawi: ". . . the official language of the National Assembly [is] English." (Peaslee 1965, Vol. 1, p. 475) Article 53: "The business of the National Assembly shall be conducted in English." One assumes then that the definitive version of laws passed in that assembly are in English, though that is not explicitly stated. (Peaslee 1965, Vol. 1, p. 504)

Table 1.2.1 (continued notes)

Malta: Article 5 stipulates that 1) The National language of Malta is the Maltese language.
2) The Maltese and the English languages and such other language as may be prescribed by Parliament (2/3 majority) shall be the official languages of Malta and the administration may for all official purposes use any of such languages. Provided that any person may address the administration in any of the official languages and the reply of the administration thereto shall be in such language. 3) The language of the courts shall be the Maltese language: Provided that Parliament may make such provision for the use of the English language in such cases and under such conditions as it may prescribe. 4) The House of Representatives may, in regulating its own procedure, determine the language or languages that shall be used in parliamentary proceedings and records. (Peaslee 1965, Vol. 3, pp. 571-572)

Nigeria: "The language of Parliament is English." (Peaslee 1965, Vol. 1, p. 591) Article 59: "The business of Parliament shall be conducted in English." (Peaslee 1965, Vol. 1, p. 622)

Philippines: Article 14:3 stipulates that English and Spanish are the official languages and Congress is to take steps to develop a common national language. On June 7, 1940 a law effective July 4, 1946, made Tagalog the official national language. (Peaslee 1965, Vol. 2, p. 1066) But see Gonzalez (1974).

Sierra Leone: ". . . The official language is English." (Peaslee 1965, Vol. 1, p. 714) Article 48: "The business of the House of Representatives shall be conducted in English." (Peaslee 1965, Vol. 1, p. 741)

Singapore: Article 37: "The languages of debate in the legislature are English, Malay, Mandarin or Tamil." (Peaslee 1965, Vol. 2, p. 1103)

South Africa: "The official languages are English and Afrikaans" (Peaslee 1965, Vol. 1, p. 807) Article 108 stipulates that the languages are on "equal footing." (Peaslee 1965, Vol. 1, p. 840)

Tanzania: "The languages [of Tanganyika] are English and Swahili" in the Tanganyika constitution of December 9, 1962. Gage and Ohannessian (1974, p. 13) claim that while the national language is Swahili, "English is still in use in the higher courts." Banks (1975) lists Tanzania as having two official languages, English and Swahili, in that order, as of January 1, 1975.

Uganda: Article 122: "The official language of the government of Uganda shall be English." (Peaslee 1965, Vol. 1, p. 981)

Western Samoa: "The languages of Parliament are Samoan and English." (Peaslee 1965, Vol. 2, p. 1227) Article 54 also stipulates that minutes and acts are to be in both languages as well.

Zambia: ". . . the working language [is] English." (Peaslee 1965, Vol. 1, p. 1026) Gage and Ohannessian (1974, p. 13) claim that English is used "for virtually all aspects of the official life of the country . . ."

---

or more co-official languages. If there is a date in the third column, the constitution of that date mentions English; the zero (0) indicates that the constitution was not available to us; and "N" means that the constitution does *not* mention English. Column 4 indicates, necessarily only for those countries where English is co-official, what the relationship is between the languages sharing official status. The plus sign (+) means English is advantaged in law over the others, the equal sign (=) indicates that the languages are co-equal in law, the minus sign (−) means that English is disadvantaged with respect to the other(s), and the zero (0) means that no relation is defined. Column 5 distinguishes four parliamentary functions where we have adequate information. The numeral "1" indicates that the business

Table 1.2.2   Non-English mother-tongue countries in which there is some official status for English, but in which English is not designated as official

Country	Sole (S) or co-official (C)	Constitutional mention	Relation	Function	Former Anglophone power
Burma	C	9/24/47	—		B
Ethiopia	C	N	—		
Israel	(C)	N	—		B
Kenya	C	12/12/63	—	2	B
Malaysia	C	8/23/57	—	3	B
Pakistan	C	3/1/62	—	2	B
Sri Lanka	C	N	—		B
Sudan	C	11/18/58	—	2	B

Note: See text (pp. 9, 11, 13) for an explanation of the symbols used. The designations in column 2 are by definition "co-official" since another language(s) is *designated* language. The relation in column 4 is also self-evident since by being designated, the other language(s) is superior.

Burma: Article 216: "The official language of the Union shall be Burmese provided that the use of the English language may be permitted." Article 217: "Two copies of the Constitution shall be made, one in the Burmese language and the other in the English language." (Peaslee 1965, Vol. 2, p. 110)

Ethiopia: English is used in the administration of government. Nearly all official documents are published in Amharic and English, the Amharic version controlling. Laws are published in both languages. Ethiopia as a whole has never been under the colonial domination of a foreign power except for the period of 1935–41 when she was under Fascist Italy, "until British liberation and the liquidation of Italy's African empire." (Banks 1975; p. 96) (The exception is the province of Eritrea, whose occupation by Italy was completed in 1889.)

Israel: There is no separate constitution, other than the entire body of law. Prior to statehood, English was one of the three official languages. After statehood, official status was revoked and English was no longer mandated in government use, but was permitted. *Transactions of the Knesset* (the congressional record) now appear in English by chapter titles only. In the case of disputes involving the laws of the British Mandate period, the English version of the laws then promulgated is still determinative. (See Fisherman and Fishman 1975)

Kenya: "Knowledge of the Swahili language is required for naturalization as a citizen and of English for being a member of the legislature." (Peaslee 1965, Vol. 1, p. 256)

Malaysia: The special status of English is to last only ten years (see Article 152). English is only now by official decree being superseded as the language used in government offices and in official correspondence. (Peaslee 1965, Vol. 2, p. 731)

Pakistan: "The national languages are Bengali [now the national language of Bangladesh, formerly East Pakistan] and Urdu but other languages, in particular English, may be used." (Peaslee 1965, Vol. 2, p. 982)

Sri Lanka: "In early 1970 court proceedings were recorded, as in the past, in English, although the Language of the Courts Act of 1961 directed that they be recorded in Sinhala as soon as

Table 1.2.2 (continued notes)

this switch was practicable; under a subsequent regulation, this transition was to begin in August 1963. In February, 1970, however, a cabinet officer acknowledged that, as far as he could ascertain, no district or magistrate's court conducted its business in Sinhala. In the Northern and Eastern provinces Tamil continued to be the medium of legal proceedings under the Tamil Language Act of 1958." (Nyrop 1971*c*, pp. 461-462)

Sudan: Parliamentary proceedings "shall be conducted in Arabic without prejudice to such use of the English language as may be convenient." (Peaslee 1965, Vol. 1, p. 846) "English has been designated the 'principal language' in the three southern provinces." (Banks 1975, p. 310)

---

of the parliament is conducted entirely in English. A "2" means that the business of parliament is conducted mainly in another language, but the use of English is permitted. "3" means that English is temporarily equal in law, but that English is to be replaced by another language at some future time. And "4" means that no relation between languages in the conduct of the parliament has been legally defined. The last column has to do with former colonial status, or colony-like status, under some Anglophone power. "B" identifies that power as the United Kingdom, and "A" indicates the United States. The tables are followed by extensive notes including direct quotations from the legal documents justifying our classifications.

A quick glance at the final columns of Tables 1.2.1 and 1.2.2 confirms the fact that English as an official language of non-English mother-tongue countries occurs almost exclusively in former colonies of the two major English speaking powers. All twenty-five countries in Table 1.2.1, those having English as a "designated" official language, are former Anglophone colonies. The only country in Table 1.2.2 not marked by former Anglophone colonial status is Ethiopia. Ethiopia as a whole has never been an Anglophone colony. When Italian domination ended, Ethiopia found itself in a world in which English was spreading rapidly and was already growing in the countries at its borders. With this single exception, English is used officially for internal governmental functions only in non-English mother-tongue countries which were, or which remain, under the political or economic hegemony of the United States or the United Kingdom.

3.0 ENGLISH IN EDUCATION

3.1 Primary and Secondary Education

Our discussion of English in primary and secondary education attempts to present in some detail (and to interpret) the use of English as a medium of instruction as well as the teaching of English as an additional language. Data given here are for 112 non-English mother-tongue countries throughout the world. There can be little doubt that there is now and will continue to be for the short term a growing demand for English instruction. The use of English as a medium of instruction, especially at the lower levels, is now found almost exclusively in former colonial countries and cannot be assumed to be a permanent feature of the worldwide situation.

In sheer numbers, however, the vast majority of people learning English in the world today are learning it in the secondary school, a fact most significant for our purpose. It is in the secondary school that the educational systems of developing countries are now experiencing their most dramatic growth. This growth, which for example in Asia shows a jump in enrollment from 22% of the secondary school age population in 1960 to 44% of the secondary school age population in 1970, accounts in the main for the growing exposure of a more and more significant part of the school age population to English instruction. Worldwide, the growth from 1960 to 1970 was a jump from 32% of the age-appropriate population in secondary school to 54% of that population. Growing school age populations coupled with a growing percentage of that population in fact enrolled in the secondary school amounts to a demand for English instruction which is growing at a substantially greater rate than the population itself. As noted above, in Asia (excluding the People's Republic of China and Taiwan) the percentage of the age-appropriate population in secondary schools doubled in the decade 1960–1970, a fact doubly significant for our purposes since overall 97% of that secondary school enrollment is in English classes.

Table 1.3.2 summarizes, by area of the world, the percentage of the total enrollment constituted by students in English classes, whether for instruction in English or through English medium, at the primary and secondary levels. Approximately 30% of the combined primary and secondary school populations are in English classes in a given year. That average, however, masks the fact—shown clearly by Table 1.3.2—that while only 15.7% at the primary level in non-English mother-tongue countries throughout the world are working through English or studying it as a subject, 76.7% are in English classes at the secondary level. Tables 1.3.3 through 1.3.6 represent country-by-country statistics, from which the summary of Table 1.3.2 was derived, on English study in the primary and secondary schools of 112 non-English mother-tongue countries arranged by continent. Enrollment figures represent totals for each country given by the *United Nations Statistical Yearbook, 1974.* "NA" indicates that enrollment figures were not available. The year with each enrollment figure is the latest year for which data are available. Primary level means, "Education whose main function is to provide basic instruction in the tools of learning (e.g., at elementary school, primary school). Its length may vary from 4 to 9 years, depending on the organization of the school system in each country." (p. 843) Secondary level, which is more important from the point of view of English instruction, is defined as "education based upon at least 4 years of previous instruction at the first level, and providing general or specialized instruction, or both (e.g., at middle school, secondary school, high school, vocational school, teacher training school) at this level." (p. 843) The estimates of students in English classes are based on Gage and Ohannessian (1974) and on British Council materials, both published and unpublished. If a school system *requires* its students to take English we include the

Table 1.3.1 Percentage of school age population attending school (at any level), 1960 and 1970, by age and by area of the world

	Primary school age		Secondary school age		Primary and secondary age		Third level: age 20-24	
	1960	1970	1960	1970	1960	1970	1960	1970
North America	98	99	90	93	94	97	30.2	48.2
Europe & USSR	96	97	57	67	79	85	8.6	19.0
Oceania	95	97	60	75	80	89	10.0	14.0
Latin America	60	78	26	49	45	65	3.1	6.3
Asia [a]	50	59	22	44	36	55	2.6	4.2
Arab States [b]	(38)	(61)	(16)	(28)	(28)	(45)	(2.1)	(4.0)
Africa	34	48	12	25	24	38	0.8	1.5
World total	63	71	32	54	50	63	6.0	11.0

Source: United Nations (1975a), p. 225.

[a]Not including China, the Democratic People's Republic of Korea, or the Democratic Republic of Viet Nam.

[b]The Arab States as a separate grouping are presented in parentheses since they are also included under Africa and Asia.

Table 1.3.2   Number of students in primary and secondary English classes, with percentage of total enrollment, by area of the world

	Primary			Secondary		
	Total enrollment	*In English classes* *Number*	*%*	*Total enrollment*	*In English classes* *Number*	*%*
Africa	32,764,741	15,438,251	47.1	5,248,162	5,085,959	96.9
Asia *a*	135,750,650	22,077,553	16.3	41,809,770	40,689,048	97.3
Europe	45,557,339	3,077,447	6.8	25,309,481	14,408,973	56.9
Latin America	43,288,487	1,110,242	2.6	10,835,663	5,849,486	54.0
USSR	39,932,000	5,000,000	12.5	9,354,600	5,000,000	53.4
Total	297,293,217	46,703,493	15.7	92,557,676	71,033,466	76.7

Sources: Enrollments are from United Nations (1975*b*). English figures are from Gage and Ohannessian (1974), as amended later in this chapter.

*a*We have excluded an estimated 1,240,000 English students listed by Gage and Ohannessian (1974) for Taiwan since we were unable to establish the total enrollment for Taiwan. Figures for the People's Republic of China are also excluded.

school population at that level in our estimate in the absence of information as to whether or not English is *in fact* taught. The percentage of enrolled students who are listed as being in English classes is then calculated and included, as an indication of the ratio of students studying English at any one time to the number of students enrolled at that same time.

The final column in each table for both primary and secondary education is included to indicate whether English is the medium of instruction or only a subject of instruction. If the column is marked "S," students are required to take English as a subject of instruction throughout the level in question; "$\frac{1}{3}$ S" means that one-third of the students study English as a foreign language. "M" indicates that instruction is provided through the medium of English throughout the level in question. "S or M" means that where English is not the medium of instruction, it is taught as a foreign language. "Some S" indicates that English is not required, but that it is taught to some students. Based on information available to us we have then estimated just what "some" means for each country. (Excluded throughout are English-medium schools for expatriate children and other private schools. They are another story.)

It has been shown for Southeast Asia (Noss 1965), and assumed to be the case for the rest of the world, that English medium schools in non-English mother-tongue countries will produce a higher proportion of students who are competent English users than will schools in which English is merely taught as a subject of instruction. For this reason, we include Table 1.3.7, which breaks down the number of students in English classes on each continent (with USSR separated out from Europe and Asia) into those studying English as a subject of instruction and those studying through the medium of English at both the primary and secondary levels. The figures are instructive. Worldwide, 70% of the primary students in English classes in non-English mother-tongue countries study English as a foreign language. Only 30% of the students studying English are in English-medium situations and all of these (more than 14 million students) are in Africa and Asia. Africa, in fact, is about equally divided between English-subject schools and English-medium schools at the primary level.

At the secondary level the situation is quite different. The percentage of students studying through the medium of English, 15.8% of those in English classes, is lower than at the primary level, but the absolute number of such students is less than 3,000,000 fewer. This is accounted for by the fact that more than half of all students studying English, are studying it as a subject of instruction at the secondary level. There is no large concentration of English-medium schooling at either level outside of Asia and Africa. Rather, at the secondary level, 84.2% of the students in English classes are studying English as a subject of instruction.

English-medium schooling in Africa is found on a wide scale only in countries which have an Anglophone colonial heritage and which also use English in governmental affairs (see Section 2.0 and Table 1.2.1) with only two exceptions, Ethiopia and Somalia. Ethiopia does not have a colonial heritage under

Table 1.3.3 Country-by-country estimates of students in primary and secondary English classes (distinguishing English medium from subject of instruction), with percentage of total enrollment: Africa

	Primary					Secondary				
	Enrolled	Year	English	%	M/S	Enrolled	Year	English	%	M/S
Algeria	2,057,048	1971	—	—	—	287,700	1971	258,930	90.0	S, 90% 9-13
Angola	485,955	1970	—	—	—	68,785	1970	68,785	100.0	S
Botswana	81,662	1972	81,662	100.0	S, M from 3	7,258	1972	7,258	100.0	M
Cameroon	930,131	1971	528,382	56.8	M (West), ¼S (East)	91,618	1971	91,618	100.0	S, M in West
Central African Republic	177,924	1971	—	—	—	12,121	1971	12,121	100.0	S
Chad	184,020	1971	—	—	—	11,500	1971	11,500	100.0	S
Egypt	3,873,297	1971	—	—	—	1,554,809	1971	1,554,809	100.0	S
Ethiopia	716,729	1971	100,697	14.0	S from 5	149,303	1971	149,303	100.0	M
Gabon	105,601	1971	—	—	—	11,507	1971	11,507	100.0	S
Gambia	19,421	1972	19,421	100.0	M	5,716	1972	5,716	100.0	M
Ghana	1,415,801	1971	1,415,801	100.0	S, M from 4	86,157	1971	86,157	100.0	M
Guinea	191,287	1970	—	—	—	63,409	1970	63,409	100.0	S
Ivory Coast	527,615	1971	—	—	—	81,738	1971	81,738	100.0	S
Kenya	1,525,498	1971	1,525,498	100.0	M	152,387	1971	152,387	100.0	M
Lesotho	171,454	1971	171,454	100.0	S	8,815	1971	8,815	100.0	M
Liberia	120,245	1970	120,245	100.0	M	16,771	1970	16,771	100.0	M
Libya	407,805	1971	—	—	—	63,138	1971	63,138	100.0	S
Madagascar	1,004,445	1971	—	—	—	114,487	1971	114,487	100.0	S

Table 1.3.3 (continued)

	Primary					Secondary				
	Enrolled	Year	English	%	M/S	Enrolled	Year	English	%	M/S
Malawi	355,004	1970	355,004	100.0	S, M from 6	11,727	1970	11,727	100.0	S
Mali	243,886	1970	–	–		8,444	1971	8,444	100.0	S
Mauritania	35,049	1971	5,556	15.9	Some S	4,444	1971	4,444	100.0	M
Mauritius	152,331	1971	152,331	100.0	M	48,551	1971	48,551	100.0	S
Morocco	1,175,227	1970	–	–		313,424	1970	313,424	100.0	S
Niger	100,892	1971	–	–		7,966	1972	7,966	100.0	M
Nigeria	3,894,539	1971	3,894,539	100.0	S, M from 3 or 4	407,734	1971	407,734	100.0	M
Republic of South Africa	3,603,256	1970	3,603,256	100.0	S	677,634	1970	677,634	100.0	S
Rhodesia	722,365	1968	722,365	100.0	S, $1/3$M	41,559	1968	41,559	100.0	M
Senegal	269,997	1971	–	–		57,124	1971	57,124	100.0	S
Sierra Leone	166,107	1971	166,107	100.0	M	35,201	1971	35,201	100.0	M
Somalia	40,222	1971	13,407	33.3	$1/3$ S	28,344	1971.	28,344	100.0	S or M
Sudan	961,411	1971	–	–		141,797	1971	141,797	100.0	S
Swaziland	76,343	1972	76,343	100.0	S, M from 5	11,347	1972	11,347	100.0	M
Tanzania	922,083	1971	922,083	100.0	S	47,470	1971	47,570	100.0	M
Togo	257,875	1971	–	–		27,255	1971	27,255	100.0	S
Tunisia	934,827	1971	–	–		173,433	1971	40,000	23.1	Some S
Uganda	786,227	1972	786,227	100.0	S or M	43,586	1972	43,586	100.0	M
Upper Volta	112,047	1971	–	–		12,113	1971	12,113	100.0	S
Zaire	3,181,242	1971	–	–		297,028	1971	297,028	100.0	S
Zambia	777,873	1972	777,873	100.0	M	64,662	1972	64,662	100.0	M

Note: Sources and an explanation of the symbols are given for Tables 1.3.3–1.3.7 in the text (pp. 14, 17)

Table 1.3.4 Country-by-country estimates of students in primary and secondary English classes (distinguishing English medium from subject of instruction), with percentage of total enrollment: Asia

	Primary					Secondary				
	Enrolled	Year	English	%	M/S	Enrolled	Year	English	%	M/S
Afghanistan	604,795	1971	—	—	—	161,839	1971	161,839	100.0	S
Bangladesh	5,494,309	1969	2,500,996	45.5	S from 4	1,299,004	1969	1,299,004	100.0	S
Burma	3,328,000	1969	—	—	—	699,615	1969	699,615	100.0	S
Cyprus	66,027	1971	—	—	—	46,150	1971	46,150	100.0	S
Hong Kong	757,152	1971	609,532	80.5	S from 2	290,468	1971	290,468	100.0	S, 2/3 M
India[a]	60,000,000	1971	6,000,000	10.0	S from 3, 4, 5, or 6	15,000,000	1971	15,000,000	100.0	S or M
Indonesia	13,474,730	1971	—	—	—	2,104,734	1971	2,104,734	100.0	S
Iran	3,230,880	1971	—	—	—	1,468,340	1971	1,468,340	100.0	S
Iraq	1,195,530	1971	294,885	24.7	S from 5	325,115	1971	325,115	100.0	S
Israel	499,705	1971	280,000	56.0	—	141,981	1971	120,000	84.5	Some S
Japan	9,595,021	1971	—	—	—	8,864,751	1971	8,864,751	100.0	S
Jordan	298,802	1971	74,700	25.0	S from 5	102,359	1971	102,359	100.0	S
S. Korea	5,775,880	1972	—	—	—	2,437,748	1972	2,437,748	100.0	S
Kuwait	63,351	1971	—	—	—	72,838	1971	72,838	100.0	S
Laos	266,790	1971	—	—	—	18,086	1971	3,000	16.6	Some S
Lebanon	175,538	1970	58,513	33.3	1/3 S	165,462	1971	55,154	33.3	1/3 S
Malaysia	1,722,941	1971	1,722,941	100.0	S, some M	660,215	1972	660,215	100.0	S or M
Nepal	449,141	1969	196,931	43.8	S from 4	103,069	1969	103,069	100.0	M
Pakistan	3,887,500	1971	—	—	—	2,266,011	1971	2,266,011	100.0	S
Philippines	7,622,424	1972	7,622,424	—	S, M from 2	1,791,176	1972	1,791,176	100.0	M
Saudi Arabia	469,800	1971	—	—	—	118,496	1971	118,496	100.0	M or S
Singapore	357,936	1971	357,936	100.0	M or S	159,585	1971	159,585	100.0	M or S
Sri Lanka	2,298,200	1969	950,000	41.3	½S at 3; ½S at 6	355,655	1969	355,655	100.0	S
Syria	1,005,739	1971	—	—	—	371,084	1971	333,975	90.0	90% S

Table 1.3.4 (continued)

	Primary					Secondary				
	Enrolled	Year	English	%	M/S	Enrolled	Year	English	%	M/S
Taiwan	NA	–	–	–	–	NA	–	–	–	–
Thailand	5,634,782	1970	1,408,695	25.0	S from 5	626,573	1970	626,573	100.0	S
Turkey	5,009,694	1971	–	–	–	1,429,654	1971	857,792	60.0	60% S
S. Viet Nam	2,375,983	1969	–	–	–	730,752	1969	365,376	50.0	½ S

aSee note 12.

Table 1.3.5 Country-by-country estimates of students in primary and secondary English classes (distinguishing English medium from subject of instruction), with percentage of total enrollment: Europe

	Primary					Secondary				
	Enrolled	Year	English	%	M/S	Enrolled	Year	English	%	M/S
Austria	912,615	1971	250,000	27.4	Some S from 5	415,041	1971	350,000	84.3	Some S
Belgium	1,008,444	1968	–			847,547	1968	800,000	94.4	Some S
Bulgaria	1,027,689	1971	–			395,242	1971	200,000	50.6	Some S
Czechoslovakia	1,939,590	1971	500,000	25.8	Some S	392,654	1971	–	–	S
Denmark	522,065	1971	180,000	34.5	Some S	329,008	1971	329,008	100.0	Some S
Finland	379,611	1971	160,000	42.1	Some S from 6	521,167	1971	400,000	76.8	Some S
France	4,853,725	1971	–			4,524,381	1971	3,981,455	88.0	Some S
W. Germany	6,476,647	1971	1,000,000	15.4	Some S from 5	4,506,317	1971	1,500,000	33.3	Some S
E. Germany	2,597,605	1972	–			474,592	1971	400,000	84.3	Some S
Greece	910,728	1971	–			612,325	1971	500,000	81.7	Some S
Hungary	1,070,017	1971	–			445,966	1971	200,000	44.8	Some S
Iceland	27,336	1971	–			24,105	1971	20,000	83.0	Some S
Italy	4,928,406	1971	–			4,018,828	1971	1,200,000	29.9	S from 9
Luxembourg	35,737	1971	25,000	70.0	Some S	19,194	1971	15,000	78.1	Some S
Malta	37,447	1971	37,447	100.0	S	27,606	1971	27,606	100.0	M
Netherlands	1,464,484	1971	100,000	25.9	S from 5	1,277,671	1971	1,213,787	95.0	Some S
Norway	386,496	1971	–			317,122	1971	317,122	100.0	S
Poland	5,052,192	1971	–			1,428,459	1971	600,000	42.0	Some S
Portugal	988,559	1971	–			486,695	1971	420,000	86.3	Some S
Romania	2,766,368	1971	300,000	10.8	Some S from 5	664,903	1971	400,000	60.2	Some S
Spain	4,182,029	1971	20,000	0.4	Some S	1,774,977	1971	354,995	20.0	Some S
Sweden	636,219	1971	380,000	59.7	S from 3	565,825	1971	450,000	79.5	S from 7-9
Switzerland	516,311	1971	125,000	24.2	Some S	491,649	1971	400,000	81.4	Some S
Yugoslavia	2,837,019	1971	–			748,207	1971	330,000	44.1	Some S
USSR	39,932,000	1971	5,000,000	12.5	Some S from 5	9,354,600	1971	5,000,000	53.4	Some S
All Europe	85,489,339		8,077,447	9.4		34,664,008		19,408,973	56.0	
Minus USSR	45,557,339		3,077,447	6.8		25,309,481		14,408,973	56.9	

Table 1.3.6 Country-by-country estimates of students in primary and secondary English classes (distinguishing English medium from subject of instruction), with percentage of total enrollment: Latin America

	Primary					Secondary				
	Enrolled	Year	English	%	M/S	Enrolled	Year	English	%	M/S
Argentina	3,443,669	1970	—	—	—	1,007,537	1971	100,000	9.9	Some S
Bolivia	694,416	1971	—	—	—	99,751	1971	50,000	50.1	Some S
Brazil	13,640,967	1971	—	—	—	4,562,123	1971	1,600,000	35.1	Some S
Chile	2,200,160	1971	—	—	—	366,099	1971	200,000	54.6	Some S
Colombia	2,669,579	1969	249,731	9.4	Some S	450,269	1971	450,269	100.0	S
Costa Rica	356,152	1971	—	—	—	77,828	1972	77,828	100.0	S
Cuba	1,631,187	1971	40,840	2.5	Some S	259,160	1971	259,160	100.0	S
Dominican Republic	823,553	1971	—	—	—	129,851	1971	40,000	30.8	Some S
Ecuador	1,016,483	1970	—	—	—	216,727	1970	216,727	100.0	S
El Salvador	509,985	1970	—	—	—	88,307	1970	40,000	45.3	Some S
Guatemala	531,122	1971	—	—	—	79,722	1970	40,000	50.2	Some S
Honduras	384,685	1970	10,161	2.6	Some S	39,839	1970	39,839	100.0	S
Mexico	9,248,290	1970	315,658	3.4	Some S	1,584,342	1970	1,584,342	100.0	S
Nicaragua	301,580	1971	—	—	—	54,690	1971	30,000	54.9	Some S
Panama	287,565	1971	—	—	—	86,616	1971	50,000	57.7	Some S
Paraguay	436,857	1971	—	—	—	58,629	1971	10,000	17.1	Some S
Peru	2,488,395	1970	—	—	—	660,063	1970	660,063	100.0	S
Puerto Rico	493,852	1971	493,852	100.0	S	281,258	1971	281,258	100.0	S
Uruguay	289,676[a]	1971	—	—	—	167,388	1969	20,000	11.9	Some S
Venezuela	1,838,314	1971	—	—	—	565,464	1971	100,000	17.7	Some S
Total	43,288,487		1,110,242	2.6		10,835,663		5,849,486	54.0	

[a] Refers to public education only.

Table 1.3.7 Summary by continents (with USSR identified separately) of total number of primary and secondary students studying English as a *subject* and through English *medium*

	Primary					Secondary				
	Total in English classes	S	%	M	%	Total in English classes	S	%	M	%
Africa	15,438,251	7,812,875	50.6	7,625,376	49.4	5,085,959	3,895,170	76.6	1,190,789	23.4
Asia	22,077,553	15,698,585	71.0	6,378,968	28.9	40,689,048	30,691,284	75.4	9,997,764	24.6
Europe	3,077,447	3,077,447	100.0	–	–	14,408,973	14,381,367	99.8	27,606	0.2
Latin America	1,110,242	1,110,242	100.0	–	–	5,849,486	5,849,486	100.0	–	–
USSR	5,000,000	5,000,000	100.0	–	–	5,000,000	5,000,000	100.0	–	–
Totals	46,703,493	32,699,149	70.0	14,004,344	30.0	71,033,466	59,817,307	84.2	11,216,159	15.8

English-speaking rule but does have English as a major "official" language. Somalia, on the other hand, is a former colony of Great Britain but does not have any notable internal official use of English. These two countries are exceptions with respect to one criterion—the generalization for Africa is, then, that English-medium schooling is almost exclusively found in former Anglophone colonial countries and in countries using English for official purposes. (See Table 1.3.3)

The same generalization holds for Asia as well, though there are fewer countries having English as a medium of instruction. Of these six countries (see Table 1.3.4), only Nepal has no English-speaking colonial heritage, though Nepal is under the wing of India.

As we read through the material we have on countries with English-medium schooling, we read of strong pressures to replace English with the vernacular, particularly at the lower levels. There are countries like Tanzania, where such vernacular-medium schooling has already replaced English at the primary levels, and Malaysia, where it has already replaced English on a large scale. The pressure is predominantly away from English-medium schooling so that changes in this situation will no doubt result in a lessening of the English-medium schooling in non-English mother-tongue countries in the world.[13]

Our discussion of English-medium schooling has so far ignored what is policy in some countries and no doubt practice in many more, the use of English as a "co-medium" of instruction. India is an example of a "multi-media" policy. "In recent years some multi-lingual states, mostly in eastern India, have introduced as a state policy, bilingual education in which a developing language in a region is used as a partial medium, together with English, Hindi, or the neighboring regional language as the major medium." (Khubchandani 1975, pp. 159-160) This phenomenon will no doubt prove to be more than a transitional stage in some countries. English co-medium schooling may provide, rather than merely an intermediate stage in the move from English-medium schooling to local language schooling, the way toward a policy through which the vernacular language may be developed in a context of greater utilization of the language of wider communication. In such a circumstance, a decline in English-medium schooling may not signal a serious decline in the knowledge of the language of wider communication.[14]

The pressures regarding English as a subject of instruction, especially in secondary schools, seem to be developing in quite the opposite direction. So-called Francophone countries are beginning to abandon their exclusive reliance on French as a second language, and the room made by this move opens the way for increased study of English as a foreign language. Further, countries in Latin America, for example, where French was the "first" foreign language are now teaching more and more English. Much of this interest in teaching English as a foreign language in secondary schools is prompted by the importance of English at the tertiary level as a library language as well as the language medium through which a great deal of tertiary level study takes place.

Growing demand for English instruction throughout the world, at the secondary and tertiary levels primarily, may be expected to continue for the foreseeable future as the importance of English as a world language continues. Such growing demand, however, is in the context of the continued development of local languages as media of elementary, secondary, and tertiary education.

3.2   Tertiary Level Foreign Students

The question of the place of English in tertiary education in the world is a complex one. Many non-English mother-tongue countries have university level work conducted through the medium of English in some advanced fields, particularly technological fields. Further, it is a safe assumption that in those countries where secondary level education is conducted mainly through the medium of English, tertiary level work is through the English medium as well. And most universities worldwide have English departments offering not only instruction in the English language, but also English major programs including the study of English literature via the medium of English. No comprehensive assessment of the tertiary level role of English worldwide is attempted here; however, one part of the issue may at least be approached by looking at the question of foreign students studying in English mother-tongue countries.

UNESCO defines a foreign student as "a person enrolled at an institution of higher education in a country or territory of which he is not a permanent resident." (UNESCO *Statistical Yearbook* 1974, 4:7) UNESCO lists the country of origin for just over 500,000 such students in the 1971 academic year,[15] in an accounting it claims represents fully 95% of the world's total. While these students constitute something less than 2% of the world's third level students, there are small countries, such as Lesotho, where as many as 58% of the third level students in the country are from foreign countries.

Table 1.3.8 presents, in summary, data on which the discussion in this section is based. Column 1 lists the major areas of the world which are the areas of origin for the more than 500,000 foreign students included in the table. The second column gives the total number of students enrolled at the third level for each area. The third column gives the number of foreign students known to be studying in the countries included in the designated area, while, by contrast, column 4 lists the number of students who have gone from countries in the designated area to a country other than their home country (not necessarily, of course, into another listed area of the world). The fifth column shows how many of the students who have gone from their country in the area of the world listed in column 1 have gone to English mother-tongue countries for study. The sixth column shows what percentage of the foreign students from the various parts of the world are studying in English mother-tongue countries, i.e., the proportion of the figure in column 4 represented by the figure in column 5. The following tables will attempt to deal in some detail with those students who are of particular

Table 1.3.8   Foreign students, 1971, showing number *in* and *from* countries of the world by area, and number and percentage *from* each area *in* English mother-tongue countries

Area	No. of third level students	Foreign students In area countries	Foreign students From area countries	Foreign students from area in English mother-tongue countries Number	%
Africa	518,000	24,332	53,616	16,945	31.6
North America	9,650,000	171,084	37,166	23,370	62.9
Latin America	1,788,000	24,942	59,064	30,357	54.9
Asia	6,396,000	70,079	218,144	94,518	43.3
Europe	5,201,000	188,004	98,712	31,509	31.9
Oceania	279,000	10,006	5,386	4,859	90.2
USSR	4,597,000	17,400	688	121	17.6
Stateless	–	–	1,523	308	20.2
Unspecified	–	–	31,608	6,140	19.4
Total	28,429,000	505,907	505,907	208,127	41.1

Source: UNESCO (1974).

interest for our purposes, those students from non-English mother-tongue countries who go to English mother-tongue countries to study.

The total number of foreign students studying in English mother-tongue countries is 208,127, or the total in column 5 of Table 1.3.8. That number represents just over 40% of the world's foreign students. While it is true that many students leaving non-English mother-tongue countries to study in an English mother-tongue country leave behind tertiary education opportunities which are English-medium, we have attempted to count those foreign students going to English mother-tongue countries on the assumption that they will return to their countries, if they return, not only with whatever skills they came to acquire, but also with a much reinforced command of the English language. Their return to their own countries constitutes an elite cadre of talent which cannot but be influential.

Of the 40%, or 208,127, foreign students studying in the English mother-tongue countries, some 80%, or 168,311, came from non-English mother-tongue countries, and it is this group in which we are most interested. (See Table 1.3.9) The five major English-speaking host countries for foreign students are, in order beginning with the largest, the United States, Canada, United Kingdom, Australia, and New Zealand. More than 120,000 of the foreign students from non-English mother-tongue countries are in the USA, while 22,120 are in Britain, 15,967 in Canada, and more than 9,000 in Australia and New Zealand.

Table 1.3.9 Foreign students *in* English mother-tongue countries showing percentage and number *from* English mother-tongue countries and *from* non-English mother-tongue countries, 1971

Country	No. of third level students in country	No. of foreign students in countries listed	Foreign students in country from Eng. m.-t.[a]		Foreign students from non-E.-m.-t.[b]	
			Number	%	Number	%
Australia	179,664	7,525	729	9.7	6,796	90.3
Canada	652,176	30,958	14,991	48.4	15,967	51.6
New Zealand	91,003	2,541	157	6.2	2,384	93.8
United Kingdom	529,080	26,977	4,857	18.0	22,120	82.0
USA	8,948,645	140,126[c]	19,082	13.6	121,044	86.4
Total	10,400,568	208,127	39,816	19.1	168,311	80.9

Source: UNESCO (1974).
[a]English mother-tongue countries.
[b]Non-English mother-tongue countries.
[c]Includes foreign students studying in Guam, Puerto Rico, and the Virgin Islands.

Table 1.3.10   Origin of foreign students studying in five major English mother-tongue host countries, 1971

Country	No. of foreign students in country	Origin of foreign students								
		Africa	N. Am.	L. Am.	Asia	Europe	USSR	Oceania	Stateless	Unknown
USA	140,126	9,591	12,397	26,976	68,927	16,144	76	2,131	304	3,580
Canada	30,958	1,468	7,029	2,198	8,361	11,208	39	655	–	–
United Kingdom	26,977	5,671	3,586	1,151	9,546	3,758	6	810	4	2,445
Australia	7,525	171	280	26	5,876	360	–	699	–	113
New Zealand	2,541	44	78	6	1,808	39	–	564	–	2
Total	208,127	16,945	23,370	30,357	94,518	31,509	121	4,859	308	6,140

Source: UNESCO (1974).

Table 1.3.11 Foreign students *from* English mother-tongue countries, 1971, by country of origin, *in* English mother-tongue host countries, with percentages

Country of origin	Total^a	USA	Canada	United Kingdom	Australia	New Zealand	Students in Eng. m.-t. Number	%	Students in non-E. m.-t. Number	%
USA	20,710	–	6,339	2,259	184	60	8,842	42.7	11,868	57.3
Canada	12,853	10,396	–	1,032	93	15	11,536	89.8	1,317	10.2
United Kingdom	12,541	3,456	6,048	–	217	26	9,747	77.7	2,794	22.3
Australia	2,230	891	437	540	–	56	1,924	86.3	306	13.7
New Zealand	1,028	333	190	207	228	–	958	93.2	70	6.8
Jamaica	2,162	1,565	424	150	0	0	2,139	98.9	23	1.1
Trinidad	2,119	1,000	903	177	2	0	2,082	98.3	37	1.7
Guyana	1,390	892	344	125	0	0	1,361	97.9	29	2.1
Ireland	1,164	385	191	297	5	0	878	75.4	286	24.6
Barbados	351	164	115	70	0	0	349	99.4	2	0.05
Total	56,548	19,082	14,991	4,857	729	157	39,816	70.4	16,732	29.6

Source: (UNESCO) 1974.

^aTotal number of foreign students *from* the English mother-tongue country *in* another country. The percentages in later columns show the proportion of each total in English mother-tongue countries (Eng. m.-t.) and in non-English mother-tongue countries (non E. m.-t.).

Table 1.3.12   Foreign students *in* English mother-tongue countries *from* non-English mother-tongue countries, by area of origin, showing percentage of the total, 1971

Area of origin	No. of students	%
Africa	16,945	10.1
North America	504	0.2
Latin America	26,914	16.0
Asia	94,518	56.2
Europe	20,884	12.4
USSR	121	0.1
Oceania	1,977	1.2
Stateless	308	0.2
Unspecified	6,140	3.6
Total	168,311	100.0

Source: UNESCO (1974).

Table 1.3.10 shows the area of the world from which the foreign students in the five major host countries came. The largest group by far is the nearly 95,000 from Asian countries, followed by the just over 30,000 each from Europe and Latin America. This table, however, includes 39,816 from English mother-tongue countries (whose origins are detailed on Table 1.3.11). As Table 1.3.11 shows, only 29.6% of the foreign students from English mother-tongue countries go to non-English mother-tongue countries to do tertiary level work.

Returning to the 168,311 students in the five major host countries who are from non-English mother-tongue countries, Table 1.3.12 details their origins. By far the largest group is from Asia (56.2%), followed by Latin America (16.0%) and Europe (12.4%).

The United States is host to more students from foreign countries than any other country in the world and is important for our purposes since all tertiary education is English medium. Fortunately, there are some 1974/75 figures available on the number of foreign students in the United States and some indication of where they come from. These figures, published in *IIE Reports*, January 1976, indicate that there were 154,592[16] non-immigrant students studying on U.S. campuses in the academic year 1974/75. The census cited counted another 65,128 immigrant students as well, but gives no details as to their origins. It is particularly helpful for our purposes that this new distinction between immigrant and non-immigrant foreign students is now being made. Even if a few non-immigrant students later get immigrant visas and remain in this country, a large number of those who might otherwise have been included in our assessment of

Table 1.3.13   Distribution of non-immigrant foreign students in the United States, by area of the world, 1974/75

Area of origin	No. in USA	%
Africa	18,400	11.9
Asia	82,370	53.3
Europe	13,740	8.9
Latin America	26,270	17.0
North America	8,630	5.6
Oceania	2,650	1.7
Stateless	150	0.1
Unknown	2,370	1.5
Total	154,580[a]	100.0

Source: IIE Reports (New York: Institute of International Education, Jan. 1976).
[a] See note 16.

Table 1.3.14   Distribution of foreign students in the United States, by area of the world, 1971

Area of origin	No. in USA	%
Africa	9,591	6.8
Asia	68,927	49.2
Europe	16,144	11.5
Latin America	26,976	19.3
North America	12,397	8.8
USSR	76	0.1
Oceania	2,131	1.5
Stateless	304	0.2
Unknown	3,580	2.6
Total	140,126	100.0

Source: UNESCO (1974).

potential linguistic impact on their home countries has been eliminated. The distribution of non-immigrant students by region, 1974/75, appears in Table 1.3.13. The figures from 1971 shown in Table 1.3.14 reflect some differences in comparison to the 1974/75 figures. These data show an increase in the number of foreign students in the United States from Africa and Asia, while the proportion from Latin American countries, Europe, and North America declined.

    The *IIE Reports* article also gives figures for the top ten non-English mother-tongue countries sending students to the USA. Table 1.3.15 shows the IIE 1974/75 figures as well as the comparable figures for 1971. Other countries with

Table 1.3.15   Top ten countries of origin of foreign students in the United States, 1974/75, with comparative figures for 1971

	No. of foreign students in USA	
Country of origin	*1974/75*	*1971*
Iran	13,780	6,771
Hong Kong	11,060	9,302
China (Taiwan)	10,250	11,435
India	9,660	11,343
Canada	8,430	10,396
Nigeria	7,210	3,077
Thailand	6,250	5,555
Japan	5,930	4,296
Mexico	4,000	2,501
S. Korea	3,390	3,490

Source: 1974/75 figures: *IIE Reports* (Jan. 1976); 1971 figures: UNESCO (1974).

sizable numbers of students in the United States in 1971 are Cuba (7,612), United Kingdom (3,456), Philippines (2,715), Pakistan (2,243), and Israel (2,000). The changes between 1971 and 1975 are no doubt related to changing economic conditions in the world as well as to shifting political relations making study in the U.S. more or less desirable and feasible.

If the patterns displayed by other English mother-tongue host countries are like the pattern in the U.S., there is growth in the number of students coming from more distant or developing countries in Asia and Africa while the proportion coming from less distant or more developed countries shows a decline. This pattern may in fact be generalizable since the 1971 U.S. pattern (Table 1.3.14) is very like the 1971 pattern for the combined host countries (Table 1.3.9). The desirability of tertiary education in an English mother-tongue country, then, is greater, or seems to be growing in this direction, for persons in the more distant and/or less developed countries of Asia and Africa than for the less distant or more developed countries of Europe, Latin America, and North America.

Of the total number of foreign students from non-English mother-tongue countries (449,359 students in 1971), 37.5%, or 168,311, chose to go to English mother-tongue countries to do their tertiary level work. More than half of them came from Asian countries, with substantial numbers also coming from Latin America, Africa, and Europe.

4.0 ENGLISH IN THE MEDIA

4.1 English-Language Newspapers

English-language newspapers in non-English mother-tongue countries are another indication of the worldwide status of English. Newspapers are listed in Table 1.4.1 by country of publication, though some of them circulate in other countries as well, a fact we note when we are aware of it. Each paper is marked "bil" (bilingual) if it is in English and another language or languages ("multi" if known to be in more than two languages). If it is in English only, the column reads "Eng." The next column indicates periodicity: "daily," "monthly," "3x weekly," etc. Following this is the circulation and finally an indication of the city of publication (if given in the source). Countries marked with an asterisk are listed in Table 1.2.1, indicating English as a "designated" official language, and those with an "x" are from Table 1.2.2, official English language use in practice.

Circulation figures are not accurate indices; thus, it is never easy to know whether they overstate or understate readership. Reported circulation figures may be high to enhance advertising revenues, to achieve political goals, or to feed the egos of publishers and editors. On the other hand, they may understate readership because it is not uncommon, especially in less affluent countries, for newspapers to be passed along from reader to reader before they are finally discarded. In the case of discrepancies between sources of circulation data, we have consistently listed the lower circulation figure so as not to run the risk of presenting a picture which overestimates the place of the English-language press in the world. In most cases the information is taken from Banks (1975), though there are many items in the list taken from the relevant area handbook.

We have omitted from the list publications prepared in English for an audience primarily external to the country of publication, such as the political journals published in some European countries, printed in English, and sold only outside the country.[17] We have also excluded business and tourist publications of the same sort, published apparently only for foreigners or for the expatriate community.

The list of English language newspapers should not be taken as a fully representative account of the English-language press in a particular country. *The International Herald Tribune* is published in France but is read all over Western Europe, in Israel, and in other Middle Eastern countries, and is also widely read in Africa (Hachten 1971, p. 32). *West Africa,* "an informed and intelligent journal of news and opinion, is published weekly in London and is read by the African elites." (Ibid.) *Time* and *Newsweek* are widely available in the non-English mother-tongue countries of the world. *Newsweek,* for example, publishes *Newsweek International,* "which is printed in English, [and] has a circulation of 325,000 throughout the Atlantic and Pacific areas, and . . . about 80% of our readers are foreign nationals, not Americans." (Quoting Thomas J. Quinn, Newsweek International Editions, New York, in *English Around the World* 5 [1971]:7.)

Of the twenty-two countries listed in Africa as having English-language newspapers, seventeen are countries in which English is designated as official or

co-official language, two are countries in which English enjoys official use in
practice, and only three are countries not mentioned on the official language
tables at all. (See Tables 1.2.1 and 1.2.2) Of these three, Somalia is a former
British colony; Egypt and Libya, with relatively small daily circulations, constitute the only exceptions. There is, then, for Africa a strong relation between
official language countries, most of which were former Anglophone colonies, and
an English-language press with substantial circulation.

The situation in Asia is even more startling in terms of circulation, if not
so remarkable in numbers of countries. Of the twenty-five countries listed in
Table 1.4.1 for Asia, five have English as one of the designated official languages
and five are listed on Table 1.2.2 as having some official role in practice for
English. These ten countries account for most of the English newspapers in Asia
on Table 1.4.1. Of the 8,366,770 daily circulation recorded there, 97.6%, or
8,165,820, is in these ten countries. Outside the ten countries listed as having
some official role for English, there is no substantial daily English-language press
except perhaps in Taiwan and Nepal; but these circulations are very small.

The only Latin American country having English as an official language is
Guyana which has such a large proportion of persons claiming English as mother-
tongue that we have included it in our list of English mother-tongue countries.
Predictably, if what we have found in Asia and Africa can be generalized, there
should be little English-language press in Latin America. We list only four
newspapers outside of Guyana: a small daily in Costa Rica, two dailies in Panama
(one circulating primarily in the Canal Zone, presumably to Americans), and one
in Caracas, Venezuela, with a daily circulation of 12,000. However, the area
handbooks for Colombia (Weil et al. 1970), Brazil (Weil et al. 1971a), and
Venezuela (Weil et al. 1971b) note that English is replacing French as the primary
second language "of the socially elite" (1971a, p. vii) and is "used increasingly in
business and professional circles" (1971b, p. vii). One suspects that major
American newspapers are relatively common in most Latin American capitals.
However, in the absence of any governmental policy to promote English, there is
little motive or purpose for English newspaper publishing, even if there is a
growing English-using elite. Most of Latin America has no colonial heritage under
an English-speaking country (Puerto Rico, Cuba, Honduras, Guyana are exceptions), and furthermore has Spanish not only as a first language of most urban
populations, but also as a viable language of wider communication (Brazil a
notable exception). While English may surpass French in Latin America as a
second language, there seems little reason to predict that English will become
anything more than that in the foreseeable future.

The large number of newspapers published in English in the non-English
mother-tongue countries of Asia and Africa show that there are many people who
are able to read English competently and that they do so on a regular basis.
English is a conduit to the wider world. This indicates, perhaps more strongly than
any of our other information, that there is widespread daily opportunity to use
English in Asia and Africa and that at least some of the growing numbers of
people learning English are in fact using it regularly.

Table 1.4.1   English-language newspapers published in non-English mother-tongue countries, by continent, giving periodicity, circulation, and city of publication

Continent, country, and newspaper	Language	Periodicity	Circulation	City of publication
Africa				
Botswana*				
Botswana Daily News	bil	daily	11,000	Gaberones
Kutlwano	bil	monthly	7,500	Gaberones
Mafeking Mail	bil	weekly	NA	Gaberones
Botswana Guardian	bil	weekly	NA	Gaberones
Cameroon*				
La Presse du Cameroun	bil	daily	15,000	Douala
Cameroon Times	Eng	3x weekly	5,000	Victoria
Egypt				
Egyptian Gazette	Eng	daily	8,500[a]	Cairo
Ethiopia[x]				
Ethiopian Herald	Eng	daily	8,000[b]	Addis Ababa
Voice of Ethiopia	bil	daily	4,000	Addis Ababa
Gambia*				
Gambia News Bulletin	Eng	3x weekly	2,000	Banjul
Gambia Echo	Eng	weekly	500	Banjul
Gambia Onward	Eng	3x weekly	NA	Banjul
Progressive	Eng	3x weekly	NA	Banjul
The Nation	Eng	fortnightly	NA	Banjul
The New Gambia	Eng	3x weekly	NA	Banjul
Ghana*[c]				
Daily Graphic	Eng	daily	125,000	Accra
Ghanian Times	Eng	daily	100,000	Accra
Star	Eng	daily	50,000	Accra
Sunday Mirror	Eng	weekly	69,827	Accra
Weekly Spectator	Eng	weekly	45,000	Accra
The Pioneer	Eng	daily	45,000	Kumasi
Kenya[x]				
East African Standard[d]	Eng	daily	36,000	Nairobi
Daily Nation	Eng	daily	35,500	Nairobi
Lesotho*				
Moeletsi on Basotho	bil	weekly	12,000	
Mohlabani	bil	biweekly	10,000	
Lesotho News	Eng	biweekly	800	
Liberia*				
The Liberian Age	Eng	daily	10,000	Monrovia
Sunday Digest	Eng	weekly	4,500	Monrovia
Saturday Chronicle	Eng	weekly	3,500	Monrovia
Daily Listener	Eng	daily	3,500	Monrovia
The Liberian Star	Eng	daily	3,500	Monrovia

Table 1.4.1 (continued)

Continent, country and newspaper	Language	Periodicity	Circulation	City of publication
Libya				
Libyan Times	Eng	daily	NA	Benghazi
Malawi*				
Moni	bil	monthly	22,000	Blantyre
Malawi News	bil	daily	18,000	Limbe
The Times	Eng	biweekly	14,700	Blantyre
The African	bil	daily	14,000	Lelongiwe
Mauritius*				
L'Express	bil	daily	18,500	Port Louis
Le Mauricien	bil	daily	15,000	Port Louis
Advance	bil	daily	12,000	Port Louis
Le Citogen	bil	daily	10,000	Port Louis
Le Cernéen	bil	daily	9,000	Port Louis
Congress	bil	daily	8,000	Port Louis
The Star	bil	daily	7,000	Port Louis
Namibia*				
Windhoek Advertiser	Eng	daily	3,391	Windhoek
Nigeria*				
Sunday Times	Eng	weekly	368,000	Lagos
Daily Times	Eng	daily	205,000	Lagos
Sunday Observer	Eng	weekly	60,000	Benin City
West African Pilot	Eng	daily	47,000	Yaba
New Nigerian	Eng	daily	45,000	Kaduna
Nigerian Observer	Eng	daily	40,000	Benin City
Nigerian Tribune	Eng	daily	30,000	Ibadan
Rhodesia*				
Sunday Mail	Eng	weekly	79,459	Salisbury
Rhodesia Herald	Eng	daily	66,358	Salisbury
The Chronicle	Eng	daily	27,645	Bulawago
Sunday News	Eng	weekly	23,630	Bulawago
Sierra Leone*				
Daily Mail	Eng	daily	15,000	Freetown
Nation	Eng	daily	10,000	Freetown
Shekpendeh	Eng	2x weekly	9,000	Freetown
African Vanguard	Eng	weekly	4,000	Freetown
Somalia				
Dawn October	Eng	weekly	NA	Mogadishu
Hoiseid	bil	weekly	NA	Mogadishu
South Africa*				
The Star	Eng	daily	187,383	Johannesburg
Rand Daily Mail	Eng	daily	142,148	Johannesburg
The Argus	Eng	daily	117,390	Cape Town
The World	Eng	daily	110,308	Johannesburg
Daily News	Eng	daily	105,545	Durban
Cape Herald	Eng	daily	83,614	Cape Town

Table 1.4.1 (continued)

Continent, country and newspaper	Language	Periodicity	Circulation	City of publication
South Africa (continued)				
Cape Times	Eng	daily	78,142	Cape Town
Natal Mercury	Eng	daily	76,305	Durban
Swaziland*				
Times of Swaziland	Eng	weekly	5,493	Mbabane
Tanzania*				
East African Standard	Eng	daily	22,274	Dar es Salaam
The Nationalist	Eng	daily	9,532	Dar es Salaam
Uganda*				
Voice of Uganda[e]	Eng	daily	27,000	Kampala
Zambia*				
Sunday Times of Zambia	Eng	weekly	65,000	Lusaka
Times of Zambia	Eng	daily	60,000	Lusaka
Zambia Daily Mail	Eng	daily	45,000	Lusaka
Asia				
Afghanistan				
Kabul Times	Eng	daily	8,000	Kabul
Bahrain				
Awali Evening News	Eng	daily	1,000	Awali
Gulf Weekly Mirror	Eng	weekly	NA	Manama
Bangladesh				
Morning News	Eng	daily	20,000	Dacca
Bhutan				
Kuensel	multi	weekly	NA	
Brunei				
Borneo Bulletin	Eng	weekly	25,921	
Salam	multi	weekly	6,500	
Burma[x]				
Working People's Daily	Eng	daily	65,000	Rangoon
Guardian	Eng	daily	15,000	Rangoon
China (Taiwan)				
China Post	Eng	daily	22,500	Taipei
China News	Eng	daily	13,000	Taipei
Fiji*				
Fiji Times	Eng	daily	20,000	Suva
Fiji Royal Gazette	Eng	weekly	NA	Suva
Pacific Review	bil	weekly	NA	Suva
India*[f]				

Table 1.4.1 (continued)

Continent, country, and newspaper	Language	Periodicity	Circulation	City of Publication
Iran				
Kayhan International	Eng	daily	15,000	Tehran
Iraq				
Baghdad Observer	Eng	daily	20,000	Baghdad
Baghdad News	Eng	daily	6,000	Baghdad
Israel[x]				
Jerusalem Post	Eng	daily	31,500	Jerusalem
Kuwait				
Daily News	Eng	daily	NA	Kuwait City
Lebanon				
The Daily Star	Eng	daily	8,250	Beirut
Malaysia[x]				
Sunday Times	Eng	weekly	172,000	Kuala Lumpur
Straits Times	Eng	daily	135,000	Kuala Lumpur
Sunday Mail	Eng	weekly	35,000	Kuala Lumpur
Malay Mail	Eng	daily	25,000	Kuala Lumpur
Nepal				
The Motherland	Eng	daily	3,500	Kathmandu
The Rising Nepal	Eng	daily	3,000	Kathmandu
The Commoner	Eng	daily	2,000	Kathmandu
New Herald	Eng	daily	1,500	Kathmandu
Pakistan*				
Nawa-i-Waqt	bil	daily	300,000	Lahore and Rawalpindi
Morning News	Eng	daily	50,000	Karachi
Dawn	bil	daily	49,000	Karachi
Daily News	Eng	daily	42,000	Karachi
Pakistan Times	Eng	daily	NA	Lahore and Rawalpindi
Philippines*				
Philippines Daily Express	bil	daily	300,000	Manila
Bulletin Today	Eng	daily	120,000	Manila
Times Journal	Eng	daily	70,000	Pasig
Qatar				
Gulf News	Eng	weekly	NA	Doha
Singapore*				
Straits Times	Eng	daily	235,000	Singapore
Sunday	Eng	weekly	235,000	Singapore
Sunday Mail	Eng	weekly	18,200	Singapore
New Nation	Eng	weekly	17,000	Singapore

Table 1.4.1 (continued)

Continent, country and newspaper	Language	Periodicity	Circulation	City of publication
Sri Lanka[x]				
Ceylon Observer	Eng	daily	91,783	Colombo
Ceylon Daily News	Eng	daily	67,537	Colombo
Times of Ceylon	Eng	daily	36,000	Colombo
Ceylon Daily Mirror	Eng	daily	31,500	Colombo
Thailand				
Bankok Post	Eng	daily	21,000	Bankok
Tonga				
The Chronicle	bil	weekly	6,500	
Viet Nam, South				
The Saigon Post	Eng	daily	15,000	Saigon
Western Samoa*				
Savali	Eng	fortnightly	6,500	Apia
The Samoan Times	Eng	weekly	5,000	Apia
South Seas Star	Eng	weekly	3,000	Apia
Latin America				
Costa Rica				
Daily News			1,000	
Guyana*				
Sunday Graphic	Eng	weekly	51,000	Georgetown
Daily Chronicle	Eng	daily	35,000	Georgetown
Guyana Graphic	Eng	daily	32,835	Georgetown
Sunday Chronicle	Eng	weekly	24,000	Georgetown
Weekend Post and Sunday Argosy	Eng	weekly	20,819	Georgetown
Mirror	Eng	daily	16,799	Georgetown
New Nation	Eng	weekly	15,000	Georgetown
Evening Post	Eng	daily	10,315	Georgetown
Panama				
The Panama American	Eng	daily	12,751	Panama City
Star & Herald	Eng	daily	12,270	Canal Zone
Venezuela				
Daily Journal	Eng	daily	12,000	Caracas
Europe				
Cyprus				
Cyprus Mail	Eng	daily	5,580	Nicosia
France				
International Herald Tribune	Eng	daily	121,317	Paris

Table 1.4.1 (continued)

Continent, country and newspaper	Language	Periodicity	Circulation	City of publication
Malta*				
Times of Malta	Eng	daily	14,700	Valetta
Bulletin	Eng	daily	12,000	Valetta

Sources: Banks (1975) and relevant *Area Handbook.*
Key: In the language column, "Eng" indicates that the newspaper is in English only; "bil" means it is in English and at least one other language; and "multi" indicates that it is known to be in more than two languages. In the circulation column, "NA" means that a figure was not available.
*English is *designated* official language.
[x]Country is listed on Table 1.2.2, meaning English plays some special official role in the country, though English is not the "designated" official language.

[a]*Egyptian Gazette,* circulation 45,000 (Smith 1970*b*, p. 260).

[b]*Ethiopian Herald,* circulation 25,000 (*English Around the World* 3 (Nov. 1970)).

[c]Kaplan (1971*a*:188) lists 4 dailies, 12 weeklies, 2 twice-monthlies, 9 monthlies, one every two months, and 6 quarterlies appearing in English.

[d]The *East African Standard* (Kenya) also circulates in Tanzania and Uganda.

[e]50.5% of total newspaper circulation (Ladefoged et al. 1971, p. 20).

[f]Banks (1975) mentions that of the 16 major dailies, English accounts for 1,300,000 of daily circulation out of 2,820,000 total. Paxton (1975) claims that English newspapers have a daily circulation of 6,479,000.

4.2 English-Language Book Production, with Comparisons to French

As yet another index of the place English plays in the life of non-English mother-tongue countries, we have collected book production figures, country by country and region by region. In the tables we give totals for each of four years, 1972, 1971, 1969, and 1967, and compare figures for the number of titles in English and the number of titles in French. Beside each language total we have given the proportion of the total book publication in the country for the given year represented by the number of titles in English and the number of titles in French, respectively. There are also various summary tables, one giving a comparison by continental region for the countries represented, comparing English in non-English mother-tongue countries with French in non-French mother-tongue countries. A second regional comparison is made for parts of Europe, comparing English in non-English mother-tongue countries with French in non-French mother-tongue countries. There are also comparisons of Scandanavia with the Warsaw Pact countries.

Table 1.4.2, which presents the number of countries for which figures are available for each of the four years we have studied, shows that these statistics do not come from the best of all possible worlds. In no year do we have figures for

Table 1.4.2   Number of countries represented in book production figures for
                1972, 1971, 1969, and 1967, by area of the world

	1972	1971	1969	1967
Africa	7	9	6	11
Asia	16	12	14	12
Americas	8	7	6	3
Europe	17	19	17	18
Others	1	1	1	2
Total	49	48	44	46

more than 49 countries. Further, we do not have figures for the same countries
each year. We have, rather, a selection, as complete as the UNESCO (1974)
statistics allow. Despite the information gaps, some tentative conclusions and
interpretations are possible.

Table 1.4.3 shows, for each of four years, the percentage of the books
published in each area of the world (excluding the USSR) in English (excluding
English mother-tongue countries) and in French (excluding French mother-tongue
countries). Several facts are highlighted in this table, and several questions raised.
First, French titles constitute a smaller proportion of the total production on each
continent of the world and in each of the years represented. Further, in no case,
with the possible exception of Europe, is there a clearly discernible growth in the
proportion of book titles in French. Second, the proportion of titles in English
seems to decrease markedly in Africa and in Asia, while showing growth in Latin
America and possibly Europe. These supposed patterns need to be examined in
light of both the raw figures in Table 1.4.4 and the details of Tables 1.4.5-1.4.9.

Table 1.4.4 shows that for the total number of countries shown in Table
1.4.2 for each year, between 7.4% and 9.3% of the book publishing was in English.

Table 1.4.3   Percentage of total book production in English (excluding English
                mother-tongue countries) and in French (excluding French mother-
                tongue countries), by continent for 1972, 1971, 1969, and 1967

	1972		1971		1969		1967	
	E	F	E	F	E	F	E	F
Africa	9.0	7.4	21.6	3.3	48.1	12.5	32.5	5.3
Asia	14.2	0.2	12.6	0.2	20.2	0.5	36.9	0.3
Europe[a]	4.5	2.8	4.3	2.5	4.4	2.6	4.2	2.0
Latin America	5.2	1.8	6.2	2.2	3.4	0.7	2.5	1.4

[a]Also excluding USSR.

Table 1.4.4 Book production, by area of the world, showing number of titles in English and in French and their respective proportion of the total number of titles for 1972, 1971, 1969, and 1967, excluding English mother-tongue countries from English figures and French mother-tongue countries from French figures

Area		1972					1971			
	Total	English	%	French	%	Total	English	%	French	%
Africa	3,147	283	9.0	232	7.4	5,781	1,246	21.6	193	3.3
Asia	60,601	8,778	14.2	139	0.2	61,123	7,673	12.6	97	0.2
Europe	129,032	5,796	4.5	3,412	2.8	125,778	5,412	4.3	3,033	2.5
Latin America	12,916	673	5.2	238	1.8	12.347	766	6.2	272	2.2
Total	205,696	15,530	7.5	4,021	2.0	205,029	15,097	7.4	3,595	1.8

Area		1969					1967			
	Total	English	%	French	%	Total	English	%	French	%
Africa	905	435	48.1	113	12.5	6,367	2,071	32.5	339	5.3
Asia	30,315	6,121	20.2	154	0.5	16,655	6,138	36.9	63	0.3
Europe	111,842	4,895	4.4	2,802	2.6	115,064	4,808	4.2	2,218	2.0
Latin America	3,113	106	3.4	21	0.7	2,304	57	2.5	33	1.4
Total	146,175	11,557	7.9	3,090	2.1	140,390	13,074	9.3	2,653	1.9

Table 1.4.5   Book production comparing English and French titles to total number of titles, country-by-country for 1972, 1971, 1969, and 1967: Americas

	1972					1971				
	Total	English	%	French	%	Total	English	%	French	%
Argentina	4,578	553	12.1	217	4.7	4,634	639	13.8	236	5.1
Canada	6,710	4,643	69.2	1,645	24.5	4,205	2,892	68.8	1,110	26.4
Chile	997	10	0.2	7	0.1	1,090	3	0.2	10	0.9
Colombia	848	18	2.1	0	0	–	–	–	–	–
Costa Rica	–	–	–	–	–	327	3	0.9	0	0
Cuba	942	72	7.6	13	1.4	885	79	8.9	13	1.5
Guyana	24	23	95.8	0	0	–	–	–	–	–
Mexico	4,513	14	0.3	0	0	4,439	15	0.3	1	.02
Panama	–	–	–	–	–	–	–	–	–	–
Peru	858	6	0.6	1	0.1	973	27	2.8	12	1.2

	1969					1967				
	Total	English	%	French	%	Total	English	%	French	%
Argentina	–	–	–	–	–	–	–	–	–	–
Canada	3,659	2,659	72.7	882	24.1	3,782	2,914	77.0	773	20.4
Chile	1,100	9	0.8	8	0.7	1,556	11	0.7	13	0.8
Colombia	–	–	–	–	–	–	–	–	–	–
Costa Rica	284	8	2.8	0	0	–	–	–	–	–
Cuba	995	78	7.8	13	1.3	748	46	6.1	20	2.7
Guyana	–	–	–	–	–	–	–	–	–	–
Mexico	–	–	–	–	–	–	–	–	–	–
Panama	199	7	3.5	0	0	–	–	–	–	–
Peru	535	4	0.7	0	0	–	–	–	–	–

Key: — = not available; 0 = no titles.

This figure does *not* represent worldwide book publishing since major publishing countries such as the United Kingdom, France, and the United States are wholly excluded. The percentage of book publishing in French is markedly lower, ranging from 1.8% to 2.1% of the total book publishing in the listed non-French mother-tongue countries. In the case of neither language is there sufficient data to note increases or decreases over time.

The highest percentages consistently, over time for English are in Asia, where English is the major language of wider communication, while, predictably, French figures are lowest in Asia, where French has no significant role in international communication. Those parts of the world where French is important—Africa, Europe, and to a lesser extent Latin America—still show English significantly ahead of French. Apparently even in countries where there is less widespread use of spoken English or of English instruction in the schools (countries such as Argentina and Egypt come to mind) English is still a widely used "library language," to a great enough extent to support some English language book publishing.

Table 1.4.5 provides a partial answer to the question raised about the possible growth in the proportion of English over time in the Americas. The figures for 1967, while helpful for the individual countries they represent, do not provide any overall picture, since only three countries are included. Further, the figures for Canada include two-thirds of the total for that year and dominate the totals, which show 48.8% English including Canada but 2.5% English excluding Canada. The figures for 1972 and 1971 are substantially higher because both Argentina and Mexico are included. Mexico deserves special mention. Apparently the English books used in Mexico in English classes (see Table 1.3.6 for primary and secondary school estimates), as well as other English books, are published in the United States and imported. The percentage is remarkably low for a comparatively large publishing total.

In Table 1.4.6, 1967 includes statistics on only eleven of the eighteen countries listed for Africa. This is the best representation of our four sample years, with 1969 the lowest (six countries). The figure for 1969 is further skewed by the absence of Egypt, a major publisher in Africa, and by the absence of South Africa, which accounts for more than 2,600 books alone in both 1967 and 1971. Further, the 48.1% English figure on Table 1.4.4 for 1969 does not represent an overall increase in English publishing for two reasons: first, there is a significantly smaller number of countries included for 1969 than for other years, and, second, two of those countries included are Ghana and Kenya with high concentrations of English book publishing. Further, the drop in 1971 is not a real drop. Nigeria, with 88.3% of its publishing in English, is one of the countries included in 1967, pushing that percentage up, but appearing only there. Nor does the 1972 figure represent a real decrease in English publishing, since all the high percentage English countries (Ghana, Kenya, South Africa, Nigeria, and Sierra Leone) are absent except for Botswana, which involves only 48 titles. Unfortunately the data are spotty and therefore continentwide generalizations are not possible.

Table 1.4.6 Book production comparing English and French titles to the total number of titles, country-by-country for 1972, 1971, 1969, and 1967: Africa

	1972					1971				
	Total	English	%	French	%	Total	English	%	French	%
Algeria	—	—	—	—	—	—	—	—	—	—
Botswana	48	41	85.4	0	0	26	22	84.6	0	0
Egypt	2,412	176	7.3	44	1.8	2,142	147	6.9	40	1.9
Ghana	—	—	—	—	—	136	88	64.7	0	0
Ivory Coast	—	—	—	—	—	—	—	—	—	—
Kenya	—	—	—	—	—	—	—	—	—	—
Lesotho	33	6	18.2	0	0	—	—	—	—	—
Libya	218	0	0	74	33.9	249	4	1.6	4	1.6
Madagascar	194	0	0	74	38.1	197	1	0.5	62	31.5
Mauritius	90	34	37.8	39	43.3	55	31	56.4	17	30.9
Morocco	—	—	—	—	—	122	0	0	70	57.4
Mozambique	—	—	—	—	—	—	—	—	—	—
Nigeria	—	—	—	—	—	—	—	—	—	—
Sierra Leone	—	—	—	—	—	—	—	—	—	—
South Africa	—	—	—	—	—	2,649	821	30.7	0	0
Sudan	152	26	17.1	1	0.6	—	—	—	—	—
Tanzania	—	—	—	—	—	—	—	—	—	—
Uganda	—	—	—	—	—	205	141	68.8	0	0

Table 1.4.6 (continued)

	1969					1967				
	Total	English	%	French	%	Total	English	%	French	%
Algeria	–	–	–	–	–	258	2	.07	238	92.2
Botswana	–	–	–	–	–	–	–	–	–	–
Egypt	–	–	–	–	–	1,819	110	6.0	32	1.8
Ghana	446	297	66.6	0	0	233	200	85.8	0	0
Ivory Coast	38	0	0	38	100.0	50	0	0	50	100.0
Kenya	193	113	58.5	0	0	162	123	75.9	0	0
Lesotho	–	–	–	–	–	–	–	–	–	–
Libya	–	–	–	–	–	–	–	–	–	–
Madagascar	156	1	0.6	52	33.3	154	41	26.6	0	0
Mauritius	42	19	45.2	23	54.8	50	32	64.0	16	32.0
Morocco	–	–	–	–	–	–	–	–	–	–
Mozambique	–	–	–	–	–	149	7	4.7	1	0.6
Nigeria	–	–	–	–	–	778	687	88.3	0	0
Sierra Leone	–	–	–	–	–	73	68	93.1	0	0
South Africa	–	–	–	–	–	2,641	801	30.3	2	.07
Sudan	–	–	–	–	–	–	–	–	–	–
Tanzania	30	5	16.6	0	0	–	–	–	–	–
Uganda	–	–	–	–	–	–	–	–	–	–

Key: – = not available; 0 = no titles.

Some country trends are noticeable, however. Egypt, while publishing a relatively stable percentage of French books, has increased the proportion of English books from 6% to 7.3% while increasing the total number of titles significantly. The percentage of English titles in Ghana has decreased with a fluctuating total, reflecting an increased role (at least in 1969) for the national languages. The drop in total publishing in 1971 may be due to economic or other internal factors.

Statistics on book production are the most complete for Europe, where we have a fairly constant number of countries (between seventeen and nineteen represented). (See Table 1.4.2) These countries, further, are consistently represented; every country listed appears for each year except Czechoslovakia (missing 1969), Luxembourg (appearing only in 1971) and Norway (missing 1972). Some major countries are missing altogether (United Kingdom and France are notable omissions) but since both are missing, any influence on the English/French comparison is neutralized. Our data show that the proportion of French titles in the total book production of these selected countries ranged from a 1967 low of 2% to a 1972 high of 2.8%. English has ranged between 4.2% in 1967 and 4.5% in 1972. The difference between the English and French figures is relatively consistent, approaching two percentage points. Only in 1967 are there more than twice as many books in English as in French in their respective non-mother-tongue countries, the difference being over 2,000 titles in each case.

The broad picture in Europe for English (and the comparison with French we are making) is brought into sharper focus when the regional comparisons of Table 1.4.8 are made. Both English and French are small contributors to the total publishing picture in Warsaw Pact countries (including the USSR), while those countries on an overall basis account for more than 60% of the non-English mother-tongue publishing in Europe. French constitutes less than 1% of publishing in Warsaw Pact countries while the English portion hovers around 2%. Clearly Russian is the most significant second language in Eastern Europe, and, while there are many students at the primary and secondary levels studying English (see Table 1.3.5), the supports one expects to find (books, newspapers, etc.) for a major second language are absent. This no doubt reflects a political decision, or a number of decisions, about which languages to promote.

The situation in Scandinavia is in sharp contrast. English is the major second language. Nearly everyone with a high school education is a reasonably competent user of English and the demand created by this large group is no doubt reflected in the relatively high percentage of the total number of titles being published in English. The number, in fact, shows a marked increase in 1972, when the total number of books fell by about 3,000 volumes while the total number of titles in English increased by 700 titles. The total drop is partly accounted for by the absence of Norway from the 1972 figures, but the increase seems to reflect a real increase; the numbers increase sharply in Finland from about 5% consistently in 1967, 1969, and 1971 to 17.8% in 1972. The increase in Sweden is slight and the increase in Denmark substantial but less dramatic than Finland's.

Table 1.4.7 Book production comparing English and French titles to the number of titles, country-by-country for 1972, 1971, 1969, and 1967: Europe

	1972					1971				
	Total	English	%	French	%	Total	English	%	French	%
Austria	5,062	123	2.4	16	0.3	4,861	70	1.4	32	0.7
Belgium	5,043	127	2.5	1,938	38.4	4,191	106	2.5	1,742	41.6
Bulgaria	3,978	94	2.4	69	1.7	4,188	76	1.8	75	1.8
Czechoslovakia	9,521	114	1.2	41	0.4	9,040	157	1.7	71	0.8
Denmark	6,547	533	8.4	28	0.4	5,339	302	5.7	19	0.4
Finland	4,522	807	17.8	67	1.5	4,407	241	5.5	8	0.2
Hungary	7,293	241	3.3	59	0.8	6,468	243	3.8	41	0.6
Ireland	556	512	92.1	1	0.2	546	485	88.9	0	0
Italy	8,381	146	1.7	148	1.8	8,283	137	1.7	100	1.2
Luxembourg	–	–		–		180	2	1.1	128	71.1
Netherlands	11,800	965	8.2	213	1.8	10,827	833	7.7	237	2.2
Norway	–	–		–		4,441	318	7.2	16	0.4
Poland	10,760	407	3.8	105	1.0	10,443	507	4.9	88	0.8
Romania	8,765	193	2.2	237	2.7	8,224	197	2.4	212	2.6
Spain	20,858	287	1.4	199	1.0	19,762	438	2.2	188	1.0
Sweden	7,782	1,079	13.9	23	0.3	7,558	898	11.9	24	0.3
Switzerland	8,449	544	6.4	2,115	25.0	7,205	293	4.1	1,877	26.1
USSR	80,555	1,377	1.7	482	0.6	85,487	1,729	2.0	671	0.8
Yugoslavia	9,715	116	1.2	46	0.5	9,815	109	1.1	45	0.5

Table 1.4.7 (continued)

	1969					1967				
	Total	English	%	French	%	Total	English	%	French	%
Austria	5,204	198	3.8	72	1.4	4,987	152	3.0	44	0.9
Belgium	5,089	159	3.1	2,026	39.8	3,888	70	1.8	1,675	43.1
Bulgaria	3,548	55	1.6	56	1.6	3,754	68	1.8	65	1.7
Czechoslovakia	–	–	–	–	–	8,079	198	2.5	74	0.9
Denmark	4,978	320	6.4	26	0.5	4,895	326	6.7	18	0.4
Finland	3,646	195	5.3	7	0.2	3,530	204	5.8	11	0.3
Hungary	4,831	111	2.3	41	0.8	5,301	100	1.9	48	0.9
Ireland	467	425	91.0	1	0.2	223	181	81.2	0	0
Italy	8,440	120	1.4	99	1.2	8,225	78	0.1	128	1.6
Luxembourg	–	–	–	–	–	–	–	–	–	–
Netherlands	11,204	799	7.1	299	2.7	11,262	730	6.5	221	2.0
Norway	3,935	292	7.4	7	.2	3,276	287	8.8	0	0
Poland	9,413	378	4.0	104	1.1	9,694	348	3.6	80	0.8
Romania	7,440	199	2.7	193	2.6	6,085	201	3.3	225	3.7
Spain	20,031	221	1.0	121	0.6	19,380	172	0.9	120	0.6
Sweden	7,404	937	12.7	25	0.3	7,218	977	13.5	22	0.3
Switzerland	7,505	351	4.7	1,678	22.3	6,041	295	4.9	1,274	21.1
USSR	74,611	952	1.3	382	0.5	74,081	1,215	1.6	548	0.7
Yuglosavia	8,708	135	1.6	73	0.8	9,226	206	2.2	88	1.0

Key: – = not available; 0 = no titles.

Table 1.4.8 Book production, regional comparisons: Europe

Region	1972					1971				
	Total	English	%	French	%	Total	English	%	French	%
USSR and Warsaw Pact countries[a]	130,587	2,542	1.9	1,039	0.8	133,665	3,018	2.3	1,203	0.9
Scandinavia[b]	18,851[c]	2,439	12.9	118	0.6	21,745	1,759	8.1	67	0.3
All non-English mother-tongue[d]	209,031	7,173	3.4	5,786	2.8	210,719	7,141	3.4	5,574	2.6
All non-French mother-tongue[e]	204,544	7,558	3.7	3,849	1.9	206,894	7,276	3.5	3,704	1.8
Non-English mother-tongue excluding USSR	128,476	5,796	4.5	5,304	4.1	125,232	5,412	4.3	4,903	3.9
Non-French mother-tongue excluding USSR	123,983	6,181	5.0	3,412	2.8	121,407	5,547	4.6	3,033	2.5

Region	1969					1967				
	Total	English	%	French	%	Total	English	%	French	%
USSR and Warsaw Pact countries[a]	108,551	1,830	1.7	849	0.8	116,220	2,336	2.0	1,128	1.0
Scandinavia[b]	19,963	1,744	8.7	65	0.3	18,919	1,794	9.5	51	0.2
All non-English mother-tongue[d]	185,987	5,847	3.1	5,209	2.8	188,922	6,023	3.2	4,621	2.4
All non-French mother-tongue[e]	181,365	5,688	3.1	3,184	1.8	185,257	5,738	3.1	2,766	1.5
Non-English mother-tongue excluding USSR	111,376	4,895	4.4	4,827	4.3	114,841	4,808	4.2	4,073	3.5
Non-French mother-tongue excluding USSR	106,754	4,736	4.4	2,802	2.6	111,176	4,523	4.1	2,218	2.0

[a] Includes Bulgaria, Czechoslovakia, Hungary, Poland, Romania, USSR, and Yugoslavia.
[b] Includes Denmark, Finland, Norway and Sweden.
[c] 1972 figures for Norway are not available.
[d] All on Table 1.4.7 except Ireland.
[e] All on Table 1.4.7 except Belgium and Luxembourg.

Table 1.4.9 Book production, comparing English and French titles to total number of titles, country-by-country for 1972, 1971, 1969, and 1967: Asia

	1972					1971				
	Total	English	%	French	%	Total	English	%	French	%
Cyprus	496	121	24.4	56	11.3	428	106	24.8	45	10.5
Greece	2,621	38	1.4	22	0.8	2,212	16	0.7	4	0.2
Hong Kong	1,238	1,190	96.1	5	0.4	–	–	–	–	–
India	14,480	5,723	39.5	0	0	13,614	5,429	39.9	0	0
Iraq	–	–	–	–	–	–	–	–	–	–
Israel	2,414	189	8.8	0	0	1,889	224	11.9	0	0
Japan	31,074	163	0.5	1	0.003	31,040	399	1.3	3	0.009
Jordan	–	–	–	–	–	–	–	–	–	–
Khmer Rep.	29	0	0	1	3.4	–	–	–	–	–
South Korea	–	–	–	–	–	–	–	–	–	–
Kuwait	–	–	–	–	–	117	2	1.7	1	0.8
Laos	179	11	6.1	20	11.2	–	–	–	–	–
Lebanon	–	–	–	–	–	–	–	–	–	–
Malaysia	1,225	524	42.8	2	0.2	1,202	480	39.9	0	0
Pakistan	–	–	–	–	–	–	–	–	–	–
Qatar	104	1	0.9	0	0	88	0	0	0	0
Singapore	508	267	52.6	0	0	574	327	57.0	1	0.1
Sri Lanka (Ceylon)	1,604	344	21.4	1	0.06	1,245	294	23.6	1	0.08
Thailand	2,579	183	7.1	1	0.03	2,174	158	7.3	0	0
Turkey	–	–	–	–	–	6,540	238	3.6	42	0.6
So. Viet Nam	729	24	3.3	32	4.4	–	–	–	–	–
Bhutan	25	0	0	0	0	–	–	–	–	–
Burma	1,569	0	0	0	0	–	–	–	–	–

Table 1.4.9 (continued)

	1969					1967				
	Total	English	%	French	%	Total	English	%	French	%
Cyprus	341	47	13.8	14	4.1	207	25	12.1	5	2.4
Greece	–	–	–	–	–	–	–	–	–	–
Hong Kong	–	–	–	–	–	–	–	–	–	–
India	13,733	4,842	35.3	0	0	10,617	4,658	43.9	0	0
Iraq	569	18	3.2	0	0	–	–	–	–	–
Israel	2,038	221	10.8	0	0	1,471	236	16.0	0	0
Japan	–	–	–	–	–	–	–	–	–	–
Jordan	224	14	6.3	0	0	162	14	8.6	0	0
Khmer Rep.	–	–	–	–	–	358	0	0	39	10.9
South Korea	2,501	135	5.4	44	1.8	–	–	–	–	–
Kuwait	80	1	1.3	0	0	–	–	–	–	–
Laos	57	0	0	2	3.5	14	0	0	3	21.4
Lebanon	685	50	7.3	42	6.1	427	15	3.5	16	3.7
Malaysia	–	–	–	–	–	483	136	28.2	0	0
Pakistan	–	–	–	–	–	3,478	612	17.6	0	0
Qatar	–	–	–	–	–	–	–	–	–	–
Singapore	533	307	57.6	0	0	322	163	50.6	0	0
Sri Lanka (Ceylon)	931	133	14.3	0	0	1,534	279	18.2	0	0
Thailand	2,457	166	6.8	4	0.2	–	–	–	–	–
Turkey	5,669	187	3.3	48	0.07	713	0	0	0	0
So. Viet Nam	497	0	0	0	0	–	–	–	–	–
Bhutan	–	–	–	–	–	–	–	–	–	–
Burma	–	–	–	–	–	–	–	–	–	–

Key: – = not available; 0 = no titles.

The figures for Asia show a stable but insignificant number of books in French. For English they show a wide divergence between 1967 and 1969 on the one hand and 1971 and 1972 on the other. (See Table 1.4.3) Part of the answer is in the figures for Japan, which show a very small percentage of English books (1971, 1.3%; 1972, 0.5%) but very high totals. The inclusion of figures for Japan in 1971 and 1972 after their absence in 1967 and 1969 accounts for the large disparity in numbers. The 1971 and 1972 figures give a fairly representative picture of Asia and include, in the main, the same countries. The increase from 12.6% English in 1971 to 14.2% is probably not significant, but it does at least indicate that English continues to maintain its position.

The proportion of books in English in India is continuing to be relatively stable. The 1969 figures show some drop in proportion but an increase in the number of titles. However, the percentage returns to just under 40% for English in 1971 and 1972, in spite of the reported decline in the growth of English since independence. (Mazrui 1975b, p. 12) The place of English books in publishing in Malaysia grew from 28.2% in 1967 to 42.8% in 1972.

5.0 CONCLUSION *

In 1938, Jespersen attributed the phenomenal growth and spread of the English language to "political ascendancy" rather than to any intrinsic superiority in the language or cultural superiority in its speakers. (p. 233) (One assumes he means

Table 1.5.1 Estimates of speakers of six European languages for the years 1500, 1600, 1700, 1800, 1900, and 1926, in millions

Year	English	German	Russian	French	Spanish	Italian
1500	4 (5)	10	3	10 (12)	8½	9½
1600	6	10	3	14	8½	9½
1700	8½	10	3 (15)	20	8½	9½ (11)
1800	20 (40)	30 (33)	25 (31)	27 (31)	26	14 (15)
1900	116 (123)	75 (80)	70 (85)	45 (52)	44 (58)	34 (54)
1926	170	80	80	45	45	41

Source: Jespersen (1938), p. 233.

first-language speakers in the absence of qualification.) He documents his claim of growth with the data in Table 1.5.1.[18] Jespersen then notes Mencken's estimates that by 1936 there were 191,000,000 first language speakers of English and 20 million second language speakers. (1938, p. 234)

Implicit in Jespersen's comment attributing the growth and spread of English to the political ascendancy of the English-speaking world is the claim that colonial domination and economic hegemony makes the spread of the language of the "master" a matter of self-interest to the dominated groups. Traunmüller (1975, p. 11) states the claim in axiomatic form: "a second language will be

Table 1.5.2   Estimation of the gross national product in 1974 in the region of certain national languages, showing the percentage of the world total

European		Orient Asian		Afro-Asian		South Asian		Other
English	34.6	Japanese	8.2	Arabic	2.2	Hindi	1.5	
Russian	13.2	Chinese	3.7	Hindi	1.5	Others	1.5	
German	9.1	Others	0.4	Others	2.7			
French	6.7							
Spanish	3.9							
Italian	2.7							
Dutch	1.3							
Portuguese	1.3							
Polish	1.1							
Others	5.0							
Total	78.9		12.3		6.4		3.0	1.0

Sources: OECD statistics for 1973, several data from *Der Fischer Weltalmanach 1975*. The value of petrol has been corrected as of 1974. [Traunmüller's notation]
Note: All values above 1% have been included.

learned if and only if the presumptive learner estimates the advantages of knowing that language to be higher than the costs." Judging, then, by his estimates, high motivation for acquiring English as a second language among people in developing countries is to be expected, and that is just what we have indeed found. While the following table from Traunmüller's paper does not take into account multinational corporations, nor English-speaking ownership of corporate enterprises in non-English mother-tongue countries, it does give some indication of the economic hegemony of the English-speaking corporate world.

While Traunmüller's conclusion seems overstated, seeming to find the whole cause of the growth and spread of English in economic factors, the discussion in this chapter and the data presented here *do* point to strong relationships between the growth of English in non-English mother-tongue countries and the political and economic hegemony, past and present, of the English-speaking powers.

Our conclusions may be summarily stated as follows:

1. English is used internally for official purposes in non-English mother-tongue countries almost exclusively in countries presently or formerly under the political or economic hegemony of English-speaking powers.

2. There is little English-medium schooling in non-English mother-tongue countries which were not or are not under the political or economic hegemony of the English-speaking powers. The information we have seems to indicate that, as the demand for English instruction continues to increase, competition from national languages (such as Malay in Malaysia, Swahili in

Tanzania, and Amharic in Ethiopia) will nevertheless bring about a decline in English-medium schooling at the primary and secondary levels.

3. Barring economic or political conditions prohibiting it,[19] English mother-tongue countries will continue to host more than 40% of the non-English-speaking world's foreign students.

4. The desirability of an English mother-tongue country as the country of study seems to be highest for students from less developed countries and from more distant countries. The proportion of students from Asia and Africa grew and the proportion from Europe fell between 1971 and 1974/75 with respect to those studying in the USA. Asia and Africa account for more than 65% of the non-English mother-tongue foreign students in the English mother-tongue countries.

5. The widespread English-language press is concentrated in countries having internal official uses for English. While some major English language papers covering international news circulate widely, the vast majority of those papers published for primarily internal readership are published in countries having some official role for English. More than 97% of the daily circulation of English language papers in Asia is accounted for by papers published in countries in which English is an official language.

6. Book production figures provided us with our most comprehensive comparison with French, and the figures in this domain show that English book production is nearly double that of French in the non-mother-tongue countries of Europe and substantially more in Latin America. The African figures are eratic, but English outstrips French in every test year. French constitutes a negligible part of book publishing in Asia, while English continues to constitute a substantial portion.

Books may be published in English for a variety of reasons, the most obvious one being the attraction of an international readership. For that reason alone, the publication of books in English in a particular country may tell us little about the place of English in that country. However, the composite figures and their comparison with French *do* tell us that there is a substantial worldwide market for English books, and that English continues to be the most viable medium through which ideas may be presented to a worldwide audience.

All in all, the data we have accumulated—which could and should be kept current with a minimum of effort and expense—indicate that English is clearly the major link-language in the world today and that it alone shows signs of continuing as such, at least in the short run, while the use of local languages for official literacy/education related purposes is also likely to increase.

6.0 NOTES

1.   *English Around the World* (2:1, May 1970) notes that of the 126 countries that were then member nations of the United Nations, 80 received their basic working documents in English. At least 15 more requested copies in English in addition to those they received in one of the other "official languages": French, Spanish, Russian, and Chinese. (Arabic has just recently—

early 1976—been included in that list.) "All but a dozen or so Permanent Representatives at the UN speak sufficient English to carry on working conversations. Each mission has at least one officer who speaks English." (p. 6) English also enjoys what might be considered a special legal status at the United Nations. The presidency of the security council is held for one month in rotation by the member states in the English alphabetical order of their names. (Paxton, 1975)

2.   Cited, for example, in *English Around the World* (3, Nov. 1970) in a proclamation by Prince Philip on the occasion of the fiftieth year of the English-speaking Union. Mazrui (1975a, p. 67) also notes this. The percentage both give is 70%, though neither gives a source.

3.   Note Mazrui's picturesque quotation, "When a Russian pilot seeks to land at an airfield in Athens, Cairo, or New Delhi, he talks to the control tower in English." (1975a, p. 67, quoting *Reporter* (Nairobi), Dec. 30, 1966, p. 13)

4.   Prince Philip claims 60% (see note 2).

5.   The estimates on mother-tongue speakers as well as additional-language speakers vary from source to source. Lewis and Massad (1975) estimate those with English as a first language at over 250 million, Gage and Ohannessian (1974) say 275 million, Müller (1964) estimates 265 million, Traunmüller (1975) gives 314 million, and there are others. The 1960–61 British Council Report suggests that "there may well be more people in the world who have learnt English as an acquired language than there are who speak it as their mother tongue." (British Council 1961, p. 3) Clearly the Lewis and Massad estimate is too low; the population of the United States alone stands at more than 220 million and the United Kingdom at over 75 million. The percentage of native speakers of English in these two countries is high, stated in Rustow (1967) as 86% for the USA and 98% for the United Kingdom. Those figures alone exceed 250 million. Taking into consideration Canada, Ireland, Australia, New Zealand, and the so-called West Indies, 300 million seems a fair estimate of first-language speakers of English. The estimate of second-language users is more difficult. The estimates start at 50–150 million (Lewis and Massad) and run all the way through the more than 275 million implied by British Council suggestion quoted above. The intense, and growing, worldwide demand for English teaching suggests that our estimate of 300 million, if wrong, is perhaps too low.

6.   For our purposes we will consider 12 nations as English mother-tongue countries. This choice is based primarily on Rustow (1967), in which there is a list of mother-tongue groups in 100 nations, including both the first and the second largest language groups and indicating the percentage of the total population. We chose the 10 countries with 45% or more of the total population having English as their mother-tongue.

1.	United Kingdom	98%
2.	Ireland	97%
3.	Australia	91%
4.	New Zealand	91%
5.	Barbados	98%
6.	Jamaica	98%
7.	Trinidad	97%
8.	United States (including Puerto Rico)	86%
9.	Canada (French 29%)	58%
10.	Guyana (Hindu-Urdu 45%)	45%

These figures represent not English-speakers as there are far higher percentages of English-speakers, for example, in Guyana, but rather represent those claiming English as mother-tongue. Many others are English-speaking multilinguals. Not included in Rustow, but included in our list of English mother-tongue countries, are (11) Granada and (12) the Bahamas.

There are, in addition, persons in nearly every country of the world who have English as their first language. Mazrui notes that there is a growing number of elite African families with parents coming from different tribal groups and sharing no language except their "additional language," English. Children in such families grow up with English as their first language. (Mazrui 1975*b*, p. 8) To a lesser, but still noteworthy, degree this development also obtains among elites in India, South East Asia, and the Pacific.

7.   See especially Kachru (1965, 1966, and 1975). The British Council specialized bibliography A-15 (available from the British Council) includes many additional references.

8.   Recent studies of this increasing *indigeonization* of English include Smith (1975), Taiwo (1976), and Achebe (1975), for example.

9.   We say "at least" because an accurate count is impossible in the light of such open-endedness as the provision in the 1974 Yugoslavian constitution under which all languages of the peoples and nationalities of Yugoslavia are accorded official status.

10.   We have listed a country as having English as a "designated" official language if Banks (1975) lists it as official. "Designated" means "designated by Banks (1975)." Citations in law, if available, are given in the footnotes for Table 1.2.1.

11.   Bengali is now the national language of Bangladesh, formerly East Pakistan.

12.   The latest (1971) figures for India in the United Nations publications are as follows:

Primary	54,326,000
Secondary	8,986,609
	63,312,609

The Times of India, Directory and Yearbook, 1975 includes the following comparative figures relevant to the question of primary and secondary enrollments. (p. 96)

Ages	1951	1971
6–11	18,200,000 or 43% of age group	60,500,000 or 80% of age group
11–14	3,100,000 or 13% of age group	14,300,000 or 35% of age group

The Statesman's Yearbook, 1975–76, gives the following figures for the year ending March 31, 1970.

Pre-primary	259,545
Primary	39,859,303
Secondary	35,097,817

These figures are based on conflicting definitions of primary and secondary. However, what is interesting is that the totals for 1970/71 are nearly identical. *The Times of India* total is 74,800,000 versus the *Statesman's Yearbook* total of 74,957,120, or 75,216,665 if the pre-primary enrollments are included. This correlation provides the basis for the figures chosen to be included for India in Table 1.3.4, namely 60,000,000 for primary, and 15,000,000 for secondary, assuming that secondary students are often older than 14 years. Since "English is generally taught as a compulsory subject" beginning in "middle school" it seems likely that an estimate of 21,000,000 students (6,000,000 primary and 15,000,000 secondary) in English classes is not high.

13.   An exception to this is a statement in the file (see Section 7.1) from March, 1972 as follows. "Only about 25% of the state and private schools (of Lebanon) are English-medium, the rest being French-medium; but by the end of the decade the figures could well be reversed." (File No. 50)

14.   The decrease in English-medium schooling, even in the event of a growth in English co-medium at the primary and secondary levels, may have another effect, perhaps

unanticipated. Platt (forthcoming) reports that in Malaysia and Singapore, students who have learned English as a foreign language speak more "correctly" from the viewpoint of educated British or Australian English while it is among the products of English-medium schooling that a distinctive variety of Singapore English has developed. The English-medium students are more fluent, but they are "less correct" in their English use. (See Platt 1975)

15.　　　　The data concerning the USSR, Spain, Holy See, Australia, Denmark, Madagascar, and Congo refer to 1970/71. The data for France, Lebanon, India, Philippines, Yugoslavia, Israel, Algeria and Colombia refer to 1969/70; for Argentina, Mexico, and Uruguay, they refer to 1968/69. No attempt is made to keep these separate.

16.　　　　*IIE Reports*, published by the Institute of International Education in New York, sheds no light on the 12 student discrepancy between the total in Table 1.3.15 and the figure 154,592 cited in the text of the report.

17.　　　　Keefe et al. (1973) notes the following English language journals published in English in Hungary for intellectuals, economists, and businessmen abroad.
　　　　　Hungarian Review (politics, economics, culture)
　　　　　New Hungarian Quarterly (politics, social and cultural affairs)
　　　　　Foreign Trade (trade journal)
　　　　　Hungarian Heavy Industries (trade journal)
　　　　　Hungarian Exporter (trade journal)
Another ready example of this phenomenon is a Czechoslovakian journal, *Czechoslovak Life*, published in English, French, German, Italian, and Swedish, as well as Czech. It is described as a pictorial monthly. Similar journals originate in Poland, USSR, China, etc.

18.　　　　"The numbers given are necessarily approximate only, especially for the older periods. Where my authorities disagree, I have given the lowest and in the parentheses the highest figure. The figures for 1926 are from L. Tesnière's *Appendice* to A. Meillet's *Les Langues dans l'Europe Nouvelle* (Paris, 1928)." (Footnote in Jespersen 1938, p. 233.)

19.　　　　Noted, for example, in Karen J. Winkler, "Closing the books on the foreign student," *International Educational and Cultural Exchange* 9 (1973): 2-3, 17-19. "SUNY at Albany with one of the highest concentrations of foreign students in the country, faces a 47% decline in foreign student aid," cited in Marckwardt (1974, p. 12).

7.0 BIBLIOGRAPHY

7.1　Guide to the Bibliography

The items listed in the bibliography represent our best effort to locate published, recent materials which provide information on the status and use of English in non-English mother-tongue countries. Many of the books listed do not focus on English; we have included them because valuable information about English is included incidentally in a discussion perhaps of the media, or of education or of the general problem of languages of wider communication in a particular country. Much of the information included in this chapter has been gleaned from such sources, sources not specifically directed to answering the questions we set out to answer.

　　　　In an attempt to make the bibliography more useful, we have reclassified the materials by country and by topic, referring to each entry by number. Such classifications are designed for use by persons interested in pursuing particular issues or countries in much greater detail.

Some unpublished material which has been made available to us was made available on the condition that we not quote it or cite it as authority for judgments it contains. These materials include British Council restricted circulation documents sent us from the British Council and others we were grateful for the opportunity to see at the Center for Applied Linguistics. We also read, but did not copy, materials prepared for the World Bank—materials which will, it is hoped, be published in the near future. We honored the conditions of use, filing this considerable material under the countries to which it has specific reference. On those occasions when we felt a note was important to indicate that a particular statistic or judgment was not a pure guess we have cited file numbers in this rather large file of unpublished materials. In every case we have relied not solely on a source considered not citable by its authors but rather on cumulative judgments or on corroborative published materials.

We have been unable to make use of any materials coming to our attention after February 1, 1976; however, items received through April 1, 1976 have been included in the bibliography. We have excluded materials not directly relevant to the sociology of English as an additional language. Materials on English-based pidgins and creoles are not included, nor have we included materials on the technical problems associated with teaching English as a second language. Older sources were eliminated if a newer source was located which covered the same ground.

For volumes in the Area Handbook series and the British Support Series, and for chapters from this volume, we included the date of the completion of research and writing whenever it was available. The heading date is the date of publication; the completion date appears in parentheses at the end of the entry. When the second date does not appear, one can assume that the work was completed sometime during the year prior to publication. All area handbooks were published in Washington, D.C. unless otherwise noted.

7.2 Numbered Alphabetical Listing

1   Abdulaziz, M.H. 1971. Tanzania's national language policy and the rise of Swahili political culture. In Whiteley 1971, pp. 160-178.

2   Achebe, Chinua. 1975. English and the African writer. Appendix B in Mazrui 1975*b*, pp. 216–223.

3   Acheson, Palmer. 1974. The English language in Saudi Arabia. *English Around the World* 11 (Nov. 1974):passim.

4   Ahmad, H.E.G. 1966. The future of English language in Pakistan. In *Pakistan Forum: I,* edited by Anwar S. Dil. Abbottabad, West Pakistan: Bookservice.

5   Ainslie, Rosalynde. 1967. *The Press in Africa: Communications Past and Present.* New York: Walker and Co.

6   Alden, Jane M. 1973. English as a foreign language: U.S. Government programs. *Georgetown University Round Table on Language and Linguistics* (1973): 157-163.

7   Alexandre, Pierre. 1972. *Languages and Language in Black Africa.* Evanston, Ill.: Northwestern University Press.

8   Alexandre, Pierre. 1971. A few observations on language use among Cameroonese
       elite families. In Whiteley 1971, pp. 254-261.

9   Alisjahbana, S. Takdir. 1974. Language policy, language engineering and literacy in
       Indonesia and Malaysia. In Fishman 1974, pp. 391-416.

10   Allen, Virginia F., and Sidney Forman, eds. 1967. *English as a Second Language.*
       New York: Teachers College Press.

11   Alleyne, Mervyn C. 1975. Sociolinguistic research in Latin America. In Ohannessian
       et al. 1975, pp. 179-190.

12   Allony-Fainberg, Yaffa. 1977. The influence of English on formal terminology in
       Hebrew. This vol., chap. 9. (Ms. 1976)

13   Amonoo, R.F. 1963. Problems of Ghanian *Lingue Franche*. In *Language in Africa,*
       edited by John Spencer. Cambridge: Cambridge University Press.

14   Ansre, Gilbert. 1975. Madina: Three polyglots and some implications for Ghana. In
       Ohannessian et al. 1975, pp. 159-178.

15   Anthony, Frank. 1972. English in India: A historical appraisal since 1947. *Indian
       and Foreign Review* 10 (Nov. 1, 1972):2, 12-13.

16   Apronti, Eric O. 1974. Sociolinguistics and the question of a national language: The
       case of Ghana. *Studies in African Linguistics* 5 (supp.):1-20.

17   Ashford, Nicholas. 1975. Afrikaans: the talking point of South Africa. *Times*
       (London), July 15, 1975, p. 12.

18   Asian-African Legal Consultative Committee, New Delhi. 1968. *Constitutions of
       Asian Countries.* Bombay: N.M. Tripath Private Ltd.

19   Austrian Institute. 1976. *News and Events: March 1976.* New York: Austrian
       Institute.

20   Bailey, Richard W., and Jay L. Robinson, eds. 1973. *Varieties of Present-Day
       English.* New York: Macmillan.

21   Bamgbose, Ayo. 1971. The English language in Nigeria. In Spencer 1971.

22   Bancroft, W. Jane. 1974. Foreign language teaching in Yugoslavia. *Modern Language
       Journal* 58:103-108.

23   Banks, Arthur S., ed. 1975. *Political Handbook of the World: 1975.* New York:
       McGraw Hill.

24   Banks, Arthur S., and Robert B. Textor. 1963. *A Cross-Polity Survey.* Cambridge,
       Mass.: MIT Press.

25   Bansal, R.K. 1969. *The Intelligibility of Indian English.* Monograph No. 4.
       Hyderabad, India: Central Institute for English.

26   Bender, M.L.; J.D. Bowen; R.L. Cooper; and C.A. Ferguson. 1976. *Language in
       Ethiopia.* London: Oxford University Press.

27   Bender, M.L.; R.L. Cooper; and C.A. Ferguson. 1975. Language in Ethiopia:
       Implications of a survey for sociolinguistic theory and method. In
       Ohannessian et al. 1975, pp. 191-208.

28   Bending, H.B. 1974. Motivation for English in an examination-geared school
       system. Paper presented at the Annual Conference of the International
       Association of the Teachers of English as a Foreign Language. Ms.

29   Blutstein, Howard I. et al., eds. 1971*a. Area Handbook for Cuba.* U.S. Government
       Printing Office. (3/70)

30   ———. 1971*b. Area Handbook for El Salvador.* U.S. Government Printing Office.
       (10/19/70)

31   ———. 1971*c. Area Handbook for Honduras.* U.S. Government Printing Office.
       (11/6/70)

32   ———. 1970. *Area Handbook for Costa Rica.* U.S. Government Printing Office.
       (7/18/69)

33   Bonenfant, J.C. 1973. Les études de la Commission royale d'enquête sur le
       bilinguisme et le biculturalisme. *Canadian Journal of Political Science*
       6:144-8.

34   Brann, C.M.B. 1975*a*. Concepts of educational language planning for Nigeria. Ms.
35   ———. 1975*b*. Language influences on pre-adolescent Nigerian children: A typology.
            International Journal of the Sociology of Language 4:7–31.
36   ———. 1975*c*. Functions of world languages in West Africa. A select bibliography.
            West African Modern Languages Association, Inaugural Congress, Ibadan,
            April 1–5, 1975.
37   ———. 1975*d*. Functions of world languages in West Africa: Retrospect, circumspect,
            and prospect. Ms.
38   Brass, Paul R. 1974. *Language, Religion and Politics in North India.* Cambridge:
            Cambridge University Press.
39   Brislin, Richard W., ed. 1975. *Topics in Culture Learning.* Vol. 3. Honolulu,
            Hawaii: East-West Center.
40   British Council. 1974*a*. *Annual Report, 1973/74.*
41   ———. 1974*b*. British support for English studies in the American continents and the
            Caribbean. Prepared by English Teaching Information Centre. Ms. (2/74)
42   ———. 1973*a*. *Annual Report, 1972/73.*
43   ———. 1973*b*. British support for English studies in tropical Africa. Prepared by
            English Teaching Information Centre. Ms. (5/73)
44   ———. 1973*c*. British support for English studies in South, South-East, and East
            Asia. Prepared by the English Teaching Information Centre. Ms. (2/73)
45   ———. 1973*d*. British support for English in Europe. Prepared by the English Teach-
            ing Information Centre. Ms. (3/73)
46   ———. 1972. *Annual Report, 1971/72.*
47   ———. 1961. *The English Language Abroad.* London.
48   ———. 1960. *Higher Education in the United Kingdom.* London.
49   Brosnahan, L.F. 1963*a*. *The English Language in the World.* Inaugural address,
            Victoria University of Wellington, New Zealand. London: British Council.
50   ———. 1963*b*. Some historical cases of language imposition. Reprinted in Bailey and
            Robinson 1973, pp. 40–55.
51   Brownell, John A. 1967. *Japan's Second Language.* Champaigne-Urbana, Ill.:
            National Council of Teachers of English.
52   Butter, P. 1960. *English in India.* Belfast: Queen's University.
53   Caldwell, Gary. 1974. *A Demographic profile of the English-speaking population of
            Quebec. 1921–1971.* Quebec City: International Center for Research on
            Bilingualism.
54   Calvert, Maurice. 1971. The elaboration of basic Wolof. In Whiteley 1971, pp.
            274–287.
55   Center for Applied Linguistics. 1967. International Conference on Second Language
            Problems: Report on eighth meeting, Heidelberg, April 26–29, 1967. Ms.
56   ———. 1966*a*. Outline report on the position and teaching of English in India.
57   ———. 1966*b*. A study of the problems of English language teaching in India. Report
            and recommendations.
58   ———. 1964. International Conference on Second Language Problems: Report of
            fifth meeting. Rome, March 18–21, 1964.
59   ———. 1961. *English Overseas.*
60   Centre for Information on Language Teaching. 1972. *A Language Teaching
            Bibliography.* 2d ed. Cambridge. (Also sponsored by the English Teaching
            Information Centre of the British Council.)
61   Chaffee, Frederic H. et al. 1969*a*. *Area Handbook for the Philippines.* U.S. Govern-
            ment Printing Office.
62   ———. 1969*b*. *Area Handbook for the Republic of China* (Taiwan). U.S. Government
            Printing Office. (11/30/67)
63   Christophersen, P. 1973. English in West Africa. *English Studies* 54:51–58.

64   Clare, Kenneth G. et al. 1969. *Area Handbook for the Republic of Korea.* U.S.
           Government Printing Office. (11/1/68)
65   Clyne, Michael G. 1973. Kommunikation und Kommunikationsbarrienen bei
           Englischen Entlehnungen im heutigen Deutsch. *Zeitschrift fur German-*
           istische Linguistik 1:2, 163-177.
66   Committee on College Composition and Communication. 1975. Students' rights to
           their own language. *College English* 36:709-726.
67   Cooper, Robert L., and Joshua A. Fishman. 1977. A study of language attitudes.
           This vol., chap. 11. (Ms. 1976).
68   Cooper, Robert L.; Joshua A. Fishman; Linda Lown; Barbara Schaier; and Fern
           Seckbach. 1977. Language, technology, and persuasion: three experi-
           mental studies. This vol., chap. 7. (Ms. 1976).
69   Cooper, Robert L., and Fern Seckbach. 1977. Economic incentives for the learning
           of a language of wider communication: A case study. This vol., chap. 8.
           (Ms. 1976).
70   Corpuz, O.D. 1967. Education and socio-economic change in the Philippines, 1870-
           1960's. *Philippine Social Sciences and Humanities Review* 32 (June 1967):
           193-268.
71   Criper, Clive, and Peter Ladefoged. 1968. Linguistic complexity in Uganda. In
           Whiteley 1971, pp. 145-159.
72   Cripwell, Kenneth R. 1975. Government writers and African readers in Rhodesia.
           Language in Society 4:147-154.
73   Crymes, Ruth, and William E. Norris, eds. 1975. *On Tesol 74.* Washington, D.C.:
           Teachers of English to Speakers of Other Languages.
74   Das, Bikram K. 1973. English for a developing country: A plea for linguistic
           relativism in teaching. *CIEL Bulletin* 9 (1972-73):18-26.
75   Das Gupta, Jyotirindra. 1975. Ethnicity, language demands, and national develop-
           ment in India. In *Ethnicity: Theory and Experience,* by Nathan Glazer and
           Daniel Moynihan. Cambridge: Harvard University Press, 1975, pp. 466-
           488.
76   DeGreve, M. et al., eds. 1973. *Modern Language Teaching to Adults: Language for*
           Special Purposes. Papers presented at AIMAV Seminar at Stockholm,
           Sweden, April 1972. Brussels, Belgium: AIMAV.
77   Dil, Anwar S. 1967. The position and teaching of English in Pakistan. Arlington,
           Virginia: Center for Applied Linguistics.
78   Dombrowski, John et al. 1970. *Area Handbook for Guatemala.* U.S. Government
           Printing Office.
79   Dunlop, Ian. 1975. *The Teaching of English in Swedish Schools.* Stockholm:
           Almqvist & Wiksell International.
80   Eng, Oor Boo. 1974. Indian poets and the use of English. *Journal of Commonwealth*
           Literature 9:entire issue.
81   *English Around the World.* A twice-yearly publication of the English Speaking
           Union of the USA, New York.
82   Epstein, E.H. 1967. National identity and the language issue in Puerto Rico.
           Comparative Educational Review 3:133-143.
83   *ESPMENA Bulletin,* edited by James Crofts and John Swales. University of
           Khartoum. (English for Special Purposes)
84   European Council for International Schools. 1975. *Annual Directory.*
85   Farine, Avigdor. 1969. Society and education: The content of education in the
           French African school. *Comparative Education* 5:51-66.
86   Ferguson, Charles A. 1966. National sociolinguistic profile formulas. In
           Sociolinguistics, edited by William Bright. The Hague: Mouton. Pp.
           309-324.

87   Ferguson, Charles A. 1962. The language factor in national development. In Rice
         1962, pp. 8-14.

88   Fishman, Joshua A. 1977a. Knowing, using and liking English as an additional
         language. This vol., chap. 13. (Ms. 1976).

89   ———. 1977b. The spread of English as a new perspective for the study of "language
         maintenance and language shift." This vol., chap. 3. (Ms. 1976).

90   ———. 1974. The Sociology of Language: An Interdisciplinary Social Science
         Approach to Language in Society. Rowley, Mass.: Newbury House.

91   ———. 1969. National languages and languages of wider communication in the
         developing nations. Anthropological Linguistics 11:111-135.

92   Fishman, Joshua A.; Robert L. Cooper; and Yehudit Rosenbaum. 1977. English
         around the world. This vol., chap. 2. (Ms. 1976).

93   Fishman, Joshua A.; Charles A. Ferguson; and Jyotirindra Das Gupta, eds. 1968.
         Language Problems of Developing Nations. New York: John Wiley &
         Sons, Inc.

94   Fishman, Joshua A., ed. 1974. Advances in Language Planning. The Hague:
         Mouton.

95   Fisherman, Haya, and Joshua A. Fishman. 1975. The "official languages" of Israel:
         Their status in law and police attitudes and knowledge concerning them.
         In Multilingual Political Systems: Problems and Solutions, edited by
         Jean Guy Savard and Richard Vigneault. Quebec: International Center
         for Research on Bilingualism. Pp. 497-536.

96   Fonlon, B. 1969. The language problem in Cameroon. Comparative Educational
         Review 5:25-49.

97   Fox, Jay. 1975. English language teaching in the Pacific. English Around the World
         12:passim.

98   Gage, William, and Sirarpi Ohannessian. 1974. ESOL enrollments throughout the
         world. The Linguistic Reporter, Nov. 1974, pp. 13-16.

99   Garrard, J.G. 1962. The teaching of foreign languages in the Soviet Union. Modern
         Language Journal 46:71-74.

100   Gendron, Jean-Denis. 1974. La Situation du Francais comme Langue D'Usage au
         Quebec. Quebec: International Center for Research on Bilingualism.

101   Ghana Library Board. 1971. Ghana National Bibliography.

102   Gokak, Vinayak Krishna. 1964. English in India: Its Present and Future. New
         York: Asia Publishing House.

103   Gonzales, Andrew. 1974. The 1973 Constitution and the Bilingual Education
         Policy of the Department of Education & Culture. Philippine Studies
         22:325-337.

104   ———. 1972. The future of English in Asia. Position paper presented at the Confer-
         ence on the National Language Policy and Language Development of
         Asian Countries in Manila, Philippines, December 18-22, 1972. Ms.

105   Gorman, Thomas P. 1971. Sociolinguistic implications of a choice of media of
         instruction. In Whiteley 1971, pp. 198-220.

106   ———. 1968. Bilingualism in the educational system of Kenya. Comparative
         Education 4:213-221.

107   Gorman, Thomas P., ed. 1974. Workpapers in Teaching English as a Second
         Language. Vol. 8. Los Angeles: University of California. (ERIC # ED
         101 591)

108   Gorokhoff, Boris I. 1959. Publishing in the USSR. Indiana University Publications,
         Graduate School Slavic and East European Series, vol. 19.

109   Gower, R.H. 1952. Swahili borrowings from English. Africa 22:154-156.

110   Grieves, D.W. 1965. English language in West African Schools. West African Journal
         of Education 9:171ff.

111   ———. 1964. English language examining: Report of an inquiry into the examining
       of English. West African Examination Council. Lagos, Nigeria: African
       Universities Press.

112   Guthrie, Malcolm. 1962. Multilingualism and cultural factors. In *Symposium on
       Multilingualism.* Second meeting of the Inter-African Committee on
       Linguistics, Brazzaville, July 16-21, 1962. London: Scientific Council
       for Africa.

113   Haarman, Harold. n.d. *Sprachpolitische Organisationsfragen der Europäischen
       Gemeinschaft.* Hamburg: Stiftung Europa-Kolleg.

114   Hachten, William. 1971. *Muffled Drums: The News Media in Africa.* Ames: Iowa
       State University Press.

115   Halverson, J. 1969. Prolegomena to a study of Ceylon English. *The University of
       Ceylon Review* 24:61-75.

116   Hancock, Ian F. 1971. Some aspects of English in Liberia. *Liberian Studies Journal*
       3:207-214.

117   Harasawa, Masayoshi. 1974. A critical survey of English language teaching in Japan.
       English Language Teaching 19:71-79.

118   Harris, George L. et al. 1973. *Area Handbook for Nepal, Bhutan, and Sikkim.* U.S.
       Government Printing Office. (11/72)

119   Harrison, William; Clifford Prator; and G. Richard Tucker. 1975. *English-Language
       Policy Survey of Jordan: A Case Study in Language Planning.* Arlington,
       Virginia: Center for Applied Linguistics.

120   Hagwood, John Arkas. 1939. *Modern Constitutions since 1787.* London: Macmillan.

121   Heine, Bernd. 1970. *Status and Use of African Lingua Francas.* Munich: Weltforum
       Verlag.

122   Henderson, John W. et al. 1971*a. Area Handbook for Thailand.* U.S. Government
       Printing Office.

123   ———. 1971*b. Area Handbook for Oceania.* U.S. Government Printing Office.
       (7/9/70)

124   ———. 1971*c. Area Handbook for Burma.* U.S. Government Printing Office. (4/71)

125   ———. 1970*a. Area Handbook for Malaysia.* U.S. Government Printing Office.

126   ———. 1970*b. Area Handbook for Indonesia.* U.S. Government Printing Office.

127   Herbert, Robert K., ed. 1975. Patterns in language, culture, and society: Sub-
       Saharan Africa. Proceedings of the Symposium on African Language,
       Culture, and Society, Ohio State University, Columbus, April 11, 1975.
       Published as No. 19, Working Papers in Linguistics, Ohio State
       Department of Linguistics.

128   Herrick, Allison Butler, et al. 1969. *Area Handbook for Uganda.* U.S. Government
       Printing Office. (8/1/68)

129   ———. 1968. *Area Handbook for Tanzania.* U.S. Government Printing Office.
       (1/31/68)

130   Hilmi, Esat. 1975. English among the Turkish Cypriots. *English Around the World*
       12:6.

131   Hofman, John E. 1977. Language attitudes in Rhodesia. This vol., chap. 12.
       (Ms. 1974).

132   ———. 1974. *Assessment of English Proficiency in the African Primary School.*
       University of Rhodesia, Series in Education, occasional paper no. 3.

133   Hopkins, Mark W. 1970. *Mass Media in the Soviet Union.* Pergasus, N.Y.: Western
       Publishing Company.

134   Hopper, Paul. 1970. The role of indigenous languages in three Third World nations.
       In *Non-Aligned Third World Annual,* 1970. Pp. 303-312.

135   Huebener, Theodore. 1962. The teaching of foreign languages in the schools of
         West Germany. *Modern Language Journal* 46:69-70.
136   Hurreiz, Sayyid Hamid. 1974. Arabic as a national and an international language:
         Current problems and future needs. Ms.
137   International Handbook of Universities and Other Institutions of Higher Education.
         Higher Education. Paris: International Association of Universities.
138   Jacobs, Robert, ed. 1966. *English Language Teaching in Nigeria.* A report of a
         special study, co-sponsored by the National Universities Commission and
         the Federal Ministry of Education. Lagos, Nigeria: National Universities
         Commission.
139   Jespersen, Otto. 1938. *Growth and Structure of the English Language.* 9th ed.
         Garden City: Doubleday.
140   Jones, Joseph. 1965. *Terranglia: The Case for English as World Literature.* Boston:
         Twayne.
141   Kachru, Braj B. 1976. Models of English for the Third World: White man's linguistic
         burden or language pragmatics? *TESOL Quarterly* 10 (June 1976):221-
         239.
142   ———. 1975. Lexical innovations in South Asian English. *International Journal of
         the Sociology of Language* 4:55-74.
143   ———. 1969. English in South Asia. *Current Trends in Linguistics* 5:627-678. The
         Hague: Mouton.
144   ———. 1966. Indian English: A study in contextualization. In *In Memory of J.R.
         Firth,* edited by C.F. Bazell. London: Longmans. Pp. 255-287.
145   ———. 1965. The Indianness in Indian English. *Word* 21:391-410.
146   Kaplan, Irving, et al. 1974. *Area Handbook for Zambia.* U.S. Government Printing
         Office.
147   ———. 1971*a. Area Handbook for Ghana.* U.S. Government Printing Office. (1/71)
148   ———. 1971*b. Area Handbook for the Republic of South Africa.* U.S. Government
         Printing Office. (2/28/70)
149   ———. 1969. *Area Handbook for Somalia.* U.S. Government Printing Office.
         (6/15/69)
150   Kearney, Robert N. 1967. *Communalism and Language in the Politics of Ceylon.*
         Durham: University of North Carolina.
151   Keefe, Eugene K. et al. 1975. *Area Handbook for Belgium.* U.S. Government
         Printing Office.
152   ———. 1973. *Area Handbook for Hungary.* U.S. Government Printing Office.
153   ———. 1972*a. Area Handbook for Romania.* U.S. Government Printing Office.
         (2/72)
154   ———. 1972*b. Area Handbook for Czechoslovakia.* U.S. Government Printing
         Office.
155   ———. 1972*c. Area Handbook for East Germany.* U.S. Government Printing Office.
         (3/71)
156   ———. 1971*a. Area Handbook for Cyprus.* U.S. Government Printing Office.
         (10/15/70)
157   ———. 1971*b. Area Handbook for the Soviet Union.* U.S. Government Printing
         Office. (3/13/70)
158   Kelly, Michael. 1974. The language picture in Cameroon. *English Around the
         World* 11:passim.
159   Khubchandani, Lachman M. 1975. Dilemmas of language transition: Challenges to
         language planning in India. In Brislin 1975, pp. 151-164.
160   ———. 1973. English in India: A sociolinguistic appraisal. *International Journal of
         Dravidian Linguistics* 2.

161   Khubchandani, Lachman M. n.d. Indian bilingualism and English: A demographic
        study. Indian Institute of Advanced Study, Simla, India. Ms.

162   Kloss, Heinz. 1968. Notes concerning a language-nation typology. In Fishman et al.
        1968, pp. 69-85.

163   Kloss, Heinz, and G.D. McConnell. 1974. *Linguistic Composition of the Nations of
        the World* Vol. 1, *Central and Western South Asia.* Quebec: Les Presses
        de l'Université Laval.

164   Knappert, Jan. 1965. Language problems of the new nations of Africa. *Africa
        Quarterly* 5:95-105.

165   Ladefoged, Peter; Ruth Glick; and Clive Criper. *Language in Uganda.* New York:
        Oxford University Press.

166   Lal, Sham, ed. 1975. *The Times of India, Directory and Yearbook.* Bombay.

167   Lambert, Wallace E.; Howard Giles; and Omer Picard. 1975. Language attitudes in
        a French-American community. *International Journal of the Sociology of
        Language* 4:127-152.

168   Lanham, L.W. 1964. *English in South Africa: Its History, Nature, and Social Role.*
        Johannesburg: Institute for the Study of Man in Africa.

169   Legters, Lyman Howard. 1967. *Language and area studies: a bibliography.* New
        York State Education Department.

170   Lehmann, Winfred P. 1975. *Language and Linguistics in the People's Republic of
        China.* Austin: University of Texas Press.

171   LePage, R.B. 1964. *The National Language Question: Linguistic Problems of
        Newly Independent States.* London: Oxford University Press (under the
        auspices of the Institute of Race Relations).

172   Lewis, E. Glyn. 1975. Attitude to language among bilingual children and adults in
        Wales. *International Journal of the Sociology of Language* 4:103-125.

173   ———. 1972. *Multilingualism in the Soviet Union.* The Hague: Mouton.

174   Lewis, E. Glyn, and Carolyn E. Massad. 1975. *The Teaching of English as a Foreign
        Language in Ten Countries.* International Studies in Evaluation IV,
        International Association for the Evaluation of Educational Achievement.
        New York: John Wiley, A Halsted Press Book.

175   Lieberson, Stanley. 1965. Bilingualim in Montreal: A demographic analysis. *Ameri-
        can Journal of Sociology* 71:10-25.

176   Mackey, William F., ed. 1972. *International Bibliography on Bilingualism.* Quebec:
        International Center for Research on Bilingualism.

177   Mackey, William F., and Albert Verdoodt, eds. 1975. *The Multinational Society.*
        Papers of the Ljubljana Seminar, June 1965. Rowley, Mass.: Newbury
        House.

178   Magner, Thomas F. 1974. The study of foreign languages in China. *Modern Language
        Journal* 58:385-391.

179   Malherbe, E.G. 1966. *Demographic and Socio-Political Forces Determining the
        Position of English in the South African Republic: English as Mother
        Tongue.* Johannesburg: The English Academy.

180   Marckwardt, Albert H. 1975. English teaching abroad: A survey of the field. In *On
        TESOL 74*, edited by Ruth Crymes and William E. Norris. Washington,
        D.C.: TESOL. (Papers from the Eighth Annual TESOL Convention,
        June 5-10, 1974.)

181   Mazrui, Ali. 1975a. The racial boundaries of the English language: An African
        perspective. In *Multilingual Political Systems: Problems and Solutions*,
        edited by L. Savard and Vigneault. Quebec: Les Presses de l'Université
        Laval. Pp. 61-86.

182   Mazrui, Ali. 1975*b*. *The Political Sociology of the English Language: An African Perspective.* The Hague: Mouton.

183   ———. 1971. Islam and the English language in East and West Africa. In Whiteley 1971, pp. 179-197.

184   ———. 1967. The English language and the origins of African nationalism. In Bailey and Robinson 1973, pp. 65-70.

185   McDonald, Gordon C. et al. 1973. *Area Handbook for Yugoslavia.* U.S. Government Printing Office.

186   ———. 1971*a*. *Area Handbook for the Democratic Republic of the Congo (Congo Kinshasha).* U.S. Government Printing Office. (12/26/69)

187   ———. 1971*b*. *Area Handbook for People's Republic of the Congo (Congo Brazzaville).* U.S. Government Printing Office. (1/30/70)

188   ———. 1969. *Area Handbook for Burundi.* U.S. Government Printing Office. (4/1/69)

189   Mead, Richard, and A.D. Lilly. 1975. The use of visual materials in teaching English to economics students. *English Language Teaching* 29 (Jan. 1975):151-156.

190   Mitchell, William B. et al. 1969. *Area Handbook for Guyana.* U.S. Government Printing Office.

191   Morrison, D.G. et al. 1972. *Black Africa: A Comparative Handbook.* New York: Free Press.

192   Mosha, M. 1971. Loan-words in Luganda: A search for guides in the adaptation of African languages to modern conditions. In Whiteley 1971, pp. 288-308.

193   Moulin, Andre. 1974. English for business. *Revue des Langues Vivantes* 40:700-703.

194   Mukerjee, Hiren. 1972. The English language and India today. *Indian and Foreign Review* 9:19, 9-11.

195   Müller, Siegfried H. 1964. *The World's Living Languages.* New York: Frederick Ungar Publishing Company.

196   Munda, Ram Dayal. 1972. Language planning in the Philippines. *Journal of the Indian Anthropological Society* 7:65-78.

197   Nadel, Elizabeth, and Joshua A. Fishman. 1977. English in Israel: A sociolinguistic study. This vol., chap. 4. (Ms. 1976)

198   Nelson, Harold D. et al. 1974. *Area Handbook for Senegal.* U.S. Government Printing Office. (9/73)

199   ———. 1973*a*. *Area Handbook for the Democratic Republic of Sudan.* U.S. Government Printing Office. (4/72)

200   ———. 1973*b*. *Area Handbook for the Malagasy Republic.* U.S. Government Printing Office. (10/72)

201   ———. 1972. *Area Handbook for Nigeria.* U.S. Government Printing Office. (7/71)

202   *Newspaper Press Directory: Benn's Guide to Newspapers and Periodicals of the World.* 1968.

203   Ney, James W. 1964. The English language center in Naha, Okinawa. *English Teaching Forum* 2(2):20-22.

204   Noss, Richard B. 1971. Politics and language policy in Southeast Asia. *Language Sciences* 16.

205   ———. 1965. *Language Policy and Higher Education in South-East Asia.* UNESCO—International Association of Universities Joint Research Program in Higher Education.

206   Nyrop, Richard F. et al. 1974. *Area Handbook for the Hashemite Kingdom of Jordan.* U.S. Government Printing Office. (9/73)

207   Nyrop, Richard F. et al. 1973. *Area Handbook for Libya.* U.S. Government Printing
Office. (9/72)

208   ———. 1972. *Area Handbook for Morocco.* U.S. Government Printing Office.
(10/71)

209   ———. 1971*a. Area Handbook for Syria.* U.S. Government Printing Office. (5/71)

210   ———. 1971*b. Area Handbook for Pakistan.* U.S. Government Printing Office.
(1/12/70)

211   ———. 1971*c. Area Handbook for Ceylon.* U.S. Government Printing Office.
(8/19/70)

212   ———. 1969. *Area Handbook for Rwanda.* U.S. Government Printing Office.
(4/1/69)

213   Obote, Milton. 1967. Language and national identification. Reprinted from *East
Africa Journal,* April 1967, pp. 3-6. In Bailey and Robinson 1971, pp.
72-76. Also Appendix A in Mazrui 1975*b,* pp. 210-215.

214   Ohannessian, Sirarpi. 1975. Scrounging for information. Paper given at the
International Conference on the Methodology of Sociolinguistic Surveys,
Montreal, May 21, 1975. Ms.

215   Ohannessian, Sirarpi, ed. n.d. *Reference List of Materials for English as a Second
Language.* Arlington, Virginia: Center for Applied Linguistics.

216   Ohannessian, Sirarpi; Charles A. Ferguson; and Edgar C. Polome, eds. 1975.
Language Surveys in Developing Nations. Arlington, Virginia: Center for
Applied Linguistics.

217   Ornstein, Jacob. 1962. English the global way. *Modern Language Journal* 46:9-13.

218   Ostrower, Alexander. 1965. *Language, Law, and Diplomacy: A Study of Linguistic
Diversity in Official International Relations and International Law.* 2 vols.
Philadelphia: University of Pennsylvania Press.

219   Pandit, Prabodh B. 1975. The linguistic survey of India—perspectives on language
use. In Ohannessian et al. 1975, pp. 71-86.

220   Parkin, David J. 1974*a.* Language shift and ethnicity in Nairobi: The speech
community of Kaolene. In Whiteley 1974, pp. 167-188.

221   ———. 1974*b.* Status factors in language adding: Bahati housing estate in Nairobi.
In Whiteley 1974, pp. 147-166.

222   Pascasio, E.M. 1975. The language situation in the Philippines. *Philippine Studies,*
special issue. Manila: Ateneo de Manila University.

223   Pattison, B. 1975. English as a foreign language over the world today. *English
Language Teaching* 20 (1):2-10.

224   Paxton, John, ed. 1975. *Statesman's Yearbook, 1975-76.* New York: St. Martin's
Press.

225   Peaslee, Amos Jenkins, ed. 1965. *Constitutions of Nations.* 4 vols. Vol. 1, *Africa*
(constitutions to 9/1/64); Vol. 2, *Asia, Australia and Oceania* (to
9/1/65); Vol. 3, *Europe* (to 9/15/66); Vol. 4, *The Americas* (to 9/1/68).
Rev. 3d ed. The Hague: Nijoff.

226   Platt, J.T. 1976. The sub-varieties of Singapore English: Their sociolectal and
functional status. In *The English Language in Singapore,* edited by
W. Crewe. Singapore, forthcoming. Ms.

227   ———. 1975. The Singapore English speech continuum and its basilect "Singlish"
as a creoloid. *Anthropological Linguistics* 17:7.

228   Polome, Edgar C. 1975. Problems and techniques of a sociolinguistically oriented
survey: The case of the Tanzania survey. In Ohannessian et al. 1975
pp. 31-50.

229   Povey, John F. 1970. The beginnings of an English language literature in East
Africa. *Books Abroad* 44 (3):380-387.

230   Povey, John F. 1975. Zaire: A summer English language program. *Workpapers in Teaching English as a Second Language.* Vol. 9. UCLA: Department of English.

231   Prator, Clifford H. 1975. The survey of language use and language teaching in Eastern Africa in retrospect. In Ohannessian et al. 1975, pp. 145-158.

232   Rafat, T. 1969. Towards a Pakistani idiom. *Venture: A Bi-Annual Review of English Language and Literature* 6:60-73.

233   Ramchand, Kenneth. 1970. The language of the master. Reprinted from *The West Indian Novel and Its Background.* London: Faber & Faber, Ltd. In Bailey and Robinson 1973, pp. 114-146.

234   Reese, Howard C. 1970. *Area Handbook for the Republic of Tunisia.* U.S. Government Printing Office.

235   Rice, Frank A., ed. 1962. *Study of the role of 2nd languages in Asia, Africa and Latin America.* Arlington, Virginia: Center for Applied Linguistics.

236   Rice, Frank A. and Allene Guss, compilers and eds. 1965. *Information Sources in Linguistics: A Bibliographic Handbook.* Washington, D.C.: Center for Applied Linguistics.

237   Riley, George A. 1975. Language loyalty and ethnocentrism in the Guamanian speech community. *Anthropological Linguistics* 17 (6):286-292.

238   Roberts, Thomas D. et al. 1972. *Area Handbook for Liberia.* U.S. Government Printing Office. (9/30/71)

239   Ronen, Miriam; Fern Seckbach; and Robert L. Cooper. 1977. Foreign loanwords in Hebrew newspapers. This vol., chap. 10. (Ms. 1976)

240   Rosenbaum, Yehudit; Elizabeth Nadel; and Robert L. Cooper. 1977. English on Keren Kayemet Street. This vol., chap. 6. (Ms. 1976)

241   Ross, Werner. 1972. *Deutsch in der Konkurrenz der Weltsprachen.* Munich: Max Hueber Verlag.

242   Rustow, Dankwart A. 1967. Language modernization, and nationhood—an attempt at typology. In Fishman et al. 1968, pp. 87-105.

243   Ryan, John Morris et al. 1970*a. Area Handbook for Nicaragua.* U.S. Government Printing Office.

244   ———. 1970*b. Area Handbook for Mexico.* U.S. Government Printing Office. (3/69)

245   Samarin, William J. 1962. Lingua francas, with special reference to Africa. In Rice 1962, pp. 54-64.

246   Saraf, R.S. 1971. Teaching of English in India. *Bulletin of the State Institute of English for Maharashtra, Bombay.* 4 (Dec. 5-9, 1971).

247   Sargent, Porter, ed. 1975. *Schools Abroad of Interest to Americans.* Boston: Porter Sargent Inc.

248   Scotton, Carol Myers. 1975*a.* Strategies of neutrality: Language use in inter-ethnic work encounters. Ms.

249   ———. 1975*b.* Multilingualism in Lagos—what it means to the social scientist. In R.K. Herbert 1975.

250   ———. 1972. *Choosing a Lingua Franca in an African Capital.* Edmonton, Alberta, Can.: Linguistic Research, Inc.

251   Seckbach, Fern, and Robert L. Cooper. 1977. The maintenance of English in Ramat Eshkol. This vol., chap. 5. (Ms. 1976)

252   Sedlak, Philip A.S. 1976. *Report on the National Taiwan Normal University/ University of Southern California Survey of English Teaching in the Republic of China.* Taipei: Wan Pang Press.

253   Senghor, Leopold S. 1975. The essence of language: English and French. *Cultures* 2 (2):75-98.

254   Shinn, Rinn-Sup et al. 1970. *Area Handbook for India.* U.S. Government Printing Office.

255   ———. 1969. *Area Handbook for North Korea.* U.S. Government Printing Office.

256   Sibayan, Bonifacio P. 1975. Survey of language use and attitudes towards language in the Philippines. In Ohannessian et al. 1975, pp. 115-144.

257   ———. 1974. Language policy, language engineering and literacy in the Philippines. In Fishman ed. 1974. pp. 221-254.

258   Sinha, Surajit, ed. 1972. *Cultural Profile of Calcutta.* Calcutta: The Indian Anthropological Society.

259   Smith, Harvey H. et al. 1974. *Area Handbook for Lebanon.* 2d ed. U.S. Government Printing Office.

260   ———. 1973. *Area Handbook for Afghanistan.* U.S. Government Printing Office. (various dates)

261   ———. 1971*a. Area Handbook for Iran.* U.S. Government Printing Office. (6/23/70)

262   ———. 1971*b. Area Handbook for Iraq.* U.S. Government Printing Office.

263   ———. 1970*a. Area Handbook for Israel.* U.S. Government Printing Office. (6/15/69)

264   ———. 1970*b. Area Handbook for the United Arab Republic (Egypt).* U.S. Government Printing Office. (12/23/69)

265   ———. 1967. *Area Handbook for South Vietnam.* U.S. Government Printing Office. (4/15/66)

266   Smith, Larry E. 1975. Teaching English in Asia—an overview. In Brislin 1975, pp. 133-136.

267   Smith, Rowland, ed. 1976. *Exile and Tradition: Studies in African and Caribbean Literature.* London: Longman.

268   Smock, David R., and Audrey C. Smock. 1975. *The Politics of Pluralism: A Comparative Study of Lebanon and Ghana.* New York: Elsevier.

269   Sofenwa, L.A. 1976. Is English a second language in Nigeria? University of Ibadan Language Seminars. Ms.

270   Sopher, E. 1974. An introductory approach to the teaching of scientific English to foreign students. *English Language Teaching* 28 (July 1974): 353-359.

271   Spencer, John Walter. 1974. Colonial language policies and their legacies in Sub-Saharan Africa. In Fishman ed. 1974, pp. 163-176.

272   ———. 1971. Language policies of the colonial powers and their legacies. In *Current Trends in Linguistics,* edited by T. Sebeok. Vol. 7, pp. 537-547. The Hague: Mouton.

273   Spencer, John Walter, ed. 1971. *The English Language in West Africa.* Harlow, Eng.: Longman.

274   Stansfield, Charles W. 1973*a.* English in Colombia—a solid position. *English Around the World* 9:passim.

275   ———. 1973*b.* The teaching of English in Colombian public secondary schools. Unpublished dissertation, Florida State University.

276   Stoddard, Theodore et al. 1974. *Area Handbook for Finland.* U.S. Government Printing Office.

277   ———. 1971. *Area Handbook for the Indian Ocean Territories.* U.S. Government Printing Office. (3/19/71)

278   Strevens, Peter D. 1973. Technical, technological, and scientific English (TTSE). *English Language Teaching* 27:223-234.

279   ———. 1971. The teaching of English in Asia: How can we maximise success and minimise failure? *Bulletin of the State Institute of English for Maharashtra, Bombay.* 4 (Dec. 10-16, 1971).

280   Symposium: The use of English in world literature. 1964. *Harvard Educational Review* 34:297-319.

281   Taiwo, Oladele. 1976. *Culture and the Nigerian Novel.* New York: St. Martin's Press.

282   Tambiah, S.J. 1967. The politics of language in India and Ceylon. *South Asian Studies* 1:passim.

283   Taska, Betty K. 1975. Teacher training for the non-native speakers in Francophone Africa. In *On TESOL, 74.* Washington, D.C.: TESOL. Pp. 67-72.

284   Tiffen, Brian. 1974. The intelligibility of African English. *ELT Documents* 74 (2): 10-12.

285   Tongue, R.K. 1974. *The English of Singapore and Malaysia.* Singapore: Eastern Universities Press.

286   Traunmüller, Hartmut. 1975. A universal interlanguage: Some basic considerations. Stockholm: Royal Institute of Technology. Ms.

287   Trifonovitch, Gregory J. 1975. Roots of bilingual/bicultural education in the trust territory of the Pacific Islands. In Brislin 1975, pp. 97-108.

288   Tsuzaki, et al. 1966. *English in Hawaii: An Annotated Bibliography.* Honolulu: University of Hawaii Press.

289   Tucker, G. Richard. 1972. A survey of English use in Jordan. Ms.

290   UNESCO. 1974. *Statistical Yearbook.* Paris: UNESCO Publications Center.

291   ———. 1965. *World Radio and Television.* Paris: UNESCO Publications Center.

292   ———. 1961. *The Education Situation in Africa Today: Final Report of the Conference of African States on the Development of Education in Africa.* Addis Ababa: UNESCO Publications Center.

293   ———. 1953. *African Languages and English in Education.* Educational Series and Documents. Paris: UNESCO Publications Center.

294   United Nations. 1975a. *1974 Report on the World Social Situation.* Dept. of Economic and Social Affairs. New York: United Nations.

295   ———. 1975b. *Statistical Yearbook, 1974.* New York: United Nations.

296   ———. 1973. *Demographic Yearbook.* New York: United Nations.

297   ———. 1971. *Statistical Yearbook, 1970.* New York: United Nations.

298   United States Agency for International Development. 1967. *English Language Programs of the AID.* U.S. Government Printing Office.

299   United States Department of State, Office of Overseas Schools. 1975. *Overseas American-Sponsored Elementary and Secondary Schools Assisted by the U.S. Dept. of State.* Washington, D.C.: U.S. Government Printing Office.

300   Viereck, Wolfgang; K. Viereck; and I. Winter. 1975. Wie Englisch ist unsere Pressesprache? *Grazer Linguistische Studien* 2 (May 1975): 205-226.

301   Walpole, Norman C. et al. 1966. *Area Handbook for Saudi Arabia.* U.S. Government Printing Office. (12/31/65)

302   Weil, Thomas E. et al. 1974a. *Area Handbook for Bolivia.* U.S. Government Printing Office. (7/73)

303   ———. 1974b. *Area Handbook for Argentina.* U.S. Government Printing Office. (1973)

304   ———. 1973a. *Area Handbook for the Dominican Republic.* U.S. Government Printing Office. (2/73)

305   ———. 1973b. *Area Handbook for Ecuador.* U.S. Government Printing Office.

306   ———. 1973c. *Area Handbook for Haiti.* U.S. Government Printing Office.

307   ———. 1972a. *Area Handbook for Paraguay.* U.S. Government Printing Office.

308   ———. 1972b. *Area Handbook for Panama.* U.S. Government Printing Office. (10/71)

309   ———. 1972c. *Area Handbook for Peru.* U.S. Government Printing Office. (3/72)

310   ———. 1971a. *Area Handbook for Brazil.* U.S. Government Printing Office. (3/5/70)

311   ———. 1971b. *Area Handbook for Venezuela.* U.S. Government Printing Office. (12/70)

312   Weil, Thomas E. et al. 1971c. *Area Handbook for Uruguay*. U.S. Government
           Printing Office. (8/21/70)
313   ———. 1970. *Area Handbook for Colombia*. U.S. Government Printing Office.
           (8/29/69)
314   ———. 1969. *Area Handbook for Chile*. U.S. Government Printing Office.
315   Whitaker, Donald P. et al. 1974. *Area Handbook for Japan*. U.S. Government
           Printing Office.
316   ———. 1973. *Area Handbook for the Khmer Republic* (Cambodia). U.S. Govern-
           ment Printing Office. (7/72)
317   ———. 1972. *Area Handbook for Laos*. U.S. Government Printing Office. (6/71)
318   Whiteley, Wilfred H. 1974. Language policies of independent African states. In
           Fishman ed. 1974, pp. 177-190.
319   Whiteley, Wilfred H., ed. 1974. *Language in Kenya*. Ford Foundation Language
           Surveys, vol. 2. London: Oxford University Press.
320   ———. 1971. *Language Use and Social Change: Problems of Multilingualism with
           Special Reference to Eastern Africa*. Papers from a conference, Dec.
           1968. London: Oxford University Press.
321   Winchell, Constance M. 1967. *Guide to Reference Books*. Chicago: American
           Library Association.
322   Wood, Richard E. 1976. English in international broadcasting. *English Around the
           World* 15:passim.
323   *World Guide to Universities: Internationales Universitäts-Handbuch*, 1972. New
           York and London: R.R. Bowker Co.
324   *The World of Learning, 1974–75*. 1974. 2 vols. London: Europa Publications.
325   World Organization of Young Esperantists (TEJO). 1974. *Report of Seminar:
           Language and Society*. Munster. Ms.
326   Za'rour, George I., and Rawdah Nashit. 1975. Attitudes towards the language of
           science teaching at the secondary level in Jordan. Beirut, Lebanon:
           Science and Mathematics Education Center, American University. Ms.

7.3   Analysis of the Bibliography

Country-by-country listing

Listings by topic

English in the media
 Book production: 108, 295, 296
 Newspapers: 5, 23, 114, 133, 202, 239, 290, 295, 296, 300
 Film: 290, 295
 Radio and television: 290, 291, 295, 322

Institutions using English or promoting English
 Libraries and museums: 290, 296, 324
 Governmental or quasi-governmental agencies: 6, 40, 41, 42, 43, 44, 46, 47, 48, 49, 298, 299
 Learned societies: 324

Information on other languages of wider communication
 French: 85, 112
 German: 241
 Arabic: 136, 326

Chapter 2

English Around the World

Joshua A. Fishman, Robert L. Cooper,
and Yehudit Rosenbaum

FACTORS IN LANGUAGE SPREAD

The great world languages of today are languages of empire, past and present. Only two, Mandarin Chinese and Russian, continue as languages of administration within single, ethnolinguistically diverse states. The others—Arabic, English, French, and Spanish—are imperial legacies, having survived the disintegration of the empires that fostered them.

The Survival of "Post-Imperial" Languages

Not all imperial languages survive within former colonial territories. Brosnahan (1963) points out that the language of Attila and his Huns vanished from Europe and that Turkish, the language of administration and authority in the Middle East for a thousand years, flowed back to Anatolia with the collapse of the Ottoman empire. In commenting on the case of three languages which did survive the empires which introduced them—Arabic, Greek, and Latin—Brosnahan isolated four features that accompanied the imposition of these languages. First, these languages spread with military conquest, becoming the languages of imperial administration. Second, the military authority which introduced them was maintained for several centuries, giving the languages time to take root. Third, these languages spread in multilingual areas. A unified administration promoted commercial, religious, and political contacts among linguistically diverse peoples,

77

and the language of administration served as a lingua franca. Fourth, the spread of these languages was marked by material advantages associated with learning them. Knowledge of the imposed languages, if not an absolute prerequisite for government employment, formal education, or commercial activity, enhanced the speaker's opportunities in these fields. According to Brosnahan, the unsuccessful imposition of Attila's language and of Turkish can be explained in terms of the absence of one or more of these four features. Attila's language disappeared in Europe because his empire dissolved too quickly for the language to become firmly established there. Turkish vanished in part because of the linguistic homogeneity of much of the Ottoman empire and in part because knowledge of Turkish did not confer material benefits on persons of non-Turkish origin. While the European portions of the Ottoman empire were linguistically diverse, the Asian and African portion was united by Arabic, which, in addition to being already spoken over most of the area, was the language of a high culture and a universal religion, one to which the conquerors themselves subscribed. In the Arabic-speaking portions of the empire, Arabic was the language of administration at all but the highest levels of authority. Turkish was used at the top level of governmental administration, to which only Turks were admitted as members. Except in the Turkish-speaking provinces, moreover, commerce and finance were carried on largely in Arabic and Greek. Thus the material advantages associated with learning Arabic, Greek, and Latin during the period of those languages' expansion, were absent in the case of Turkish.

Subject populations probably adopted Arabic, Greek, and Latin only for specialized purposes initially—for commerce, finance, education, religion, law, or dealings with governmental authorities—and maintained their mother tongues for other purposes. It is likely, in other words, that at first the conquerors' languages only partially displaced the indigenous languages and even then not for all sections of the population. Eventually, however, in many portions of the original empires, the imperial languages either pushed out the people speaking indigenous languages or absorbed the indigenous languages completely, becoming adopted as mother tongues. For example, as Brosnahan (1963, p. 13) points out with respect to the spread of Arabic, that language absorbed all the other Semitic dialects of Arabia, completely displaced Coptic, and pushed Berber back into the desert, becoming the general language and in most places the only language "of all the peoples from Aleppo to Aden and from Oman to Morocco."

Of the other modern world languages which are no longer the language of a unified empire but which are themselves imperial legacies—English, French, and Spanish—the last probably comes closest to Arabic in the degree to which it has displaced indigenous languages as mother tongue. Spanish has become the general mother tongue within the former Spanish empire in Central and South America. However, many of the Central and South American Indian languages have survived, although usually in reduced circumstances, and exist side by side with Spanish, which has displaced them for some but not all purposes among substantial numbers of speakers.

English and French have also been adopted as mother tongues by indigenous peoples living within the territories of the former British, French, and Belgian empires, but such adoption has generally been the exception rather than the rule. One can point to some elite families in India, Indochina, and Africa which have adopted the imperial language as the language of the home (see, for example, Alexandre 1971), but by and large where English and French are spoken by indigenous populations in former Anglophone and Francophone colonies, they are learned as additional languages and not spoken as mother tongues. English and French have been maintained as mother tongues by the descendants of colonial settlers, as in the United States and Canada, and have been acquired as mother tongues by the descendants of immigrants to such territories and by the descendants of persons forcibly removed to such territories. Although there are important exceptions, particularly with respect to North American Indian populations, when English and French are spoken as mother tongues within the territories of former colonies, they are spoken by the descendants of the displaced and not by the descendants of the original inhabitants. Unlike Spanish, the use of which as an additional language is confined principally to the territories originally conquered by Spain, the use of English and French is by no means limited to former colonial territories. Both languages are used throughout the world as additional languages.

Are the forces which promote the spread of a language as an additional language the same as those which promoted the spread of Arabic, Greek, and Latin as mother tongues? Although all are likely to promote the spread of a language as an additional language (after all, before a language can spread as a mother tongue it must first spread as an additional language), it seems clear that not all are prerequisites for such expansion. English and French, for example, are spoken as additional languages in countries which were never part of an Anglophone or a Francophone empire. No one would claim that military conquest is a prerequisite for bilingualism, whether the additional language is a world language or not. Within those countries which formerly were colonies, moreover, it is doubtful that the expansion of the imperial language as an additional language depended on the duration of military authority for several generations. It is plausible that less time is required for one language to supplant another partially—being employed for some of the functions for which the mother tongue was originally used, or being learned for entirely new functions which are introduced along with the language— than for one language to supplant another as mother tongue. Duration of authority may be less important in determining whether an imperial language remains in a former colonial territory as an additional language than it is in determining whether the language spreads there as a mother tongue.

With respect to the four conditions—military imposition, duration of authority, linguistic diversity, and material incentives—it is not clear what their independent contribution is to the promotion of a language, whether as an additional language or as a mother tongue. Territories formerly under imperial rule are, for example, more likely to be linguistically diverse than other countries. If an imperial language has a more important status in former colonies than in other countries, to what extent is the enhanced status a function of linguistic diversity and to what extent is it a function of the forces, motivations, and interactions implied by former imperial rule? Besides asking what the independent contribution of each of the four factors is, one can also ask what other factors promote the spread of a language as an additional language. This chapter summarizes the results of a study designed to answer such questions for English.

Hypotheses as to Additional Promotional Factors

What factors, besides those identified by Brosnahan, might promote the spread of a language as an additional language? Some of these factors, which are among those suggested in connection with the spread of Amharic (Cooper 1976), are likely to be urbanization, industrialization or economic development, and educational development. In addition, we can suggest religious composition and world-power political affiliation.

Urbanization

Towns often serve as loci for the spread of an additional language. A good example is Amharic, which appears to be spreading out from Ethiopia's towns and from the roads connecting them (Cooper and Horvath 1973). For one thing, towns tend to be more linguistically diverse than the surrounding countryside. Persons from different linguistic areas create linguistic diversity within the towns to which they migrate and they must often use an additional language as a lingua franca there. Second, governmental agencies tend to be concentrated in towns. People who do not speak natively the language of governmental administration may need to use an additional language when transacting government business. Third, there are apt to be greater educational opportunities in towns, particularly in developing countries. If the additional language is learned mainly in schools, urbanization would be related to its acquisition by the population. These factors can be seen at work in Kampala (Scotton 1972), for example, where English is the official language and where it serves, with Swahili, as one of the two chief lingua francas. Learned only in school, it is employed as a lingua franca only by those who have stayed long enough in school to have learned it.

Economic development

Educational language policy, while often based on political considerations, is influenced by economic constraints. A language of wider communication sometimes serves as a medium of instruction if there are not enough teachers to teach via local languages or if textbooks and other teaching materials have not been developed in local languages. Teacher training and the development of teaching materials may be more expensive in the short run than the hiring of expatriate teachers and the use of texts written in languages of wider communication. The use of additional languages for other than educational purposes may also be determined by economic considerations. Languages of wider communication may be employed as technical languages, in manuals for the use and maintenance of equipment, for example, if local languages have not been developed for such uses. Local languages are less likely to be used for such purposes if the industrial work sphere is relatively unimportant, employing relatively few workers. Economic underdevelopment may also retard the work of language academies or other language planning agencies in modernizing local languages and in disseminating their recommendations. On the one hand, economic underdevelopment promotes reliance upon languages of wider communication for functions that might be fulfilled by local languages in more developed economies. On the other hand, economic development promotes the spread of languages of wider communication to the extent that the acquisition of such languages is school-dependent. Thus the direction of the relationship between economic development and the status of a language of wider communication is likely to depend on the criterion which is employed.

Educational development

To the extent that an additional language is learned primarily in school, the proportion of persons who know that language will be a function of educational opportunity. Since educational opportunity varies with economic development, it may seem unnecessary to posit educational development as another factor promoting the spread of an additional language. Its probable importance, however, makes it worth listing separately even if its independence as a predictor is open to question.

Religious composition

That economic advancement is not the only incentive for learning an additional language can be seen in the case of Arabic, which is a classical language for educated persons throughout the Islamic world. As a language of revealed religion, Arabic is perhaps unique among languages of wider communication. It is unlikely that one would learn English, French, or Spanish for religious purposes inasmuch as sanctity is not among the claims that can be made for those languages. Besides, Christian missionaries take pains to translate the Gospels into local languages. On the other hand, in areas in which universal religions or religions associated with high cultures are not dominant, religious beliefs are likely to be relatively particularistic, reflecting ethnic and linguistic diversity, which in turn promotes the spread of lingua francas. Such areas also tend to be underdeveloped economically and educationally. Thus religious composition may serve as a kind of mediating variable with respect to the spread of English, to which it may be related either via linguistic diversity or via economic and educational development.

Political affiliation

It is possible that a country's position vis-à-vis the superpowers will be reflected in the languages taught as subjects and used as media of instruction in their schools and in the languages used when dealing with foreign governments. Thus Russian, for example, is more likely to be taught as a subject of instruction in Eastern

European schools than in South American schools. It is of course not the political affiliation itself that promotes second-language acquisition but rather the interactions which are encouraged or facilitated by such affiliation, for example, in international trade.

Independence of additional factors

Economic and educational development are not the only suggested additional promotional factors which are related to one another. All are related to one another. Economic development is related to urbanism, which in turn is related to educational development. Similarly, particularistic, folk religions are more likely to be dominant in countries which are less economically developed. With respect to political affiliation, the Third-World countries are in general less economically developed than countries which are firm allies of either of the two great superpowers. Thus, just as the independence of Brosnahan's four factors as facilitators of language spread is problematic, so too is the independence of the five additional factors that have been suggested here.

STUDY PROCEDURE

Information from secondary sources was gathered for each of 102 countries with respect to the position of English and with respect to various demographic, economic, educational, and other factors. In none of these countries was English the mother tongue of a substantial proportion of the population. These data were intercorrelated and then multiple regression analyses were performed on a number of criterion variables pertaining to the status of English.

Criterion Variables

The criterion variables employed were as follows.

1. *The use of English as a medium of instruction in secondary schools.* This information, obtained from Gage and Ohannessian (1974), was scored as follows for purposes of data analysis: 2 = used as a medium of instruction throughout the school system; 1 = used as a medium in some schools or in some classes; 0 = not used as a medium of instruction.

2. *The use of English as a medium of instruction in primary schools.* This information, obtained from Gage and Ohannessian, was scored in the same way as was the first criterion variable.

3. *The use of English as a subject of instruction in secondary schools.* This information, also obtained from Gage and Ohannessian (1974), was scored as follows: 2 = taught as a subject of instruction throughout the school system; 1 = taught in some schools or in some classes; 0 = not taught as a subject of instruction.

4. *The use of English as a subject of instruction in primary schools.* This information, obtained from Gage and Ohannessian, was scored as in the third criterion variable.

Table 2.1   Correlations between the composite criterion and each of its components (all countries)

Component	N	Correlation with composite
Official status	94	.89
Language of government administration	102	.87
Lingua franca within country	88	.43
Technical language	49	.66
First foreign language studied by most students	102	.63
Use in universities	32	.80
Percentage of daily newspapers in English	96	.84
Use on radio	80	.62
Percentage of books published in English	38	.81
Medium of instruction in secondary schools	88	.87
Medium of instruction in primary.schools	88	.75
Subject of instruction in.secondary schools	88	.50
Subject of instruction in primary schools	88	.79
Percentage of population in primary and secondary school English classes	87	.65

5. *The percentage of the population enrolled in English classes in primary and secondary schools.* The number of students enrolled in English classes (whether as subject or medium) at the primary and secondary school levels in each country, as estimated by Gage and Ohannessian, was divided by the total population for that country as reported in U.S. Government (1972).

6. *A composite score based on fourteen items with respect to the status of English.* The components of this score were the five items previously described as well as the following: the use of English as an official language; the use of English as a language of governmental administration; the use of English as a lingua franca within the country; the use of English as a technical language; the use of English as the first foreign language for most students; the use of English in universities; the proportion of daily newspapers published in English; the use of English on the radio; and the percentage of books published in English. These variables were converted to standard scores to equalize their weight in the composite. The composite was computed by summing the standard scores and dividing by the number of variables for which there was information. Averages were employed because there were no countries for which information could be obtained on all variables. The number of countries for which each of these components was obtained and the correlation of each component with the composite variable are presented in Table 2.1. It can be seen that the components with the highest relationship to the composite were official status ($r = 0.89$), use as a language of administration ($r = 0.87$) and use as a medium of instruction in secondary school ($r = 0.87$). The components with the lowest correlation to the composite criterion were used as a lingua franca within the country ($r = 0.43$), use

Table 2.2   Intercorrelations among criterion variables (all countries)

Criterion	Coefficient					
	1	2	3	4	5	6
1. Medium in secondary schools	—	.79	.33	.76	.58	.87
2. Medium in primary schools		—	.27	.69	.40	.75
3. Subject in secondary schools			—	.27	.21	.50
4. Subject in primary schools				—	.61	.79
5. Percentage population in English classes					—	.65
6. Composite						

as a subject of instruction in secondary school ($r = 0.50$), and the use of English on the radio ($r = 0.62$). The median correlation of the components with the composite was 0.77.

The intercorrelations among the six criterion variables are presented in Table 2.2. These coefficients ranged between 0.21 and 0.87, with the median at 0.61. Thus these criteria appear independent enough to justify separate treatment.

Predictor Variables

The variables chosen to represent the four conditions described by Brosnahan for Arabic, Greek, and Latin and the five conditions we have suggested as possible contributors to the spread of an additional language are as follows:

1. *Military imposition*. While not all colonies were obtained through military conquest, the use of force is a common enough feature to justify former colonial status as an indicator of former military imposition. Thus all countries were classified as to whether or not they had been former Anglophone colonies.

2. *Duration of military authority*. This variable was measured indirectly and inversely as recency of independence (Stebbins 1970). The decade in which independence was achieved was scored, with all decades prior to 1801–1810 scored as zero, with that decade scored as one, and with subsequent decades scored from two (1811–1820) to seventeen (1961–1970).

3. *Linguistic diversity*. The linguistic complexity of each country at the national level was classified according to the categories suggested by Criper and Ladefoged (1971). The language situation of a country was classified as *dominant* if the language spoken by its largest mother-tongue group was spoken natively by at least twice as many people as in the next largest mother-tongue group and if no other language was spoken natively by more than 10% of the population. The language situation of a country was classified as *predominant* if the language spoken by the largest mother-tongue group was spoken natively by twice as many people as were in the next largest mother-tongue group but there was also at least one language, in addition to the predominant one, that was spoken natively by at least 10% of the population. The language situation of a country was characterized as *mixed* if it was not classified as either dominant or predominant. These classifica-

tions were treated as three dichotomous variables, with each country being classfied as belonging to only one. In addition, each country was classified with respect to the proportion of the population made up of the largest mother-tongue group and with respect to the communicability of the language spoken by the largest mother-tongue group. The latter variable was scored on a four-point scale, with the lowest point representing a language which was spoken in parts of the country only and the highest point representing a language spoken in more than three other countries.

4. *Material benefits.* No relatively direct index of the material benefits to be gained from learning English was employed, although it might have been possible, if expensive, to do so. For example, the proportion of help-wanted ads in the daily press which specified English as a requirement for employment might have been used (see, for example, Cooper and Seckbach, this vol., chap. 8). Two indirect measures were used. These were based on the percentage of exports sent to English-speaking countries and the percentage of imports originating from English-speaking countries (U.S. Government 1972), i.e., the relative importance of English-speaking countries as suppliers of a country's imports and the relative importance of English-speaking countries as customers for a country's exports. Relative importance was scored in each case on a nine-point scale. While it is true that one need not know English in order to participate in foreign trade with English-speaking countries and while it is also true that direct participation in such trade represents a small proportion of a nation's gross national product, foreign trade may have a multiplier effect with respect to the material advantages associated with a knowledge of English. Thus, not only some of the employees of import-export firms might be expected to know the language of their principal customers but also some of the employees of the companies through which the imported or exported goods travel (manufacturers, wholesalers, retailers).

5. *Urbanization.* Urbanization was measured as the percentage of the population living in urban centers, as reported by U.S. Government (1972).

6. *Economic development.* The following measures were selected to represent economic development: per capita gross national product, life expectancy, average daily caloric intake, and number of infant deaths per 1,000 live births. These statistics were taken from U.S. Government (1972).

7. *Educational development.* Four measures were employed to represent educational development. These were the number of years of compulsory education, the proportion of the school-age population attending school, the proportion of the secondary school-age population enrolled in secondary school, and the rate of illiteracy. These statistics were taken from UNESCO (1973).

8. *Religious composition.* The percentage of the population falling within each of the following categories was scored: Roman Catholic, non-Roman Catholic Christian, Muslim, Hindu, Buddhist and Confucian, traditional beliefs, and other. The main sources consulted were Paxton (1972) and *The Europa Year Book* (1972).

9. *Political affiliation.* Each nation was scored as belonging to one of four rather primitive categories: neutral, leaning to the West, leaning toward the

Soviet Union, or leaning toward China. In addition, nations falling into either of the last two categories were also scored as belonging to a fifth category, leaning toward the East. The principal source here was Stebbins (1970).

10. *Other variables.* In addition to the thirty predictor variables enumerated previously, the following twenty-three variables were employed: population size, annual population increase, population density per square mile, total area, number of acres in the country per capita, percentage of total area used for agriculture, percentage of the labor force engaged in agriculture, gross national product, growth rate of the gross national product, growth rate of per capita income, number of radio receivers per 1,000 population, number of daily newspapers, television broadcasting, number of universities, public expenditure on education as a percentage of total public expenditure, total imports, total exports, proportion of imports from the United States, proportion of exports sent to the United States, English the official language of a neighboring country, extent of genetic relationship between English and the language spoken by the largest mother-tongue group, former Francophone colony, and former colony of a nation other than an Anglophone or Francophone country. Most of these data were taken from U.S. Government (1972).

All in all, then, about fifty predictor (independent) variables were employed to predict each of six criterion (dependent) variables expressing the status of English around the world.

RESULTS

Before summarizing the intercorrelations and regression analyses, we will present some summary data with respect to the status of English in the 102 countries surveyed.[1]

English was the only official language or co-official language in 20 countries. In an additional 36 countries it held a privileged status, i.e., it was used as a medium in courts, as a principal medium of instruction in schools, or as the chief foreign language employed by the government in its dealings with foreigners and with foreign governments. In only 38 countries did English have no official use whatsoever. In 56 countries it was the foreign language which most students were taught first. Of the 88 countries for which data were available from Gage and Ohannessian (1974), English was a medium of instruction throughout the secondary schools in 18 countries and a subject of instruction throughout the secondary schools in 61. It was a medium of instruction in at least some elementary schools in 35 countries. Gage and Ohannessian estimated that approximately 115 million persons in the non-English mother-tongue states they surveyed were currently exposed to English in the primary and secondary schools, either as a medium or as a subject of instruction. Their data with respect to the number of persons enrolled in English classes were available for 87 of our countries. Of these, the average percentage of persons exposed to English in the schools was 6.3%.

When the status of English was examined according to whether or not a country was a former Anglophone colony, there were of course substantial differences. Thus, for example, whereas almost 60% of the 29 former Anglophone colonies for which we had information used English as a medium of instruction in at least some secondary schools, only 3% of the other countries did so. Whereas all the former Anglophone colonies taught English as a subject in at least some high schools, about two-thirds of the other countries did so. Whereas almost 50% of the former Anglophone countries used English as a medium of instruction in at least some primary schools, less than 2% of the other countries did so. Finally, whereas almost three-fourths of the former Anglophone countries taught English as a subject of instruction in at least some primary schools, less than one-fourth of the other countries did so. With respect to the percentage of the population exposed to English as a subject or medium of instruction in the primary and secondary schools, the average percentage in the former Anglophone colonies was 11% as contrasted with 4% in the average country which had never been an Anglophone colony. The sharpest difference between former Anglophone colonies and other countries with respect to the status of English can be found in terms of that language's official status. All the countries that employed English as their only official language or as a co-official language were former Anglophone colonies.

Zero-order Correlations

How well did the variables previously suggested—military imposition, duration of military rule, linguistic diversity, material benefits, urbanization, economic development, educational development, religious composition, and political affiliation—predict the status of English? Because there was a sharp difference between the former Anglophone colonies ($N = 31$) and the other countries ($N = 71$), it is worthwhile to examine these relationships not only for all countries combined but also separately for those countries that were never Anglophone colonies.

Military imposition

We have already seen that there were substantial differences between former Anglophone colonies and other countries with respect to our six English criterion variables when expressed in terms of percentages. When expressed in terms of correlation coefficients, we see that former Anglophone colonial status was the single best predictor of five of these criteria, with coefficients ranging from 0.41 (use of English as a subject of instruction in secondary schools) to 0.77 (the composite criterion), with the median at 0.53. Former Anglophone colonial status was the third best predictor of the remaining criterion (use of English as a medium of instruction in primary schools), with a coefficient of 0.53. These coefficients are presented in Table 2.3.

Duration of colonial rule

There was a positive relationship between recency of independence and all but one of the criterion variables, but these relationships were modest ones. Excepting the use of English as a subject of instruction in secondary schools, which had

Table 2.3   Relationship between former Anglophone
colonial status and English criterion variables

Criterion	Correlation
Medium in secondary schools	.62
Medium in primary schools	.53
Subject in secondary schools	.41
Subject in primary schools	.53
Percentage population in English classes	.50
Composite	.77

a negligible relationship to recency of independence, the other criteria displayed correlation coefficients ranging from 0.25 (percentage of the population in English classes) to 0.38 (use of English as a subject of instruction in primary schools). However, these relationships were largely due to the fact that almost half (31 of 64) of the former colonies had been former Anglophone dependencies. Most recently independent nations, in other words, tended to be former Anglophone colonies, and thus more recently independent nations tended to rely on English more than did countries that had been longer established. When the correlations were computed only for those countries which had never been Anglophone colonies, the positive relationship between recency of independence and the use of English in educational contexts disappeared. With respect to the composite English criterion, a slight negative relationship (−0.27) was found. Thus when former Anglophone colonies were not considered, the more recently independent nations tended to use English less, when measured in terms of the overall composite criterion. This negative relationship can be explained partly on the grounds that former Francophone colonies ($N = 25$), which presumably rely more heavily on French than on English, tended to be more recently independent ($r = 0.38$). Thus recency of statehood does not appear to have been independently related to the English criterion variables. The relationships between recency of independence and the criterion variables can be found in Table 2.4.

Linguistic diversity

Former Anglophone colonies were found to be more linguistically diverse than the other countries. Whereas almost 80% of the countries which had never been Anglophone colonies were characterized as having a dominant language, only a little over one-third of the former Anglophone colonies were so characterized. Conversely, whereas less than 10% of the countries which had never been Anglophone colonies were described as linguistically mixed, about one-third of the former Anglophone colonies were so described.

     When coefficients were computed for all countries combined, linguistic diversity (language situation—mixed) proved to be positively correlated to all the

Table 2.4   Correlations between recency of independence and
English criterion variables

Criterion	All countries	All countries but former Anglophone colonies
Medium in secondary schools	.35	−.04
Medium in primary schools	.35	.14
Subject in secondary schools	.06	−.21
Subject in primary schools	.38	.13
Percentage population in English classes	.25	−.12
Composite	.27	−.27

English criterion variables. Substantial correlations were observed between linguistic diversity and use of English as a medium of instruction in primary schools ($r = 0.64$) and secondary schools ($r = 0.58$). Even after former Anglophone colonies had been excluded from consideration, substantial relationships were observed between linguistic diversity and these two criteria. Linguistic diversity was, in fact, the variable with the highest correlation with the use of English as a medium of instruction in primary school not only when the correlation was computed for all countries combined ($r = 0.64$) but also when it was computed for only those countries which had never been Anglophone colonies ($r = 0.70$). Thus linguistic diversity appeared to be related to the use of English as a medium in the schools, particularly primary schools, independently of former Anglophone colonial status.

Three variables expressed linguistic homogeneity: relative size of the largest mother-tongue group, communicability of the language spoken by the largest mother-tongue group, and dominant language situation. These measures were inversely related to the variable "mixed language situation," with correlation coefficients in the 0.50s. The relationships between the homogeneity measures and the criterion variables were similar to those between mixed language situation and the criterion measures except that, of course, the direction of the relationships were reversed. The relationships between the linguistic diversity and the homogeneity measures on the one hand and the criterion variables on the other are presented in Table 2.5.

Material benefits

There was a modest positive relationship between the overall composite criterion and the relative importance of English-speaking countries as customers for exports ($r = 0.38$). This coefficient was only slightly reduced ($r = 0.31$) when former Anglophone colonies were excluded, and in fact the relationship between former Anglophone colonial status and the relative importance of English-speaking countries to a nation's exports was almost negligible ($r = 0.12$). Thus countries for which English-speaking nations were relatively important customers tended to

Table 2.5   Correlations between linguistic diversity measures and English criterion variables

Linguistic diversity measure	Countries	Medium in secondary schools	Medium in primary schools	Subject in secondary schools	Subject in primary schools	% in English classes	Composite
Language situation—mixed	All	.58	.64	.24	.49	.23	.36
	Without former A-p colonies	.48	.70	.17	.23	–.13	.12
Language situation—predominant	All	.07	.09	.08	.03	.01	.14
	Without former A-p colonies	.20	–.05	–.03	–.04	–.05	.03
Language situation—dominant	All	–.46	–.51	–.23	–.36	–.17	–.36
	Without former A-p colonies	–.41	–.29	–.05	–.07	.11	–.06
Relative size of largest mother-tongue group	All	–.48	–.51	–.28	–.46	–.25	–.33
	Without former A-p colonies	–.26	–.29	–.22	–.26	–.10	–.10
Communicability of main language	All	–.50	–.51	–.11	–.51	–.25	–.42
	Without former A-p colonies	–.23	–.23	.03	–.34	–.04	–.14

Table 2.6 Correlations between the relative importance of trade with English-speaking countries and the English criterion variables

Trade measure	Countries	Medium in secondary schools	Medium in primary schools	Subject in secondary schools	Subject in primary schools	% in English classes	Composite
Exports	All	.30	.24	.20	.14	.11	.38
	Without former A-p colonies	.09	.01	.18	-.13	.00	.31
Imports	All	.09	.08	.27	-.04	.03	.22
	Without former A-p colonies	-.03	.05	.29	-.22	.05	.24

Table 2.7 Intercorrelations among urbanism, economic development, and educational development variables (all countries)

Variable	1	2	3	4	5	6	7	8	9
1. Illiteracy	—	-.43	-.80	-.81	-.72	.84	-.76	-.85	-.71
2. No. yrs. compulsory education		—	.51	.51	.46	-.46	.39	.43	.44
3. School enrollment ratio			—	.84	.76	-.78	.67	.78	.62
4. Secondary school enrollment ratio				—	.79	-.83	.78	.83	.84
5. Urbanism					—	-.77	.70	.76	.70
6. Infant death rate						—	-.67	-.85	-.72
7. Average daily calories							—	.76	.75
8. Life expectancy								—	.73
9. GNP per capita									—

have a greater overall use of English than countries for which English-speaking nations were relatively less important, and this relationship was independent of former Anglophone colonial status. The relationships of the export and import variables to the criterion variables are shown in Table 2.6.

Urbanism, economic development, and educational development

Urbanism, economic development, and educational development can be considered together as predictor variables because they proved to be substantially correlated with one another. (See Table 2.7) Countries which were more urban also tended to be more economically and educationally developed. The correlations between urbanism and the four measures of economic development ranged from 0.70 to 0.77; the correlations between urbanism and the four measures of educational development ranged from 0.46 to 0.79, with three of these coefficients above 0.70; and the correlations between the four measures of economic development and the four measures of educational development ranged from 0.39 to 0.85, with the median coefficient at 0.77 and with all but four of the sixteen coefficients above 0.60. Only one of these variables yielded substantially lower intercorrelations. This was the number of years of compulsory education, whose correlations with the other variables ranged from 0.39 to 0.51, with the median coefficient at 0.45. The coefficients among urbanism, economic development, and educational development, which are presented in Table 2.7 for all countries combined, were substantially the same when the former Anglophone colonies were excluded.

Urbanism, economic development, and educational development were all modestly related to former Anglophone colonial status, which was negatively correlated to urbanism $(r = -0.26)$, number of years of compulsory education $(r = -0.44)$, school enrollment ratio $(r = -0.26)$, secondary school enrollment ratio $(r = -0.27)$, average caloric daily intake $(r = -0.26)$, and gross national product per capita $(r = -0.25)$, and which was positively related to the rate of illiteracy $(r = 0.28)$. Former Anglophone colonies, in other words, showed a modest tendency to be less urbanized and less developed economically and educationally than other countries.

All the criterion variables except the proportion of the population enrolled in English classes showed modest relationships with most of these predictors when the correlations were computed for all countries combined. Countries which were less urbanized and less economically and educationally developed tended to place more reliance on English than did other countries. Because former Anglophone colonial status was related to these predictors, however, we can expect that some of these relationships would disappear when former Anglophone colonies were excluded. This in fact occurred for most criteria except the use of English as a medium of instruction in secondary schools and the use of English as a subject of instruction in secondary schools. The former criterion continued to display negative, although reduced, correlations with urbanism and with economic and educational development, and the latter criterion continued to show a negative, although reduced, relationship to economic development. The proportion of the population enrolled in primary and secondary school English classes, which showed negligible relationships with urbanism and with economic and educational development when the correlations were computed for all countries combined, showed modest positive relationships with urbanism and with economic and educational development when the former Anglophone colonies were excluded. Thus, when former Anglophone colonies were removed from consideration, urbanism and economic and educational development were negatively related to the use of English as a medium of instruction in secondary schools and positively related to the proportion of the population enrolled in primary and secondary school English classes.

Developing nations apparently find it more difficult than other nations to provide secondary school education via indigenous languages. Expatriate teachers using foreign languages as media of instruction must sometimes be employed until the educational system can be sufficiently expanded to provide a sizable number of teachers who can teach via indigenous languages. Since it is usually more expensive to produce secondary school teachers than it is to produce primary school teachers, the widespread use of foreign languages as media of instruction is more commonly found at the secondary school level than at the primary school level. Thus there is a tendency for the widespread use of foreign languages as media of instruction in secondary schools to be more commonly found in poorer nations than in richer ones, which have greater resources for the development of teachers and materials and which can more readily afford to develop local languages for educational purposes.

The percentage of the population enrolled in primary and secondary school English classes, on the other hand, is partly a function of the proportion of the population enrolled in school, which in turn is a function of economic development. In general, the more economically developed a country, the greater the proportion of its population enrolled in school, and therefore the greater proportion of the population enrolled in English classes. The relationship between economic development and the proportion of the population enrolled in English classes was negligible when computed for all countries combined because former Anglophone colonies, which are typically poorer, also typically have a greater proportion of the population enrolled in English classes. The relationship could be seen when these countries were excluded from the computation. The correlations of urbanism, economic development, and educational development with the criterion variables can be seen in Table 2.8.

Religious composition

The only religious category to be substantially correlated with the criterion variables was that of "traditional beliefs," i.e., local systems of folk beliefs as distinguished from universal religions or religions associated with high cultures such as those of Christianity, Hinduism, and Islam. The highest of these correlations were with the use of English as a medium of instruction in primary schools ($r = 0.62$) and in secondary schools ($r = 0.53$). The substantial relationships with

Table 2.8 Correlations of urbanism, economic development, and educational development variables with English criterion variables

Variable	Countries	Medium in secondary school	Medium in primary school	Subject in secondary school	Subject in primary school	% in English classes	Composite
Urbanism	All	-.42	-.41	-.16	-.36	-.02	-.26
	Without former A-p colonies	-.30	-.19	-.03	-.02	.33	.07
Infant death rate	All	.45	.39	.37	.28	.01	.19
	Without former A-p colonies	.26	.12	.32	-.24	-.57	-.13
Average daily calories	All	-.33	-.27	-.31	-.18	-.04	-.27
	Without former A-p colonies	-.24	-.18	-.23	.09	.27	-.11
Life expectancy	All	-.33	-.32	-.32	-.18	.08	-.16
	Without former A-p colonies	-.23	-.12	-.26	.14	.53	.00
GNP per capita	All	-.33	-.28	-.33	-.11	.06	-.21
	Without former A-p colonies	-.17	-.12	-.26	.30	.47	.10
Illiteracy	All	.33	.29	.24	.16	-.04	.16
	Without former A-p colonies	.23	.07	.13	-.20	-.41	-.18

Table 2.8 (continued)

Variable	Countries	Medium in secondary school	Medium in primary school	Subject in secondary school	Subject in primary school	% in English classes	Composite
No. yrs. compulsory education	All	-.54	-.42	-.24	-.26	-.13	-.46
	Without former A-p colonies	-.25	.05	-.09	.40	.45	.02
School enrollment ratio	All	-.34	-.32	-.21	-.23	.14	-.21
	Without former A-p colonies	-.23	-.02	-.11	.06	.39	.03
Secondary school enrollment ratio	All	-.43	-.38	-.29	-.28	.04	-.27
	Without former A-p colonies	-.24	-.15	-.18	.09	.45	.06

these two variables remained when former Anglophone colonies were excluded from the computations. (The correlation between former Anglophone colonial status and the traditional belief percentage was only 0.21.) These relationships can be explained in part by the fact that countries with relatively high proportions of the population categorized as subscribing to traditional beliefs tended to be relatively unurbanized and relatively undeveloped economically and education-ally. The correlation between the traditional belief percentage, on the one hand, and urbanism and the economic and educational development indices, on the other, ranged from 0.28 to 0.55, when computed for all countries combined, with five of these nine coefficients above 0.40. Countries with high traditional belief percentages, furthermore, tended to be linguistically mixed ($r = 0.50$). While linguistic diversity itself was negatively related to urbanism and to economic and educational development, these relationships were on the whole smaller than between the traditional belief percentage and the urbanism, economic develop-ment, and educational development indices. The relationships between linguistic diversity and the urbanism and development indices ranged from 0.12 to 0.46, with only two of the nine coefficients above 0.40. These relationships were about the same when computed without the former Anglophone colonies. Thus the localism reflected both by traditional beliefs and by linguistic diversity were substantially related to reliance upon English as a medium of instruction in the schools, this reliance being mediated at least in part by lack of economic develop-ment. The correlations between the traditional beliefs percentage and the criterion variables are presented in Table 2.9, and the relationships of linguistic diversity to the traditional belief percentage, urbanism, and the economic and educational development indices are presented in Table 2.10.

Political affiliation

Political affiliation, in terms of associations with the Big Powers, proved to have little relationship to the criterion variables. None of the five political categories had a substantial correlation with any of the criterion variables. The highest coefficient observed, when computed for all countries, was 0.19. When computed without the former Anglophone colonies, the highest coefficient was 0.22.

The highest zero-order correlations between predictors and criteria

When correlations were computed across all countries, the single most important predictor of the criterion variables was former Anglophone colonial status. With coefficients ranging from 0.41 (use of English as a subject of instruction in secondary schools) to 0.77 (the overall composite), it proved to be the best single predictor for five of the six criteria. The second best predictor was linguistic diversity (mixed language situation), which was the single best predictor of the use of English as a medium of instruction in primary schools ($r = 0.64$) and which was the second best predictor of the use of English as a medium of instruction in secondary schools ($r = 0.58$). A related measure, the communicability of the language spoken by the largest mother-tongue group, was the second best predictor

Table 2.9   Correlations between the traditional beliefs percentage and the English criterion variables

Criterion	All countries	All countries but former Anglophone colonies
Medium in secondary schools	.53	.56
Medium in primary schools	.62	.65
Subject in secondary schools	.23	.17
Subject in primary schools	.49	.24
Percentage population in English classes	.21	−.15
Composite	.22	−.15

Table 2.10   Correlations between linguistic diversity (language situation— mixed) and selected variables

Variable	All countries	All countries but former Anglophone colonies
Traditional beliefs percentage	.50	.73
Urbanism	−.38	−.40
Infant death rate	.44	.46
Average daily calories	−.31	−.24
Life expectancy	−.46	−.49
GNP per capita	−.28	−.22
Illiteracy	.38	.37
No. yrs. compulsory education	−.12	−.18
School enrollment ratio	−.36	−.37
Secondary school enrollment ratio	−.36	−.33

of the use of English as a subject of instruction in primary schools ($r = -0.51$). The third best predictor of the criteria was the percentage of the population whose religion was categorized as that of traditional beliefs. This was the second and third best predictor of the use of English in primary schools, as a medium ($r = 0.62$) and as a subject ($r = 0.49$) of instruction. Another good predictor was the number of years of compulsory education, which was the second highest predictor of the overall composite ($r = -0.46$) and which was the third best predictor of the use of English as a medium of instruction in secondary schools ($r = -0.54$).

When the former Anglophone colonies were excluded from the computations, the single best predictors of the criteria were linguistic diversity and the traditional beliefs percentage. These were either the best or second best predictors for the use of English as a medium of instruction in secondary and primary schools, with the four coefficients ranging from 0.48 to 0.70. Number of years of compulsory education was the best predictor of the use of English as a subject of instruction in primary school ($r = 0.40$). The best single predictors of the proportion of the population studying in primary and secondary school English classes were the infant mortality rate ($r = -0.57$) and life expectancy ($r = 0.53$). The best single predictor of the overall composite criterion was percentage of exports to English-speaking countries ($r = 0.31$).

All in all, then, when former Anglophone colonial status was not considered, the best predictors of the criteria were linguistic diversity, traditional beliefs percentage, number of years of compulsory education, economic development indicators, and exports to English-speaking countries. In general, countries with greater linguistic diversity, a greater traditional beliefs percentage, fewer years of compulsory education, and relatively less economic development tended to place greater reliance on English both as a medium of instruction and as a subject of instruction. Conversely, countries which were more economically developed tended to have a greater percentage of the population enrolled in primary and secondary school English classes.

As we have seen, the interrelationships among these predictors were complex. How much did each contribute to the prediction of the criteria when the predictors were combined with one another? To answer this question we turn to the multiple regression analyses.

Multiple Regression Analyses

Just as the zero-order correlation coefficient expresses the degree of relationship between two variables, a multiple correlation coefficient expresses the degree of relationship between a criterion variable and two or more predictor variables taken together. In general, a multiple correlation coefficient will be higher than a zero-order correlation coefficient to the extent that the multiple correlation combines predictors which have both high correlations with the criterion *and* low correlations with one another.

Just as a zero-order coefficient squared expresses the percentage of the variation (variance) of one variable that is associated with or "accounted for" by the other, so the multiple correlation coefficient squared expresses the percentage of the criterion's variance that is associated with or accounted for by the predictor variables jointly. Multiple regression analysis tells us how much additional variation in the criterion variable is associated with the addition of a new predictor.

Let us take as a concrete example the use of English as a medium of instruction in secondary schools. The single best predictor of this criterion was former Anglophone colonial status ($r = 0.62$). Another variable with a high correlation with this criterion was the traditional beliefs percentage ($r = 0.53$). Adding traditional beliefs percentage to former Anglophone colonial status increased the percentage of the criterion's variance that we can account for only to the extent that these two predictor variables did not overlap with one another. In fact they were related to one another slightly ($r = 0.21$). Thus adding traditional

Table 2.11   Multiple regression analysis: Use of English as a medium of instruction in secondary schools

Step[a]	Variable	R	R^2	$\triangle R^2$	r
1	Former Anglophone colony	.623	.388	.388	.623
2	Traditional beliefs percentage	.747	.558	.170	.535
3	Exports to English-speaking countries	.790	.624	.066	.302
4	Language situation—mixed	.819	.671	.046	.583

[a]All steps shown until first step at which $\triangle R^2$ fell below 0.036.

beliefs percentage to former Anglophone colonial status increased the correlation of 0.62 (between the criterion and former Anglophone colonial status only) to 0.75. If we square each of these coefficients and then subtract the smaller from the larger figure we find a difference of 17%. In other words, by adding traditional beliefs percentage to former Anglophone colonial status we can account for an additional 17% of the variance in the use of English as a medium of instruction in secondary school.

We present the following results from our multiple regression analyses for each of the criterion variables in turn, based on all countries. For each regression analysis we show the effects of including each additional predictor variable until the addition of a predictor results in an increment of *less* than 4% in the amount of the criterion's variance that has been accounted for or "explained." Each additional predictor resulting in an increment of at least 4%, in other words, is shown. In the tables summarizing these results, the following symbols are used:

R = multiple correlation coefficient

R^2 = square of the multiple correlation coefficient
This expresses the proportion of the criterion's variance which has been explained by the predictor variables up to and including the new predictor.

$\triangle R^2$ = increment in R^2
This is the increment in the proportion of the criterion's variance that has been explained by adding the new predictor.

r = the zero-order correlation coefficient between the additional predictor variable and the criterion variable.

The use of English as a medium of instruction in secondary schools

By combining the traditional beliefs percentage, exports to English-speaking countries, and linguistic diversity (mixed language situation) to former Anglophone colonial status as a predictor of the use of English as medium of instruction in secondary schools, we obtained a multiple correlation of almost 0.82. These results are presented in Table 2.11.

Table 2.12   Multiple regression analysis: Use of English as a medium of
instruction in primary schools

Step[a]	Variable	R	R^2	ΔR^2	r
1	Language situation—mixed	.639	.408	.408	.639
2	Traditional beliefs percentage	.729	.531	.123	.624
3	Former Anglophone colony	.797	.635	.103	.530
4	Exports to English-speaking countries	.819	.671	.036	.244
5	Percentage Hindu	.844	.712	.040	−.013

[a]All steps shown until first step at which ΔR^2 fell below 0.036.

The use of English as a medium of instruction in primary schools

The single best predictor of the use of English as a medium of instruction in
primary schools was linguistic diversity ($r = 0.64$). By adding the traditional
beliefs percentage, former Anglophone colonial status, exports to English-speaking
countries, and percentage Hindu, the multiple correlation coefficient rose to 0.84
(see Table 2.12). It should be noted that the last of these predictors was negligibly
correlated with the criterion but nevertheless raised the proportion of variance
accounted for by 4%. A predictor which is not correlated to a criterion can
sometimes raise the multiple correlation coefficient by serving as a "suppression
variable," if it correlates substantially with another predictor variable which is
correlated with the criterion. In the present case, percentage Hindu was correlated
with former Anglophone colonial status ($r = 0.36$), which in turn was correlated
with the criterion. Former Anglophone colonial status contained some variance
which was not shared with the criterion and which reduced the correlation that
otherwise might have been obtained with the criterion. Presumably, some of this
"unwanted" or useless variance that was unshared with the criterion was shared
with percentage Hindu, which acted in such a way as to suppress the effect of
part of the unwanted variance, thus raising the contribution that could be made
by former Anglophone colonial status to the prediction of the criterion.

Three variables, then, in addition to former Anglophone colonial status,
were important in the multiple prediction of the use of English as a medium of
instruction both in primary schools and in secondary schools: linguistic diversity,
the traditional beliefs percentage, and exports to English-speaking countries.

The use of English as a subject of instruction in primary schools

Three variables increased our ability to account for variance in the use of English
as a subject of instruction in primary schools by more than 3% when added to
former Anglophone colonial status (see Table 2.13). These were, in order, the
traditional beliefs percentage, the non-Roman Catholic Christian percentage, and
the relative size of the largest mother-tongue community. The last of these was in
part an inverse measure of linguistic diversity ($r = 0.52$). Thus religion composi-

Table 2.13   Multiple regression analysis: Use of English as a subject of instruction in primary schools

Step[a]	Variable	R	R^2	ΔR^2	r
1	Former Anglophone colony	.533	.284	.284	.533
2	Traditional beliefs percentage	.659	.435	.151	.493
3	Percentage non-Roman Catholic Christian	.717	.514	.079	.114
4	Relative size of largest mother-tongue community	.754	.568	.054	−.460

[a]All steps shown until first step at which ΔR^2 fell below 0.036.

Table 2.14   Multiple regression analysis: Use of English as a subject of instruction in secondary schools

Step[a]	Variable	R	R^2	ΔR^2	r
1	Former Anglophone colony	.415	.172	.172	.415
2	Former non-Anglophone, non-Francophone colony	.512	.262	.090	−.374
3	Infant death rate	.575	.330	.068	.369
4	Urbanism	.632	.399	.069	−.159
5	Percentage Buddhists	.683	.466	.067	.104
6	Illiteracy	.717	.514	.048	.241
7	Acres per capita	.750	.562	.048	−.200

[a]All steps shown until first step at which ΔR^2 fell below 0.036.

tion and linguistic diversity appeared to be important predictors for this criterion, much as they were for the use of English as a medium of instruction in secondary and primary schools.

English as a subject of instruction in secondary schools

Six variables in addition to former Anglophone colonial status added at least 4% to the incremental prediction of English as a subject of instruction in secondary schools (see Table 2.14), yielding a multiple correlation coefficient of 0.75. These were, in order, status as a former colony of a non-Anglophone, non-Francophone power, infant death rate, percentage of the population living in urban areas, percentage Buddhist and Confucianists, percentage of illiteracy, and number of acres per capita (total area of the country divided by the population). All but the last of these, for the incremental contribution of which we can advance no principled explanation, was a measure either of urbanism, religious composition,

Table 2.15   Multiple regression analysis: The percentage of the population
enrolled in primary and secondary school English classes

Step[a]	Variable	R	R^2	$\triangle R^2$	r
1	Former Anglophone colony	.499	.249	.249	.499
2	School enrollment ratio	.570	.325	.076	.138
3	Relative size largest mother-tongue community	.653	.427	.101	−.251
4	Genetic relationship to English of main language	.695	.483	.056	−.310
5	Political affiliation—West	.721	.520	.037	.195

[a]All steps shown until first step at which $\triangle R^2$ fell below 0.036.

former colonial rule, or economic development. The multiple prediction of this criterion, then, contrasts with that of the three criteria previously described—the use of English as a medium of instruction in secondary and in primary schools and the use of English as a subject of instruction in primary schools—which did not include urbanism, economic development, or educational development among their important incremental predictors. It may be recalled that these three criteria were substantially related to one another but only moderately related to the use of English as a subject of instruction in secondary schools. It is of interest that the addition of urbanism and illiteracy improved prediction although an economic development variable, to which both were substantially related, had entered the multiple correlation before them. Thus economic development, urbanism, and educational development were in part independently related to the use of English as a subject of instruction in secondary schools.

*Percentage of the population studying English
in primary and secondary schools*

Four variables improved prediction by as much as 4% when added to former Anglophone colonial status as predictors of the proportion of the population studying English in primary and secondary schools (see Table 2.15). These were, in order, proportion of the school-aged population enrolled in school, relative size of the largest mother-tongue community, genetic relationship to English of the language spoken by the largest mother-tongue community, and Western political affiliation. The importance of the next-to-last of these is probably due to the fact that non-Indo-European languages tend to be spoken in countries which are less economically and educationally developed, less urbanized, and less homogeneous linguistically. (India, of course, is a notable exception to this tendency.) Although the school-enrollment ratio had a low correlation with the criterion ($r = 0.14$), it has a moderate correlation with it after the non-Anglophone countries had been removed from consideration (r = 0.39). Important incremental contributions, then, were made to the prediction of the proportion of the population enrolled in English classes, by variables assessing both linguistic diversity (in this case, homogeneity) and educational development, which had not appeared together as important incremental predictors of the other criteria.

Overall composite variable

The overall composite variable represented both educational and non-educational variables with respect to the status of English, including its status as a language of administration and its use in mass media (see Table 2.1). It was substantially predicted by former Anglophone colonial status (r = 0.77). Only two additional variables contributed incrementally more than 3% to the prediction of the criterion (see Table 2.16). These were, in order, exports to English-speaking countries and the communicability of the language spoken by the largest mother-tongue group. The second of these was in part an inverse measure of linguistic diversity (r = −0.53). Relative importance of exports to English-speaking countries, which was an important incremental contributor to the use of English as a medium of instruction in secondary and in primary schools, was also an important

Table 2.16   Multiple regression analysis: Overall English composite criterion

Step[a]	Variable	R	R^2	ΔR^2	r
1	Former Anglophone colony	.766	.586	.586	.766
2	Exports to English-speaking countries	.819	.671	.084	.378
3	Communicability of language of largest mother-tongue group	.844	.712	.041	−.423

[a]All steps shown until first step at which ΔR^2 fell below 0.036.

contributor to the incremental prediction of the overall composite criterion. Similarly, linguistic diversity (or homogeneity), important in three of the other four criteria, was also important in the cumulative prediction of the composite criterion. Absent as important incremental contributors of this criterion, however, were variables indicating economic or educational development, which were important to the multiple prediction of the use of English as a subject of instruction in secondary schools, and the proportion of the population enrolled in primary and secondary school English classes.

Summary of the multiple regression analyses

Table 2.17 indicates the categories of variables which contributed at least a 4% increment to the multiple prediction of each of the criterion variables: former

Table 2.17 Categories of variable contributing at least four percent to the incremental prediction of the English criteria

Category	Percentage added[a]					
	Medium in secondary schools	Medium in primary schools	Subject in secondary schools	Subject in primary schools	% in English classes	Composite
Former colonial status	39	10	26[b]	28	25	59
Linguistic diversity/homogeneity	5	41		5	10	4
Economic incentives (exports)	7	4				8
Urbanism			7			
Economic development			7			
Educational development			5			
Religious composition	17	16[b]	7	23[b]	8	
Political affiliation					4	
Other			5		6	

[a]Percentage contribution to the multiple prediction of criterion variance until the first step at which ΔR^2 fell below 0.036.
[b]Sum of the incremental contribution of two predictors.

colonial status, linguistic diversity, material benefits, urbanization, economic development, educational development, religious composition, and political affiliation. It can be seen that the most important contributors, in addition to former colonial status, were religious composition and linguistic diversity, each contributing incrementally to four or five of the six criteria. The next most important was the relative importance of English-speaking countries to exports, contributing to the incremental prediction of three criteria. Educational development variables contributed to two, and variables indicating urbanism, economic development, and political affiliation each contributed to the multiple prediction of one criterion.

SUMMARY AND CONCLUSIONS

Statistics were gathered from secondary sources for 102 non-English mother-tongue countries with respect both to the status of English and to economic, educational, demographic, and other variables in an attempt to determine which variables, singly and in combination, are related to the use of English as an additional language around the world. We hypothesized that the variables isolated by Brosnahan (1963) with respect to the spread of Arabic, Greek, and Latin as mother tongues—military imposition, duration of authority, linguistic diversity, and material advantages—would also be related to the spread of English as an additional language. We also hypothesized that five additional factors would be related to this expansion—urbanization, economic development, educational development, religious composition, and political affiliation. Of these nine categories, we found that all but political affiliation showed at least a moderate relationship to the status of English. However, the direction of the relationships depended on the criterion. Urbanization and economic and educational development were positively related to the percentage of the population enrolled in primary and secondary school English classes when former Anglophone colonies were excluded from consideration, but negatively correlated to the other criterion variables. Poorer countries, in other words, were more likely to rely on English as a medium of instruction and to stress English as a subject of instruction than were richer nations, but poorer nations were less likely to provide equal opportunity to learn English through formal schooling.

The most important categories of predictor, in terms of their zero-order correlations with the English criteria, were former Anglophone colonial status, linguistic diversity, religious composition, and educational and economic development. The most important categories in terms of their incremental contribution to the prediction of the status of English, after former Anglophone colonial status had been considered, were religious composition and linguistic diversity, followed by material benefits (exports to English-speaking countries). Urbanism and economic and educational development indicators contributed relatively little, independently of the other predictors.

It is of interest that exports to English-speaking countries proved to be a better predictor, both singly and jointly, than imports. This result is reminiscent of the finding that in Ethiopian markets, sellers accommodated themselves to buyers by using the latters' language (Cooper and Carpenter 1969). That exports were a better predictor than imports provides additional support for the notion that material gains provide an important incentive for second-language acquisition inasmuch as it is plausible that, all things being equal (which of course is rarely the case), one has more incentive to learn the language of one's customers than of one's suppliers.

Seven of the nine categories of predictor variables were related both singly and jointly to the spread of English as an additional language. Political affiliation, which showed at best a very slight relationship to the status of English, contributed incrementally to the prediction of one of the criteria. Conversely, duration of military rule, while moderately related to the status of English, showed no independent relationship to the criterion variables after former Anglophone colonial status had been considered. It is likely that the duration of military rule is more important for the spread of a language as a mother tongue than as an additional language.

This study has taken numerals found in the small print of books, and related them to one another. It is sometimes easy to forget that these numerals reflect, if palely and imperfectly and waveringly, human activities and human passions. To say that English is spreading around the world as a function of the combination of particular variables is a summarizing statement, based on the effects of innumerable human interactions and motivations. Individuals, not countries, learn English as an additional language. An individual learns English, moreover, not because of abstractions such as linguistic diversity or international trade balances but because the knowledge of English helps him to communicate in contexts in which, for economic or educational or emotional reasons, he wants to communicate and because the opportunity to learn English is available to him. That the summarizing statistics employed here revealed pleasing symmetries and sensible regularities should not allow us to forget the human behavior underlying them. The study of language spread, then, must proceed not only from the manipulation and analysis of summary data at very great levels of abstraction but also from the observation of human behavior at first hand. Why do particular individuals in particular contexts want to learn English? How do they go about learning it? What are the circumstances in which they use it once they have learned it? What effect does their knowledge of English have upon their knowledge and usage of other languages? Primary data of great contextual specificity must be sought, as well as secondary data far removed from the everyday arenas in which languages are learned and used and abandoned, if we are to construct a satisfactory explanation of language maintenance and language shift in general and of the expansion and decline of languages of wider communication in particular.

NOTE

1.   The small differences between the summary data presented here and the summary data presented by Conrad and Fishman in Chapter 1 are due to differences in the number and composition of the countries surveyed by the two studies.

REFERENCES

Alexandre, Pierre. 1971. A few observations on language use among Cameroonese *élite* families. In *Language Use and Social Change,* edited by W.H. Whiteley. London: Oxford University Press. Pp. 254–261.

Brosnahan, L.F. 1963. Some historical cases of language imposition. In *Language in Africa,* edited by J. Spencer. Cambridge: Cambridge University Press. Pp. 7–24.

Conrad, Andrew W., and Joshua A. Fishman. 1977. English as a world language: The evidence. This vol., chap. 1.

Cooper, Robert L. 1976. The spread of Amharic. In *Language in Ethiopia,* by M.L. Bender et al. London: Oxford University Press. Pp. 289–301.

Cooper, Robert L., and Susan Carpenter. 1969. Linguistic diversity in the Ethiopian market. *Journal of African Languages* 8 (part 3):160–168.

Cooper, Robert L., and Ronald J. Horvath. 1973. Language, migration, and urbanization in Ethiopia. *Anthropological Linguistics* 15:221–243.

Cooper, Robert L., and Fern Seckbach. 1977. Economic incentives for the learning of a language of wider communication: A case study. This vol., chap. 8.

Criper, Clive, and Peter Ladefoged. 1971. Linguistic complexity in Uganda. In *Language Use and Social Change,* edited by W.H. Whiteley. London: Oxford University Press. Pp. 145–159.

The Europa Year Book, 1972, A World Survey. Vols. 1 and 2. London: Europa Publications, 1972.

Gage, William W., and Sirarpi Ohannessian. 1974. ESOL enrollments throughout the world. *The Linguistic Reporter* 16(9):13–16.

Paxton, J., ed. 1972. *The Statesman's Year-Book: Statistical and Historical Annual of the World for the Year 1971-1972.* London: Macmillan.

Scotton, Carol Myers. 1972. *Choosing a Linga Franca in an African Capital.* Edmonton and Champaign: Linguistic Research.

Stebbins, R.P., ed. *Political Handbook and Atlas of the World.* New York: Simon and Schuster, 1970.

UNESCO Statistical Yearbook 1972. Paris: UNESCO, 1973.

U.S. Government, Department of State. 1972. *World Data Handbook.* Washington, D.C.: U.S. Government Printing Office. (Department of State Publication 8665, General Foreign Policy Series 264).

Chapter 3

The Spread of English as a New Perspective for the Study of "Language Maintenance and Language Shift"

Joshua A. Fishman

A dozen years have transpired since I first advanced the notion of "language maintenance and language shift" (LMLS) as a pivotal topic for the sociolinguistic enterprise (Fishman 1964).[1] In that time the sociology of language has become a reality and the study of language maintenance and language shift has become one of its recognized topics, with very definite links to all of the theoretical as well as all of the applied ramifications of the parent field. Nevertheless, in all of this time, the perspective on language maintenance and language shift has remained the one from which I originally approached it: the minority language or the small national language faced by pressures related to a much bigger national or inter-national language. Although considerable progress has been made from that vantage point, a different approach to LMLS, namely, one whose perspective is that of the more powerful (the waxing, the spreading) language—the spread of English, e.g.—might now provide further stimulus to this topic. Conversely, the sociology of English and other languages of wider communication (LWCs), a relatively new area of concentration within the sociology of language, might also now benefit by being examined within the context of such more general concerns as language maintenance and language shift.[2]

The author is grateful to Andrew Cohen, Andrew Conrad, Robert L. Cooper, Vladimir Nahirny, Jonathan Pool, and Carol Scotton for their helpful comments on an earlier draft of this paper.

HABITUAL LANGUAGE USE
(AT MORE THAN ONE POINT IN TIME)

The volume in which this chapter is included brings together as much evidence as possible concerning the substantial, and apparently still growing, use now being made of English throughout the non-English mother-tongue world. Surprisingly enough, this volume does not have an exhaustive benchmark predecessor whose findings could be utilized in order to systematically pinpoint whether, where, and why this use has increased (or decreased). I hope, then, that this volume itself will have some value as a benchmark for other volumes yet to come, as these others in turn will be benchmarks for still others that will come after them. Obviously, neither *where* nor *why* can be studied unless the issue of *whether* is fully explored. This issue, then, is the first and basic topic of the study of language maintenance and language shift, and it is itself divisible into considerations of *degree of bilingualism* (i.e., *how much* each language is employed) and *location of bilingualism* (i.e., in *what social contexts* each language is employed). At this juncture the second subdivision is more intriguing than the first, precisely because more sociolinguistic progress was needed, and has been made, in connection with it during the past dozen years.

Degree and Location of Bilingualism

A dozen years ago the concept of "bilingual balance" was at its zenith. It conceived of bilingualism in overall, global terms and proceeded, via various measures, to determine whether individual bilinguals were X dominant, Y dominant, or balanced. The measures employed were generally reflections of speed or automaticity of response and, presumably, context free. That language that was "globally" stronger would, it was believed, issue forth more quickly, more effortlessly, more flawlessly.

The past decade has witnessed the well-nigh complete abandonment of the global approach. Almost all measurement of degree of bilingualism today is sociofunctionally contextualized, i.e., measures of degree are still employed but with as much societal embeddedness as possible. Thus, were we to study any population today with respect to use of English, or were we to compare any two populations in this respect, our inquiry would immediately be in terms of how much English is spoken, heard, read, or written *in one context or another* (at home, in school, at work, in connection with government, etc.), rather than merely in terms of how much English is spoken, heard, read, or written. This certainly represents a sociolinguistic victory over earlier societally detached approaches.

Our concern for English as an additional language must particularly sensitize us to certain degree and location intersections. Additional languages are often more characterized by contextual specificity than are first languages; they may be more widely heard and read than spoken or written, i.e., they may be more frequently utilized on the level of comprehension than on that of production. Thus, more refined measures may be needed—measures that can not only make the above media and overtness *distinctions* but also focus upon particular combinations of degree and location of bilingualism with considerable precision.

Domains of Language Behavior

Not only is the principle of societal contextualization rather well established now (in comparison to a dozen years ago) insofar as the measurement of bilingualism is concerned, but the particular type of contextualization referred to as "domain analysis" is also quite widely accepted. It has traveled the often rocky road from theoretical construct (Fishman 1964) to operational and theoretical validation (Fishman, Cooper, and Ma 1971) and has been found useful in a great variety of discussions and research on bilingualism, far and beyond language maintenance and language shift alone (e.g., most recently, Clyne 1976; Solé 1975; Zirkel 1974). Certainly the notion of institutional domain (and all of the lower level social interaction notions upon which it depends, particularly role relationship, topic, and situation) should be utilized in the study of English as an additional language. The phenomenological reality of major social institutions (family, education, government, work, religion, etc.) is a guide to the normative allocation of languages in within-group bilingual settings and probably in between-group bilingualism as well (since this is the locus of initial LWC spread).[3] Consciously or not (depending on more general factors related to level of awareness and sophistication relative to sociocultural norms), members of speech (-and-writing) communities utilize such major social institutions, and the situations most commonly pertaining to them, as guides for navigating through the unpredictable currents of interpersonal communication in bilingual settings. Certainly the researcher too must discover and then utilize these as well, whether in their macrolevel or in their microlevel realizations.

The same greater specificity that marks additional languages with respect to media and overtness variance undoubtedly also marks them with respect to domain variance. Whether they are disproportionately *absent* (other than *metaphorically*) in the family and religion domains (an *atypical* situation insofar as social phenomenology is concerned) and whether they are disproportionately *present* in the (higher) education, (technological) work, (imported) mass media and intergovernmental domains, our measures must be able to make these distinctions and then to reflect usage in the more crucial domains with sufficient precision to be able to capture changes in degree of usage over time. These would, of course, be desirable features for LMLS measures under *any* circumstances, but the sociofunctional imbalance of LWCs is often so great that the relevance of these desiderata becomes much clearer. Indeed, the typical domain distribution of additional languages may be so skewed that it may be instructive to compare LWCs in non-mother-tongue settings not only in terms of the domains or patterns in which they predominate (e.g., technological higher education: reading) but also in terms of a measure of domain dispersion/concentration per se.[4]

Domain dispersion measures must be related to a particular population, of course, whether it be that of a network, a neighborhood, a city, or a nation. The sociolinguistic question that comes to the fore—once any socially contextualized measurement of language use is obtained—is whether it implies the absence or the presence of a speech (-and-writing) community in the technical sociolinguistic sense (Fishman 1972*b*, see pp. 81–83) of situational variance predominating over demographic variance. The full answer to this question is obviously not determinable from an analysis of language use data per se, but *without* rather sensitive language-use data the answer cannot be pursued at all.[5]

The Dominance Configuration

Our quest for a configurational recognition of bilingualism is part and parcel of our dissatisfaction with global designations or dominance, whether these be psychological (stronger/weaker), sociological (upper/lower) or otherwise. Configurational thinking has led us as far as dummy tables (whether with qualitative or quantitative entries) implying data on language use by media, overtness, domains, role-relations, etc. (Fishman 1972*b*). For whatever reason, we have not passed beyond the dummy-table stage to the actual-table stage for anything resembling a complete configuration (see Tables 3.1 and 3.2, reproduced from Fishman 1972*b*), although there have been a few approximations thereto both in early research (e.g., Greenfield and Fishman 1970) as well as in this volume. It may be that this is as it should be, or must be, since dummy tables are merely ambitious theoretical exercises and as such, they lack the substantive focus of all empirical research. On the other hand, it may be that something not only simpler but also more revealing, more intercomparable (across studies) is what is called for. Certainly, if pattern analysis were more advanced than it is as a data analysis approach, some might prefer to develop LMLS configurational thinking in that direction. At the moment that does not appear to be very promising and has largely been abandoned even in the area of personality/preference measurement from which it was derived. Perhaps it is better that we struggle with the demands of overambitious theory (to which we have now added the domain dispersion concept) than that we settle for premature and artificial mathematical parsimony.

Continuing Issues in Domain Analysis

The limits of domain analysis must also be recognized. They come to the fore more evidently when dealing with actual samples of speech or when restricting one's self to a particular domain. Both of these foci of the study of interlingual variation are quite common and share an emphasis on the analysis of *social dynamics*, rather than on the analysis of *social location*, for which domain analysis was initially advanced. While it is not necessarily true that institutional domains are static constructs (since domain boundaries are neither obvious nor set), they are, nevertheless, normative, cognitive-affective orientations. As such, they must always be distinguished from interactional behavior per se and their precise relationship to such behavior must be studied as a separate issue. However,

Table 3.1   Intra-group Yiddish-English maintenance and shift in the United States: 1940-70; summary comparisons for immigrant generation "secularists" arriving prior to World War I ("dummy table" for dominance configuration, Table 3.2)

Sources of Variance

Media	Overtness	Family role-rels. 1 2 3	Neighb. role-rels. 1 2	Work role-rels. 1 2 3	Jew Rel./Cult. role-rels. 1 2
Speaking	Production				
	Comprehension				
	Inner				
Reading	Production				
	Comprehension				
Writing	Production				
	Comprehension				

Source: Fishman (1972*b*).

Table 3.2   Part of "dummy table" (Table 3.1) in greater detail

Media	Overtness	*Domains*	Role-Relations	*Summary Ratings* 1940	1970
Speaking	Production	Family	Husband-Wife	Y	Y
			Parent-Child	Y	E
			Grandparent-Grandchild	–	E
			Other: same generation	Y	Y
			Other: younger generation	E	E
		Neighborhood	Friends	Y	E
			Acquaintances	Y	E
		Work	Employer-Employer	E	E
			Employer-Employee	E	E
			Employee-Employee	E	E
		Jewish Rel./Cult.	Supporter-Writer, Teacher, etc.	Y	Y
			Supporter-Supporter	Y	Y

Source: Fishman (1972*b*).

cognitive-affective norms along macroinstitutional lines are phenomenological guides to verbal behavior in bilingual settings. As such, they have a certain validity vis-à-vis behavior; as such, they can be differentially self-reported by members of speech communities; and, as such, they can be investigated and revealed by skillful investigators. However, as mentioned, often the investigator's interest is in subdomain dynamics rather than in domains per se. In that case, and that is very frequently the case when we are dealing with a corpus of texts derived from interactions in a particular domain, domain analysis per se is no longer at issue and no longer of particular interest (e.g., Scotton ms., Basso ms.).

Whether or not there is a Heisenberg indeterminacy phenomenon at play here, such that one cannot *simultaneously* study institutionalized domain location and subdomain interactional dynamics, it is still true that the two types of analyses must be interrelated if an exhaustive understanding is to be arrived at of the "sociolinguistic economy" of any total speech community or speech network. Only such an exhaustive effort can reveal whether the dynamic factors that are documented for a particular domain, or for a given set of social relationships, also obtain for *all* domains. If they do, then domains per se are of clearly secondary importance (note Fishman 1966, p. 438; Fishman 1972*b*, p. 93). If they do *not* (i.e., if there are *domain-specific* role-relationships, situational places, situational times, network types, interaction types, etc.), then domains must be retained, precisely so that the societal location of different social dynamics can be indicated. Certainly, domains must also be defined if self-report data *does* reveal domain distinctions even if the sociodynamic analysis of texts does not. Finally, since many anthropologists, linguists, and ethnomethodologists are more inclined to study texts and their concomitant interactional behaviors whereas many sociologists and political scientists are more likely to study more macroscopic self-report data, the latter are far more likely than the former to find domain analysis necessary and useful. However, whether or not domain analysis is undertaken should not be the result of disciplinary considerations as much as it should flow from "level of abstraction" considerations, "kind of data" considerations, and ultimately from "purpose of study" considerations.[6] It seems particularly likely that many studies of the spread of English as an additional language *will* find domain analysis useful, precisely because the presumed skewedness in locational use, skewedness in medium, and skewedness in overtness of use still remain to be documented.

SOCIOCULTURAL PROCESSES RELATABLE TO LMLS

The first dozen years of work on LMLS recorded the bulk of progress, theoretical, methodological, and empirical, in connection with the first subsection of the field as a whole, namely, that concerned with the measurement of habitual language use. If the next dozen years were to record similar progress in conjunction with the field's second major subsection, sociocultural processes leading to or inhibiting LMLS, then we would really have come a long way toward our basic goal. Unfortunately, this second step is far more difficult to take than the first, if only because it requires detailed understanding of social organization, social change, and social indicators, topics which are rather new and difficult for sociology as a whole. In the absence of such understanding, descriptive studies that proceed via ad hoc lists of social categories (generation, social class) and social agencies (press, church, radio, schools) will continue to be reported without adding at all to our systematic knowledge of LMLS in general or of LWC spread in particular.

Our two basic societal questions relative to the spread of English (or any LWC) can be put very easily: (a) Why is it that some non-English mother-tongue countries (or other political units of analysis) have witnessed greater utilization or acceptance of English over the past decade or two (e.g., China: Lehmann 1975; Senegal: Senghor 1975) than have others (e.g., Philippines, Tanzania)?, and (b) Why is it that the spread of English, wherever it *has* occurred abroad, has *not* resulted in the kind of massive mother-tongue replacement with which we are so familiar in immigrant settings in the USA, Anglo-Canada and Australia? Although the first question is more basic for our purposes in this volume, both questions confront us with the need to find parameters that can clarify settings varying all the way from no language shift at all through to complete language shift, so that we can explain the relative absence of the former vis-à-vis English, as well as the well-nigh complete absence of the latter. Interestingly enough, there are very few indications of ideologized and organized opposition to English abroad for particular societal functions. Nevertheless, we do *not* have the impression that it is therefore "merely a question of time, resources, and priorities" such that "sooner or later, the entire world will have some control of English as an additional language." In other words, it is not simply that all LWCs reach their functional limits—in part, because of competing spheres of interest with other LWCs—but that there may, in addition, be something about the particular auspices and processes through which English and other LWCs have been diffused during the past quarter century or so that sets these limits at a lower level than those formerly set for Latin, Arabic, and Spanish and even for French, Chinese, and Russian.

Generally speaking, social change theory is the weakest link of modern sociology, but there are, nevertheless, a few promising points at which to start in seeking to push closer to answering the questions posed. Some of these are discussed next.

Language, Power, and Resources

Spreading languages that are not being imposed by force[7] must provide (or promise to provide) entree to scarce power and resources or there would be little reason for indigenous populations to adopt them for intergroup use, or, by extension, for certain subsequent intragroup use as well. Thus we must begin tracing the spread of a LWC to the power differentials with which its possession is associated. Obviously these differentials have their cognitive, affective, and overt behavioral counterparts (about which see the later section, "Behavior Toward Language"), but it is their objective distributional documentation that is being referred to here. Entree to better positions, to useful specialized knowledge, to more effective tools, to more influential contacts (and thereby to control over human and material resources), to more desirable consumable goods, to more satisfying high culture behaviors (and to their low culture counterparts), or merely to the new and different in whatever domain, as long as that too is considered desirable—these are among the basic desiderata of intergroup contact and, therefore, of LWC spread as well.

We must begin with actual or assumed need for resources and power at any point of intergroup contact and with language as a possible key to a desired (re)distribution of such resources and power on an intragroup basis as well. In those settings in which either the myth or the reality of social mobility is widespread, bilingualism is repeatedly skewed in favor of the more powerful, with the language of greater power being acquired and used much more frequently than that of lesser power.[8] When the *same* language is the language of greater power (or power-sharing trends) in setting after setting then we are dealing with a LWC and with a spreading LWC as well. In the case of English it is clear that two centuries of British and American colonial, commercial, industrial, scientific, and fiscal power have left a substantial legacy in higher education, government, trade, and technology. It is this legacy, in its domain and social-dynamic realizations, that needs to be investigated in all non-English mother-tongue settings that may be of interest in connection with the actual or possible spread of English.

The underlying concept is simple enough but it has rarely been fully documented. What is needed, in any setting, are hypotheses concerning the resources, privilege, and powers differentially related to knowledge and use of English (or any other LWC) and the cross-tabulation of such with degree and location of bilingualism involving English (or any other LWC). Such cross-tabulations should reveal stronger and weaker correlations, some that are more class or age dependent and some that are less so, and, all in all, provide excellent clues to the processes that are fostering the spread of English as well as to the mechanisms upon which these are dependent and the domains in which these are concentrated. Settings which hold no interest for mother-tongue speakers of English or for other (i.e., foreign) speakers of English as an additional language, and settings where the indigenous population has (or sees) little of rather tangible worth to gain by acquiring English, are likely to be settings that will lag behind others with respect to the spread of English. Languages are rarely acquired for their own sake. They are acquired as keys to other things that are desired. We must first identify and document what these are,[9] if only because such documentation will help us explain why, how, and among whom English as an additional language is or is not spreading.

The Diffusion Process

To have identified the sources or forces upon which the spread of English is dependent is one thing; to identify the processes via which the spread proceeds is another. Where English itself is an import (i.e., it is *not* accompanied by the massive presence of at least semifluent speakers of English from abroad, as often occurs in settings of tourism, student concentration, resource exploitation, military bases, etc.), then its spread is, of necessity, from the top down, i.e., from governmental, commercial, industrial, cultural, or other elites to the populace. This type of spread will often follow established patterns and channels of elite to mass influence, although, on occasion, special methods have been attempted in connection with language spread (e.g., "going to the people" in pre-revolutionary literacy efforts of Russian *narodniki*, or resettlement and mixture of populations in Zionist Hebraization efforts). Cities have long been the focal points of organized propagation efforts (and, it must be noted, of organized resistance efforts as well). For language spread, schools have long been the major formal (organized) mechanisms involved, particularly for those considered to be of school age and school-worthy. Those who are beyond school age or who are not considered school-worthy[10] are sometimes also reached via special mechanisms (such as mass media, after-work educational programs, and vacation programs). Serious elitist efforts on behalf of an additional language often take on ideological overtones and involve an interlocking network of reward and communication options (e.g., those utilized in Canada in the mid-sixties to "encourage" Anglos to learn French, those utilized until recently in Ireland on behalf of Irish, those used to encourage Spanish immersion for Anglos in the American Southwest). The efficacy of all of these efforts, formal and informal, seems to vary considerably.

A number of possibly important considerations that have been mentioned so far should be reviewed before proceeding:

1. Diffusion as the ultimate or long-term context, even when an initial imposition stage obtains
2. Spread from the top (*gesunkenes Kulturgut*) rather than from the bottom (*gehobenes Primitivgut*): the determining role of elites
3. Urban focal points of spread (and of organized resistance thereto)
4. Normal propagation channels as well as special ones
5. Schools as major formal vehicle of additional language acquisition; post-school populations require special handling
6. Ongoing reward efforts, including access to power and resources
7. Efficacy determination (evaluation) and reformulation of program

Of course, all of the preceding considerations must be viewed in the context of general resource availability, priorities in national development, countermovements from indigenous and external counter- (proto-) elites, reinforcement from other ongoing developments (e.g., transfer of populations, tourism, and political alignments), and general effectiveness of education and other large scale governmental operations. We still have no study encompassing all of these factors and viewing the acquisition of English as an additional language as a process which interacts with the major social, cultural, economic, and political processes of the national (let alone the international) context—not the least of which is the common need to foster *internal ethnic consolidation* via a national language which, in many cases, is also no more than an *additional* language. When viewed in the above light, the *relative* impotence of the school—certainly when it is denied vigorous societal support—becomes more obvious. Indeed, English is learned best when there are extraschool social forces abetting and rewarding its acquisition (Fishman 1976). Little wonder then that LWCs are not widely replacive of indigenous mother tongues (MTs), particularly if the stage of vigorous imposition is brief and relatively nondislocating of populations and their more normal social processes. The usual problem is learning them at all and maintaining, rather than containing, them.

Concomitant Processes

Some of the processes accompanying efforts on behalf of English or other LWCs deserve a few words of separate attention.

The LWC setting versus the immigrant setting

For our purposes it is particularly instructive to note that the LWC setting (in which a powerful language enters into the social space of an established population) and the immigrant language setting (in which a normally powerless population enters into the social space of an established language) may well reveal appreciably different patterns in this connection. Whereas immigrant settings have been hypothesized regularly to go through the cycle of domain overlap (MT dominant), domain separateness, and domain overlap (OT dominant), the LWC spreading by diffusion among indigenous populations may commonly stabilize at the second stage. Certainly the history of language spread among indigenous populations (see, e.g., Tabouret-Keller 1968, 1972; Lewis 1971, 1972, 1976; Kahane ms.) is far *less* marked by mother-tongue replacement and far *more* marked by the sociofunctional separation of languages than is the typical history of (im)migrant language settings (Hofman and Fisherman 1971; Lewis 1975). The lesser dislocation of indigenous populations attendant upon the spread of unimposed (or post-imposition) LWCs—(leaving intact a great deal of the indigenous family, community, government, religious, and cultural structures with their established authorities and mutually established responsibilities)—is certainly the decisive difference between the two settings. Indigenous populations have a firm base to hold on to while seeking the rewards that are (said to be) contingent upon the acquisition of an additional language; immigrant populations do not characteristically have any such base. (For an interesting exception, see Pryce 1975).

The reverse phenomena obtain but are rare. Immigrant "language islands" *have* maintained themselves for centuries (usually on the basis of *primum mobile*: massive numbers and control of resources sufficient to firmly establish authoritative institutional structures of their own and, therefore, to regulate intergroup contacts). In such cases (e.g., German in parts of the USA, French in Quebec,

Chinese in Malaysia, and Tamil in Sri Lanka) their acquisition of the "other tongue" (the national or bridging language) may well follow the LWC model rather than the typical immigrant language model. Similarly, a few nonimpositional LWC settings *have* resulted, not only in mother-tongue *displacement* (from one domain or another) but in mother-tongue *replacement* as a whole (e.g., the very slow but steady Aramization, Hellenization, or Romanization of various populations in the classical world, as well as the Anglification and Francofication of indigenous European, African and Asian elites in the modern world). In such cases the reward system related to the initially additional language was sufficiently open, strong, and dislocative (often involving intermarriage, resettlement, and sociocultural change to an unusual degree, at least for certain select networks) that the resultant constellation may have been more similar to the usual immigrant case than to the usual unimposed LWC case.

Thus, the typical "immigrant case" and the typical unimposed "LWC case" are merely abbreviated labels for the extreme poles of sociocultural processes accompanying language maintenance and language shift. Mother-tongue replacement is an indication of a dislocated society undergoing other massive changes and unable to establish or maintain institutional protection for its MT (mother tongue). Such dislocation is less common under circumstances of the diffusion-based spread of LWCs. As a result, it is possible for the host society to control the propagation of LWCs in accord with its own designs, and these are frequently quite specific and restrictive. They may involve mother-tongue displacement from a few domains (even this may not be the case where the domains themselves and the LWC "arrive together," so to speak, as part and parcel of the same broader forces and tendencies), but certainly not its replacement in the most ethnically encumbered domains of family, religion, and other cultural preserves and value systems.

Ethnic and ideological encumberedness

Ethnicity—whether ideologized or not—is a strong bastion of immigrant languages, although rarely strong enough to withstand the onslaught of change. A diffusion-based LWC must also come to grips with the ethnicity values, sentiments, and overt behaviors of an indigenous population. These expressions of ethnicity are likely to be far better protected among indigenous populations than they are in the typical immigrant case and, in modern times in particular, they are likely to be explicitly related to the indigenous language(s). A spreading LWC can be viewed as a threat to indigenous ethnicity and to its symbolically elaborated structures. If the LWC itself is also ethnically or ideologically encumbered, it is more likely to be viewed as a threat (or actually to be so) than if the LWC is relatively unencumbered in the ethnic or ideological sphere (Fishman 1976, see chap. 9). It is part of the relative good fortune of English as an additional language that neither its British nor its American fountainheads have been widely or deeply viewed in an ethnic or ideological context *for the past quarter century or so.*

To some extent this de-ethnicized (or minimally ethnicized) posture was also part of the earlier spread of Latin and Greek, and, to an even greater extent, of the even earlier spread of Akkadian and Aramaic. The obvious more recent contrasts are with Arabic, Russian, and Spanish, each of which were (and often still are) strongly associated with a particular nationality, religion, or ideology. English is, of course, identified by some with capitalism, colonialism, and bourgeois values, but it is not as *uniquely* identified with any of them, nor as *strongly* identified with any of them (because of its competing association with democracy, individual liberty, civil rights, religious tolerance, e.g.) as is Arabic with Islam, Russian with Marxist communism, Chinese with Maoist communism, or as was Spanish with conquistador Catholicism. Indeed, in much of the Third World, and elsewhere as well, the image of English may well be ethnically and ideologically quite neutral, so that it may be related much more to appreciably generalized, de-ethnicized, and de-ideologized *process variables* (modernization, urbanization, technological know-how, consumerism, and a higher standard of living in general) than to any ethnicity or ideology viewed as particularly English or American. Furthermore, English as an additional language abroad often has a momentum that is hardly related to Anglo-Americandom (through the auspices of Dutch, Arab, Japanese, and various other non-Anglo-American English publications and broadcasting abroad). It would be interesting to determine whether this is recognized or not (see next section, "Behavior toward Language") and whether views concerning ethnic and ideological encumberment do or do not effect the actual knowing, using, and liking of English as an additional language. At the level of elitist planning for (or against) LWC spread, the presence or absence of overt ethnic or ideological entanglement of the target language is obviously of importance and should also be examined in conjunction with the next section. At this point, however, it is germane to inquire whether there may not be certain stages in the sociocultural development of a host society when ethnic or ideological encumberedness is more of a handicap for the spread of a LWC than such encumberedness would be at other stages. Current theory points to host factors and contact factors as being just as important as are pre-contact factors in determining the outcome of any diffusion process (Schermerhorn 1970). In line with these and other considerations it would seem reasonable to posit pre-ideologization and post-ideologization periods of easiest penetration for LWCs. Thus, either before or a good while after any host population has experienced its own intense and conscious ethnicization or ideologization (often coinciding with the early period of more focused urbanization, industrialization, modernization, and political integration efforts), it would be most likely to be more permeable by LWCs related to foreign ethnicity or ideology. During the white-heat period of indigenously organized ethnicity even ethnically and ideologically unencumbered LWCs may face difficulties. In line with these considerations English would probably be viewed most negatively today in Latin America, where its negative referents—imperialism, capitalism, exploitation, *"el coloso del norte"*—are highlighted not only by nationalisms but by the increasing pace of local economic growth (Solé, personal communication).

All in all, it would seem to be highly desirable to be alert to the current plethora of research on ethnicity (and the few attempts to conceptually integrate that research, e.g., Cohen 1974; Glazer and Moynihan 1975; Fishman ms.) in our efforts to understand the variable acceptance and rejection of English and other LWCs.

Cross-polity and social indicators

Another approach to social change that merits our attention—and a relatively rigorous and quantitative approach to that—is the entire social indicator "movement" that has come to the fore in the past decade (Sheldon and Moore 1968; Fox 1974; Sheldon and Parker 1975). For the field of LWC study, the selective utilization of social indicators would make it unnecessary to construct and conceptualize de novo the large number of societal measures that have already been suggested and, indeed, operationalized by others. Measures (and accompanying theories) have been developed dealing with the allocation of time, quality of life in metropolitan areas, resource allocation in education, dimensionality of national goals at the small community level, interstate and international measures of social, political, and economic circumstances, and so forth.

In addition, the various cross-polity compendia (e.g., Banks and Textor 1963; Russett et al. 1964; Ernst 1967; Kloss and McConnell 1974; and others) are also good sources of operational and theoretical leads. All in all, I would urge careful consideration of "piggy-back" possibilities such as these in conjunction with future LMLS research in general and research on the spread of English and other LWCs in particular. Since social change theory and research are among the fundamental bodies of societal knowledge and speculation with which LMLS and LWC research must be in contact, the cross-polity and social indicators fields currently strike me as being two potentially useful areas with which to stay in close touch.[11] Both of these approaches are "good bets" for picking up early macrosociological indicators pertaining to the socioeconomic and sociocultural processes that are most pertinent predictors of the spread of English (or any other LWC). Among the dimensions well worth monitoring in this respect are Anglo-American investments (though even Dutch, Japanese, and Arab investments are probably English-related in many countries with the exception of their own homelands), in view of the fact that English instruction (and perhaps other types of English use) is noticeably high in many countries in which such investments are also noticeably high (e.g., Mexico, Brazil, Peru)—notwithstanding the reversibility of these relationships in the course of growing cultural nationalism and related tendencies to impose indigenous controls on foreign investors.

The selection of indicators that complement each other across a range of sociocultural, socioeconomic, and related sociopsychological dimensions promises to be particularly rewarding (Land and Spilerman 1975). The fact that development is not linear, and that its relationship to LM and LS is often reversed, does not mean that properly executed studies (repeated at sufficient and appropriate intervals) cannot pick up changes that occur—in whatever direction.

Summary

In the early and mid-sixties, when I first attempted to organize the field of LMLS study, the idea of organizing an international LMLS file did not seem as impossible as it does today. Not only has the whole notion of culture and area files elicited far less interest in recent years than it did in the fifties and before, but there are obviously too few workers in the LMLS and LWCs fields to handle the volume of data collection and processing that would be necessary in order to render such a file operative. Nevertheless, when viewed in connection with a particular LWC (English, French), the matter is far less discouraging. The materials accumulated in conjunction with this very project (see Conrad and Fishman, this vol., chap. 1) move us a little distance along the way toward providing what is needed. With a little continuous effort and support such a file could be kept current, could be transformed into more quantitative and accessible shape, and could be subjected to periodic analyses and interpretations. [12]

In review, before proceeding to the third and final broad topic area within the field of LMLS, the following concerns and sensitivities have come to the fore more clearly by virtue of considering concomitant sociocultural change processes from the vantage point of the spread of English and other LWCs.

1. The diffusion-based spread of LWCs to relatively undislocated indigenous populations is likely to be controlled by the elites of these populations rather than being entirely under the aegis of outside propagators. Such control (ideological and institutional) normally results in the stabilization of LWCs at a domain separation stage (diglossia). Mother-tongue *displacement* among elites and other relatively favored population segments, rather than mother-tongue *replacement,* is thus the rule (in contrast with the typical pattern in the immigrant setting).

2. Ethnic and ideological encumberedness can pose problems for the spread of diffusion based LWCs, particularly during those periods of sociocultural development when host societies are experiencing heightened ethno-ideological concerns of their own.

3. Social indicator theory/research and cross-polity files are two promising approaches to documenting the spread of LWCs in general and of English in particular.

During the past dozen years there has been only slight progress in systematizing knowledge of the social processes that facilitate or inhibit LMLS. LWC perspective on this topic is valuable, providing, as it does, sensitivities and hypotheses that cannot be derived as readily from work on immigrant and minority settings alone. Nevertheless, much still remains to be done, not only in conjunction with LMLS but also in conjunction with the basic fields in sociology upon which LMLS study must depend.

BEHAVIOR TOWARD LANGUAGE

This entire area of concern not only appears to be much more important to current researchers, but also strikes them as more understandable and system-atizable than I would have predicted (but not more than I would have hoped for) a dozen years ago. I suspect that the turning point for many American students was the burgeoning of scholarship on (and scholarly involvement in) *language planning*, particularly with respect to its policy formulation, linguistic codifica-tion, linguistic elaboration, and overall evaluation stages. The undeniable evidence and experience gained with languages that were being fostered (or curbed) and consciously altered (rather than merely liked or disliked) made the entire area of behavior toward language come alive far more than could my own attempts to portray it and my urgings that it be given attention a dozen years ago. I hope that this momentum can now be transferred to the consideration of behavior toward language in contexts of LMLS in general and of LWC spread in particular. There is some evidence that this is being done (e.g., Cooper 1975a).

Affective Behaviors: A Component of the Attitudinal Constellation

The past dozen years have witnessed considerable progress in the entire language-attitude area (e.g., Fishman and Agheyisi 1970; Fishman 1969; Shuy 1973; Cooper 1974; Cooper 1975b; Lewis 1975)—much of it in the context of LMLS and LWC study. Since the state of general theory and methodology relative to language attitudes is so much more advanced than it was then, the time has come to focus the systematic views and methods that have been developed more squarely upon the substantive issues of concern to us here. Some of the studies in this volume attempt to do just that (Fishman: chap. 13; Hofman: chap. 12; Cooper and Fishman: chap. 11).

Several investigators have recognized the need to distinguish between (and then to try to relate) affect toward particular *languages* and affect toward the *speakers* of these languages. This can only be done if study designs are adopted that do not confound these two dimensions (as sociolinguistically uninformed researchers in the sixties confounded them). This distinction would seem to be particularly apropos to English, in view of the growing body of simultaneous impressions that "everyone is trying to learn it," that "no one particularly likes it," and at the very same time, that "Americans are less popular than they were a quarter century ago." Actually, we have little enough data on the first component of this trio and practically none at all on the remaining two in relation to the first.

If it were to prove true that there is little affect toward English (of the kind lavished upon MTs but upon few LWCs, French being a noteworthy modern exception) it would still be desirable to find out which features of the language "are considered attractive or unattractive, proper or improper, distinctive or commonplace" by various populations, including judgments of " 'beautiful' or 'ugly,' 'musical' or 'harsh' " relative to other languages, be they MTs or LWCs (Fishman 1964). However, given the generally low affective profile that is assumed to obtain for English, it may well be necessary for all of our affective measures that pertain to it to be even more sensitive and subtle than would otherwise have to be the case. It is obviously more difficult to differentiate between subareas of low (or no) affective intensity than between subareas of high intensity.

The general relationship between learning, using, and *liking* English has been found to be low in this volume (Fishman: chap. 13; Cooper and Fishman: chap. 11) as well as in other studies (e.g., Riley 1975). This compounds the dilemma that we reported a dozen years ago vis-à-vis various immigrant languages in the USA and in Australia, many of which were *liked* (by their former users and their children and grandchildren) but *not used*. In the case of English, we may be witnessing the complementary occurrence: a language being *used* but *not* much *liked*. Certainly this needs to be much better documented than it is at the moment, as do the interrelationships between affect toward English and attitudes (including affects, cognitions, and overt behaviors) toward modernization, language consciousness, national consciousness, and other aspects of sociocultural tension and change. Obviously, languages are not liked or disliked in a vacuum, but rather liked or disliked as symbolic of values, of peoples, of ideologies, of behaviors. It is the symbolic nature of English and affect with respect to its associations that we must seek to explore more widely. A beginning in this direction has been made by Spina (1974).

Cognitive Behaviors: Knowledge and Beliefs

We have accomplished far less with respect to what people *know* and *believe* about English than we have with how they *feel* about it. Not only has the ethnic and ideological encumberedness (or lack thereof) of English not been studied, but even the dimensions of language feeling, belief, and action posited a decade ago by Stewart (1968) have remained largely unstudied. (These dimensions are vitality, historicity, autonomy, and standardization.) Less systematically interrelated parameters of knowledge and belief have also been ignored—utility of the language in social advance (i.e., the necessity for learning English in order to qualify for particular positions or privileges), perceived difficulty of the language "globally" as well as in terms of related-unrelatedness to the first language, growth or decline in number of local speakers, specific features of recognized similarity/dissimilarity of the language relative to own MT, and national language or other LWC among others. The entire cognitive response to language has gone largely unrecognized with respect to English (see, however, parts of Riley 1975). Perhaps highlighting the distinction between the affective and the cognitive components of language attitude, one of the contributions of this volume, will result in as much attention being devoted to the latter as to the former. The current imbalance between the two—or, alternatively, the current tendency to make no distinction between them and, therefore, constantly to study the one confounded with the other—is much to be regretted. [13]

Overt Behavior toward Language

The final component of the attitudinal constellation is overt behavior, the obvious heartland of the entire topic of "behavior toward language." It represents an area waiting for explorers, all the more so since many of its dimensions have now been anticipated. The area of status planning with respect to English remains unexplored in most settings in which English *is* already a widely available additional language (e.g., Scandinavia, the Near East, West Africa, India, Southeast Asia, Oceania). It is even all the more unexplored in settings in which no such availability is possible or desirable. The same is true with respect to corpus planning vis-à-vis similarity/dissimilarity between the national integrating language and English. [14] We are certainly ignorant with respect to commitment-readiness on behalf of English (Fishman 1969), although some populations have gone to considerable pains to enable their children to have access to it (e.g., "New Canadians" in Quebec) and although the impression remains that there is "no love lost" on behalf of English. Certainly English is put to considerable use by many of the major foes of American and British capitalism in order to spread their own counter philosophies among nonnative users (readers, understanders) of English (see particularly, Lehmann 1975 for evidence of Chinese preparation to use English abroad in order to spread the doctrine of Mao).

Notwithstanding the relatively neutralized ethnic and ideological image of English it still seems to be true (both from IRPLPP data [Fishman 1974] as well as from our own) that English is considered to be more acceptable for technology and natural science use than for political and social science use, and that it is least acceptable of all for local humanistic and religious purposes. The same progression might also obtain for any foreign language—LWC or not—but the differences in acceptability for these various uses might be less in the case of English than for ethnically or ideologically more encumbered LWCs. Similarly, younger populations (indigenous "nationals," *not* minority group members) seem less resistant to English (whether affectively or overtly) than were their parents and teachers during their own adolescent years (Fishman 1974 and this vol., chap. 13). This may be an aspect of their lesser general ideological involvement relative to that of their elders, as well as a reflection of the generally lower level of nationalism throughout the world today in comparison to the 1875–1950 period. If all of the foregoing could be documented—and a small international documentation center could do so over a period of years—the topic of overt behavior toward English would come into its own and, simultaneously, so would the study of the spread of English relative to other LWCs.

SUMMARY AND CONCLUSIONS

A new look at LMLS reveals several promising developments and changes in this field, not only since 1964 but even since 1972. Certainly, a new look at LMLS from the point of view of spreading LWCs in general, and from the point of view of the spread of English as an additional language in particular, prompts a number of hypotheses or emphases that might not otherwise come to the fore.

All in all, it appears that most progress has been made in conjunction with the measurement of habitual language use, and the least in conjunction with sociocultural change processes. Intermediate between these two is the progress made in conjunction with behavior toward language. Apparently, the more societally embedded a topic has been, the less progress there has been in connection with it; conversely, the more language-focused the topic, the more progress there has been. In part, this relationship reflects the greater precision of scholarly work with language as a result of the more highly systematic nature of language and language behavior. The social sciences in general and sociology in particular simply have not reached the same level of precise and systematic analysis, in part because they are focused upon behavior which is simultaneously more complex and less systematic than language or language use per se. The discrepancy between these two parent fields, from which LMLS (and all of the sociology of language) must derive its basic theories and methods, is reflected in the discrepancies between one subtopic and the other within the area of LMLS itself.

As far as the spread of English and other LWCs is concerned the following points have come to the fore.

With respect to habitual use

1. Since additional languages, including LWCs are often marked by great contextual specificity, more refined measures are required—measures than can focus upon particular combinations of *degree* and *location* of bilingualism with considerable precision.

2. In view of the greater contextual specificity that seems to mark LWC use, future dominance configurations might well benefit from a measure of skewedness or of domain dispersion/concentration. Such a measure would be useful in comparing configurations across networks within the same or similar communities.

3. Domain location, social dynamics, and conversational interaction each represent worthwhile and interrelatable levels of analysis for the study of LMLS.

With respect to sociocultural change relatable to LMLS

4. The distinction between the military imposition of LWCs or their diffusion, on the one hand, and the distinction between their spread from the top downward or from the bottom upward, on the other hand, are crucially related to the rate and degree of LWC spread, as well as to the mechanisms of spread most likely to be involved.

5. During the past quarter century or so, the spread of English has usually been via diffusion. Its spread has most commonly proceeded from the top downward and has depended upon real or hoped for entree to governmental, technological and industrial, commercial, or modern cultural rewards. Its spread has depended not only upon schooling but also upon special channels pertaining to the above institutional domain-related substantive fields and their associated social behaviors.

6. The indigenously controlled spread of LWCs among relatively undislocated populations commonly stabilizes in the pattern of domain separation (diglossia) and mother-tongue displacement (rather than replacement) among elitist and relatively favored population segments. The continued spread of English as an additional language, outside of initially elitist networks, is dependent on the more widespread availability of the rewards (real or imaginary) with which *it* is associated as compared to the availability of rewards associated with its national or international competitors.

With respect to behavior toward language

7. The spread of English is currently apparently accompanied by relatively little affect—whether negative or positive—and by correspondingly meager American and British ethnic or ideological connotations. The staying power of LWCs may derive from ethnic neutrality every bit as much as the staying power of minority languages may derive from ethnic relatedness.

8. On the whole, English as an additional language is more learned than used and more used than liked. The three (learning, using, and liking) are little related to each other.

9. Consistent exploration of this area, in conjunction with the sociolinguistic parameters of institutional domains, social behaviors, and conversational interactions, may help to clarify it further as well as relate it more fully to the other topics of LWC study.

In attempting to conceptualize the spread of English from the point of view of LMLS more generally, as well as in relation to the spread of other LWCs in particular, it also becomes clear that the possibilities for inter-LWC language planning at an international level have been all too ignored both in research and in policy. Intrastate LWC planning has proven possible both in Canada and in India. More such planning at an international level, involving both trade-offs and cooperation, may yet prove to be feasible and advantageous to all concerned.

NOTES

1.   This paper assumes that the reader is familiar with at least one of the three versions of my original paper (Fishman 1964, 1966, 1972b [in Spanish: 1974]), although its major points can be followed without such familiarity by those familiar with the language maintenance and language shift field per se.

"Language maintenance and language shift"

2.   Our basic concern in this volume, and in this chapter, is with *the sociology of English as an additional language* in all countries, but particularly in countries where English is the mother tongue of a minority of the population. Most of our comments will be focused directly upon this concern. Nevertheless, other languages such as Russian, French, Arabic, Chinese, and Swahili, that are also widely used today as second languages, as well as Akkadian, Aramaic, Greek, and Latin, that were once so used, will also be referred to for purposes of greater cross-national and diachronic perspective. Although further specification is possible, a LWC will be defined simply, to begin with, as any language widely used as a second or additional language, thus subsuming, for the time being, international languages, linga francas, vehicular languages, contact languages, and other intergroup communication varieties (such as Hausa, Lingala, Pidgin English).

3.   When LMLS is pursued from the point of view of the threatened/minority/smaller language in an intergroup context, it is necessarily its *intragroup* maintenance that is the focus of attention and the spread of the intrusive language is also monitored relative to the same intragroup base. However, when LMLS is pursued from the point of view of the more power-ful language, *intergroup bilingualism* must be studied first and only then can the question of new intragroup functions for the spreading LWC be examined. Thus, the study of LWCs represents a two way broadening of concern, from a primarily intragroup orientation to a more balanced concern for both intergroup and intragroup bilingualism, and from a primarily maintenance orientation to a more balanced concern for both maintenance and shift. Finally, note that the domains of intergroup use of LWCs may well be indicative of the first domains of intragroup use of a spreading LWC (at least nonmetaphorically).

4.   This suggestion is not to be interpreted as implying that a universal set of domains be sought or utilized. Such a universal set would doubtlessly render more commensurable the dispersion measures obtained from various settings in which English (or another LWC) is an additional language, but spurious commensurability is worthless elegance. The domains utilized must have local validity from within. They must be tentatively derived and then confirmed or revised on the basis of internal evidence of various kinds. In any speech-and-writing community of interest to us there will be not only language use variance due to the within-group use of English but also variance due to such use of (varieties of) the mother tongue and, possibly, of other languages as well. Such variances in language use must be carefully examined in initially positing and ultimately validating domains and in computing dispersion indices for the various languages and varieties (including English) that are employed by particular networks.

5.   At this point in my original treatment(s) of LMLS I discussed the compound/coordinate distinction which has fallen somewhat into disuse in the past dozen years, and it is to be doubted whether better language-use data can revive it. While it is still a heuristically appealing distinction, its neuropsychological base has not been nearly as certain as was originally thought to be the case. At this very writing, psychoneurological interest in bilingualism is again growing and new evidence has again been adduced to the effect that the languages utilized by bilinguals are differently processed (Kaplan and Tenhouten 1975). This new evidence is not yet unambiguous with respect to the compound/coordinate distinction but, rather, merely implies such evidence might be forthcoming. At any rate, the attitudinal-phenomenological and the sociofunctional validity of the distinction may be quite substantial, regardless of its neurological status.

         The above-mentioned appeal of the distinction is based upon its commensurability with the *extremes* of social contextualization and its absence. It is not a distinction that can assist us directly in measuring degree or location of bilingualism, but, rather, one that may help further enrich the location consideration, in view of the different stages of English use that may obtain in any setting in which it is an additional language. As such, we will return to it in the next section ("Sociocultural Processes Relatable to LMLS").

6.   There is, of course, a finer-grained level of analysis that may well be related to sociodynamic analysis, just as the latter is to domain analysis. I have in mind the explication of a *particular* interaction, an exercise to which ethnomethodologists and symbolic anthropologists are so inclined. I do not rule the latter type of analysis out of the total sociolinguistic enterprise. Indeed, I believe that such analyses provide many worthwhile clues for more generalized social dynamics analyses, just as the latter, in turn, provide vital clues insofar as domain location and verification are concerned. In this light, Table 3.2 could also have a subtable contributing to it, detailing the social behavioral dimensions of, e.g., family or work interaction alone. Furthermore, there could be still finer-grained tables contributing to that subtable, and so forth.

          Finally, it is in conjunction with a dynamic model of the use of English as an additional language—one that is concerned with the recurring situational and interactional implementation of normative expectations—that the metaphorical or meta-communicational use of English would be reported. A bit of English—and sometimes more than a bit—creeps into mother-tongue conversations, both among those who know more than a bit of English and those who do not know any more than that—for purposes of emphasis, humor, sarcasm, status stressing, leg-pulling, rank-pulling, etc. Such use of English is not always due to circumstances similar to those that govern the use of English terminology when the mother tongue still lacks a handy term for referents in the world of technology or other "Western wisdom." Metaphorical phrases are typically motivationally contrastive or connotative rather than referentially denotative. They point to the speaker, to his/her relationship to the interlocutor, to their temporary withdrawal from the "conventions of speaking" that normally obtain between co-members of a speech community. Under such circumstances English is often employed, just as French or German were in a former generation, to imply rather than to specify, even though perfectly good mother-tongue phraseology is available to all concerned and would be handled with facility. Nevertheless, English is used precisely because it is *not* what is normatively expected and because doing so *does* italicize a snatch of conversation and more clearly mark it as special in the speaker's intent and, it is hoped, in the hearer's interpretation as well.

7.   "The question of whether a given language is imposed by force is an objective, as well as subjective, one. Even if a language is not believed by its promoters or by its targets to be imposed, it may in fact be imposed. But the whole voluntarism-coercion debate tends to be metaphorical, if not metaphysical . . . There are substantial forces pushing for English across state boundaries, and these are accompanied by laws within many countries that make English a compulsory subject of instruction in compulsory schools, and by professional recruitment patterns that make a knowledge of English a prerequisite to many kinds of advancement. If this be voluntarism . . ." (Jonathan Pool, personal communication).

          All of the dimensions mentioned by Pool deserve to be retained for study, viz., the objective/subjective distinction vis-à-vis imposition, the advocate's phenomenology versus the target's phenomenology with respect to imposition, and finally, the distinction between armed intervention or enforcement and the more ordinary compulsion of social life with its legal and normative pressures. However, it is my view that this very complexity (i.e., the multiplicity of forces within any notion of force) makes the topic of imposition a multidimensional continuum worth retaining rather than dispensing with. In this chapter, wherever gradations are not explicitly mentioned, the term "imposition" implies the use of obvious military force and not the reliance upon nonmilitary means of compulsion (the laws and conventions to which Pool perceptively refers). (Note my use of the term "diffusion" which is here employed to refer to a *type* of spread rather than to spreading per se.)

          The military, the police, and the secret service are ubiquitously in the background, as we have all come to realize in the past decade, often as part of the conventions of everyday social life. However, their background rather than foreground presence, their invisibility rather than visibility in social processes, may be a useful primitive indicator of whether imposition is in effect. Of course imposition may fade into "diffusion via regular channels," and of course participants, observers, and analysts may differ about when or whether direct imposition has ended. Considerations such as these, as mentioned earlier, are eminently worthy of study.

As for voluntarism, I do not see how it can be utilized as a variable in social research. Its societally patterned manifestations must be studied in relation to societal structures, societal functions, societal values, and societal symbols. (Also see Ravetz 1971)

8.   "The direction of language-acquisition is not always in favor of the language of higher socioeconomic status when a lingua franca is needed. Note use of Swahili in East Africa and Pidgin in West Africa. The 'big' man learns the low status language; the 'little' man doesn't have to learn English . . . Explanation exists on a more abstract level than demographic variables." (Carol Scotton, personal communication) (Also see Scotton 1972, 1975, 1976)

The above observation is doubtlessly of value, in that it serves to correct an unconscious view as to the availability of social mobility, both as a motive and as a reality, which is quite widespread among American and other Western investigators. Nevertheless, it must also be realized that it pertains to a very small proportion of the contact conditions involving English or other LWCs today. With decolonization and modernization, the "big man" has not disappeared (nor even been replaced by a local counterpart) as much as acquired a rather large corps of active associates at various levels of government, economy, and education. This associative role, often accompanied by all of the accoutrements of political, economic, and cultural independence, does foster the widespread myth (see "tunnel effect" discussion in note 9)—even if not the equally widespread reality—of social mobility opportunity. Western largess is increasingly funneled through nationals rather than through outsiders. These nationals, as co-gatekeepers, are the initial locus and constant wellspring of LWC spread, as long as power-sharing and resource-sharing processes, pretenses, and aspirations continue. For internal counterprocesses, see the next section, "The Diffusion Process."

9.   Again, the foregoing is not to say that all those among whom English may be spreading will actually gain access to the power or resources with which English is associated. Indeed, there may be considerable discrepancy between aspiration and achievement in this respect. However, the fact that the relationship between English and resources does hold for some (or even for most) may long have a strong motivating effect even upon those for whom it does not (yet) hold. For a discussion of this possibility, in terms of general economic development, see Hirschman (1973). Hirschman calls this phenomenon of delayable and indefinite gratification "the tunnel effect" and points to its greater applicability in societies marked by still traditional extended-family responsibilities, relative ethnic homogeneity and avowedly earned status. He points out, however, that the tunnel effect (i.e., imagining that one is about to see the light at the end of the tunnel) cannot last indefinitely. To the extent that the acquisition of an additional language is dependent upon institutionalized (rather than function-oriented) instruction, it may well become stabilized for far longer periods than the economic behaviors to which the tunnel effect initially applies.

There are, of course, contexts in which indigenous elites seek to limit both the spread of their own ethnic mother tongues as well as the spread of outside LWCs associated with Western power and resources development and, instead, foster the spread of a third option associated with neither (e.g., Swahili). Note, however, that these elites themselves do increasingly acquire English (or another international and interregional LWC), that their position is often motivated or rationalized in terms of supra-ethnic authenticity integration, and, finally, that their ability to sustain their initial position will depend on political factors ultimately linked to power sharing and to social mobility for wider segments of their national societies. Both ideological and resource links to the outside world need to be considered in this connection.

10.   The economic development literature contains many cost-benefit studies comparing, among other things, the costs of educating students (short term), the benefit of their increased productivity (long term), and their decreased productivity during the very time that they are in the classroom or literacy program (short term). It is to such considerations, as well as to others mentioned by Thorburn (1971) and Jernudd (1971), rather than to more obviously ideological or academic ones, that I am referring with the term "school-worthy."

11.   When writing on LMLS a dozen years ago I was fortunate enough to relate this topic to Schermerhorn's theoretical model of intergroup relations which was then at a very early stage (1963) of its development. Subsequently it struck the fancy of Verdoodt (1968) and later, after it was developed into book-length dimensions, it also proved to be of interest to Paulston (1975). On the whole, however, Schermerhorn's model has proved to be too complex, too qualitative, and too immigrant/host related (and, perhaps, too focused upon minority groups in the American sense) to be of widespread interest to sociolinguistic researchers in general or to LMLS students in particular.

12.   It is regretable that the International Center for Bilingualism Research has not been able to keep such files for monitoring the fortunes of French as a LWC and that the Center for Applied Linguistics has not been able to do so for English. Both Centers have been able to keep exhaustive country files, but these need to be combed and integrated at fixed intervals—across countries as well as for international agencies and for such functions as trade and diplomacy—if LWC information is to be derived from them.

13.   A good example of cognitive (and affective) response to English is cited by Levenson (1971) in his discussion of Chinese "bourgeois cosmopolitanism" in the 1920s: "And what was more cosmopolitan, anyway, than to be a French, not an English translator? The relative eclipse of France in the twentieth century, except in culture, made French the language of the purest cultural.sophisticate; English speakers were more likely and more than likely, to be just gross utilitarian lackeys, serving imperialist business and politics, not Shakespeare." (p. 25) Various national (and international, e.g., Esperantist) literatures would yield a rich harvest of quotations that could not only be treated as data but also help generate hypotheses and empirical-data-gathering instruments.

14.   It is likely that English is recognized as lexically richer than most other LWCs today in connection with high status roles pertaining to technology, industry, commerce, finance, weaponry, etc. This makes English a useful model in corpus planning, whether this is consciously recognized as such or is masked under the label of internationalisms and translation loans. However, it also gives English lexical items a power that is greater than the ability of corpus planners to control (Fainberg 1974). Indeed, these may diffuse via *gehobenes primitivgut* routes, from below, rather than being at all dependent on elitist populations, institutions, or mechanisms. As a result, the foreign-markedness of Englishisms may be appreciably briefer than that of other foreignisms that are more dependent on trickling down from above.

REFERENCES

Agheyisi, Rebecca, and Joshua A. Fishman. 1970. Language attitude studies. *Anthropological Linguistics* 12:137–157.

Banks, Arthur S., and Robert B. Textor. 1963. *A Cross-Policy Survey.* Cambridge, Mass.: MIT Press.

Basso, Keith H. Language use and cultural symbols: English, Western Apache, and the "Whiteman." Ms.

Clyne, Michael. 1976. Nieuw-Hollands or Double-Dutch. *Dutch Studies.*

Cohen, Abner, ed. 1974. *Urban Ethnicity.* London: Tavistock.

Cooper, Robert L. 1975a. Sociolinguistic surveys: The state of the art. In *Conference Proceedings: International Conference on the Methodology of Sociolinguistic Surveys.* Arlington, Virginia: Center for Applied Linguistics.

———. 1975b. Language attitudes II. *International Journal of the Sociology of Language* 6: entire issue.

———. 1974. Language attitudes I. *International Journal of the Sociology of Language* 3: entire issue.

Ernst, Morris L. 1967. *The Comparative International Almanac.* New York: Macmillan.

Fainberg, Yaffa Allony. 1974. Official Hebrew terms for parts of the car. *International Journal of the Sociology of Language* 1:67–94.

Fishman, Joshua A. Recent research and theory concerning ethnicity: concepts and findings. Ms.

———. 1976. *Bilingual Education: An International Sociological Perspective.* Rowley, Mass.: Newbury House.

———. 1974. The comparative dimensionality and predictability of attitudinal and usage responses to selected centralized language planning activities. In *Proceedings* (of the Association Internationale de Linguistique Appliquee, Third Congress, 1972), edited by Albert Verdoodt. Vol. 2. Heidelberg: Julius Gross. Pp. 71–80.

———. 1972a. *The Sociology of Language: An Interdisciplinary Social Science Approach to Language in Society.* Rowley, Mass.: Newbury House.

———. 1972b. Language maintenance and language shift as a field of inquiry: Revisited. In his *Language in Sociocultural Change.* Stanford: Stanford University Press. Pp. 76–134. In Spanish, in *Estudios de Etnolingüistica y Sociolingüistica*, edited by P. Garvin and Y. Lastra. Mexico City: Universidat Nacional, 1974.

———. 1969. Bilingual attitudes and behaviors. *Language Sciences* 5:5–11.

———. 1964. Language maintenance and language shift as a field of inquiry. *Linguistics* 9:32–70. Revised in *Language Loyalty in the United States.* The Hague: Mouton, 1966.

Fishman, Joshua A.; Robert L. Cooper; Roxana Ma et al. 1971. *Bilingualism in the Barrio.* Language Sciences Monograph No. 7. Bloomington: Indiana University.

Fox, Karl A. 1974. *Social Indicators and Social Theory: Elements of an Operational System.* New York: Wiley.

Glazer, Nathan, and Daniel P. Moynihan, eds. 1975. *Ethnicity: Theory and Experience.* Cambridge: Harvard University Press.

Greenfield, Lawrence, and Joshua A. Fishman. 1970. Situational measures of normative views in relation to person, place and topic among Puerto Rican bilinguals. *Anthropos* 65: 602–618.

Hirschman, Albert O. 1973. The changing tolerance for income inequality in the course of economic development. *Quarterly Journal of Economics* 87:544–566.

Hofman, John E., and Haya Fisherman. 1971. Language shift and maintenance in Israel. *International Migration Review* 5:204–226.

Jernudd, Bjorn H. 1971. Notes on economic analysis for solving language problems. In *Can Language be Planned?*, edited by Joan Rubin and Bjorn H. Jernudd. Honolulu: University Press of Hawaii. Pp. 263–276.

Kaplan, Charles D., and Warren D. Tenhoutten. 1975. Neurolinguistic sociology. *Sociolinguistics Newsletter* 6(2):4–9.

Kahane, Henry. 1975. The rise and spread of the Lingua Franca in the medieval Mediterranean world. In *Proceedings of a Conference on Bilingualism and Applied Linguistics.* Champaign-Urbana, University of Illinois. Ms.

Kloss, Heinz, and Grant D. McConnell. 1974. *Linguistic Composition of the Nations of Word: I. Central and Western South Asia.* Quebec City: Laval University Press.

Land, Kenneth C., and Seymour Spilerman, eds. 1975. *Social Indicator Models.* New York: Russell Sage.

Lehmann, W.P., ed. 1975. *Language and Linguistics in the People's Republic of China*. Austin: University of Texas Press.

Lieberson, Stanley. 1970. *Language and Ethnic Relations in Canada*. New York: Wiley.

Levenson, Joseph R. 1971. *Revolution and Cosmopolitanism*. Berkeley: University of California Press.

Lewis, E. Glyn. 1976. Bilingualism and bilingual education: The ancient world to the Renaissance. In *Bilingual Education*, by Joshua A. Fishman. Rowley, Mass.: Newbury House.

———. 1975. Attitude to language among bilingual children and adults in Wales. *International Journal of the Sociology of Language* 4:103-126.

———. 1972. *Multilingualism in the Soviet Union*. The Hague: Mouton.

———. 1971. Migration and language in the USSR. *International Migration Review* 5:147-179.

Paulston, Christina Bratt. 1975. Questions concerning bilingual education. (Note: provisional title.) In *Proceedings of the 1974 InterAmerican Conference on Bilingual Education*. Arlington, Virginia: Center for Applied Linguistics.

Pryce, W.T.R. 1975. Industrialism, urbanization and the maintenance of cultural areas: North East Wales in the mid-nineteenth century. *The Welsh History Review* 7(3):307-340.

Ravetz, Jerome R. 1971. *Scientific Knowledge and its Social Problems*. Oxford: Clarendon.

Riley, George A. 1975. Language loyalty and ethnocentrism in the Guamanian speech community. *Anthropological Linguistics* 17:286-292.

Russett, Bruce M. et al. 1964. *World Handbook of Political and Social Indicators*. New Haven: Yale University Press.

Schermerhorn, Richard A. 1970. *Comparative Ethnic Relations: A Framework for Theory and Research*. New York: Random House.

———. 1964. Toward a general theory of minority groups. Paper presented at the annual meeting of the American Anthropological Association, November 21, 1963, San Francisco, California. Published: *Phylon* 25:(1964).

Scotton, Carol M. A proposal to study language choices. Ms.

———. 1976. Language in East Africa: Linguistic patterns and political ideologies. In *Advances in the Study of Societal Multilingualism*, edited by J.A. Fishman. The Hague: Mouton.

———. 1975. Multilingualism in Lagos—what it means to the social scientist. *Sixth Annual African Linguistics Conference, Ohio State Working Paper in Linguistics* No. 19, 78-90.

———. 1972. *Choosing a Lingua Franca in an African Capital*. Edmonton, Alberta: Linguistic Research.

Senghor, Leopold S. 1975. The essence of language: English and French. *Cultures* 2(2):75-98.

Sheldon, Eleanor Bernert, and Wilbert E. Moore, eds. 1968. *Indicators of Social Change: Concepts and Measurements*. New York: Russell Sage.

Sheldon, Eleanor Bernert, and Robert Parke. 1975. Social indicators. *Science* 188 (no. 4189, May 16, 1975):693-699.

Solé, Yolanda R. 1975. Language maintenance and language shift among Mexican American college students. *Journal of the Linguistic Association of the Southwest* 1:22-48.

Spina, Joseph M. 1974. Adolescent attachment to Canada and commitment to a national community. Ms.

Stewart, William A. 1968. A sociolinguistic typology for describing national multilingualism. In *Readings in the Sociology of Language*, edited by J.A. Fishman. The Hague: Mouton. Pp. 531-545.

Tabouret-Keller, Andree. 1972. A contribution to the sociological study of language maintenance and language shift. In *Advances in the Sociology of Language*, edited by Joshua Fishman. Vol. 2. The Hague: Mouton. Pp. 365-376.

Tabouret-Keller, Andree. 1968. Sociological factors of language maintenance and language shift: A methodological approach based on European and African examples. In *Language Problems of Developing Nations*, edited by Joshua A. Fishman et al. New York: Wiley, Pp. 107-118.

Thorburn, Thomas. 1971. Cost-benefit analysis in language planning. In *Can Language be Planned?*, edited by Joan Rubin and Bjorn H. Jernudd. Honolulu: University Press of Hawaii. Pp. 253-262.

Verdoodt, Albert. 1971. The differential impact of immigrant French speakers on indigenous German speakers: A case study in the light of two theories. *International Migration Review* 5:138-146.

———. 1968. *Zweisprachige Nachbarn*. Vienna: Braunmüller.

Zirkel, Perry A. 1974. A method for determining and depicting language dominance. *TESOL Quarterly* 8:7-16.

PART TWO

English in Nation and Neighborhood

Chapter 4

English in Israel: A Sociolinguistic Study

Elizabeth Nadel and *Joshua A. Fishman*

The importance of a language of wider communication for small developing countries is generally recognized by sociolinguists. Yet its precise role in national life can vary depending upon historical circumstances, the status of the local languages, and future national goals.

In any study of a multilingual situation, the following questions need to be asked: Under what circumstances are each of the languages learned? When are they used? What are the attitudes of the government and of the people toward each language? This case study of English in Israel attempts to answer the above questions in order to better understand this particular setting as well as to generalize about the role of English as a language of wider communication.

One typology for national languages and languages of wider communication in developing countries—that of Fishman (1971)—designates three types of planning decisions. Type A decisions are found in those new countries which lack any established national traditions and widely accepted history and which are presently concerned with their own political integration. Here a language of wider communication is likely to be officially designated as the "permanent, national symbol." Local, tribal languages may be officially subordinated to the language of wider communication, which is seen as part of the transition to modernity. For example, in Botswana, a former British protectorate, English was named the first official language in 1966 when the state received its independence. There was one predominant local language, Setswana, but it lacked a literature and the prestige associated with English. In spite of the fact that even now there are very few native English speakers other than the British expatriates, education from the third grade upward is carried on in English. The government is conducted in English, and the emphasis, particularly during the first years of statehood, was on English as a key to social, political, and economic advancement. It is of interest to note that since 1973 more articles in Setswana have begun to appear in *Kutlwano*, the national magazine. Also, the letters to the editor are beginning to sing the praises of the tribal customs and language, and to call for greater pride in the indigenous culture. It would appear that Botswana is beginning to shift away from the strictly type A decisions, and this may be a natural step in statehood development.

In contrast, there is the type C decision, which (according to Fishman) occurs when there are *several* competing, established local cultures and languages. The language of wider communication may be officially adopted as a unifying compromise. English was thus designated in India, to try to overcome at the national level the tremendous conflicts between entrenched local languages of this subcontinent. On a regional level, one or more of the local languages—Hindi, Urdu, Bengali—were to be used. The very lack of ethnic ties toward English was one of the reasons it was preferred as a modernizing factor. In India the complex local and religious ties to dozens of languages have not been fully overcome, and the introduction of local languages, even on a regional level, has not always been successful. Here the role of English for the elite, for the federal government, and for sciences comes closest to type C designation.

Type B decisions exhibit one great tradition which at the national level elicits the approval of the population. Nationalism, and with it the national language, are stressed. A language of wider communication is not overlooked, but is adopted for specific functions which serve the transition to modernity. According to Fishman (1971): "*That* bilingualism which involves the indigenous national language and the (usually Western) Language of Wider Communication is seen as having current functional significance but only transitional ideal significance at the national level, with the latter (the LWC) rather than the former (the indigenous language) destined to 'go'." The implication is that eventually the indigenous language will dominate and the importance of the language of wider communication will decline.

In this three-category classification, Israel has usually been placed in category B regarding its Jewish population. (This chapter does not consider the use of English among the Arab population.) The first official language, as well as that most used for internal purposes, is Hebrew. English has become that foreign language most strongly supported by government policies as well as being recognized as important by the individual citizen. Though indeed closer to category B than to either A or C, a close study of Israel's use of its national language and language of wider communication will reveal that it may have developed beyond this categorization.

RESEARCH METHODS

This study was conducted during the first half of 1973. To obtain statistical data regarding English in Israel, the authors turned first to the Israeli Central Bureau of Statistics. Their published results of the 1960 national census were available but not those of 1970. Various government ministries, several universities, and a large number of people working in the communication media were kind enough to grant interviews and to discuss their attitudes and activities regarding English in Israel.

In addition, a 1970 survey of Israeli culture, *Tarbut Yisrael*, conducted by Professors Elihu Katz and Michael Gurevitch, included questions relevant to this study. The authors were fortunate enough to have access to their results and were able to conduct secondary analyses of their data. There were also a number of other relevant surveys conducted by graduate students at various Israeli universities which included findings about attitude, knowledge, and use of English in this country. Finally, there were the authors' personal observations of local residents, which will be cited as such. It is hoped that these various sources will give a more valid, more complete picture than would any one source by itself.

HISTORY OF THE ISRAELI CASE

Prior to the British Mandate in Palestine, which began in 1917, there were few reliable statistical surveys conducted there, particularly regarding language use. It appears from the tables published by Bachi (1956) that English was used as the main or first language by one out of every 1000 residents of Palestine in 1916–18. When the British took control, the status of English changed drastically. It became the first of three official languages of Palestine—English, Arabic, and Hebrew— mentioned in that order for official documents. Its legal status was defined in 1922 in the King's Orders in Council:

> All ordinances, official notices and official forms of the government and all official notices of local authorities and municipalities in areas to be pre- scribed by order of the High Commissioner, shall be published in English, Arabic, and Hebrew. The three languages may be in use in debates and discussions of the Legislative Council, and subject to any regulations to be made from time to time, in the government offices and the law Courts.
> *(Quoted in Fisherman 1972)*

In education English was to become the first foreign language taught in schools of the settlement. Yet the change to this position (which had been held by French during the Ottoman rule) did not take place immediately in 1917, but only some years later, when the Mandate government began financial support of Jewish schools and in this way influenced both teaching methods and the number of hours of English lessons in government schools (Bamberger 1971).

The Mandate government agreed that for the Jewish population there would be Hebrew-language "public" schools and that English would be taught as one of the subjects beginning in grade 5, with four hours of instruction each week in grades 5–8. The subject was also compulsory during the high school years, with the goal being preparation for the matriculation examination. Five years before the cessation of the Mandate, the British demanded an extra hour per week of English lessons in the fifth and sixth grades—that is, five hours per week. Jewish teachers were strongly opposed to this proposal, hand in hand with their opposition to the Mandate rule as a whole. They even proposed at one time that any foreign language *but* English be taught (Bamberger 1971).

The political attitudes of the Jews toward the British during the 1930s and 1940s were reflected in language usage. Many young activists refused to speak any language but Hebrew and adamantly opposed their English lessons. Consequently, many of these now middle-aged Israeli citizens do not know English, and some regret this, forty years later. English is not a symbol of colonial domination for Israelis today. On the other hand, many Israelis served in the British Army during World War II, putting anti-Nazi sentiments over anti-English ones. These people generally retain good to excellent colloquial English. The fact that there was a more terrible enemy than the British probably unconsciously eased resentment to them and their language.

The lack of statistics regarding actual knowledge of English or use of it in the media during the 1930s and 1940s is probably due to the current Israeli effort to write the history of steady growth in the use of the Hebrew language.[1] During the first stage of independence, commencing in 1948, tremendous emphasis was put on Hebrew—increasing its oral use, the knowledge of its written forms, and its availability in the cultural and communication media. In that period of stressed nationalism, the Hebrew language was considered one of the corner-stones of the Jewish state. Since then, the government, the schooling, and the communication media are officially in Hebrew, with certain accommodations made for other languages. Hebrew is not only the official language of the government, it is also used daily (although far from exclusively) by almost 90% of the Jewish population over fourteen years of age (Central Bureau of Statistics, *The Educational Level Attainment and Use of Language,* 1973). From just these facts, it would seem that Israel fits perfectly into the type B category with respect to the development, spread, and use of its national language among its Jewish population.

In the period between 1948 and 1967, the percentage of the Israeli population which knew and used Hebrew vacillated. The waves of immigrants that doubled the population in the first few years of statehood often knew no Hebrew on arrival. A 1950–51 survey of immigrants indicated that only 16% of the immigrants over sixteen years of age reported that they could read, write, and speak Hebrew while still abroad and another 15% reported partial knowledge (Schmelz and Bachi 1972). Yet by 1954, according to the Statistics Bureau, the use of Hebrew was regaining, and by 1961 had once more reached, its 1948 level. Bachi states that any wave of immigrants can now only present a temporary setback for Hebrew's prominence among the Jews of the state. This statement reflects the policy not only of encouraging the increased use of Hebrew among all sections of the population but likewise of discouraging the use of mother tongues brought from the diaspora.

During the first year of statehood, when there was a pronounced rise in nationalism, there was also a greater official stress on Hebrew. Yet English was not dismissed along with British political domination. Legally, one was no longer required to use English for any official function. Still its use was never outlawed, and major Israeli legal thinkers feel that "the right to use English is not negatively affected" by the deletion of the Orders in Council reference to English (Fisherman 1972). For example, the official gazette of the Knesset (Israel's parliament), as well as a compilation of its enactments, have continued to date to be published in English. Even immediately following the removal of the British, English continued to be taught as the first foreign language. However, there was a slight decrease in the number of study hours, negating the increase the British had imposed five years earlier (Bamberger 1971).

Thus, even at the height of the nationalistic period, there seems to have been reluctance to dictate the use of one language. The fact that there is no separate law regarding official languages in the State of Israel and that one must still rely on the revised 1922 King's Orders in Council is revealing in itself. First, legislators probably realized that the subject was an extremely delicate one— because of the Arabic-speaking non-Jewish minority in the country as well as because of a multitude of Jewish immigrant groups speaking various mother tongues. Second, it may have been realized early that Hebrew alone would not be a sufficient tool for international communication between Israel and the rest of the world. Thus, the lack of laws specifically forbidding second-language use left the door open for the spread of English.

Yet prior to 1967 the amount of English spoken in Israel was consistently low, according to official sources. In 1948 and again in 1961 surveys revealed that of every 1000 Jews only 4 spoke English as their main language. An American sociologist, Harold Isaacs, found that English-speaking parents had great difficulties trying to raise children in English. When he personally interviewed children of American parents, they were unwilling to answer in English, though they were able to do so (Isaacs 1967). English in this instance functioned as an in-group language and by no means as a lingua franca. And it seems that Anglo-Saxon parents were no more successful in perpetuating in their children regard for or use of English as a mother tongue than were other immigrant parents. Yet because its native speakers formed such a tiny percentage of the Israeli population, English was generally viewed as a foreign language and not widely seen as a between-group language or as a lingua franca.

The year 1967 and the aftermath of the Six Day War brought some significant changes in Israeli life which affected the use of English. The nation grew more open to Western, particularly American, influence. Dozens of new

American-backed companies sprang up, the economy boomed, and Israelies began to travel abroad much more for business and pleasure. In addition there were now many more imported products, more American journals, and more popular American music, all of which boosted the position of English.

Also following the 1967 war there was a rise in immigration from Western countries. Never before had so many Americans come to settle here.[2] Many more visiting professors came to lecture in English at Israeli universities. Thousands of volunteers came to kibbutzim speaking English, Swedish, Dutch, and Spanish, among other languages, and almost always using English as the common language among themselves and with the kibbutz members.

In politics as well as in economics, English became more important for Israelis. The ties between the United States and Israel, as well as between Israelis and Jews, grew much stronger after 1967, and these ties necessitated continual negotiations and discussions at various political and military levels. The election and success of Prime Minister Golda Meir also probably strengthened the status of English; Israelis who used to laugh at her American-accented Hebrew now praised her successful dialogues with top American politicians. Keeping in mind these major changes, we shall now study the specifics of English education and proficiency in Israel today.

Education

In comparison with post-independence days there has been in recent years an increase in the number of class hours of English required of every pupil. The language of instruction for all other subjects is Hebrew—with few exceptions—and there has been no movement since 1948 to alter this. Since 1960 it has been compulsory in all government-recognized schools to begin the study of English in the fifth grade for four hours per week. Thus, virtually every student studies English as his or her first and major foreign language, continuing to do so throughout high school.

The current official goals stress oral usage and comprehension during the elementary years. During high school there is said to be approximately equal stress upon reading and oral comprehension. The shift is away from emphasis on writing skills, which the Ministry of Education and Culture has concluded are less important than other skills. The Ministry of Education and Culture's Inspector of English summarizes the goals of English studies as "international communication." (Gefen 1973)

Greater interest in the English language by students has been noted by the Ministry of Education and Culture. It attributes this to the following factors which reflect the oral rather than the written use of the language: (1) increased consciousness of English, caused by greater contact with foreigners, and (2) the advent of Israeli television in 1968. Israeli students now are more likely to travel abroad than in the past, and they have greater contact with Arabs, tourists, and kibbutz volunteers within Israel. In all instances the first language of communication with foreigners is English. Therefore the study of English is the key to communication in a very tangible sense. One studies the language no longer to eventually be able to appreciate Shakespeare, but to speak to that new volunteer who has come to work at the kibbutz and does not yet know any Hebrew. The existence of Israeli television means that English is heard by Israelis of all ages much more than in the past. In addition to regular programs, which will be discussed later, there are also special educational programs in English. The locally-produced televised English lessons have been quite well received, and again encourage the learning of oral skills.

The mass media and the school system may work together in other ways. Pop songs on the international hit parade, generally in English, are very popular here. Teachers often use the lyrics to teach vocabulary which is of great interest.

With English now seen by many as a key to advancement it is emphasized by parents and pupils more than ever before. This trend has been on the rise for a number of years; in fact, the Ministry of Education and Culture is on the defensive concerning the reasons for not beginning English classes before the fifth grade. Lack of adequate funds, lack of fully qualified teachers in the lower grades, and uncertainty that all the pupils are secure enough in the Hebrew language (which is still a second language in many Israeli homes) are given as the official reasons, but it is admitted that the first is the most relevant. (Gefen 1973)

According to the Ministry of Education and Culture, a growing number of regular schools are trying to organize English classes in the fourth grade (Gefen 1973). In addition, vocational school pupils and parents have demanded and received more English studies, particularly to learn terminology in mechanics, hotelry, and agriculture. There has even been an effort to increase the amount of English studied in special slow classes, as it has been found that being given the opportunity to study this subject is psychologically encouraging for the slow learner.

To emphasize just how far English had replaced French, which had been the major language of wider communication under Ottoman rule, the English supervisor told this anecdote: About ten years ago when new North African immigrants arrived, it was decided to teach them French before English, as many were already familiar with that language and would, therefore, presumably be able to excel and feel more comfortable in their new school environment. Contrary to the desired effect, the parents felt insulted, felt that their children were being downgraded by being taught French and not English, and demanded that English be taught, even if it proved to be much harder.

In spite of public recognition of the importance of learning English, the marks on the high school matriculation exams in this subject are extremely poor. This may have been caused by unrealistically high standards or unsuccessful teaching methods. In 1972, a greater percentage (43%) failed this subject than any other required subject or any other language (see Table 4.1). Perhaps with changes in emphasis in the new curriculum and in the corresponding examination, the results will change for the better in the future. Today it is still a fact that the

Table 4.1   Failures according to subject on matriculation exams 1972

Subject	Percentage failing	Number failing
Bible	17.6	2327
Hebrew Literature	10.8	1358
English	43.1	5246
French	14.3	145
Arabic	21.8	351
History	25.8	1262

Source: Israel, Ministry of Education and Culture, "Summary of results of matriculation examination, 1972."

level of attainment does not meet the expectations. The results of a survey of pupils' attitudes to different subjects of study show that in grades 4 through 10 English is consistently considered to be important but is not especially liked or considered interesting (Levi and Kaplan 1972). Students in the many privately sponsored courses reflect the same attitude. Their number appears to be growing, through it is impossible to get complete statistics in this connection. The directors of these courses report that their students are strongly motivated to study "in order to advance in their work or profession, to travel, and to do business with non-Hebrew speakers." (Letter, July 15, 1973) Yet, at the same time, there were complaints of "overambitious demands set by the Ministry of Education." (Letter, June 28, 1973) In sum, young Israelis are very aware of the importance of English. Their attitude to the language and its mass culture are positive, though their competence is not as great as they themselves or the Ministry of Education would like it to be.

At Israeli universities a similar pattern exists. There has been an increase in the number of students taking English as their major subject for the B.A. as well as an increase in the number and level of advanced courses available at universities. (Letters from major universities' English departments, 1973) In addition, every student, regardless of his major field of study, is required to pass a basic English course or show proficiency in reading university English-medium texts. The aim here is practical: to master enough of this language of wider communication to handle the reading lists and bibliographies for most university courses. Though there are no published statistics regarding the level of actual reading proficiency in contrast to pro forma standards at universities, it would appear that the student who reads and understands more than a few pages in English for any B.A. course is the exception rather than the rule, though such a student would indeed be respected and envied by his peers for his competence. However, student interest in English is undeniably growing and even students who are not at ease reading an English textbook will glance at *Time* and will intersperse their native Hebrew speech with many English phrases. Thus "lighter English" in popular mass culture fares better than "heavy English."

Table 4.2   Israeli students studying abroad, according to
countries in which they study

Country	Number	Country	Number
Australia	8	Ireland	1
Austria	79	Italy	1105
Belgium	67	Ivory Coast	2
Canada	122	Japan	2
Czechoslovakia	12	Mexico	2
Denmark	16	Poland	5
France	158	Romania	4
Germany	201	Spain	16
Great Britain	182	Switzerland	168
Greece	3	United States	1105
Holland	50	Yugoslavia	3
Hungary	3		
India	2	Total	2288

Source: UNESCO (1972), p. 466.
Note: 62% of Israeli students abroad study in English-speaking
countries—Australia, Canada, Great Britain, India, Ireland, and
United States.

Another reason for the increased popularity of English could be the
number of Israelies studying abroad. Figures from the *1972 UNESCO Statistical
Yearbook* show that almost 60% of these were in English-speaking countries (see
Table 4.2). They may be attracted to the United States and England because of
the quality of their schools and/or the relative ease of study in English rather than
in Dutch or Swedish, for example. Likewise, these Israelis, on their return, are
very likely to favor English phrases and other cultural traits.

General Proficiency in English

Though attainment does not yet match expectation, training in English is
considered increasingly important by both the government and the individual.
Hence, hours of study in both compulsory and voluntary classes tend to be on the
rise. Yet what are the statistics for overall language proficiency in English and
Hebrew in this immigrant society?

According to self-report, as recorded in the *Tarbut Yisrael* study, more
than one-third of those in the 18–24 age category can speak, read, and write
English in contrast to just half that proportion in the 65-and-over group. Likewise
the number of the youngest age group who reported having no knowledge of
English whatsoever was half that of the oldest age group—36% versus 69% (see
Table 4.3). In other studies,[3] neither French nor Arabic was found to be nearly
this closely related to age in the Israeli population. The apparent fact that
English—and only English—has a pronounced correlation to youth is undoubtedly

Table 4.3   English proficiency of Israelis (eighteen years and older), according to age

Age	Speak only	Read only	Speak, read only	Speak, read, write	None	Total
18–24	12	9	8	36	36	100
25–29	10	3	8	31	49	100
30–34	8	4	5	25	58	100
35–39	9	4	4	25	58	100
40–44	16	1	4	22	57	100
45–49	7	3	5	20	64	100
50-54	4	1	5	22	68	100
55–64	6	3	4	15	72	100
65 +	8	3	2	18	69	100
Average	9	4	5	24	58	100

Source: Katz et al. (1972): *Tarbut Yisrael* data.
Note: Results are given as percentages. *N* = 1483.

a result of the fact that young people are increasingly given the opportunity to learn English. As English is the mother-tongue of less than 1% of Israelis, it would seem that it is learned for the most part in the school setting. This is confirmed by the fact that 84% of those Israelis in the *Tarbut Yisrael* study who can speak, read, and write English have eleven or more years of education.

It follows from the preceding data that competence in English, related as it is to education, is also presently related to socioeconomic class—as higher education is substantially a reflection of socioeconomic class. Proficiency in English is seen as a key to economic advancement. Research is needed into the number and type of jobs which demand competence in English (see Cooper and Seckbach, this vol., chap. 8). A study of the level of competence expected in comparison to that found would also be revealing. For example, Fisherman (1972) found that the police are generally unable to handle English although they are expected to be able to do so. In contrast, it appears that many Israeli-born scientists use English rather than Hebrew orally and in writing—and seem to find it more precise and natural for their purposes.

Hebrew is spoken by 99% of the population and read by 83% (Katz et al. 1972, *Tarbut Yisrael* data). However, it is generally not used for the same functions as English. But Israelis who can at least read English are far more likely to be fully fluent in Hebrew than those Israelis who know no English at all (see Table 4.4). Thus, knowledge of one of these languages does not detract from knowledge of the other.

According to as yet unpublished statistics of the 1972 national census, English is spoken every day by 9.1% of the Jewish population age 14 or over. There are no data available on the percentage that reads and/or listens to English, but it is surely even higher. Only 11.7% of those who speak English daily use it as

Table 4.4   English language proficiency in relation to proficiency in Hebrew

	Hebrew					
English	Speak only	Read only	Speak, read only	Speak, read, write	None	Total
Speak	5	0	2	92	1	100
Read	2	0	0	98	0	100
Speak, read	1	0	0	99	0	100
Speak, read, write	2	0	1	96	0	100
None	24	0	9	65	1	100
Average	15	0	6	78	1	100

Source: Katz et al. (1972): *Tarbut Yisrael* data.
Note: Results are given as percentages. $N = 1484$.

Table 4.5   Country of birth in relation to English language proficiency

Country of birth	Speak only	Read only	Speak, read only	Speak, read, write	None	Total
Israel	15	3	10	46	27	100
East Europe and Mediterranean	9	3	6	23	59	100
South Europe	8	4	2	18	67	100
West Europe	14	2	4	65	16	100
English-speaking countries	0	0	0	92	8	100
North Africa	5	4	3	10	78	100
Near East	7	5	3	10	75	100
Far East	5	0	5	42	47	100
South America	43	14	0	14	29	100
Average	9	4	5	24	58	100

Source: Katz et al. (1972): *Tarbut Yisrael* data.
Note: Results are given as percentages. $N = 1481$.

their sole or principal language. In contrast, 87.7% of those who reported using Hebrew every day used it as their principal language. The corresponding figures for the other languages listed by the census bureau are: Rumanian, 39.0%; Hungarian, 34.1%; Yiddish and Spanish, 28.9% each; and French, 20.8%. That English had a substantially smaller percentage of users speaking it as their principal language suggests that English is used for specific functions which do not seem to compete with those of Hebrew. Yet this very specific use among non-native speakers is an indication of its importance in Israel.

According to the *Tarbut Yisrael* data, the native-born Israeli is twice as likely as the average adult in the population to be fully proficient in English—46% versus 24% (see Table 4.5). This finding goes hand in hand with that confirming

Table 4.6 Main language spoken at home in relation to English language proficiency

English language proficiency	Hebrew	Yiddish	Arabic, Eastern langs.	East European langs.	Central and West European langs.	Balkan, Latin, langs.	Other	Two langs.	Total
Speak only	87	2	2	3	2	1	0	1	100
Read only	76	4	7	9	2	2	0	0	100
Speak, read only	87	3	5	1	1	0	0	3	100
Speak, read, write	80	1	2	5	8	1	0	3	100
None	63	10	11	6	2	2	0	4	100
Average	71	7	8	5	4	2	0	3	100

Source: Katz et al. (1972): Tarbut Yisrael data.
Note: Results are given as percentages. N = 1480.

that young people know more English than their elders. It appears that English is learned primarily in the classroom and that the more years of education an Israeli has, the more English he learns. If this is true, then there should not be any conflict between the main language spoken in the home and an individual's proficiency in English. In fact, 71% of the *Tarbut Yisrael* sample speak Hebrew at home (see Table 4.6); and knowledge of English is a bit higher among this Hebrew-speaking group than among the total population. As a group, people who speak a Central or Western European language as their main language know somewhat more English, but other groups not speaking Hebrew at home—such as those speaking Yiddish, Slavic, or Latin languages at home—all report far lower knowledge of English. Thus, in spite of the vast differences between their linguistic structures and learning situations, Hebrew and English proficiency seem to be increasingly correlated.

USE OF ENGLISH IN THE MASS MEDIA

Next we will examine many of the specific functions for which English is popular in Israel, discussing first the oral and then the written communication media. We shall see that the popularity of English in certain instances is not at the expense of the national language.

Radio

The radio is the medium which affords the easiest access to a variety of languages, and many Israelis take advantage of this fact and listen to foreign language broadcasts. Israeli broadcasting includes programs in English and in nine other languages in addition to Hebrew. Obviously Hebrew receives the bulk of programming time, and Arabic receives the second largest time allotment. English programs on AM/FM currently include two five-minute and two fifteen-minute daily newscasts plus a half-hour news magazine. This is as much as the total time allotted to French programs and more than that allotted to languages other than French, Hebrew, and Arabic.

The local broadcasting authority maintains that its foreign language programs are a courtesy to new immigrants in the transitional period before they are capable of understanding Hebrew broadcasts. In the case of English, though, when less than 1% of the population are native speakers, one suspects that there are other reasons as well. The use of English on the Israeli radio is also a courtesy to tourists, who are an important factor in the Israeli economy. The prestige of English as the first language of wider communication in Israel today is also reflected in the radio time allotment.

More available and more popular than Israeli English broadcasting are the BBC and the Voice of America. The former has programs beamed at the Near East virtually twenty-four hours each day and the latter twelve. These are the major English language radio programs for Israelis. According to the *Tarbut Yisrael* study, 31% of the respondents said they listen sometimes to the BBC, 19%

Table 4.7   Exposure to the BBC according to age and education level

Age – Education	Listen to Eng.[a]	Listen to other languages	Do not listen to B.B.C.	Total
18–30				
low	0	0	100	100
medium	18	6	76	100
high	51	3	43	100
30–50				
low	4	11	86	100
medium	12	11	76	100
high	44	5	50	100
50 +				
low	4	14	82	100
medium	15	5	79	100
high	31	3	66	100
Average	24	7	68	100

Source: Katz et al. (1972): *Tarbut Yisrael* data.
Note: Results are given as percentages. $N = 951$.
[a]Listen to English only *or* listen to English and other languages, too.

to the Voice of America, and 11% to locally produced English language programs. Though availability must play a role in amount of audience exposure, there seem to be other reasons for the popularity of English broadcasts.

In contrast to the Radio Authority claim that listening to foreign radio stations in general increases with age, the audience of the BBC and the Voice of America is decidedly young (see Table 4.7). Not only age but education is a determining factor. The more education an Israeli has, the more likely he is at any age to listen a lot to the BBC and the Voice of America. He is even more likely to do so if he is also under thirty years of age.

The standard claim that foreign language listening increases with age is true for broadcasts appealing to non-Hebrew mother-tongue populations, but this is not generally the situation of English in Israel. Israelis do not listen to the BBC because it is easier for them to understand than local Hebrew broadcasts. This is not at all a reversion with age to a more familiar language but a trend, sparked by higher education, to listen to a language which is usually a second or third language. Listeners to the BBC and the Voice of America are just as likely to speak Hebrew as their main language at home as are all other Israelis. It was also found that Hebrew language proficiency is very high for listeners to both local and foreign English language broadcasts. As the same cannot be said for listeners to broadcasts in other languages, one must conclude that the function of English for Israelis is not the same as that of the immigrant languages per se (Katz et al. 1972).

We may speculate about the reasons for English language popularity on radio. Perhaps content of programming is a factor. Probably the more international point of view in news, cultural features, and music also attracts Israelis. Radio also offers an opportunity to practice English. Finally, the status factor—that is, being able to relate at a party a story heard on the BBC—might be an additional motivation.

Even Israeli Hebrew radio is more influenced today by the English language than it was ten years ago. Interviews with personalities from abroad are likely to be heard in their complete English version with a brief Hebrew summary, instead of the full Hebrew quote without the first person interview, as was common here some years ago. Secondly, in spite of the stress on excellent or "pure" Hebrew, once known to characterize the Broadcasting Authority, the use of English words seems to be growing in news broadcasts, feature shows, and surely in advertisements. The status—call it even the snob appeal—of using English is evident, particularly in advertising. If the English phrase for a product is announced in the middle of a Hebrew commercial, the product is somehow thought to be popular abroad. Supposed popularity in the English-speaking world is thought to help sell a product in Israel. In contrast, it is rare to hear a Hebrew radio ad with Russian or Yiddish or Ladino words prominently interspersed.[4]

The local radio bows to English in yet another way. While Hebrew lyrics are very popular, there has been a clear rise since 1967 in the amount of English lyrics heard on Hebrew programs. Most of these records—not traditional folk music but international pop culture—are also popular in Black Africa, Australia, and Sweden. But this is a new trend in Israel, a change from the official emphasis on Hebrew songs and Hebrew culture only. Currently, there are radio programs devoted to foreign songs translated into Hebrew. An Israeli pop group which can say that it was organized in New York or had a successful concert series in England seems to have some points in its favor. Israelis hear this music not only on radio but also on phonograph records. Though expensive, records are popular and are another means of exposure to English lyrics and international pop culture.

In sum, though exposure to Hebrew language broadcasts is consistently extremely high, exposure to English radio programs—especially those from abroad—seems to be on the rise, particularly among the young and the well-educated. The influence of such English programs on Israeli radio and radio audiences seems to be growing.

Television

Another medium which has recently exposed Israelis to more English is television. Israeli television was initiated in 1968 and the market for television sets was quickly saturated. Though a television set costs several times what it would in the United States, virtually every newly married couple receives or buys one straightaway—along with the refrigerator and the washing machine. There is only one channel and its policies are directed by the Ministry of Communications. It broadcasts several hours of locally produced educational programs in the morning, Arabic programs in the early evening, and what is officially termed Hebrew programs for about three hours nightly. The educational programs are indeed in Hebrew, except for the English lessons. The Arabic portion has Hebrew subtitles approximately half of the time. As for Hebrew, the nighttime viewer hears the news in Hebrew, sometimes a Hebrew panel or entertainment show, but always one or two episodes of imported serials, usually detective or Western shows obtained from American networks. These are shown with Hebrew (often Hebrew and Arabic) subtitles, but are always heard in the original English. Native-spoken English is heard nightly by most Israelis—by those who understand the dialogue as well as by the many who read the Hebrew translation. Since 1968 virtually all Israelis, including preschool children, listen daily to such English telecasts. Thus this language is less than new to them when studies officially begin in school. It is plausible that being exposed to an hour or two of spoken English nightly should contribute to greater fluency, greater motivation for learning the language, and more English colloquial expressions flowing from these shows into Hebrew slang. Indeed, the provision of Hebrew subtitles may lessen or even eliminate any conflict between the two languages in the minds of Hebrew language "protectors." Nevertheless, it is high time for research into the exact influence of English television programs on Israeli comprehension, pronunciation, and attitudes toward this language.

Films

Films in Israel are virtually never shown without subtitles. The government policy is that all commercial films have subtitles in two languages—Hebrew, English, or French. This is in response both to the linguistic heterogeneity of the population of Israel and to the variety of languages in which films are produced.

The Israeli film scene, then, is varied. The local resident has his choice of films imported from a range of countries and cultures. The percentage of Israeli-made, Hebrew-language, full-length films available is less than 4% of the total, according to Ministry of Interior statistics (1968–72), though relative to their number they are quite popular. In contrast, there are many English-language films to be seen. According to the Ministry of Interior, movies in English were something under half of those approved for showing the years of 1969–72.[5] Surveying the notices in the English-language *Jerusalem Post* for the same period, it was found that actually approximately 60% of the movies to be seen in the cities were in English. The difference in figures is explained by the popularity of the English-language movies. The same film may be shown simultaneously in two or three theaters in contrast, for example, to a Turkish film which appears at only one theater. These findings were confirmed by the *Tarbut Yisrael* survey which revealed that 60% of the public reported that the last film they had seen was in English.

Attendance at an English movie may not necessarily reflect proficiency in that language. As previously stated, there are always subtitles in Hebrew, if

Table 4.8   Language of last movie seen according to English language proficiency

Language of movie	Speak only	Read only	Speak, read only	Speak, read, write	None	Total
Hebrew	12	5	6	18	60	100
English	12	4	6	34	43	100
French	9	5	7	40	39	100
Arabic	25	0	0	25	50	100
Other European languages	8	3	5	38	46	100
Other Eastern languages	7	5	1	5	81	100
Don't remember	7	2	7	16	68	100
Average	10	4	6	28	52	100

Source: Katz et al. (1972): *Tarbut Yisrael* data.
Note: Results are given as percentages. $N = 1155$.

that language is not spoken in the movie, and therefore an audience thoroughly literate in Hebrew would have no difficulty attending movies narrated in English or any other language.

For the audience at ease reading Hebrew subtitles, which tends to be the younger generation Israeli, no films present a problem of language. If the English is only partially understood, it is disregarded to a great extent by the audience which relies on its fluency in reading Hebrew. There can be no doubt that these subtitles are essential for the Israeli audience. As Professor Katz has said (Katz et al. 1972), the campaign to revive the Hebrew language has succeeded so well that it is now necessary to retranslate foreign works of culture so that they can be understood by the Israeli audience. Thus, though 60% of the films viewed are narrated in English, this does not represent any real linguistic tensions for Hebrew speakers. The vernacular in this instance, as with television, complements the language of wider communication and is probably not felt to be in competition with it.

The statistics for language proficiency and movie attendance confirm our theory. Of the *Tarbut Yisrael* respondents who reported that the last movie they saw was in English, 43% said they knew no English at all (see Table 4.8). Nevertheless this same audience is more literate in Hebrew than is the overall population. The movie audience was found to be younger, better educated, and more likely to be native-Israeli than the nationwide average. Yet we do not know if it was the English language which attracted them to such films or rather the content and type of culture these films display. We cannot know if they actually listen to the English or rely instead on subtitles entirely. Certainly they are exposed to the sound of English and the sights of Western culture through movies, as in the case of Israeli television. Yet research is needed to determine just how much English is absorbed by the Israeli movie audience—consciously or unconsciously.[6]

Theater

In contrast to the case of English movies, which comprise such a large portion of all the movies to be seen in Israel, plays in English are not common. Amateur acting groups—often from English departments at local universities—do present infrequent, short-running productions. These are parallel to the Yiddish or German theater (though far less professional than either), being restricted largely to a special group in the population. None of them competes with Hebrew plays, for the audience of one are rather unlikely to attend the other. While no statistics are as yet available regarding the growth or decline in English-language plays, nor on the demographics of their audiences, one suspects English plays are closely related to the Anglo-Saxon immigration and should be studied as an aspect of English as a group language among one immigrant community in Israel. The reason for this may well be that English stage plays demand a higher level of understanding than do other English media. English television programs and films have Hebrew subtitles. English plays, on the other hand, are produced almost entirely for Israelis of English mother tongue, and there are no facilities for simultaneous translation into Hebrew.

A more profound, though indirect effect of English plays is their translation and production in Hebrew by the national theater groups. This is a widespread phenomenon which might be of interest to study. Here again, it is the foreign culture—style, subjects, and trends—not language to which the Israeli audience is exposed.

Books

In the written media of communication there is much material available in English. In this instance, though, individual exposure is more selective. Reading demands language proficiency, as there are no subtitles to aid the nonnative speaker. Still, we shall see that English books, journals, and signs are plentiful in Israel.

English book publishing in Israel

In the field of Israeli book publishing, the major emphasis by government and establishment has been in encouraging Hebrew books. Statistics consistently report that there have been yearly increases in the number and proportion of Hebrew publications (*Monthly Bulletin of Statistics,* 1970–74). And recent surveys of readers here reveal that 70% reported that the last book they read was indeed in Hebrew (Katz et al. 1972).

Nevertheless, there is also a substantial amount of local book publishing in English, far more than in any language other than Hebrew. English-language publishing is also more openly cited and discussed by official sources than is book publishing in other languages. For example, the Central Bureau of Statistics annually reports in tabular form on local publications. The tables which relate to languages of print are divided into the following categories: Hebrew, English, other languages, and two languages. True, there is no other language in which as much is published as in English, but it is also true that these other languages are not equally encouraged or even mentioned (*Monthly Bulletin of Statistics,* 1970–74).

English books are published on an increasing variety of subjects. In contrast to the 1968/69 figures, in which half of the books were related to the natural sciences, the most recent statistics, 1972/73, reveal an increase in fields such as political science, art, literature, and children's books (see Tables 4.9 and 4.10). While local English publications in the natural sciences have decreased somewhat, it is likely that more Israeli scientists now publish abroad in English. The rise in other fields reflects the effort to export books in these subject areas. Both Hebrew and English book publishing are on the rise, but as English books are "an increasingly important export item" (*Jerusalem Post,* April 25, 1973, p. 7), this limits the range of confrontation between the two. As was seen with other Israeli media, there is a definite official effort to elevate the level and amount of English production, but not at the expense of the national language. The chairman of the Book Publishers' Association of Israel made this revealing statement in the spring of 1973: "By comparison we have nothing like the richness of English literature. Somebody who wants to read even a good mystery, for instance will read an English one (or a translation). But I don't believe a Sabra will read poetry in English." (*Jerusalem Post,* April 25, 1973, p. 7) There is no longer the claim, as there was twenty or thirty years ago, that Hebrew must fulfill all functions for all Israelis. But for the native Israeli—the Sabra—the most personal form of written language—poetry—will always be best expressed and understood in Hebrew. From the sociolinguistic point of view this seems a valid interpretation. For example, Garvin (1972) has distinguished the functions of a language in the technological realm from those in the literary. In the former he sees a world language as "most practical," but in the latter "the desire to participate in world-wide development will often be subordinate to the need for cultural self-expression and the search for cultural identity—hence, the separatist function will predominate."

Book imports

English books published in Israel are only a small fraction of the material available in that language. While government statistics do not list the number of books imported annually, it is clear from interviews with the major book distributors that this number is a very substantial one. The following figures are approximations, as neither Steimatzky nor Bronfman, the major sellers of imported material, were anxious to divulge exact statistics—apparently in light of competition with each other.

Paperback books far outnumber hardcover imports. In 1973, there were between 2,000 and 3,500 new titles imported in paperback form from the United States and the United Kingdom. No other foreign language had even half this number. An average of 100 copies of each English book are sold in Israel—with the notable exception of bestsellers, such as *Love Story,* which sold 150,000 copies in its English-language paperback edition. According to distributors, the rising

Table 4.9 Books in first or renewed edition according to subject and language of print, absolute numbers and percentages, 1965/66–1968/69

Subject	Number (1968/69)					% in Hebrew	
	Total[a]	In Hebrew	In English	In other languages[b]	In two languages	1968/69	1965/66–1967/68
General	21	16	2	–	3	(76.1)	(95.5)
Judaism and other religions	165	156	3	3	3	94.5	89.1
Humanities	178	124	22	19	13	66.3	78.0
Education	45	39	3	1	2	(86.7)	(92.6)
Social Science	47	37	6	1	3	(78.7)	(85.3)
Economics	65	53	8	2	2	(81.5)	67.9
Political Science	76	64	7	5	–	(84.2)	86.3
Law	21	16	5	–	–	(76.2)	(86.7)
Natural Science and Mathematics	149	44	104	–	1	29.5	18.9
Agriculture	75	42	5	–	28	(56.0)	(31.2)
Medicine	30	10	16	1	3	(33.3)	(37.1)
Engineering and technology	62	38	15	2	7	(61.3)	(46.4)
Art	48	28	3	–	17	58.3	66.1
Literature—total	812	726	19	54	13	89.4	89.2
Literature—Six Day War	92	82	3	1	6	(89.1)	(77.7)
Children's books	179	174	–	4	1	97.2	98.1
Textbooks	56	44	3	8	1	(78.6)	(93.1)
Total	2029	1611	221	100	97	79.0	78.1

Source: Israel, Central Bureau of Statistics, *Monthly Bulletin of Statistics, Supplement* (1970).

[a] Of these, 9 dictionaries.

[b] Including 35 books whose language of print is Yiddish (mainly literature).

Table 4.10   Number of books in first or renewed edition according to subject and language of print, 1972/73

Subject	Total	Language of print			
		Hebrew	*English*	*Other*	*Two*
General	8	3	2	2	1
Judaism and other religions	251	241	4	3	3
Humanities	273	220	32	20	1
Education	78	71	4	1	2
Social Science	117	92	9	1	15
Economics	93	85	5	–	3
Political Science	119	102	15	2	–
Law	54	51	3	–	–
Natural Science and Mathematics	173	88	85	–	–
Agriculture	49	41	6	2	–
Medicine	45	41	4	–	–
Engineering and technology	69	55	14	–	–
Art	49	22	12	–	15
Literature	549	424	65	59	1
Children's books	164	138	25	1	–
Textbooks	48	45	1	2	–
Total	2139	1719	286	93	41

Source: Israel, Central Bureau of Statistics, *Monthly Bulletin of Statistics, Supplement* (1974).

Table 4.11   Newspapers and periodicals according to language, type, and frequency, 1969

Language and type	Total	More than once/month Daily[a]	More than once/month 2/wk.	More than once/month 2/month	Frequency 8–12/yr.	Frequency 5–7/yr.	Frequency 2, 3, 4/yr.	Frequency 1/yr.	Irregular
Total	481	24	69	15	111	30	131	42	59
General periodicals and press	128	24	43	15	29	3	8	–	6
Specialized periodicals and press	353	–	26	–	82	27	123	42	53
Hebrew total	314	14	40	8	73	23	77	28	51
General	65	14	17	8	16	3	4	–	3
Specialized	249	–	23	–	57	20	73	28	48
English total	46	1	5	4	8	3	18	5	2
General	13	1	4	4	1	–	2	–	1
Specialized	33	–	1	–	7	3	16	5	1
Other languages	60	9	19	3	14	1	8	1	5
General	44	9	19	3	10	–	1	–	2
Specialized	16	–	–	–	4	1	7	1	3
Two languages[b]	61	–	5	–	16	3	28	8	1
General	6	–	3	–	2	–	1	–	–
Specialized	55	–	2	–	14	3	27	8	1

Source: Table adapted from Israel, Central Bureau of Statistics, *Monthly Bulletin of Statistics Supplement* (1970), p. 2.

[a] Of these, two evening papers are in Hebrew.

[b] Most publications in two languages are in Hebrew and English

Table 4.12   Circulation of *The Jerusalem Post*, 1965, 1972

	Total paid subscribers	
	1965	*1972*
The Jerusalem Post daily	17,850	31,500
The Jerusalem Post Friday-weekend edition	25,200	42,000
The Jerusalem Post weekly-overseas edition	6,500	35,000

Source: The Jerusalem Post (1973): statistics supplied in correspondence with authors.

sales of English-language books can be accounted for by several factors: (1) the recent increase in the number of English-speaking immigrants; (2) the rise in the number of tourists; and (3) the greater amount of money which Israelis have to spend. One may couple to the last factor the positive attitude toward English which Israelis now have, and the language's special status relative to all other foreign languages in Israel.

Newspapers and periodicals

Paralleling the popularity of English books is that of English newspapers and periodicals. Approximately 10% of the newspapers and periodicals published in Israel are in English; and there are additional local bilingual publications, most of which are in Hebrew and English (see Table 4.11). In addition, over one-fifth of the adult population reads an imported newspaper (Katz et al. 1972), and of these newspapers 40% are in English (Aronson 1973). *Time* alone sells 20,000 copies weekly, which means statistically that nearly 100,000 people in Israel look at this international magazine. Even the rather expensive *International Herald Tribune* sells about 2,000 copies daily, which is a threefold jump in circulation in the past four years (Aronson 1973). The only locally-published English daily is the *Jerusalem Post*, which sold almost twice as many daily copies in 1972 as in 1962 (31,500 versus 17,850). (See Table 4.12)

Regarding the local English press, it is interesting to note that the number of titles of general English periodicals (such as *Israel Magazine* or *Israel Book World*) decreased between 1969 and 1972; in contrast, the local English specialized press (such as *The Israel Economist* or *Israel Shipping Research Institute Journal*) has experienced an increase of 33%, from thirty-three to forty-three titles. The reasons for the latter occurrence seem to rest with increased Israeli recognition of the importance of English for specialized technical communication. In contrast, general subject matter in English published in Israel is less popular than imported material because the international point of view is lacking.

An observation should be made regarding the imported press: foreign serials may be read for many reasons. The *Tarbut Yisrael* survey reported that the two major reasons cited for reading foreign press were (a) reading in a language

Table 4.13   Percentage of material in English in Israeli libraries, 1973

Type of library	No.	% of total book collection	% of total periodical collection	% new books	% new periodicals	% books wanted	% periodicals wanted
Medical	15	84	81	84	82	89	91
Universities	40	74	74	75	79	74	74
Industry	27	70	67	80	77	77	70
Research inst.	25	66	64	74	73	69	70
Government	17	60	62	66	59	58	57
Museums	11	59	51	57	61	60	60
School	18	13	12	11	12	10	10
Moshav, kibbutz	94	10	8	9	7	13	13
Public	54	6	9	6	9	10	14
Other	6	56	57	52	57	NR	NR
Total	307	37	36	39	38	39	39

Note: NR = no response.

more easily understood and (b) desire to know what is thought of Israel through-out the world. It would have been most informative to be able to cross tabulate these and other reasons for reading the imported press with the particular language read. It may well be that interest in world opinion is much more likely to be an attitude of English-language readers. The largest English-language serials, such as *Time* and the *International Herald Tribune*, are indeed international in nature.

Library Survey

The above figures reveal one part of the trend in the book and periodical world of Israel. In addition, one can study the holdings of Israeli libraries to discover the current reading habits in various fields as reflected in different types of libraries. More than 300 Israeli libraries responded to a brief questionnaire (1973) concerning the proportion of their collection in English as compared to Hebrew and other languages. The results, shown in Table 4.13, reveal that of the 307 libraries surveyed (which included the majority of special libraries and a small sampling of school and public libraries) the overall average of English material in the collections is 37%. The lowest percentage of English material is found in Israeli public libraries. Six percent of the book collection in such libraries is in English, and this figure matches the Ministry of Education and Culture figures of 1970 (Golan 1971). In the more specialized libraries (e.g., those of museums, universities, hospitals) the percentage of English is dramatically higher. The shift is not a gradual one—public, elementary, and high school libraries as well as kibbutz and *moshav* (collective agricultural settlements) collections are all quite low in the proportion of English books and periodicals in their total collections and in their 1973 annual acquisitions. Contrastingly, all special libraries reported that over 50% (and as much as 84% in medical collections) are English.

Several observations may be made regarding responses to the 1973 survey. The respondents said in most cases that their recent acquisitions were comprised of approximately the same language distribution as their overall holdings. In other words, there are no dramatic recent changes regarding acquisition of English-language materials. In a few cases, for example in private industry and research institute libraries, there is a trend toward purchasing more English today than in the past. When asked the amount of English, Hebrew, or other language material they would like to have in their collection if budget were of no concern, the more specialized libraries and even the public and kibbutz libraries state that they would request somewhat more English. School libraries, though, indicated that 10% would be adequate. The difference between elementary and high school collections and those of universities in Israel (74% in English) is most striking. Though there is an official effort to stress both Hebrew and English there nevertheless appears to be a gap in actuality between training virtually exclusively in Hebrew at early levels and expectations for English proficiency at higher, more specialized stages.

Table 4.14   Reading of English books according to years of education

Amount of reading in English [a]	None	Up to 4	5-8	9-10	11-12	Post high school	B.A. at least	Total
					Years of education			
Lot	0	0	2	8	33	30	28	100
Little	0	1	7	11	45	23	14	100
None	5	5	34	21	28	6	2	100
Average	4	4	26	18	31	11	6	100

Source: Katz et al. (1972): data derived from *Tarbut Yisraeli*.
Note: Results are given as percentages. *N* = 1149.
[a] As reported by the respondents.

Summary of *Tarbut Yisrael* Results

The very strong connection between educational level and reading of English was confirmed by results of the *Tarbut Yisrael* survey (see Table 4.14). The more education a person had, the more English books he reported reading. Ninety percent of all of the respondents who read at least one English book per month had eleven or more years of education. No other demographic factor—age, sex, main language spoken at home—had this direct a relationship with reading habits. These results mean that the greater emphasis on English in the school system is not misplaced. English is acquired as a school-learned skill in the main, and proficiency in English is linked to success in university and advanced professions. The abundance of English in the media—television, movies and books—will not be fully appreciated unless the population has achieved a sufficient level of language proficiency at school. Without this, total dependence on Hebrew translations will be the rule.

ENGLISH ON SIGNS

We have discussed various examples of the functions of English in Israel. Among the attitudes connected with the use of English, we have noted the association of English with modernity and with what is new on the world market in business, science, and culture as well as its connection with tourism and status in the eyes of Israelis. Another visible verification of the attitudes relates to storefront signs.

A count was made of the prominence of Hebrew and Roman lettering on storefront signs on Jaffa Road, perhaps the busiest shopping area in Jerusalem. The signs were tabulated on a five-point scale: Hebrew letters only, Hebrew dominant though Roman script appears, the two types of lettering equivalent, Roman dominant though Hebrew script appears, and Roman lettering only. Next, the signs were divided into two broad categories regarding their age—the new signs being easily distinguished by neon lights and modern lettering in contrast to those which are decades old, often gray, and usually less prominent. The results (noted in Table 4.15) show that Roman letters, which in almost all cases on Jaffa Road means English words, are increasingly important in trade. Of the older signs there were none with Roman script dominant over Hebrew, whereas of the new signs close to 10% were in this category. In both old and new signs the consistently largest group has equal prominence for the two languages. The sharpest contrast is the drop in number of signs with only Hebrew letters from one-third of the older to one-fifth of the newer signs. Though the exact age of each store sign was not determined, it seems clear that the more recent the sign, the more prominence is given to English. Increase in tourism as well as increase in use and status of the English language for advertising and trade are the reasons for this trend.

Comparison between the signs on Jaffa Road (the downtown shopping district) and Keren Kayemet Street (a local neighborhood district) is revealing (Rosenbaum, Nadel, and Cooper, this vol., chap. 6). In the latter district though the citizens are well educated, the amount of English on signs is considerably less

Table 4.15   Use of Hebrew and Roman lettering on signs in Jerusalem

Signs	Number	Type of lettering (% of total)				
		Hebrew only	Hebrew prominent	Both equal	Roman[a] prominent	Roman[a] only
Jaffa Road						
Old signs	75	33.3	26.7	38.7	0	1.3
New signs	53	20.8	30.2	39.6	9.4	0
Total	128	28.1	27.3	39.1	3.9	0.8
Keren Kayemet	50	34.0	32.0	34.0	0	0

Note: Keren Kayemet Street data (see Rosenbaum et al., this vol., chap. 6) pertain to both office and storefront signs in contrast to the Jaffa Road data which pertain only to storefront signs.

[a]Roman lettering almost always indicates English words.

than in the heart of the business section of Jerusalem. Use of English in addition to Hebrew for commerce and tourism is shown on Jaffa Road. The busier the focus of communication, the more likely we are to find more use of English; in most cases this is not at the expense of the Hebrew, which is found side by side on signs. The percentage of signs with equal prominence for both languages is extremely consistent in both settings; yet Jaffa Road reveals that recent signs are less likely than older ones to have Hebrew only and more likely to have English script predominantly. The distribution on Keren Kayemet Street today is similar to that on the old signs on Jaffa Road—that is, before the rise in international tourism.

CONCLUSION

A survey of various primary and secondary sources leads to the following conclusions: exposure to English, particularly through second-language classroom and through the mass media, is on the rise. The Israeli does not seem opposed to this, for Hebrew, the national language, retains undisputed prominence for conversational, educational, and governmental purposes on the domestic level. Israelis frequently make a distinction between internal and external use of language; hence Hebrew is without rival on the local scene while English is used increasingly for international communication in various fields. The use of English *within* Israel is also often legitimized on this same basis: tourists from English-speaking countries and the world at large or specialists in a given field of international inquiry are the ultimate "target." Having passed the stage specifically labeled type B, nationalism— at least in language—seems to be somewhat less emphasized, and we do not expect the use of English to be merely transitional.

English in Israel

Israel seems to be at a crossroad in language development and planning. While English is recognized as being extremely important, as shown by its increased study hours and prominence in all the mass media, its actual use—for example, the amount of books read voluntarily—and proficiency as judged by matriculation examinations are less outstanding.

Research is needed concerning the specific effects of exposure to English both in the mass media and in the classroom. Regarding the media, we need to study the effects of English television and films on the population, both in Israel and in other developing and developed nations. In education, we need to evaluate how much English is learned in high school and at the university. To date we lack adequate information concerning what students *can* do with English as distinct from what they actually *do* do with it. Comparative research on this subject is needed in Israel and in other countries. The balance between national and international needs is not a stable one.

English, even in Israel, which was formerly under British rule, is no longer seen as a sign of colonialism or of attachment to another nation. Its status is no longer connected strictly to political considerations, certainly not exclusively to ties to Great Britian. For a language to spread as a language of wider communication without political imposition, it must have connotations greater than being just the language spoken in one state. Research would probably reveal the tremendous advantage of English in contrast to other languages of wider communication (such as Russian, French, or Chinese) which are associated more closely, both politically and culturally, to one mother country. The popularity of English for mass pop culture, scientific writings, and lingua franca usage among tourists is an international phenomenon. The current trend in Israel is to stress the language of wider communication, but presumably not at the expense of the national language. If this policy in language planning continues with public support we may expect increased understanding of and exposure to English as well as Hebrew. Jewish Israelis may cease to be multilingual in the various European and Middle Eastern languages known by the immigrant generations, and become increasingly bilingual in Hebrew and English only.

The general conclusion to be derived from this study is that a language of wider communication can be retained for international and intergroup functions without perceived threat to the national language. At the stage of development typified by greater security and subsided nationalism, the benefits of the language of wider communication can be viewed dispassionately and without guilt or conflict.

NOTES

1.	Cf. Bachi (1956) for material collected from surveys conducted since World War I recording the rise of Hebrew in Israel.

2.	According to the Association of Americans and Canadians in Israel, between 1967 and 1974 approximately 30,000 Americans came to settle in Israel. It is not yet known how many of them remained permanently.

3.　　　Unfortunately, the *Tarbut Yisrael* survey did not study proficiency in other languages—particularly Jewish languages—to see their relation to demographic factors.

4.　　　In fact, there are many foreign words used in modern Hebrew but they have been absorbed to such an extent that they are now not recognized as such by young people who hear these terms on the radio or elsewhere. In contrast, English words used in Israeli advertising are assumed to appeal because listeners recognize them as being foreign, specifically as English.

5.　　　All films shown commercially in Israel must first be approved by a council of the Ministry of Interior, Ha-Moetzah La-bikoret S'ratim.

6.　　　About two-thirds of the university-bound, Jerusalem high school students surveyed by Cooper and Fishman (this vol., chap. 11) reported that they had to read less than half the subtitles in American films in order to understand the dialogue.

REFERENCES

Published Material

Bachi, Roberto. 1956. A statistical analysis of the revival of Hebrew in Israel. In *Scripta Hierosolymitana*, Vol. 3. Jerusalem: Magnes Press. Pp. 179-248.

Bamberger, Y. 1971. [Teaching of English in Israel since the establishment of the State]. *English Teachers' Journal* (Israel) (no. 8, Dec. 1971):86–92. (In Hebrew)

Dudman, Helga. 1973. People of the book's reading habits change. *Jerusalem Post*, April 25, 1973, p. 7.

Fisherman, Haya. 1972. The 'official languages' of Israel: Their status in law and police attitudes and knowledge concerning them. *Language Behavior Papers* (no. 1, winter 1972):3–23.

Fishman, Joshua A. 1971. National languages and languages of wider communication in developing nations. In *Language Use and Social Change*, edited by W. Whiteley. London: Oxford University Press. Pp. 27-57.

Golan, M. 1971. [The public library in Israel] n.p.: Ministry of Education and Culture. (In Hebrew)

Guthrie, M. 1962. Multilingualism and cultural factors. In *Symposium on Multilingualism*. Commission de Coopération Technique en Afrique (CCTA)[Brazzaville: Commission de Coopération Technique en Afrique (CCTA). P. 107.

Isaacs, Harold. 1967. *American Jews in Israel*. New York: J. Day Co.

Israel, Central Bureau of Statistics. 1973. *The Educational Level Attainment and Use of Language*. Jerusalem: Central Bureau of Statistics.

Israel, Central Bureau of Statistics. *Monthly Bulletin of Statistics Supplement* 21 (no. 4, April 1970), 24 (no. 1, Jan. 1973), 25 (no. 3, March 1974). Jerusalem.

Katz, Elihu; Michael Gurevich et al. 1972. *Tarbut Yisrael* [The Culture of Israel]. 2 vols. Jerusalem: Israel Institute of Social Research and the Communications Institute of the Hebrew University. (In Hebrew)

Levi, Arie, and Ilana Kaplan. 1972. *Attitudes of Pupils toward Different Subjects of Study*. Jerusalem: Ministry of Education and Culture Curriculum Center.

Noss, Richard B. 1970. Politics and language policy. Paper presented at the Ford Foundation Meeting on Education, Singapore, October 1970.

Rice, Frank, ed. 1962. *Study of the Role of Second Language in Asia, Africa, and Latin America*. Washington, D.C.: Center for Applied Linguistics of the Modern Language Association of America.

Schmelz, Uriel, and Roberto Bachi. 1972. [Hebrew as the everyday spoken language of Jews in Israel]. *Leshonenu* 37 (no. 1, 1972):50–68. (In Hebrew)

The Teaching of English in Israel, A Survey. 1964. Jerusalem: Hebrew University, John Dewey School of Education.

UNESCO (United Nations Educational, Scientific and Cultural Organization). 1972. *UNESCO Statistical Yearbook.* Paris.

Unpublished Material

Aronson, C. (of Bronfman). Interview with first author, Tel-Aviv, February 11, 1973.

Errie (of Steimatzky). Telephone interview with first author, February 15, 1973.

Garvin, Paul. 1972. Some comments on language planning. Draft for presentation at 23rd Annual Roundtable on Linguistics and Language Study, Georgetown University, March 1972. (Ditto)

Gefen, Raphael (Chief Inspector of English, Ministry of Education). Interview with first author, Jerusalem, June 14, 1973.

Goldfarb, Robert. Letter to first author, Jerusalem, July 15, 1973.

Goldman, Esther (of *Jerusalem Post*). Letter to first author, Jerusalem, July 26, 1973.

Israel, Central Bureau of Statistics. 1975. Unpublished manuscript of 1972 national census. Jerusalem.

Israel, Ministry of Education and Culture. 1973. [Summary of results of matriculation examination, 1972]. Jerusalem. Mimeographed, March 1973. (In Hebrew)

Israel, Ministry of Interior, Film Control Board. [Annual statistical reports, 1968–72]. Mimeographed.

Letters from all Israeli universities to first author re English courses given and student registration, June 1973.

Starr, Laura, and Sissy Laster. 1971. Attitudes to English: A sociolinguistic case study. Seminar paper, Hebrew University.

Rosenbaum, Yehudit et al. 1977. English on Keren Kayemet Street. This vol., chap. 6. (Ms. 1974)

Weissbrot, E. Letter to first author, Jerusalem, June 28, 1973.

Chapter 5

The Maintenance of English in Ramat Eshkol

Fern Seckbach and *Robert L. Cooper*

In Israel there is a wide variety of immigrant groups which can be classified by the languages they speak as well as by geographic origins, ethnic groupings, socio-economic status, and so on. As each group passes through different stages of assimilation into or accommodation to the local society, one might assume that the use of Hebrew inside and outside of the home would increase. If the language of the immigrant group is one which offers benefits—social, educational, or commercial—to the native residents who have to learn it as a second language, the immigrant group might be assumed to give some emphasis to the maintenance of its valuable language even if this retards in some ways the complete social absorption of the individual. Parents of young children would have to decide whether to insist on continued usage of the mother tongue with their children or to let the children become totally engulfed by the local language. If parents were convinced of the value of language maintenance, they would have to find practical methods for maintaining, and even improving, their children's knowledge of their home tongue, particularly if there were little out-of-home provision for doing so.

English in Israel had not held any special position among its native speakers prior to the Six Day War of June 1967. In a study by an American sociologist, Harold Isaacs (1967), it was reported that English-speaking parents had great difficulties in raising their children in English. The children were reluctant to use English with outsiders, even in the interview situation. The native English-speaking population was quite small and the language was not needed as a lingua franca among Israelis because Hebrew served that purpose. Although

English is a language of international import, to the children of English-speaking immigrants it was just another immigrant language.

Following the Six Day War, Israel became more open to the influence of English (see Nadel and Fishman, this vol., chap. 4). There was more English-language printed matter available, more American movies and music gained public acceptance, and more visitors came from English-speaking countries (and elsewhere) using English as a lingua franca. The numbers of Americans coming to settle in Israel increased significantly, although figures are not available to tell us how many remained. As political and military ties with the United States became closer, the acceptance and recognition of English as being important grew.

Another factor which may have positively influenced the attitude of Israeli adults and children—specifically English-speaking children—toward the English language is the establishment of a local television station. Many programs for adults and children are in English, and the children who understand English are pleased to be able to comprehend the broadcasts. In fact, the children's programs encourage the young English-speaking audience to increase its vocabulary in order to get full benefit or enjoyment from television viewing. In view of the increased recognition among the Israeli public of the usefulness of English, we can ask whether immigrants from English-speaking countries are more successful in raising their children in English now than they were at the time of the Isaacs study (1961). In order to help answer this question, we studied the pattern of use of English by native speakers in Ramat Eshkol, a new neighborhood in Jerusalem.

Ramat Eshkol is an urban neighborhood planned by the government and located in the northeast section of Jerusalem. Its borders are well defined by a highway to the east and north, an older neighborhood to the south, and a shallow valley to the west. The land was not available for use by Israel prior to June 1967. Today the community has over 2,000 families. Buildings, whether individual houses or apartments, are quite close to each other, yet various apartment complexes are clustered around either common parking lots or malls. All building was initiated by the government, although the housing itself was built by a number of private contractors. Apartments were initially assigned for purchase through various savings programs (for Israelis) or by the Jewish Agency for Israel (for new immigrants). The first residents moved in at the end of 1969 and others came as the buildings were finished. The original distribution was to be something like 60% Israelis and 40% new immigrants.

The immigrants were assigned to buildings as space became available, so "pockets" of speakers of a given language are found, although the individuals themselves did not seek housing as a group nor ask to be put in any "ethnic colony." There are Israelis in the neighborhood who criticize English speakers for living near each other, but the choice was not in the hands of the immigrants, since the apartments were not originally available on the open market. Now people can buy into the buildings on a private basis, so shifts have taken place in the population and there is no longer any control on the ratio of natives to immigrants.

The purposes of the present survey, which was confined to English-speaking mothers, were to determine whether or not English is being maintained in the home and used in the street or at play, and to assess the Hebrew-language skills of English mother-tongue parents and children.

PROCEDURE

Forty-five respondents filled out a specially constructed fifty-six-item questionnaire. The answers to the questions provided us with biographical data and information on educational background (with emphasis on the study of Hebrew), current proficiency in and usage of Hebrew, and the languages used in various contexts. There were also a few items which inquired into the respondents' attitude towards the use of English and their desire to teach it to their children.

The respondents in this study were all English-speaking mothers with at least one child still living at home. All families had lived in Israel three years or more. All but five mothers were native speakers of English. The nonnative speakers were included because the exclusive language of their households prior to coming to Israel was English and the husbands were also found to be native speakers of English. Most of the nonnative English-speaking mothers learned English before entering school. In the cases where the husbands were not native speakers of English and the mothers were, the family was included in the survey if the husbands spoke English freely enough to allow the household to be English-speaking.

The topic itself seems to be of significant interest to the mothers in the neighborhood, who are well aware of the children's increased usage of Hebrew. Only one family approached refused to take the questionnaire and forty-five of the forty-seven who did take it returned it. Everyone had an opinion on the subject of language maintenance and was only too glad to share with the first author in impromptu discussions before or after filling out the form. From these conversations we learned that people realize that English is an important language and want their children to continue with it, yet they are unsure of the methods necessary for achieving this goal. For example, a special class was established for native English speakers in the fourth grade in one of the Ramat Eshkol schools on the initiative of the school. Yet parents were disappointed because poetry and literary appreciation were stressed, rather than basic skills, such as writing, spelling, and composition.

RESULTS

Biographical and Family Data

The majority of our respondents were born in English-speaking countries: twenty-one in the United States, nine in England, and five in Canada. The other ten were born in Europe. Even though only thirty-five of the respondents were born in

English-speaking countries, forty women claimed to be native speakers of English. There were two each who were native speakers of Yiddish and German and one native speaker of Dutch. The respondents ranged in age from twenty-six to fifty-seven, with the average being thirty-three. These women were between nineteen and fifty upon immigration to Israel, with the average age at entry being twenty-eight. The families surveyed had been in Israel from three to twenty years and more than half had been in the country between five and six years.

Although Ramat Eshkol itself was barely six years old at the time the survey was made, fourteen of the families had been living there for five years, and nineteen had resided in it for four years. Of the remaining twelve families, nine had been there for three years and three for only two years.

The respondents and their husbands were fairly well educated. The majority (55%) of women had B.A. degrees. Thirteen women only completed high school and nine more studied for some time in college but did not complete a degree. Seven women had Master's degrees. We found that nine of the husbands had completed high school or the equivalent, fourteen had a B.A., ten had a Master's degree, and twelve had doctorates.

Many of the respondents and their husbands had a wide exposure to Jewish education, but since the quality of Jewish education varies from place to place and from school to school, there is not necessarily a linear relationship between the number of years of Jewish education and the amount of Hebrew learned. There were three women who had no Jewish education. Twelve women and eight men studied only at the elementary level, sixteen women and six men continued through the secondary level, and eleven women and twenty-two men (including four rabbis) continued the study of Jewish subjects through college.

Every household had a mother, a father, and a number of children. Three families had grandmothers living with them, two of whom were English-speaking. Twenty of the families surveyed had three children living at home, twelve had four, eight had two, three had five, and two had one. The families' children ranged in age from only a few months to twenty-five years. Thirty-three children were of preschool age, fifty-four were in elementary school, forty-one were teenagers, and ten were between twenty-one and twenty-five.

Almost half of the women and all of the husbands were currently employed. The women were found in a variety of occupations, such as office work, teaching, librarianship, nursing, occupational therapy, and editing. The husbands were mostly in business or the free professions and several held managerial positions. There were also a number of teachers among them.

The main language used at work was English for fourteen women and eleven men and Hebrew for eight women and twenty-six men. The others used both languages. Some of the women, especially the editors and secretaries, were hired because of their knowledge of English. For only a few of the men was English a prerequisite for their jobs. The greater importance of English for the women's work is consistent with the results of a survey of language requirements specified in newspaper ads in the Hebrew press, in which English was specified

Table 5.1   Spoken Hebrew: Claims of proficiency
             and usage

Skill	Proficiency		Usage	
	No.	%	No.	%
Ask directions	45	100	40	88
Make purchases	44	98	41	91
Describe illness to physician	43	95	28	62
Discuss child's work with teacher	41	91	34	76
Socialize at party	34	76	23	50
Participate in PTA meeting	29	64	22	49
Discuss economics or politics	18	40	16	36

more often for women's jobs than for men's (see Cooper and Seckbach, this vol., chap. 8).

Knowledge and the Use of the Hebrew Language

Hebrew speech. Nineteen of the respondents had studied Hebrew as a spoken language prior to coming to Israel, in college or *ulpan*-style classes or in summer camps. Ten of these women felt no need to take additional Hebrew language classes after coming to Israel. Thirty-two of the women (71%) did attend some type of language class or *ulpan* in Israel and twenty-two of them considered it a worthwhile effort. When we combine those who studied spoken Hebrew abroad and in Israel we find that forty-two of the forty-five respondents studied Hebrew formally.

When asked to tell which tasks they could do and which they typically did do in Hebrew, almost everyone could do and actually did perform the most basic tasks, such as asking for directions or making daily purchases (see Table 5.1). There was a progressive decline in claimed proficiency and usage as the difficulty of the tasks increased, and in general the usage claims were lower than the proficiency claims. For example, while forty-three respondents (95%) said they could describe illnesses to a doctor in Hebrew, only twenty-eight actually did so (62%). Several individuals, in fact, used English-speaking physicians. The ability to socialize at a party seemed to represent a second stage of difficulty, with thirty-four respondents (76%) indicating that they could do this. But only twenty-three (50%) actually did it. The most difficult type of task, that of discussing economics or politics, was within the ability of only eighteen of the women (40%).

Hebrew composition. The same general situation existed with regard to Hebrew composition, except that fewer people claimed ability for each level of task and many fewer actually performed the tasks. In fact, eight of the women indicated that they could not do even the simplest written task. About three-fourths of the women said that they could compose the less demanding items

Table 5.2 Hebrew composition: Claims of proficiency and usage

	Proficiency		Usage	
Written item	No.	%	No.	%
Party invitations	35	78	19	42
Notes to the teacher	33	73	29	64
Ads for household help	33	73	13	29
Ads to sell items	32	71	14	31
Personal letters	30	67	19	42
Office memos	30	67	17	38
Job applications	24	53	11	24
Letters to editor of newspaper	16	36	9	20
Essays	14	31	5	11
Songs or poems	12	27	8	18

(ads, invitations), but only about one-third felt that they could compose the more difficult items (letters to the editor, essays), and only 20% or less claimed that they actually composed such items (see Table 5.2). There was one item in which the difference between claimed proficiency and usage was small: the category of "notes to the teacher," with 73% claiming proficiency and 64% actually claiming to write them. This is apparently an item which is an integral part of a mother's existence in Israel as elsewhere.

Hebrew reading habits. Respondents were asked about their Hebrew reading ability and habits in relation to newspapers, magazines, novels, nonfiction, and cookbooks or craftbooks. Again we found that many more people claimed the ability to read than actually did read any of the types of literature mentioned (see Table 5.3). The most commonly read items were the newspapers (76% claimed ability, 33% actually read them) and the cookbooks and craftbooks (60% claimed the ability, 31% indicated that they did read them).

Improvement in Hebrew. While thirty-four of the women claimed to want to improve their Hebrew, only ten were doing anything about it. The areas which

Table 5.3 Hebrew reading: Claims of proficiency and usage

	Proficiency		Usage	
Item	No.	%	No.	%
Newspapers	34	76	15	33
Cookbooks and craftbooks	27	60	14	31
Magazines	24	53	7	15
Nonfiction books	19	42	7	15
Novels	19	42	6	13

they felt needed improvement were speech, composition and reading comprehension, in that order.

Language used in public with children and friends. The respondents said that they used English in public with their English-speaking friends and two-thirds used English with their children in public. One-third of the women said they tried to use Hebrew in public with the children, although at home they used English with them. The majority of women (91%) were not self-conscious about using English in public. These results are consistent with the findings in a survey of language usage in public (Rosenbaum, Nadel, and Cooper, this vol., chap. 6)—that English was the foreign language most frequently heard and that while almost half of those heard speaking Hebrew spoke it with a foreign accent, most of those speaking English spoke it with a native accent.

Hebrew with nonnative English speakers. The respondents indicated that if their conversation partner spoke good English, the majority would prefer to use English as the medium of conversation. This was true whether or not the other party was a native Israeli. Hebrew was used most often when a third party who did not understand English was present, or when speaking on the telephone. Many respondents claimed that on the telephone they spoke Hebrew to individuals with whom they most usually spoke English when speaking face to face. Just why the telephone should induce people to use Hebrew is unclear. Perhaps telephone conversations tend to be more routinized and thus easier than face-to-face conversations.

General reading and listening habits: Library usage. Two-thirds of the women and about two-fifths of the husbands used an English-language library regularly. Many fewer used a Hebrew library—only 9% of the women and 33% of the men. The children of thirty families (66%) used a Hebrew-language library and those of twenty-seven families (60%) used an English library. The latter were, for the most part, children who read English prior to coming to Israel.

Reading material in English. In addition, almost all the women indicated that they tried to obtain English reading matter for themselves. There was much trading of reading matter between families. The most commonly read English-language publications were *Time, Newsweek, Jerusalem Post,* and a variety of women's magazines.

Television and radio. Forty-two of the families owned television sets and twenty-seven women (60%) indicated that they specifically watched for English-language television programs. Twenty-nine women (64%) listened regularly to English news broadcasts.

Language Used within the Family

Oral communication between parents and children was conducted exclusively in English in thirty-seven of the families surveyed. There were five families which consistently used Hebrew and in each case the father was not a native speaker of English (see Table 5.4). When the children spoke to each other, the situation was

Table 5.4   Languages spoken within the family

Speaker-addressee	English No.	English %	Hebrew No.	Hebrew %	English and Hebrew No.	English and Hebrew %
Parent to parent	41	91	4	9	0	0
Mother to child	39	87	4	9	2	4
Father to child	38	84	5	11	2	4
Child to mother	38	84	5	11	2	4
Child to father	34	75	9	20	2	4
Child to child	20	44	16	35	9	20

Table 5.5   Languages used within the family for written messages

Writer-addressee	English No.	English %	Hebrew No.	Hebrew %	English and Hebrew No.	English and Hebrew %
Parent to parent	40	89	4	9	1	2
Mother to child	25	55	10	22	5	11
Father to child	25	55	13	29	1	2
Children to parents	19	42	15	33	6	13
Child to child	11	24	17	38	6	13

somewhat different. Only in twenty families (44%) did the siblings use English with each other; in sixteen families (35%) Hebrew was exclusively used between the children. There were nine families in which the children used both Hebrew and English. The indication is that the children were more comfortable in Hebrew than their parents even though the children had grown up in an English-speaking home.

English was still the predominant choice for written messages between parents and children and between the parents themselves but not as strongly as with speaking (see Table 5.5). Twenty-five mothers said they and their husbands left messages in English and about half that number said they used Hebrew. When the children left messages for the parents it was about as likely to be in one language as the other. The written messages the children left for each other were most often in Hebrew. It is important to note that it was mostly older children who wrote English, and these were the ones who learned to do so abroad.

The respondents indicated that even if the language of the house was English, a knock on the door was most usually answered by a Hebrew reply; if no response was heard, the inquiry was likely to be repeated in the other language.

It was stated by the mothers of 44% of the families that when their children have English-speaking friends visiting they most often play in Hebrew. In the 26% of the families where English was indicated as the language of play, some mothers noted that when they leave the room the children switch to Hebrew.

The impact of the English-speaking family on the neighbors. Non-English-speaking families are often interested in help from their English-speaking neighbors in the form of translations of words or language lessons. The respondents who lived in concentrated English-speaking areas had less opportunity to influence or aid their neighbors. The respondents who had fewer English-speaking neighbors were called upon rather frequently for translations of words and passages.

The nature of the children's English. More than half the mothers felt that their children's English was not as good as that used by children of the same age in English-speaking countries. The differences were noticeable to the mothers in vocabulary, pronunciation and accent, self-expression, and grammar. Few mothers mentioned the fact that the children tend to mix words of one language with the other in the same utterance and that some of the resulting statements are almost unintelligible to someone who does not know both Hebrew and English.

The children in about half of the families came to Israel already knowing how to read English and they are the ones who continued to read it for pleasure. However, only about half of them were felt to write English correctly.

While only thirteen families (28%) had their children study English in private lessons, it would be improper to conclude that the others were not interested in having their children learn more English. Thirty-six mothers (78%) said that if free lessons were provided after school they would have their children attend. The issue seems to be clearly one of economics.

Respondents' attitudes toward Hebrew, English, and English usage. The majority of women (64%) felt that they would be using the same amount of English in Ramat Eshkol in five years' time, although 40% indicated that the quality of their English had already deteriorated. Many felt that they more frequently had to grope for the right word in English.

About half the women belonged to organizations which conduct their meetings in English. Since all the groups sponsor a predominant number of chapters whose meetings are conducted in Hebrew, we see that many respondents were still happier to be surrounded by the more familiar language, even if this somewhat limited their integration into these organizations.

The mothers of small children answered in a ratio of two to one that they would not care if a daily babysitter could not speak English (twenty-four versus twelve). Apparently the parents felt that they could do an adequate job of transmitting the language to the children.

The respondents felt that spoken Hebrew was necessary for being a "good Israeli" (57%) and for being an "integral part of the neighborhood" (66%), somewhat less necessary for being a good parent (37%), and not necessary for being a "good Jew" (10%). This can perhaps be interpreted as meaning that Hebrew is more essential for public goals and less necessary for the home.

When asked if they would be disappointed if their grandchildren did not speak English natively, twice as many women said no as said yes, twenty-six to thirteen. The reasons given for not feeling disappointed were that the respondents would be proud to know that their offspring were well integrated as Israelis or that they knew that English could be learned well as a second language. Others said that it would only be natural for Israeli-born children of Israeli parents to be native speakers of Hebrew.

Those who would prefer native English-speaking grandchildren offered personal reasons, such as their own potential lack of ability to communicate with the grandchildren (15%), or more universal reasons, such as the fact that English is and remains an important language even to someone outside of English-speaking countries and is an asset in education and business and for the broadening of one's views (70%).

Social contexts. We found that only seventeen families (34%) were frequently visited by native Israelis and those families included the couples in which the husband was Israeli and the majority of the long-term residents among our respondents. If our respondents had little social contact with native Israelis there may have been lessened incentive for them to improve their Hebrew. Conversely, lack of a good knowledge of Hebrew may limit one's social contacts with Israelis. However, many Israelis speak good English, and three-fourths of the respondents claimed to know enough Hebrew to socialize at a party. Thus one might have expected more social contacts between immigrants and Israelies than we found.

Length of stay in Israel and Hebrew usage. When we divide our respondents into three groups according to their length of stay in Israel—Group I (three to four years): ten respondents; Group II (five to six years): twenty-five respondents; Group III (over six years): ten respondents—we find a gradual increase from group to group in claimed proficiency and usage of spoken and written Hebrew. The longer one is in the country, the more his skills improve or the more they are needed and demand improvement. The same applies to reading Hebrew, since 10% of Group I, 40% of Group II, and 60% of Group III read Hebrew publications regularly. Correspondingly, the longer the families had lived in Israel, the more the children used Hebrew among themselves at home.

DISCUSSION

How does the language behavior of the English speakers in this study compare to that of other immigrant groups? Some broad comparisons can be made to the study by Hofman and Fisherman (1972) in which the language maintenance of Rumanian immigrants was described. Only 7% of the Rumanians had a Hebrew education abroad compared to 95% of our respondents. Nevertheless, in the work sphere it was found that 70% of the Rumanians used Hebrew at work, while for our English speakers only 17% of the women (and 37% of husbands and wives) used Hebrew as the main language at work. While 40% of the long-time resident Rumanian-speaking mothers had shifted to Hebrew as their principal language, there was almost no shift to Hebrew among the English-speaking mothers. It was found that 25% of the Rumanians preferred Hebrew newspapers. Of the English-speaking mothers, 33% read Hebrew newspapers regularly, although we do not know which paper they preferred.

With regard to maintenance, we find that both Rumanian and English continued to be used in the home, but it was English which was also preserved in public. Both groups preferred to read literature in their own languages and would continue to do so as long as material is easily obtainable. Radio broadcasts in Rumanian were listened to by 40% of the respondents, and we found that 64% of the English-speaking mothers continued to listen to the English news broadcasts.

From the above comparisons, it seems that the course which the two languages follow is not the same. Part of the answer must lie in the fact that English is viewed as more valuable and the speakers are aware of it. Many of the women felt that they would be doing their children a disservice if they let their English usage slip away, and they tried to prevent that from happening. They were happy to see their children integrated into the local society, yet they were not pleased if the children's use of English or interest in English-language skills declined.

In addition, one must remember that many of the English-speaking women still had strong, positive attachments to the countries they voluntarily left. Their language, English, was a strong link to that country and served as a symbol of positive experiences in the past which the women did not wish to relinquish.

Almost all of the English-speaking mothers had studied Hebrew and several had become quite proficient in it, yet there was no household with a native English-speaking father in which the mother indicated a willingness to forego English usage. Only in homes with Israeli fathers was a shift to Hebrew obvious. As long as English remains useful and necessary in Israel for economics and education, there is no reason to believe that it will be displaced in the English-speaking households of Ramat Eshkol. As far as the children's usage of Hebrew and English is concerned, however, our data suggest that English will not be maintained as the children's principal language once they set up their own households. In spite of its importance to Israelis, English appears to be just another immigrant language to the children of English-speaking immigrants.

REFERENCES

Cooper, Robert L., and Fern Seckbach. 1977. Economic incentives for the learning of a
    language of wider communication: A case study. This vol., chap. 8.
Hofman, John E., and Haya Fisherman. 1972. Language shift and language maintenance in
    Israel. In *Advances in the Sociology of Language*, edited by Joshua A. Fishman.
    Vol. 2. The Hague: Mouton. Pp. 342-364.
Isaacs, Harold 1967. *American Jews in Israel*. New York: J. Day Co.
Nadel, Elizabeth, and Joshua A. Fishman. 1977. English in Israel: A sociolinguistic study.
    This vol., chap. 4.
Rosenbaum, Yehudit; Elizabeth Nadel; and Robert L. Cooper. 1977. English on Keren
    Kayemet Street. This vol., chap. 6.

Chapter 6

English on Keren Kayemet Street

Yehudit Rosenbaum, Elizabeth Nadel,
Robert L. Cooper and *Joshua A. Fishman*

By observing the proficiency, usage, and attitudes of urban dwellers with respect to a single language or language variety, confining the initial investigation, perhaps, to one or two restricted social contexts, a beginning can be made in disentangling the complex web of interrelationships which exist between urban linguistic and social organization. This chapter reports the results of one such attempt. The language was English, the city was Jerusalem, and the social contexts were set inside the shops and offices and outside on the sidewalks of a busy street: Keren Kayemet Street.

The linguistic situation of Jerusalem is exceedingly complex. Among the Jewish population, a substantial proportion are functionally bilingual, speaking at least two languages every day, and many speak Hebrew as a second language.[1] Continued immigration to Israel from the Jewish diaspora promotes linguistic diversity among the Jewish population of the city. Among the non-Jewish population, who make up about one-third of the city's population, Arabic is the chief language of everyday life. However, many of the non-Jewish population know Hebrew, just as many of the Jewish population, a large number of whom immigrated from Muslim countries, know Arabic.

In this complex linguistic situation, English has a special place. It is at the same time a language of wider communication, a language with important local scientific and technological uses, and the mother tongue of a small group of immigrants who come from English-speaking countries. It is the language associated with American Jewry, a group which has extended important material and moral

The authors are grateful to Andrew D. Cohen and Fanny Eliash for their criticisms of an earlier version of this paper.

179

support to Israel. In addition, all public school students study English as a foreign language, beginning in the fifth grade. It is the foreign language most frequently specified by job requirements (Cooper and Seckbach, this vol., chap. 8). Finally, it is the language most closely associated with tourism from abroad.

The special place which English occupies in Israel can be seen from as yet unpublished data collected by the Central Bureau of Statistics, which show that whereas about 9% of the Jewish population aged fourteen and above in 1972 claimed to use English every day, less than 12% of these claimed to use it as their principal language. Of all foreign languages claimed to be in daily use, in fact, English had the smallest percentage claiming it as a principal language. Thus, when English is used by Israelis, it must be used mainly for specialized functions. Among the specialized roles which languages of wider communication typically fill is that of lingua franca, i.e., a medium of communication between persons who do not share the same mother tongue (Greenberg 1965). While English undoubtedly serves this function between Israelis and foreigners, it is not clear to what extent it is used as a lingua franca between Israelis themselves. Thus, one question we can ask about the use of English in Israeli urban settings is the extent to which it serves as a lingua franca between Israelis.

Another question we can ask is the extent to which Israelis in urban settings are able to use English as a lingua franca. While English is universally taught in Israel, it is far from universally known there. Mailmen, for example, sometimes seem to have trouble correctly delivering mail with addresses written in Roman script, and complaints are sometimes seen in the press about the standard of high school students' English attainment. In a sample survey of the urban Jewish population, 24% of persons aged eighteen or more claimed to be able to speak, read, and write English (see Nadel and Fishman, this vol., chap. 4). However, native-born Israelis were almost twice as likely to claim competence in English as the average respondent, and younger persons were more likely to claim English than older persons. Inasmuch as 84% of the respondents with eleven or more years of schooling claimed proficiency in English, and inasmuch as younger and native-born Israelis are more likely than immigrants and older persons to have had the opportunity to study English in school, it appeared that in Israel knowledge of English is largely a function of education. Nonetheless, we do not know the actual (as distinguished from self-reported) English proficiency of these respondents. To what extent, for example, could they use English to give directions to tourists on the street?

A third question which can be asked about the use of English in urban settings is the extent to which Israelis are favorably disposed to foreigners who attempt to use it as a lingua franca. Are Israelis resistant to the use of English as a lingua franca by foreigners? Are they surprised by its use?

A fourth question concerns the extent to which English is used in public. Are immigrants who speak it natively reluctant to use it in public? To what extent is English heard in public and to what extent is it encountered in public signs?

We can summarize the questions which motivated our collection of data in the urban context of Keren Kayemet Street as follows:

1. To what extent is English used as a lingua franca between Israelis?
2. To what extent can Israelis use English as a language of wider communication in the specific context of giving directions to tourists?
3. To what extent do Israelis accept being addressed in English by foreigners?
4. To what extent is English encountered in public?

Keren Kayemet Street, which is less than a kilometer long, runs from King George Street, a heavily trafficked thoroughfare, to an old, quiet, religiously observant neighborhood perched on a bluff with a magnificent view of Israel's parliament building. For more than half its length, Keren Kayemet is a narrow, winding, busy street, and it is this section of the street that was studied. Here the street contains almost all of the stores and services needed by the people who live within its immediate vicinity as well as several institutions which serve a wider public. It has about thirty shops, including grocery stores, kiosks, and service establishments such as those of an electrician and a barber; three restaurants; ten private offices, such as those of attorneys and physicians; and nine government offices, including a post office. Most of the shops and service establishments are small enough to be adequately served by only one or two shopkeepers or clerks at any one time, and most are on the ground floor of small, three- or four-story apartment houses. Near the commercial center of town, Keren Kayemet Street is surrounded by a heterogeneous collection of neighborhoods, which vary with respect to ethnic origin, degree of religious observance, and economic status. It is not, however, representative of all of Jerusalem's shopping streets. First of all, it is in West (Jewish) Jerusalem. Second, it runs along the edge of a prosperous neighborhood, characterized by a relatively high proportion of persons of European background and by a relatively low proportion of new immigrants. Thus the proportion of pedestrians and shoppers on this street who can use English is likely to be higher than in other parts of Jerusalem or in other Israeli towns. Keren Kayemet Street, then, is likely to yield an upper limit to our estimate of the extent to which English serves as a lingua franca between Israelis and to our estimate of the extent to which English serves as a lingua franca between Israelis and to our estimate of the extent to which it can be used in urban settings. While not completely representative, Keren Kayemet Street is clearly an urban microcosm and thus an excellent site for the study of the urban interpenetration of linguistic and social structure.

PROCEDURE

Data collection proceeded via the "measurement of outcroppings" (Webb, Campbell, Schwartz, and Sechrest 1966), whereby available techniques are applied to the available points of observation. If different types of method, each with its own sources of error, yield overlapping data, the investigator can be more confident in the validity of his results. Accordingly, four different methods of data collection were employed:

1. *Transaction counts* (Bender, Cooper, and Ferguson 1972), by which the number of persons heard speaking in each of various languages was counted
2. *Sign counts*, by which the degree of English used in public signs was determined
3. *Planted encounters*, by which English proficiency as well as attitudes to the public use of English were naturally and anonymously elicited
4. *Interviews*, by which shopkeepers were directly questioned about their language usage and proficiency and their attitudes toward the use of English on Keren Kayemet Street.

All field work was carried out by the first two authors during May and June of 1973. The four methods of data collection were initiated and were completed in the order listed, although there was some overlapping of the periods in which they were carried out. No interviews were attempted until the first three procedures had been completed.

Transaction Counts

The primary purpose of the transaction-count procedure was to record the percentage of persons heard using English and the characteristics of the persons using it. The observers made the transaction counts independently during a three-week period on various days, hours, and locations on the street. Some observations were made from a parked car, which was never kept in the same location for more than thirty minutes. Other observations were made as an observer walked up and down the street and in and out of the shops, restaurants, and offices that line it.

In all, over 900 persons were overheard talking ($N = 936$). About three-fourths were overheard as they were walking or standing on the sidewalk. The distribution of locations at which the remaining persons were overheard was as follows: about 9% in restaurants (some of which were at sidewalk tables), about 8% in the post office, about 3% in grocery stores, about 2% at kiosks (small, self-standing structures at which ready-to-eat foods and other items of very low cost are sold), and about 1.5% at service establishments and other stores. The reasons for the smaller percentages of persons overheard inside than outside the establishments which line the street were: (a) the practical difficulty of conducting observations at small enterprises without arousing the suspicion of the shopkeepers and (b) the fact that there were typically more interactions taking place outside the establishments than inside them at any one time.

With the exception of the post office and restaurants, where an observer could unobtrusively watch the same speakers for relatively long streteches of time, the amount of speech overheard in most interactions was quite brief, usually not more than a sentence or two and often less than that. Thus the opportunity to observe language switching or bilingual conversations was small. Typically, only one person in an interaction was overheard talking. Therefore the number of interactions observed was close to that of the number of speakers overheard.

For each of the speakers overheard, three classes of observation were recorded: (1) situational characteristics (judged relationship between the speaker and his interlocutor, location, day of the week, time of day); (2) demographic characteristics (sex, approximate age, judged ethnic origin, and judged degree of religious observance); and (3) linguistic characteristics (language used and foreign accent in the language used if the language was English or Hebrew).[2] Because most of these characteristics were impressionistically judged, it must be remembered that, for example, a judgment that a speaker was young and not religiously observant meant that the speaker *appeared* this way to the observer.

The transaction-count observations were recorded on sheets designed to be minimally obtrusive. On each sheet there was a place for recording information for twenty speakers, ten on each side. An observation sheet could be folded so that it could be kept in a pocket when not in use. When folded, it looked like a shopping list.

Sign Counts

For each of the fifty establishments which displayed a sign identifying the name of the establishment and the type of goods or services it offers, the prominence of Roman script on the sign was determined. Signs were rated on a three-point scale: no Roman script; some Roman script, but Hebrew script dominant; both Roman and Hebrew script with about equal prominence for each. (No signs employing only Roman script were found.) Inasmuch as virtually all words written in Roman script were English words (except, of course, for proper names), Roman script in effect represented English. Scripts other than Hebrew and Roman were not encountered on the identifying signs.

Planted Encounters

Like the transaction- and sign-count procedures, the planted encounter was a non-reactive device (Webb, Campbell, Schwartz, and Sechrest 1966) designed to avoid the biases implicit in situations in which the respondent or subject knows that he is participating in an investigation. Unlike the first two techniques, which required only that the observer act as a passive recording agent, the planted encounters required the observers to actively intervene in the observational process by creating the situations the outcome of which was described.

One purpose of the planted encounters was to determine the English proficiency of the "man on the street" and of the "man behind the counter." Whereas the transaction-count procedure provided a measure of *actual* usage of English, the planted encounters provided a measure of the respondents' *ability* to use English. The second purpose of the planted encounters was to determine the attitudes of respondents toward the use of English in the public context of the street and of the establishments along the street.

In the planted encounter, each observer, acting alone, initiated transactions in English with randomly chosen persons. Each observer walked from one end of the street to the other and stopped every tenth adult (persons who appeared to be at least of secondary-school age), except people who were personally known to her. Half of the persons stopped were asked (in English) "How can I get to the Old City?" The Old City is a few kilometers away from Keren Kayemet Street. The other half were asked (in English) "Can you tell me where I can find this address?" and were then presented with a slip of paper with an address in English. Half of the slips of paper contained the name and address of the Ministry of Tourism, which is a few blocks away from Keren Kayemet Street, and the other half contained the name and address of a youth hostel on the other side of town. Half the slips of paper to each address were typewritten and the other half were handwritten. If the person understood the first request for help with a written address, he was also asked for help with a second written address. The order of presentation of addresses and the order of presentation of typed versus handwritten addresses were counterbalanced.

The observers who staged the encounters are both women in their twenties. They tried insofar as possible to dress and to behave similarly during their independently staged encounters. The outstanding difference between them, from a methodological point of view is linguistic. One is a native speaker of English, the other speaks English with a foreign accent. This difference, of course, could be exploited as an independent variable.

For each encounter, the same situational and demographic characteristics were noted as for the transaction count. In addition, the following were noted: the characteristics of the question (oral or written, and if written, the order in which the different types of address were presented); the identity of the initiator (native English speaker or not); and the reaction of the person encountered (degree of helpfulness exhibited; the language, if any, in which a response was made; and if the response was in English, fluency and degree of foreign accent in English). Like the notations for the transaction counts, the notations for the planted encounters were made unobtrusively.

The planted encounters were staged over a three-week period on different days of the week and at different times of the day. There were 265 such encounters staged, about half of which employed written addresses. In addition to the planted encounters in which directions were asked, a small group of encounters were staged inside some of the establishments along the street. In seventeen of the retail enterprises, one or the other of the observers asked the shopkeeper in English for the price of an item carried in stock. The same information was noted for these encounters as for the encounters in which directions were asked.

Interviews with Shopkeepers

In twenty-four of the retail establishments, interviews were held with a shopkeeper. In almost all cases, the person interviewed was male and was the owner or manager of the shop. Whereas the transaction counts and planted encounters had been carried out by individual observers, the interviews were carried out by both observers together, acting as a team. The interviews were based on a questionnaire, which included open-ended questions about the respondent's proficiency in various languages, his use of English at work, his estimate as to the amount of English spoken in his store and on the street, and his attitude toward the use of English by Hebrew-speaking customers in his shop. The interviews, which were carried out in Hebrew, typically lasted for about ten minutes.

RESULTS

The presentation of the results is organized in terms of the four data-gathering procedures which were employed: transaction count, sign count, planted encounter, and interview.

Transaction Counts

Hebrew was, of course, the language most frequently overheard, but it was by no means the only language heard. Over one-quarter of the speakers employed a language other than Hebrew. Of the non-Hebrew languages, by far the most frequently heard was English, which was used by 14% of the speakers. The next two most frequently heard non-Hebrew languages were used only about 3% (German) and 2% (Yiddish) of the time. The distribution of languages overheard is summarized in Table 6.1.

Table 6.1 Languages overheard on Keren Kayemet Street

			Persons			
	Outside		*Inside*		*Total*	
Language	*No.*	*%*	*No.*	*%*	*No.*	*%*
Hebrew	546	76.2	133	60.2	679	72.5
English	81	11.2	42	19.0	123	14.1
German	11	1.5	12	5.4	23	2.5
Yiddish	14	1.9	3	1.3	17	1.8
Bilingual	16	2.2	18	8.1	34	3.6
Other	47	7.0	13	6.0	60	5.4
Total	715	100.0	221	100.0	936	100.0

Most (85%) of the persons heard using English were native speakers of English, whereas only a little more than half (55%) of the speakers who were heard using Hebrew were native speakers of Hebrew. While some of the native speakers of English were presumably tourists or new immigrants who knew little Hebrew, a more likely explanation for the relatively large proportion of transactions heard in English lies in the status of English (and of Americans) compared to that of other non-Hebrew languages (and of other immigrant groups). Considerations of relative status would account for the small proportion of transactions heard in Yiddish (2%) and Arabic (1%), languages which are spoken natively by more Israelis than any other non-Hebrew language but which are not held in particularly high esteem by Israelis. In a study reported by Herman (1961), for example, Israeli high school students, asked to rate languages in terms of prestige, gave the highest ratings to Hebrew and English and substantially lower ratings to Arabic and Yiddish. Similarly, in an extensive study of Israeli high school students' language attitudes, Yiddish and Arabic usually received less favorable ratings than the other four languages studied—English, French, Hebrew, and Russian (Cooper and Fishman, this vol., chap. 11). While it can be argued that the proportion of persons able to speak Arabic and Yiddish is likely to be lower on Keren Kayemet Street than elsewhere, it is unlikely to be as low as the proportions heard using them. Among the shopkeepers interviewed, for example, Yiddish and Arabic were the languages most frequently claimed as mother tongues. Herman hypothesizes that when a language provides a cue to low status and when a person does not wish to be so identified, he is less likely to speak that language in public settings. The results of the present study are clearly consistent with this hypothesis.

The persons heard speaking English did not seem different from the other observed speakers with respect to age and degree of religious observance. Since most of the English speakers were native speakers of English, almost all were judged to be Westerners, but about one-quarter of the total sample were judged to be Easterners. One other difference between the English speakers and the total sample was noted: a greater proportion of women was found among the English speakers (52%) than among the total sample (48%). Since English was more likely to have been spoken by native speakers than was Hebrew, it is tempting to speculate that native speakers of English are slightly less likely to learn Hebrew if they are female and to explain such a difference on the hypothesized grounds that occupational and religious obligations exert more pressure on men than on women to learn Hebrew. However, such speculations are suggested by a slender difference and remain to be substantiated by future research.

About the same percentage of transactions in English were overheard by each observer and on each day of the week and hour of the day at which observations were made. Did the location of the interaction or the relationship between the speakers make a difference with respect to the use of English? Both location and relationship did make a difference. The percentage of persons overheard in English was greater inside the street's establishments (19%) than outside on the street (11%). This suggests that the proportion of native speakers of English was greater among the establishments' clientele than among the passersby on the street, inasmuch as most speakers of English were native speakers.

Within the establishments themselves, the percentage of customers talking to other customers in English (37%) was almost five times as great as the percentage of customers and shopkeepers talking to each other in English (8%). Inasmuch as most of the shopkeepers could speak some English and inasmuch as the proportion of customers using English with shopkeepers was quite small, it appears that English was not used as a lingua franca, but rather as a medium for within-group communication. Thus, it appears that most native speakers of English observed in the street's establishments knew enough Hebrew to communicate with the shopkeepers, chose Hebrew rather than English to talk to them, and reserved English for use with other native speakers of their mother tongue. The idea that customers who can speak both English and Hebrew will choose English for use with shopkeepers in order to obtain better service is not at all supported by the data collected here. Less English was used between customers and shopkeepers than the English proficiency of either would lead one to predict. Differences were observed in the percentage of persons using English in the different types of establishment on the street. The smallest percentage was observed in shops (10%) and the largest percentage was observed in restaurants (31%). These differences, however, were primarily a function of differences in the percentage of customer-customer interactions found in the different types of enterprise. Whereas about two-thirds of the speakers in restaurants were customers talking to other customers, only one-fifth of the speakers in shops were so characterized. Inasmuch as English inside enterprises was used mostly between customers, the percentage of persons observed using English was larger in restaurants than in the shops. Differences between the proportions of customer-customer interactions in English found in the different types of establishment were fairly small, considering the relatively small number of cases involved. The proportion of speakers using English in different types of establishments according to the relationships between speakers is presented in Table 6.2.

Sign Counts

Since English was used by a relatively small proportion of the speakers overheard on Keren Kayemet Street, one might have expected to find little English on the signs identifying the street's shops and offices. This was not the case, however, as can be seen in Table 6.3, which summarizes the use of Roman and Hebrew script on the signs. Roman and Hebrew script were equally prominent on about one-third of the establishments' identifying signs and on only one-third was there no Roman script at all. The signs on the grocery stores were in Hebrew only, whereas less than one-third of the other stores used Hebrew-only signs. Inasmuch as the latter sell merchandise or services which have a higher per-unit cost, the use of Roman script (which in almost all cases was English) on the identifying signs may indicate an attempt to exploit the snob appeal of English. The signs of private offices tended to use Roman script more than the signs of government offices. Three-fifths of the former used signs in which Roman and Hebrew script were

Table 6.2 The use of English overheard inside Keren Kayemet Street's establishments

| | Transactions | | | | | | | | |
| | Customer-customer | | Customer-shopkeeper | | Shopkeeper-shopkeeper | | Total | | |
Location	Total number	% in English	Total number	% in English	Total number	% in English	Number	% in English
Shops	12	50.0	37	0.0	12	0.0	61	10.0
Post office	34	23.6	36	5.6	7	0.0	77	13.0
Restaurants	56	42.9	17	11.8	10	0.0	83	31.4
Total	102	37.3	90	7.6	29	0.0	221	19.0

Table 6.3 The use of Roman script on the identifying signs of Keren Kayemet Street's establishments

| | Prominence of Roman script[a] | | | | | | | |
| | Equal to Hebrew script | | Some, but less than Hebrew script | | No Roman script | | Total | |
Establishment	No.	%	No.	%	No.	%	No.	%
Grocery stores and kiosks	–		–	–	6	100.0	6	100.0
Shops offering services	1	20.0	2	40.0	2	40.0	5	100.0
Other shops	8	47.0	4	23.6	5	29.4	17	100.0
Restaurants	1	33.3	1	33.3	1	33.3	3	100.0
Public offices	1	11.1	5	55.5	3	33.3	9	100.0
Private offices	6	60.0	4	40.0	–	–	10	100.0
Total	17	34.0	16	32.0	17	34.0	50	100.0

[a]No signs employing only Roman script were found.

equally prominent, whereas this was true for only one of nine government offices.[3] While one-third of the government offices used Hebrew-only signs, none of the private offices did so. The different use of Roman script by public and private offices may be in part a function of the snob appeal of English, but it probably also reflects the gap between the official language policy, which was set at the independence of the State and which stresses the dominance of the national language, and the much higher tolerance towards foreign languages in general and English in particular that is expected by the general public today. Thus English could be seen as well as heard on Keren Kayemet Street, and it was relatively more seen than it was heard.

Planted Encounters

Since English was used by only a small proportion of the speakers who were overheard, would the proportion of people who were able to use English be similarly small? The opposite was true. About three-fourths of the persons who were stopped for directions appeared to understand the English which the investigators used, and about the same proportion used at least some English in their replies. Eleven percent of the people who were stopped proved to be native speakers of English (the proportion of persons on the street who were observed, via the transaction-count procedure, speaking English natively was the same), and about 50% spoke accented but fluent English. Of those who were asked for help in finding a written address, a slightly smaller proportion (70%) appeared able to read the address. There were no meaningful differences between responses to the typed and handwritten addresses or to the two different addresses or to the order in which they were presented. Among the shopkeepers with whom planted encounters were staged, the proportion who appeared able to understand the question and who spoke at least some English in reply was about the same as for the pedestrians outside. No significant differences were associated with the day of the week or the time of day the encounter was staged. Also, no difference was associated with the identity of the questioner. That is to say, the English proficiency observed did not appear to be a function of whether or not the initiator of the planted encounter was a native speaker of English.

What characteristics distinguished those whose English proficiency was good from those whose English proficiency was poor? To answer this question, three proficiency criterion scores were computed and then correlated with several demographic variables. The criterion variables were each composed of a set of subscores which had been converted to z-scores. The criterion scores and their component subscores were as follows: *oral proficiency*—degree of comprehension of the investigator's speech, degree of spoken proficiency, and whether or not the person replied that he knew no English; *reading comprehension*—degree of understanding of the written address and degree of confidence displayed in reading it; and *general proficiency*—oral proficiency and written proficiency as previously indicated.[4] It may be noted in passing that the correlation between the oral and written criterion scores was quite high ($r = 0.84$), which suggests that the criterion scores were stable ones.

The best single predictors of English proficiency were those characterizing ethnic origin. Persons characterized as Westerners tended to have higher scores than persons characterized as Easterners. Correlations between membership in each of these two groups (each scored as a separate variable) and the criterion variables ranged from 0.39 to 0.61. There was a slight tendency for men to have greater proficiency scores than women, with correlations from −0.15 to −0.18 between sex (female) and the criterion variables. In general, non-religiously observant persons tended to be better in English than those characterized as religiously observant, but again the relationship was slight, with correlations from 0.21 to 0.26. Age proved to have no relationship substantial with the criterion variables. The multiple correlations between demographic variables and each of the criterion variables turned out to be little better than the best zero-order coefficients. With ten predictors, the multuple correlations were 0.54, 0.67, and 0.66 for oral, written, and total English proficiency scores, respectively. The best zero-order correlations with these criteria were 0.44, 0.61, and 0.60, respectively.

Consistent with the conclusion by Nadel and Fishman (this vol., chap. 4) that English proficiency is primarily a function of educational opportunity, educational differences appear to underlie these correlations. Westerners and men tend to have greater educational opportunity and thus greater opportunity to learn English through formal instruction than do Easterners and women. The tendency for non-religiously observant persons to have higher proficiency scores can also be explained, at least in part, by educational differences, since a secular education is likely to give more attention to English than a religious one. The better proficiency of the non-religiously observant may also be due to greater participation in the modern, secular, and Western-oriented sectors of society, which tend to demand more knowledge of English than do the more traditional sectors. The correlations between English proficiency ratings and demographic ratings can be seen in Table 6.4.

What reaction did people display toward being addressed in English? Almost no one seemed surprised to find someone asking for directions in English, and this was true whether or not the questioner was a native speaker of English. Most people tried to be helpful, with about four-fifths showing positive or very positive attitudes. Only three persons showed signs of rejection. Most of the people addressed appeared anxious to display their knowledge of English. Most people probably considered the questioners to be tourists, as the questions asked were ones likely to be asked by a tourist. (When the questioners became involved in longer conversations and said that they were new immigrants, a frequent reaction was "Don't you know any Hebrew?") Favorableness of attitude, as judged by the questioners, was related to English proficiency scores. Those with greater proficiency tended to show more favorable attitudes, with correlations between attitude ratings and the proficiency criteria ranging from 0.47 to 0.66.

Table 6.4   Correlations between demographic variables
and English criterion scores

Demographic variable[a]	Correlation with criterion		
	Oral (N = 282)	Written (N = 133)	Total (N = 133)
Ethnicity			
Eastern	−.44	−.61	−.60
Western	.39	.56	.55
Non-Jewish	−.02	−.09	−.07
Religiosity: secular	.27	.21	.26
Age			
Old (65 +)	−.13	−.03	−.05
Middle-aged (30–64)	.08	.05	.01
Young (20–29)	.04	−.05	.03
High school (15–19)	−.07	.05	−.02
Sex: female	−.15	−.17	−.18

[a]Each demographic variable was scored dichotomously.

Interviews

Only three of the twenty-four shopkeepers claimed to speak Hebrew as their first language, the largest numbers claiming Yiddish (eight) and Arabic (six) as mother tongues. The shopkeepers were a multilingual group; the average shopkeeper claimed to be able to speak 3.4 languages including his mother tongue. Next to Hebrew, English was the language in which the shopkeepers most often claimed some proficiency, followed by Yiddish and Arabic. In most cases, if English was claimed, it was the language mentioned next after Hebrew.

Although only one shopkeeper spoke English natively, almost 80% claimed to be able to understand at least some English, but 16% claimed only to be able to understand a little. The proportion who claimed literacy skills was much lower. Only about one-third said they could read at least a little in an English newspaper and only about one-fifth claimed to be able to write letters in English.

Inasmuch as planted encounters had been staged with seventeen of the twenty-four shopkeepers who were subsequently interviewed, it was possible to correlate the shopkeepers' self-reported English proficiency with the judgment of their proficiency made earlier by the observers. The coefficients were 0.60 for the ability to understand and 0.64 for speaking ability. Considering the brevity of the planted encounter procedure, the subjective nature of the proficiency ratings, and the fact that understanding and speaking were only two subscores (combined with a third to form the oral proficiency criterion score), the coefficients between self-reported and observed proficiency are substantial.

The shopkeepers' perception of the role of English on Keren Kayemet Street was generally in accordance with the findings of the transaction-count procedure. In answer to the question about the percentage of customers who speak to them in English, all but one said that at least some of their customers speak English to them. More than half said that English is spoken to them more than any other language except Hebrew. (The language cited next most frequently, German, was mentioned by only two shopkeepers.) Also, about half thought that English was the language, next to Hebrew, most heard on the street. (The language cited next most frequently, again German, was mentioned by only three shopkeepers.)

When asked if they thought some of their customers use English with them when in fact the customers know Hebrew, almost half of the shopkeepers said yes. Only one of those who thought so expressed a negative opinion toward such customers. If customers use English when they know Hebrew, the status of the former language was typically not invoked as an explanation. On the contrary, most of those who believed that customers do *not* use English if they know Hebrew cited spontaneously either Hebrew's emotional appeal ("They love to speak Hebrew") or its practical value ("If he lives in Israel he knows that he has to speak Hebrew"). It is unlikely that any language, even English, surpasses Hebrew in the eyes of Israelis.

CONCLUSION

The data of the present study, obtained in different ways, were in substantial agreement with respect to the status of English on a busy street in Jerusalem. English was the foreign language which was most in evidence. Its native speakers did not scruple to use it in public, unlike the native speakers of other languages, who tended to use Hebrew in this context.

While the man on the street was found to know some English, proficiency was not evenly distributed throughout the population studied. Knowledge of English appeared to be a marker of inequality of educational opportunity as well as of differences in the communicative networks in which Israelis participate. In spite of the high potential usefulness of English as a lingua franca for Israelis, they appeared to use English as a lingua franca only when their interlocutor did not know Hebrew. As Greenberg (1965) has pointed out, the only thing which stops the spread of a lingua franca among a linguistically heterogeneous population is the existence of another lingua franca. In Israel, Hebrew is the lingua franca par excellence.

The English-speaking tourist would have little difficulty in communicating with Israelis on Keren Kayemet Street, inasmuch as most of the Israelis he met there would be able to cope with at least simple communicative requirements in English and almost half would be fluent in English. Furthermore, most of the persons he turned to for assistance would be helpful and not at all surprised to find someone asking a question in English.

The immigrant whose mother tongue is English, however, would be expected by Israelis to learn and to use Hebrew. In addition, many an English-speaking immigrant feels an ideological commitment to learn and to use Hebrew from the same motivations which led him to settle in Israel. However, the high practical value of his mother tongue as a potential lingua franca might well slow him in learning Hebrew, and, if he learns it, from adopting it as his principal language of everyday life. The outcome of these conflicting pressures with respect to the maintenance of English in Israel, for differentiated communicative functions and by demographically and ideologically differentiated subgroups of English mother-tongue speakers, remains a fascinating subject for future research.

NOTES

1.   The first provisional data of the Population and Housing Census of 1972 show that more than half (57%) of the Jewish population above the age of fourteen speak two or more languages daily (Central Bureau of Statistics 1973). As yet unpublished data from this census show that about 88% claimed to use Hebrew daily and of these 88% claimed to use it as their principal language. If all Hebrew mother-tongue speakers in Israel used Hebrew every day and used it as their principal language, and if all respondents who claimed to use it daily as their principal language were mother-tongue speakers of Hebrew, then about 77% (0.88×0.88) of the Jewish population aged fourteen or more would speak Hebrew natively. However, inasmuch as many of those who use Hebrew as their principal language do not speak it natively, the proportion of the Jewish population aged fourteen or more who speak Hebrew as their mother tongue must be substantially less than 77%.

2.   Degree of (Jewish) religious observance was judged primarily on the basis of hair and dress styles. Ethnic membership was judged primarily on the basis of physical character-istics, but speech characteristics sometimes played a part as well, inasmuch as ethnicity is often identified by the speaker's accent in Hebrew. The use of speech characteristics to help identify ethnicity did not contaminate identification of the language spoken. If it had, considerably higher proportions of Arabic and Yiddish would have been reported.

3.   This was the post office, which used French and Hebrew. This was one of the rare examples of Roman script being used for a language other than English.

4.   Oral proficiency scores were computed for all persons ($N = 282$) engaged in the planted encounters, including the seventeen shopkeepers. Reading and general proficiency scores were computed only for those who were given written addresses ($N = 133$).

REFERENCES

Bender, M. Lionel; Robert L. Cooper; and Charles A. Ferguson. 1972. Language in Ethiopia: Implications of a survey for sociolinguistic theory and method. *Language in Society* 1:215–233.
Central Bureau of Statistics, Prime Minister's Office, State of Israel. 1973. *The Educational Level Attainment and the Use of Language.* Jerusalem. Mimeographed.

Cooper, Robert L., and Joshua A. Fishman. 1977. A study of language attitudes. This vol., chap. 11.

Cooper, Robert L., and Fern Seckbach. 1977. Economic incentives for the learning of a language of wider communication: A case study. This vol., chap. 8.

Greenberg, Joseph H. 1965. Urbanism, migration, and language. In *Urbanization and Migration in West Africa,* edited by Hilda Kuper. Los Angeles: University of California Press. Pp. 50–59.

Herman, Simon N. 1961. Explorations in the social psychology of language choice. *Human Relations* 14:149–164.

Nadel, Elizabeth, and Joshua A. Fishman. 1977. English in Israel: A sociolinguistic study. This vol., chap. 4.

Webb, Eugene J.; Donald T. Campbell; Richard D. Schwartz; and Lee Sechrest. 1966. *Unobtrusive Measures: Nonreactive Research in the Social Sciences.* Chicago: Rand McNally.

PART THREE

*The Economic and
Technological
Power of English*

Chapter 7

Language, Technology, and Persuasion: Three Experimental Studies

Robert L. Cooper, Joshua A. Fishman, Linda Lown, Barbara Schaier, and *Fern Seckbach*

The languages associated with science and technology are often foreign or second languages for the speech communities in which they are used. This is frequently the case in communities whose principal language is not a language of wider communication. It is also commonly the case in communities which are ethno-linguistic minorities within a larger community in which the dominant language is a language of wider communication. Thus, for example, English is a language of science and technology not only for Israelis but for Mexican Americans as well.

In speech communities in which a second or foreign language is associated with scientific and technological uses, it is employed for purposes such as the following: as a medium of instruction in scientific and technological institutes of higher learning, in industrial training programs, and in work-oriented literacy campaigns; as a medium of science textbooks and of technical manuals for the operation, maintenance, and repair of imported machinery; as a medium of communication with professional colleagues from abroad; and as a lingua franca among the industrial work force. When a foreign or second language assumes functions such as these, is it a better medium than the mother tongue for conveying technological arguments when the purpose is not so much to inform as to persuade? In this chapter we summarize the results of three studies designed to explore this question.

For the past quarter century, the study of persuasion has been a central focus of communication research (see McGuire 1969 for a review of the extensive

The authors wish to thank Andrew D. Cohen for his criticism of an earlier draft of this essay.

literature on this subject). Although numerous studies have been published which deal with the persuasive effect of manipulating various elements of the communication process, there has been little attention paid to the effect of language on persuasion. The few studies that do examine the relationship between the language of a message and its persuasive effectiveness have focused on the importance of within-language differences. Thus, the number of emotional words and metaphors (Reinsch 1971) and the interaction between the word and the degree of abstractness of the referent (Kanouse and Abelson 1967) have been found to influence a receiver's response to a message. Perhaps the research which is most relevant to the differential persuasiveness of two languages is that of Giles (1973), who found that although the quality of an argument in English was perceived as better when presented in Received Pronunciation than when presented in various regional accents, only the regional accents were effective in eliciting opinion shifts.

In order to explore the relative persuasive effectiveness of second languages associated with scientific and technological uses, we conducted three studies. The first employed Arabic and Hebrew; the second and third employed English and Hebrew. The Arabic-Hebrew study was carried out in the Israeli-administered West Bank in Jericho, with Arabic-Hebrew bilingual Muslims. The English-Hebrew studies were carried out with Jewish residents of Jerusalem, one study with university students, the other with housewives.

In the Jericho study, our assumption was that West Bank Arabs are beginning to associate Hebrew with scientific and technological uses because Israeli scientific and technological achievements are recognized by residents of the West Bank and because Hebrew is a medium for participation in the urbanized and industrialized sectors of the administering power. There can be no question that West Bank Arabs view Arabic as the vehicle par excellence for Arabic culture and traditional Muslim values. The use of both scientifically-based and traditionally-based appeals would throw into sharp relief the relative persuasive effectiveness of Arabic and Hebrew. One would expect that Hebrew would have a greater opportunity for persuasiveness with a scientifically-based argument than with a traditionally-based argument and that the reverse would be true for Arabic.

With respect to the Jerusalem studies, out assumption was that one of the contexts with which Israelis associate English is that of science and technology. English is frequently the medium of the bibliographies assigned to university students; foreign university lecturers typically lecture in English; and the study of English in public schools is often justified to students by its usefulness at institutions of higher learning. English, furthermore, is the source of many technical and scientific terms in common use, and it is the medium in which the technical manuals for imported machinery and appliances are often published. While English has other functions in Israel—e.g., as a medium of international pop culture and as the most common medium of communication with foreigners—Israelis also encounter it in scientific and technological contexts. Thus, in the Jerusalem studies we assumed that English was associated with science and technology, whereas in the Jericho study we assumed that Hebrew had such an association.

The polarization between English and Hebrew in Jerusalem, however, is probably not as great as between Arabic and Hebrew in Jericho. Whereas in Jericho scientific and technological uses are more associated with Hebrew than with Arabic, it can be argued that Hebrew and English are equally associated with science and technology in Israel—although there may be important differences in the political and emotional associations with which they are involved. Accordingly, it was not at all clear what types of appeal ought to be employed in our persuasive messages in order to reveal potential differences in the persuasive effectiveness of English and Hebrew. In both Jerusalem studies we employed a technologically-based appeal. In one study, however, we also used an appeal to national solidarity, whereas in the other study the second appeal was to traditional values of hearth and home.

THE JERICHO STUDY

Four one-minute passages were recorded by a fluent speaker of Arabic and Hebrew. He was a Muslim from Jerusalem. Two of the passages presented scientific evidence for tobacco's harmful effects on health. One of these was recorded in Arabic and the other was recorded in Hebrew. The Arabic and Hebrew versions were translations of one another, obtained by the back-translation method. The other two passages presented a traditional Islamic argument with respect to the evils of drinking alochol. Again, one was in Arabic and the other in Hebrew, with each version a translation of the other. The varieties of Arabic and Hebrew which were used were those which would be appropriate for a radio news broadcast.

The four recordings were rerecorded onto a cassette tape in the following order: Side I—the argument against drinking (Arabic), the argument against smoking (Hebrew); Side II—the argument against drinking (Hebrew), the arguments against smoking (Arabic). Before each pair of arguments (i.e., at the beginning of each side), the following announcement by the speaker was recorded, once in Arabic and once in Hebrew: "You are now about to hear two arguments, one in Arabic and one in Hebrew." This preliminary announcement was used so that the listeners would know that both passages were spoken by the same person. Thus any differences obtained between responses to the Arabic and Hebrew versions of an argument could not be attributed to differences in the perceived ethnic identity of the speaker.

Respondents

Thirty Muslim men from Jericho, with good listening comprehension of Hebrew, served as respondents in interviews which were carried out in the spring of 1973. These respondents included almost all of the city's Arabic-Hebrew bilinguals. In all cases, Arabic was the language the respondent spoke first as a child. Most had learned Hebrew through interaction with Hebrew-speaking Israelis, although a few had attended formal classes. Most of the men, who were between twenty and forty years old, had completed or nearly completed high school. It was not known exactly how many were strict teetotalers, but it was known that all but one were smokers.

Interviews

Each respondent was approached individually by the fourth author and an Arabic-speaking Israeli who served as interviewer and who was well known to all of the respondents. Each of the interviews lasted about ten minutes and was conducted entirely in Arabic. The respondents were interviewed during working hours at their places of employment, either in Jericho or in Ein Feishcha, a nearby nature reserve. The interviewer asked each respondent to cooperate with a research project that was being undertaken by the Hebrew University. The fourth author was introduced as a person from the University and as one who did not know Arabic. The purpose of the research was not mentioned. The interviewer then explained that a tape recording of two passages would be played, one in Arabic and one in Hebrew, and that the respondent would have to listen carefully because a few questions would be asked after each passage had been played. Each respondent heard either Side I or Side II, with alternate respondents hearing alternate sides. In this way, all of the respondents heard the arguments against drinking and smoking, but half heard the former in Arabic and the latter in Hebrew, whereas the other half heard the former in Hebrew and the latter in Arabic.

After the respondent had heard a passage, he was asked the following questions:

1. What was the main argument of the passage?
2. To what extent do you agree with each of the following statements?
   a. The reasons presented were good ones.
   b. The reasons presented were logical ones.
   c. The speaker was persuasive.
3. Do you think it is all right to drink/smoke a little?
4. Do you think that the price of liquor/cigarettes should be raised in order to discourage people from drinking/smoking?

The first item was asked in order to assess comprehension of the passage. Items 2 and 3 were relatively direct questions and item 4 a relatively indirect question with respect to the respondent's attitude toward the referent of the message. After these questions had been asked in connection with the second passage, an attempt was made to obtain a behavioral (as distinguished from purely verbal) measure of attitude. This was done as follows. After the interviewer stated that the interview was over, he said that he personally did not agree with the reasons advanced for not drinking. He then said something to this effect: "When I come home from a hard day's work and am tired from the day's activities I like to take one or two drinks. They relax me and make me feel good. I don't think that getting drunk is good at all, but one doesn't get drunk from only one or two drinks!" After the respondent had had an opportunity to react to this statement,

Table 7.1   Should the price of this commodity be raised in order to discourage consumption? Number and percentage of Jericho respondents answering "yes," according to language of message and appeal heard

Commodity	Appeal	Language of message	Respondents answering "yes" Number	%
Tobacco	Science	Arabic	2	13
		Hebrew	8	53
Liquor	Tradition	Arabic	8	53
		Hebrew	4	27

the interviewer took a cigarette for himself and matter-of-factly offered one to the respondent. For each respondent, it was noted (a) whether he argued against the interviewer's position with respect to the anti-drinking message and (b) whether he refused the cigarette.

Results

Everyone who was asked to participate agreed to do so, and no one appeared to be suspicious about the purpose of the research. The interviews proceeded smoothly. The respondents answered the questions willingly and thoughtfully and they seemed to be entirely unaware of the intent of the research.

All of the respondents understood each message, whether in Arabic or in Hebrew. With respect to the direct attitudinal questions (items 2 and 3), there was little difference between the average responses of those who heard the Arabic and Hebrew versions of a given argument. Over 90% of the respondents said that they agreed with the anti-drinking and anti-smoking arguments. Almost all also said that the reasons advanced in each message were good ones, that they were logical, and that the speaker was persuasive. There was no difference in overt behavioral responses associated with language. Twenty-two of the men argued with the interviewer about the evils of alcohol. Of these, half had heard the anti-drinking message in Arabic and half had heard it in Hebrew. Similarly, twenty-two men refused the cigarette, and half had heard the anti-smoking argument in Arabic and half had heard it in Hebrew.

With respect to the indirect attitude questions (item 4), however, there was a dramatic difference in response associated with the language in which the message was presented (see Table 7.1). Eight (53%) of the respondents who heard the anti-drinking argument in Arabic thought that the price of liquor should be raised to discourage consumption of alcohol, whereas only four (27%) of those who heard that argument in Hebrew thought so. In contrast, eight (53%) of those who heard the anti-smoking argument in Hebrew agreed that the price of cigarettes should be raised, whereas only two (13%) of those who heard that

argument in Arabic thought so. In other words, with respect to the indirect attitude question, the traditionally-based argument (anti-drinking) appeared to be
more effective in Arabic than in Hebrew and the scientifically-based argument
(anti-smoking) appeared to be more effective in Hebrew than in Arabic.

If the responses to the indirect questions indicated differential
persuasiveness according to an interaction between language and the type of
argument used, why did not the direct question do so well? One explanation lies
in the nature of the topics and of the type of arguments used. Most people today,
smokers as well as nonsmokers, recognize the statistical relationship between
smoking and various types of disease, and most are prepared to accept the
relationship as a casual one. Similarly, most Muslims recognize Islam's ban on the
consumption of alcohol, even if not all always follow the prohibition in practice.
Within the formal framework of an interview situation, it was probably difficult
to disagree explicitly with the obvious, scientifically-based argument that smoking
is harmful to health, and it was probably equally difficult to disagree explicitly
with the traditionally-based argument that drinking is immoral. In such a situation
it was unlikely that one would wish to appear either irrational or irreligious. There
was a socially accepted stereotyped response to questions about the suitability of
drinking and smoking, and the direct questions elicited such responses. The
indirect question, however, did not have a single, socially acceptable response. It
elicited far less agreement among the respondents than did the direct questions.
Thus the indirect question permitted the language in which a message was encoded
to exhibit a differential effect.

THE FIRST JERUSALEM STUDY—UNIVERSITY STUDENTS

One of the problems with the Jericho study was that there were socially approved
answers to many of the questions we asked. In our second study, we tried to
employ topics which would not elicit such stereotyped responses. The topics we
chose involved traffic regulations. In one message we argued for stronger
enforcement of rules which require pedestrians to cross the street at crosswalks
and to cross only when the traffic light permits crossing. In the other message,
we argued for stronger enforcement of rules prohibiting unnecessary sounding of
automobile horns. The first message was based on an appeal to national solidarity.
The second message was based on an appeal to research studies showing the
harmful effects of noise.

Each message was prepared in English and in Hebrew. The English and
Hebrew versions were translations of one another. All versions were recorded by
an Israeli woman whose first language is Hebrew and who is fluent in English.
All four versions, each lasting about one minute, were rerecorded onto a cassette
tape in the following order: Side I—enforcing pedestrian crossing laws (Hebrew),
enforcing horn-sounding laws (English); Side II—enforcing pedestrian crossing laws
(English), enforcing horn-sounding laws (Hebrew). Before each pair of arguments,
the speaker introduced the task in Hebrew and in English.

Respondents

Forty students at the Hebrew University served as respondents. All were studying for either a B.A. or an M.A. degree. The third author approached people at random on the Givat Ram (western) campus of the Hebrew University. Once she had determined that they were students and that their first language was Hebrew, she asked them to listen to a short tape and to answer some questions. The first twenty respondents heard Side I of the tape and the second twenty students heard Side II. An equal number of men and women participated, with twelve women and eight men hearing Side I and eight women and twelve men hearing Side II. There were eight drivers in the first group and eleven drivers in the second.

Interviews

All interviews, each of which lasted about ten minutes, were conducted in Hebrew and carried out in the spring of 1975. After determining that the respondent had understood the message by asking him to summarize it, the following questions were asked:

1. In your opinion, did the speaker use good arguments in presenting the issue?
2. Should greater efforts be made by law enforcement authorities to enforce this law?
3. Are you willing to participate in a broad campaign of bringing this matter to the attention of the public by handing out fliers at the main gate of the University?

Results

If the persuasive effectiveness of our messages is judged by the students' willingness to hand out fliers, then the messages were unsuccessful, inasmuch as the largest number indicating an unequivocal willingness to do so after hearing a message was only three. For the message based on a scientific appeal, language appeared to have little effect on the students' answers; the number of unequivocally positive responses to the three questions was about the same for the English version as it was for the Hebrew version. Language did seem to make a difference, however, for the argument based on a solidarity appeal. Students who heard this message in English more frequently thought that the argument was good (ten students, 50%) than those students who heard in in Hebrew (seven students, 35%). On the other hand, those who heard it in Hebrew agreed with the message more frequently than those who heard it in English, with thirteen students (65%) agreeing with the Hebrew message as compared to nine students (45%) agreeing with the English message. These results, which are summarized in Table 7.2., are reminiscent of Giles' (1973) findings—that an argument was thought to be better when spoken in Received Pronunciation than when spoken in regional dialects, but that only the latter appeared effective in promoting attitude change. It should

Table 7.2 University students' responses to three questions about enforcement of traffic laws, according to language of message and appeal heard

Question	Number answering "yes"				Percentage answering "yes"			
	Science		Solidarity		Science		Solidarity	
	English	Hebrew	English	Hebrew	English	Hebrew	English	Hebrew
Is argument good?	9	8	10	7	45	40	50	35
Should there be greater enforcement?	14	13	9	13	70	65	45	65
Are you willing to hand out fliers?	3	3	1	2	15	15	5	10

be noted that whereas Hebrew appeared to be as persuasive for one message as for the other, there was a marked discrepancy in the persuasiveness of English for the two messages, as determined by the number of students agreeing that there should be greater enforcement of the regulation in question. Only nine (45%) of the students who heard the solidarity argument in English agreed that there should be greater enforcement. In contrast thirteen (65%) of those who heard the scientific message in English supported greater enforcement.

THE SECOND JERUSALEM STUDY—HOUSEWIVES

In our attempt to obtain messages for the university students which would not elicit stereotyped responses, we may have resorted to messages which were overly bland. We felt, at any rate, that these messages did not particularly interest many of our respondents. In our third study, therefore, we tried to construct messages which would be both interesting and unlikely to elicit stereotyped reactions. The topic we hit on was food—in particular, ways to prepare tasty and economical substitutes for meat. Almost everyone, we reasoned, likes to eat and to feel thrifty—housewives, in particular, ought to be interested in learning to prepare appetizing substitutes for meat. We wrote two messages. One advocated the use of nuts as a meat substitute. The other advocated the use of legumes. Neither food is commonly used by Jerusalem housewives as a meat substitute. Each message made the points that the food in question is economical, nutritious, an excellent source of protein, and that appetizing dishes can easily be prepared from them. The message promoting nuts emphasized an appeal to traditional Jewish ways. It mentioned Biblical references to nuts and various traditional Jewish dishes for which nuts could serve as the main ingredient. The other message emphasized an appeal to scientific evidence of legumes' nutritional value, but it also appealed to modernism and fashion as well. It referred to a recent article in *Time* magazine which reported on the fashion of using legumes as a main dish in the United States. English and Hebrew translation equivalents were prepared for each message and were recorded, each as one-minute passages, by a male Israeli who speaks fluent Hebrew and English. His first language was German, but he began speaking Hebrew at the age of four and speaks Hebrew without any foreign accent whatsoever. His English is accented, but the accent is not readily identifiable as either Hebrew or German. The four passages were rerecorded onto a tape cassette in the following order: Side I—legumes (Hebrew), nuts (English); Side II—legumes (English), nuts (Hebrew). Each side was introduced by the speaker's announcement, made both in Hebrew and English, that he was going to deliver a message in each language.

Respondents

Thirty women served as respondents. Primarily a middle-class lot, one-third had studied at a university and about one-quarter had studied at teachers' seminaries. About one-third had lived abroad for a year or more; of these, eight had lived in

English-speaking countries. Almost all were native speakers of Hebrew, and all used Hebrew as their principal language. All but two were currently married, and many worked outside the home. Each respondent heard either Side I or Side II, with alternate respondents hearing alternate sides. The two groups were equivalent with respect to educational status and foreign residence.

Interviews

The fifth author interviewed each of the women individually, usually in the respondent's home. All interviews, which were carried out in the fall of 1975, were conducted in Hebrew. After determining that the respondent had under-stood the message, by asking her to summarize it, the interviewer asked the following questions:

1. Are you interested in trying this food as a meat substitute?
2. Do you think that using this food as a meat substitute is a good idea?
3. In your opinion, was the argument which was presented a good one?
4. Do you agree with the message?
5. Do you think your family would like to eat this food as a meat substitute?
6. If someone gave you a recipe for the use of this food as a meat substitute, would you try it?
7. If you could buy a reasonably priced cookbook which was devoted to the use of this food as a meat substitute, would you buy it?

After the respondent had answered the seventh question in response to the second passage, the interviewer said that she had available a printed recipe for nuts as a meat substitute and a printed recipe for legumes as a meat substitute, each on a separate sheet. The interviewer said that the respondent could have either or both but that she should take one only if she really wanted it, since supplies were limited.

In addition to the above procedure, which was followed for all thirty respondents, the last twenty-two respondents were asked four questions at the beginning of the interview, before any of the tapes were played, in an attempt to determine what they knew about legumes and nuts. These questions were about each food's nutritional value, its relative value as a source of protein, its cost per portion, and the effort required to prepare it into appetizing dishes. Those who did not know the correct answer to a question initially were asked the question again at the conclusion of the relevant message, in order to determine whether they had learned (or had been persuaded to believe) the correct answer after having heard the message.

Results

Unlike those with university students, the messages which the housewives heard appeared to be effective, if we can accept the number taking a recipe as evidence for the persuasiveness of the messages. All but three housewives took the recipe for nuts and all but four took the recipe for legumes. It is of course more agreeable to take a recipe than to hand out fliers, but most of the women seemed genuinely interested by the topic. The language in which the message was heard made a difference for one of the messages. For the message which appealed to scientific authority (legumes), those who heard the Hebrew version more frequently gave positive responses to six of the eight items than did those who heard the English version. In contrast, the differences between responses to the Hebrew and English versions of the traditional message (nuts) were in most cases so small as for us to call the responses almost identical. For the scientific message, the between-language differences were substantial for four of the eight items. These were all "conative" items, i.e., items which assessed the respondent's readiness to use the food as a meat substitute (items 1, 6, 7, and 8). To be specific, thirteen (87%) of the women who heard the Hebrew version of the scientific message said they were interested in trying legumes as a meat substitute, whereas only eight (53%) of those who heard the message in English said so (item 1). All the women who heard the message in Hebrew said they would try a recipe for legumes, whereas eleven (73%) of those who heard the message in English said so (item 6). The same difference was found for those who actually took a recipe when given the opportunity to do so (item 8). And nine (60%) of those who heard the Hebrew version said they would buy a cookbook, whereas only five (33%) of those who heard the English version expressed a willingness to do so (item 7). Thus, the Hebrew version seemed to be substantially more effective than the English version for the scientific message and about as effective as the English version for the traditional message. These results are summarized in Table 7.3.

To what extent did our messages actually inform the housewives or change their minds about the properties of legumes and nuts? With respect to the questions about nutritional value and relative value as a source of protein, most of the women who had not given the correct answer before hearing the messages, did give the correct answer after hearing them. Relatively few, however, changed their minds with respect to cost per portion or ease of preparation after hearing the messages. There was virtually no between-language difference for the traditional message. The women who heard the English versions improved their responses proportionally about as those who heard the Hebrew version. For the scientific message, however, there was a between-language difference. Women gave improved responses proportionally after hearing the Hebrew version than after hearing the English version. Again, Hebrew appeared more effective than English for the scientific message but not for the traditional message. These results are presented in Table 7.4.

SUMMARY AND DISCUSSION

Three studies were carried out to investigate the persuasive effectiveness of languages associated with scientific and technological uses, particularly for

Table 7.3 Housewives' responses to eight items connected with the use of legumes and nuts as meat substitutes, according to language of message and appeal heard

Items	Number giving positive response				Percentage giving positive response			
	Science		Tradition		Science		Tradition	
	English	Hebrew	English	Hebrew	English	Hebrew	English	Hebrew
1. Are you interested in trying it?	8	13	10	11	53	87	67	73
2. Is it a good idea?	12	13	11	11	80	87	73	73
3. Is the argument sound?	9	9	6	7	60	60	40	47
4. Do you agree with the message?	8	6	5	7	53	40	33	47
5. Would your family like it?	6	8	11	12	40	53	73	80
6. Would you try a recipe?	11	15	13	14	73	100	87	93
7. Would you buy a cookbook?	5	9	6	8	33	60	40	53
8. Respondent took recipe	11	15	13	14	73	100	87	93

Table 7.4   Number of women who gave incorrect answers before hearing message and gave correct answers after hearing message, according to language of message and appeal heard

Question topic	Science		Tradition	
	English	*Hebrew*	*English*	*Hebrew*
Nutritional value	2/3	5/5	5/6	3/3
Source of protein	1/3	5/6	4/4	5/8
Cost per portion	1/3	2/3	1/8	2/8
Ease of preparation	0/4	1/5	1/6	2/6
Total	4/13	13/19	11/24	12/25
	(31%)	(68%)	(46%)	(48%)

Note: These questions were asked *before* the message was played only to the last 22 of the 30 women interviewed. Results are given as the number giving *correct* answer *after* hearing message divided by the number giving *incorrect* answer *before* hearing message.

messages based on appeals to scientific authority. The languages and samples involved were: (1) Arabic and Hebrew with thirty Muslim men in Jericho, (2) English and Hebrew with forty university students in Jerusalem, and (3) English and Hebrew with thirty housewives in Jerusalem. The language marked for scientific and technological uses was assumed to be Hebrew in the first study and English in the second and third studies. Each respondent heard two messages, one in each language, each message based on a different appeal. In each study, one of the appeals was to scientific authority. In the first and third studies, the other appeal was to traditional values, and in the second study the other appeal was to national solidarity. In each study the language-message combinations were counterbalanced so that all the respondents heard two messages, each in a different language, and each message was heard by half the respondents in each language.

     We found some evidence in the Jericho study to support the idea that an appeal to scientific authority was more successful when spoken in a language associated with science and technology and that an appeal to traditional authority was more successful when spoken in a language associated with traditional values. In neither of the Jerusalem studies, however, did we find that English was more persuasive than Hebrew for messages that appealed to scientific authority. In the study of university students, only in the message based on an appeal to solidarity was there a between-language difference. Here, students who heard that message in English more frequently thought the argument to be sound than did those who heard it in Hebrew, but those who heard it in Hebrew were more apt to agree with the message than those who heard it in English. In the study of housewives, on the other hand, only in the message based on an appeal to scientific authority was there much of a between-language difference, and here the Hebrew version seemed more effective than the English version.

How can we explain these differences? If the language associated with science and technology appeared more persuasive, for a scientific message, than the mother tongue in Jericho but not in Jerusalem, we can attribute it perhaps to the greater polarity between the languages involved in Jericho. In Jerusalem, Hebrew as well as English is associated with scientific and technological uses, particularly for our sample of university students. It can be argued, after the fact, that since both English and Hebrew are associated with university course work, the message based on an appeal to national solidarity had a greater opportunity to show a between-language difference, since English is not associated with solidarity values. This argument could explain why the university students more often tended to agree with this message when they heard it in Hebrew than when they heard it in English, but it would not explain why they tended to think the reasoning was better when they heard it in English than when they heard it in Hebrew. That the Hebrew version of the scientific appeal was more successful for the housewives than the English appeal can perhaps be explained, again on an ex post facto basis, on the nature of the message, which resorted to other appeals, such as modernism and fashion, in addition to scientific authority. It may be that scientific authority was less influential than the other appeals employed by the message.

While English was not found to be more persuasive than Hebrew for scientific appeals in either of the Jerusalem studies, in one of these studies (university students) English appeared to be more persuasive when used as the medium for a scientific appeal than when used as the medium for a nonscientific appeal. This result is consistent with the notion that when a group uses a language for restricted functions, that language is apt to be more persuasive for messages associated with such functions than for messages which are not. How then can we explain our lack of a between-appeal difference for either language in the other Jerusalem study (housewives)? Perhaps we can attribute this also to our dilution of the scientific appeal in that study.

Differences among the results of these three studies can also be explained, of course, in terms of differences between the populations studied and the messages employed as well as in terms of differences in the language situations involved. However one explains these differences, our results seem to us to justify the notion that the relationship between the language of a message, the appeal on which the message is based, and the persuasiveness of a message for a bilingual audience is complex. One cannot assume that the audience's mother tongue is necessarily the best vehicle for all types of persuasive messages.

REFERENCES

Giles, Howard. 1973. Communicative effectiveness as a function of accented speech. *Speech Monographs* 40:330-331.

Kanouse, David E., and Robert Abelson. 1967. Language variables affecting the persuasiveness of simple communications. *Journal of Personality and Social Psychology* 7:158-163.

McGuire, William J. 1969. The nature of attitudes and attitude change. In *The Handbook of Social Psychology*, edited by G. Lindsey and E. Aronson. 2d ed. Vol. 3. Reading, Mass.: Addison Wesley. Pp. 136-314.

Reinsch, Lamar N. 1971. An investigation of the effects of the metaphor and the simile in persuasive discourse. *Speech Monographs* 38:142-145.

Chapter 8

Economic Incentives for the Learning of a Language of Wider Communication: A Case Study

Robert L. Cooper and *Fern Seckbach*

Bread-and-butter considerations can provide a powerful incentive to learn a language. Lingua francas, for example, often spread along trade routes and radiate from market centers, carried by traders who need a common language in order to do business. In colonial territories, the language of the imperial administration often spreads in part because proficiency in the language becomes a prerequisite for government employment and school attendance (Brosnahan 1963). When knowledge of a language becomes associated with material benefits, and when people have the opportunity to learn it, they are likely to do so.

It is clear that economic considerations are at least partly responsible for the spread of trade lingua francas and imperial languages. To what extent do they also play a role in the spread of languages of wider communication? Such languages (Fishman 1969) enable a community whose primary languages are not widely spoken outside the community to communicate with foreigners and to gain access to those scientific, technical, and literary materials that exist primarily in world languages. It is plausible that economic considerations, at least in part, motivate the acquisition of such languages. The automobile mechanic who needs to read repair manuals of cars manufactured abroad, the secretary who has to type letters to foreign customers or suppliers, the hotel clerk who must deal with foreign guests, the scientist who has to read articles published abroad, all need, to a greater or lesser extent, a language of wider communication in order to carry out their work.

Economic incentives for learning

Within communities which require a language of wider communication as an additional language, the importance of the language of wider communication probably varies partly with the importance of foreign trade and foreign tourism to the community's economy (see Fishman, Cooper, and Rosenbaum, this vol., chap. 2). It probably also varies partly with the extent to which the community's primary languages are vehicles for technical and scientific literature and partly with the extent to which such literature is important to the workings of the economy. In addition, the importance of a language of wider communication depends on the extent to which it occupies additional roles. In many African countries, for example, the language of the former imperial administration has become the official language and an important lingua franca between fellow nationals.

Just as differences in the importance of a language of wider communication may exist between communities, differences may exist within communities as well. In Kampala for example, almost all respondents to a sociolinguistic sample survey (Scotton 1972) believed that the following positions required a knowledge of English: lawyer, typist in a government office, and administrator in a government office. Fewer than a third of the respondents believed that porters in an office building, carpenters, or bus conductors needed to know English as part of their work.

Given such differences in the importance of languages of wider communication, both between communities and within communities, how crucial can economic considerations be in promoting the spread and maintenance of a language of wider communication? Israel provides a good place for investigating this issue. This is so because among the Jewish majority the functions of a language of wider communication have been largely concentrated on one language, English, and because the primary function of that language in Israel is that of a language of wider communication. English is spoken natively by only a small fraction of the country's population, and it has only a minor role as a lingua franca among Israelis who typically employ Hebrew as the medium of communication if they do not share the same mother tongue (see Rosenbaum, Nadel, and Cooper, this vol., chap. 6). While it is true that English was a colonial language in Israel during the period of the British Mandate, the mandatory period was relatively brief and it ended a generation ago, before mass immigration began. Thus the colonial residue of English is slight. Its chief role is that of language of wider communication. The present chapter summarizes the results of a study of the economic importance of English in Israel insofar as this can be judged by an analysis of the language requirements which are stipulated in help-wanted advertisements published in the Hebrew press.

PROCEDURE

In Israel there are many daily newspapers published in a number of languages. Of all newspapers, the three Hebrew newspapers not affiliated with a political party have the largest circulations. They are *Ha-arez, Yediot Aharonot,* and *Ma'ariv.* The first two newspapers publish a combined want-ad section, and it was this section which was chosen for analysis. Because the Friday editions contain the week's largest number of advertisements, the Friday editions were the ones which were studied. Every eighth Friday edition of the combined *Ha-arez-Yediot Aharanot* want-ad section was analyzed for the year 1973, beginning with the first Friday edition (January 5). This yielded seven sections for analysis. To provide a diachronic perspective, the same procedure was also followed for the 1953 want-ad sections of these papers.

In these sections there are two types of advertisements offering jobs. One consists of short, classified ads, in very small print, which are listed one beneath the other and provide the necessary information in a telegraphic style. Most of these offer positions for blue-collar employment and specify relatively few requirements. The other type of advertisement consists of "framed" ads, within black borders, of various sizes and individual layout. In framed ads, the name of the employer is usually listed at the top and is often accompanied by the symbol or trademark of the firm. Framed ads are often designed to catch the eye. The print containing the main information is large, and the requirements listed are typically quite specific.

The language requirements specified in the classified and framed advertisements were tabulated according to the languages mentioned and the level of proficiency desired. When a language was mentioned as a characteristic of the prospective employee, it was counted, whether it was listed as an absolute requirement for employment or simply as "desirable." Languages which were mentioned as part of the job title, e.g., English typist, were also counted, even if they were not mentioned as a wanted characteristic of the applicant, because it can be assumed that proficiency in the language mentioned in the job title was essential for performance of the job. Although most ads offered one job only, some offered more than one. Thus the unit of analysis which was employed was the individual job and not the individual advertisement.

RESULTS

The seven 1973 editions surveyed yielded almost 4,500 jobs, of which about half were found in framed advertisements and about half in classified advertisements. Most of the language requirements were found in the framed advertisements. Of the jobs in the classified ads, only 6% mentioned a language, whereas over 20% of the jobs in the framed ads did so. For both types of advertisement, the foreign language most commonly mentioned was English, which was mentioned slightly more often than Hebrew in the framed advertisements and slightly less often than Hebrew in the classified advertisements. All the other languages which were found, when combined, accounted for fewer than 15% of the jobs in which languages were mentioned. Of these, the languages mentioned most commonly were French

Economic incentives for learning

Table 8.1   Language requirements for jobs appearing in a sample of Israeli newspaper advertisements, 1973

Language specified	Framed ads No.	Framed ads %	Classified ads No.	Classified ads %	Total No.	Total %
English only	105	4.7	26	1.1	131	2.9
English and Hebrew	194	8.8	37	1.6	231	5.1
English and other	25	1.1	4	.2	29	.6
English, Hebrew, and other	41	1.8	5	.2	46	1.0
Hebrew only	74	3.7	44	1.9	118	2.6
Hebrew and other	8	.4	3	.1	11	.2
Other only	21	1.0	12	.5	33	.7
None	1,750	78.9	2,142	94.2	3,892	86.7
Total	2,218	100.0	2,273	100.0	4,491	100.0
English	365	16.5	72	3.2	437	9.7
Hebrew	317	14.3	89	3.9	406	9.0
Other	95	4.3	24	1.1	119	2.6

and German. The distribution of language requirements in the 1973 advertisements is summarized in Table 8.1.

English was mentioned in about 10% of all the 1973 jobs surveyed and in about 17% of the jobs found in the framed advertisements. Of the jobs mentioning English, most stated that English proficiency was a required rather than "desirable" characteristic. Fewer than half the ads mentioning English stated a wanted level of proficiency, but of those which did, almost all specified "full knowledge" of the language. Almost none asked for one skill only (e.g., reading) or stated that "some" knowledge would be adequate. Most of the jobs mentioning Hebrew mentioned English as well. Less than 30% of the jobs mentioning Hebrew specified Hebrew alone. It is likely, therefore, that the specification of Hebrew was often motivated by a desire to avoid giving the impression that jobs which required a foreign language did not require Hebrew as well.

What kinds of jobs were likely to require English? The categories mentioning English most frequently were nonscientific and nontechnical jobs requiring a university degree (30%) and white-collar jobs (26%). In contrast, jobs for skilled technicians and for scientific or technological workers with university degrees specified English a smaller percentage of the time. Inasmuch as white-collar jobs represented almost one-quarter of all the jobs surveyed and a substantial proportion of them required English, it may be worthwhile to list the principal jobs included by this category. These were office receptionist, switchboard operator, secretary, clerk-typist, straight typist, stenographer, bookkeeper, bank clerk, and hotel clerk. The distribution of English requirements over the different occupational categories is presented in Table 8.2.

Table 8.2 English requirements by occupational category: Jobs appearing in a sample of Israeli newspaper advertisements, 1973

Occupational category	Framed ads			Classified ads			Total		
	No. jobs	English mentioned No.	%	No. jobs	English mentioned No.	%	No. jobs	English mentioned No.	%
White-collar	613	215	35.1	460	61	13.3	1,073	276	25.7
Skilled technician	571	52	9.1	216	1	.1	787	53	6.7
Blue-collar	477	9	1.9	1,358	4	.3	1,835	13	.7
Academic—science and technology	167	20	12.0	16	0	.0	183	20	10.9
Academic—other	110	33	30.0	1	0	.0	111	33	29.7
Teacher	95	7	7.4	17	0	.0	112	7	6.3
Other	185	29	15.7	205	3	1.5	390	32	8.2
Total	2,218	365	16.5	2,273	69	3.0	4,461	434	9.7

Table 8.3   Language requirements for jobs
appearing in a sample of Israeli
newspaper advertisements, 1953

Language specified[a]	No.	%
English only	2	1.1
English and Hebrew	20	10.9
English and other	0	.0
English, Hebrew, and other	3	1.6
Hebrew only	6	3.3
Hebrew and other	0	.0
Other only	4	2.2
None	148	80.9
Total	183	100.0
English	25	13.7
Hebrew	29	15.8
Other	7	3.8

[a]Of the 183 jobs in the sample, 129 were found in framed
ads and the remainder in classified ads. All language
requirements, except 3 of the "Hebrew only" requirements,
were found in the framed advertisements.

A much larger proportion of the jobs offered specifically to women
required English than did those offered specifically to men, presumably reflecting
the substantially larger proportion of white-collar jobs among the positions offered
specifically to women than among the jobs offered specifically to men. English
was mentioned only slightly more often in jobs which required the employee to
meet the general public or in jobs which involved supervision of other workers
than it was in all jobs combined. There was no relationship between the mention
of English and the level of education which was required.

The same sampling procedure carried out for the 1953 newspapers
yielded a dramatically smaller sample of jobs, less than 200 compared to the 1973
sample of almost 4,500, an eloquent testimony to the growth of the Israeli
economy during the intervening twenty years. The distribution of language
requirements, however, was much the same for the two years. As in 1973, English
was the foreign language most frequently specified, with 14% of the 1953 jobs
mentioning that language, about the same percentage as in 1973. As in 1973, the
largest number of jobs specifying English was found in the white-collar category.
The languages required in 1953 and the distribution of English requirements
over different job categories in 1953 are presented in Tables 8.3 and 8.4
respectively.

Table 8.4   English requirements by occupational category: Jobs appearing in a sample of Israeli newspaper advertisements, 1953

	Number of jobs			Jobs mentioning English[a]	
Occupational category	Framed	Classified	Total	No.	%
White-collar	36	7	43	22	51.2
Skilled technician	19	1	20	0	.0
Blue-collar	18	43	61	3	4.9
Academic– science and technology	18	1	19	0	.0
Academic–other	3	0	3	0	.0
Teacher	8	1	9	0	.0
Other	27	1	28	0	.0
Total	129	54	183	25	13.7

[a] All jobs mentioning English were found in framed ads.

DISCUSSION

English has been an important job requirement in Israel since the early days of the State's independence. The importance of English as a job requirement in Israel can be appreciated when we look at foreign language requirements in the United States. In a survey of almost 88,000 help-wanted advertisements appearing in *The New York Times* (all help-wanted ads in every eighth Sunday edition of 1973 were analyzed), less than 200 advertisements mentioned a foreign language as a requirement (Moher 1975). In contrast to the United States, where foreign-language ability appears to be of negligible importance in the job market, knowledge of English as a language of wider communication appears to be of considerable importance in the Israeli job market.

It is surprising that jobs requiring technical and scientific training did not demand as much English as did other jobs requiring an equivalent amount of education, in view of the importance of English as a medium for technical and scientific information. It is possible that enough technical and scientific material has been translated into Hebrew to have reduced the importance of English proficiency for the types of technical and scientific jobs surveyed. Alternatively, if the scientific and technical training which was required for these jobs could not have been obtained without knowledge of English, then employers could have assumed English proficiency and not have needed to specify it.

It is of interest that Hebrew was specified as a job requirement in 1973 about as often as English, indicating that in a land whose population contains a large proportion of persons whose first language is not Hebrew, competence in Hebrew cannot be taken for granted. By the same token, although instruction in

English is universal, competence in English cannot always be assumed. The statement often repeated by Israelis that "one can't get a good job without knowing English" does not appear to be literally true. Nonetheless, the percentage requiring English was substantial, representing a large number of jobs, and it constitutes a considerable kernel of truth for the notion that knowledge of English is an economic advantage in Israel.

The importance of English for white-collar jobs suggest that a strong incentive to learn English exists among ordinary citizens, persons who are not likely to continue their formal education beyond high school and who will thus not need English for post-secondary school studies. Thus for many of the students who do not plan to continue their studies beyond high school, English can be viewed with some justification as a bread-and-butter skill, much as is shorthand, typing, and bookkeeping.

The results of the present survey of job requirements suggest that economic considerations do indeed play an important role in promoting the spread and maintenance of languages of wider communication and are consistent with a study by Fishman, Cooper, and Rosenbaum (this vol., chap. 2), in which the importance of exports to English-speaking countries was found to be related to overall use of English in countries around the world. If anything, the present survey probably underestimates the importance of economic considerations, inasmuch as there are many jobs which do not require proficiency in a language of wider communication but for which the training requires such knowledge. In Israel, candidates for a university degree in social work, for example, are assigned most of their texts in English, even though most of them will not need English on the job when dealing with their clients. It appears, therefore, that the economic incentives which promoted the spread of great imperial languages in the past, continue, in the absence of empire, to promote the spread of languages of wider communication today.

REFERENCES

Brosnahan, L.F. 1963. Some historical cases of language imposition. In *Language in Africa*, edited by J. Spencer. Cambridge: Cambridge University Press. Pp. 7–24.

Fishman, Joshua A. 1969. National languages and languages of wider communication in the developing nations. *Anthropological Linguistics* 11:111–135.

Fishman, Joshua A.; Robert L. Cooper; and Yehudit Rosenbaum. 1977. English around the world. This vol., chap. 2.

Moher, Deena. 1975. Foreign language ability, an important job requirement in the U.S.A.? Unpublished term paper, Hebrew University.

Rosenbaum, Yehudit; Elizabeth Nadel; and Robert L. Cooper. 1977. English on Keren Kayemet Street. This vol., chap. 6.

Scotton, Carol Myers. 1972. *Choosing a Lingua Franca in an African Capital.* Edmonton and Champaign: Linguistic Research.

PART FOUR

The Impact of English on Local Terminology, Planned and Unplanned

Chapter 9

The Influence of English on Formal Terminology in Hebrew

Yaffa Allony-Fainberg

In a study of the acceptability and use of the formal Hebrew terms published in the *Dictionary of Automobile Terms* (DAT), as seen in written sources, it was found that in addition to the many original Hebrew terms published, there were others translated from languages of wider communication such as German, English, or French (Allony-Fainberg 1973). However, the DAT contained a greater number of terms translated from German than from any other language, though in the terminology used by speakers and appearing in written sources of later dates, it was easily discernible that English terms had greater influence. Several examples were given there, such as the term *Hilazon* in the DAT, a direct translation from the German *Schnecke* for what is called *worm* in English. In later sources there appears *Tola'at*, which is the Hebrew translation for *worm*.

As the paper cited above did not deal directly with the influence of English, that subject was not elaborated any further. This chapter demonstrates that, in time, the influence of English terminology greatly surpassed that of German in the formal Hebrew nomenclatures created by the Academy of the Hebrew Language.

INFLUENCES ON TERM-FORMATION

One of the ways of creating new terms in developing languages is to translate terms from languages of wider communication. That mythic hero (Bar-Adon 1973, p. 88; Rubin 1973, p. *viii*) of the development of the Hebrew language,

Ben Yehuda, used to make direct translations from German such as: *Sah Rahoq* (for *telephone*) from *Fernsprecher; Et Oferet* (*pencil*) from *Bleistift,* etc. Many of the terms of that type were not accepted, and were later replaced by others. At that time the only language that could compete with German as a source for neologisms was French. However, as most Jewish scientists and linguists who lived and worked in Israel then were from East European countries and had received their higher education mainly in Germany or Austria, the only naturally influencing language was German. There were additional factors that strengthened the influence of German at that time, such as the Ezra Foundation and its activities on behalf of education in Israel (Palestine).

After World War I, when England was entrusted with the Mandate over Palestine, the influence of English on the cultural life of Israel increased. The arrival of the British army and police force, and later of the many British officials, greatly affected social life and language in Israel. English became a compulsory subject of study in all schools and its influence naturally increased.

Still later, with the arrival of immigrants from other countries, the establishment of the State of Israel, and the overpowering influence of America, English certainly became a most influential factor in the development of the Hebrew nomenclature, formally and informally. Americanisms even invaded well-developed languages of wider communication such as French and German. No wonder, then, that English words and expressions easily found their way into languages of lesser prestige and national power. In addition, the mass media (television, radio, records, and movies) contributed their not insignificant share to the influence of English on other languages.

ANALYSES OF THE INFLUENCE OF ENGLISH

In Israel the influence of English can easily be traced not only on colloquial Hebrew, but also on the neologisms approved by the Academy of the Hebrew Language and accepted by the Minister of Education and Culture.

A Comparison of Dictionaries of Various Dates

In order to examine the influence of English on formal modern Hebrew terminology in earlier times in comparison with that of today, four dictionaries were chosen from among those published by the Academy of the Hebrew Language and its predecessor group, the Va'ad Halashon Haivrit (Council of the Hebrew Language). Two were chosen at random from among the dictionaries published by the earlier Council, and two at random from those published by the Academy itself (necessarily more recent). These four are: *Dictionary of Kitchen Terms* (Jerusalem, 1938), *Dictionary of Locksmith's and Blacksmith's Craft* (Jerusalem, 1942), *Dictionary of Joinery Terms* (Jerusalem, 1971), and *Dictionary of Technical Drawing* (Jerusalem, 1974).

In addition, another dictionary published by the Academy was examined: *Dictionary of Work Study* (1973). This one is analyzed separately because of its different form. Unlike the other dictionaries, its terms are translated into English only, without any mention of French or German.[1]

Two hundred terms from the first four dictionaries were examined—the first 100 and the last 100 of each. This is quite a significant number of terms as most of the dictionaries examined do not contain many more (*Kitchen*, 507 terms; *Locksmith's and Blacksmith's*, 335 terms; *Joinery*, 247 terms; and *Drawing*, 246 terms). Table 9.1 shows the number of terms in Original Hebrew (i.e., *not* loan translations (calques) such as "wing—*Türflügel—agaf*"), the number of terms which were translated equally from English and German (e.g., "door closer—*Türschlieser—megif delet*"), the number of terms translated directly from German only (e.g., "sliding door guide—*Schiffchen—sirit*"), and the number of those translated directly from English only (e.g., "box cover—*Laufschienen verkleidung—teivat kisuy*"). Only very rarely can one notice a direct translation from any other language, such as a term translated from French (e.g., "louvered window—*fenêtre à lames de verre—halon rfafot zehuhit*," or "to ink in—*ausziehen—passer à l'encre—ha'avir betush*").

Table 9.1 clearly shows that in earlier times there was a tendency to form original Hebrew terms, to adapt and revive indigenous roots; therefore in the earliest dictionary (*Kitchen Terms*, 1938) such terms comprise 59.5% of all terms, whereas in later dictionaries the percentage decreased (33% in 1974). The small number of Jewish settlers in Palestine thirty years ago fought for the use of Hebrew in every area of life and made a great effort to find Hebrew words for all of life's needs. Wherever one went there were large posters calling on the Jewish inhabitants to speak Hebrew, such as "*Ivri Daber Ivrit*" ("Hebrew, speak Hebrew"). It is interesting to note an example in the 1938 dictionary of an adaptation of a word taken from the religious life (in this case the name of an Aramaic chant sung on Shavuot, a Jewish holiday) for secular purposes as "*Vorspeise—entrée—Aqdamot.*"

Another observation that can be made is that there were many more terms translated from German in dictionaries published before the establishment of the State (19.5%, 18%) than in dictionaries that were published later (9%, 7%). In the case of terms translated from English, the trend was in the opposite direction. In the earlier dictionaries there are very few terms formed in this way (3.5%, 4.5%), whereas in the dictionaries published in the seventies, the number of such terms increases considerably (23%, 11.5%). An informal comparison of other (non-Academy) dictionaries published before and after the establishment of the State yielded a similar trend, with a greater proportion of English sources and a smaller proportion of German sources after 1948.

Analysis of the *Dictionary of Work Study Terms* (1973)

The *Dictionary of Work Study Terms* is quite new and unique in form in comparison with the other dictionaries published by the Academy of the Hebrew language. It contains no French or German translation or Index. It refers only

Table 9.1 Formal Hebrew terms and their origin: Four dictionaries

Dictionary	Year of Publication	Source[a]									
		Hebrew		English and German equally		German only		English only		Other languages	
		No.	%	No.	%	No.	%	No.	%	No.	%
Kitchen Terms	1938	119	59.5	46	23.0	27	13.5	7	3.5	1	.5
Locksmiths and Blacksmiths	1942	92	46.0	62	31.0	36	18.0	9	4.5	1	.5
Joinery	1971	81	40.5	53	26.5	18	9.0	46	23.0	2	1.0
Technical Drawing	1974	66	33.0	95	47.5	14	7.0	23	11.5	2	1.0

[a]From a sample of the first 100 and last 100 terms in each dictionary.

Table 9.2 The origin of Hebrew terms from the Dictionary of Work Study Terms (1973)

Source	Number	%
Hebrew	29	14.5
Hebrew translated from English	145	72.5
Both English and Hebrew	14	7.0
Untranslated English	9	4.5
English abbreviations	3	1.5

[a]From the first 200 terms.

to English terms, and looks rather like an attempt to translate directly from English rather than an attempt to create an indigenous-sounding Hebrew terminology.

The first 200 terms in running order, out of the total of 364 terms contained, were chosen for examination. The data are quite significant, as they demonstrate a different approach to term-formation in Hebrew from that manifested in former dictionaries, especially those published before the establishment of the State. It seems to point to a rapprochement with Western terminology mainly with the English, without any real search for new indigenous Hebrew words or any attempt to revive suitable words existing in older layers of the language.

Among the 200 words examined here, there are only 29 Hebrew terms (14.5%) that are *not* a direct translation from English (e.g., "consistency—*aḥidut bizua*"), whereas with respect to directly translated terms from English (e.g., "empty transport—*hovalat reyq*") there are 145 items (72.5). In addition, there are 14 terms (7%) which are a mixture of Hebrew and English words (e.g., "foreign element—*element zar*," or "normal performance—*bizua normi*"). Another 9 terms (4.5%) keep their English form as it is, or with a slight change (e.g., "element— *element*," histogram—*histograma*"). Some of these may quite easily be accepted as being in keeping with the trend of using widespread international terms. However, the final acceptance of such a purely English term as *work factor* is very doubtful. Many Hebrew-speakers will not even pronounce it properly, as according to the transcription in the dictionary it should be pronounced "work factor" with the vowels as pronounced in Latin. The same may happen to the term *wink*, which will be pronounced "vink."

A specific and especially strange case, quite new in the field of term-formation in Hebrew, is the inclusion of English abbreviations as Hebrew terms. They are transcribed as names of letters (e.g., "M.S.D.—*Em-es-di*," "M.T.M.—*em-ti-em*," and "B.M.T.—*bi-em-ti*"). English words appear next to the letter abbreviations, e.g., "M.T.M. (Methods Times Measurement)." The term is clear and it makes sense. Such terms may be familiar only to the small number of people who deal professionally with the subject of work study, as they may know these abbreviations and use them as part of their occupational jargon. However, such people do not need the sanctifying power of the Academy in order to go on using such terms.

The normal way of writing abbreviations in Hebrew is quite different from the one appearing in the case of these terms. "Methods Time Measurement" could have been translated into clear and comprehensible Hebrew, e.g., "*Shitot medidat zman*," which could even be nicely abbreviated as *Shamaz*, the regular Hebrew form of abbreviation.

SUMMARY

There certainly are other English influences on Hebrew which can be seen in loanwords (see Ronen, Seckbach, and Cooper, this vol., chap. 10); idiomatic

Impact of English on Local Terminology

expressions; and specific grammatical formations, such as the use of the passive voice—modeled on English usage—instead of the active—the natural form in Hebrew. The influence of English syntax on Hebrew is especially worth systematic examination and calls for a special research paper. All in all, however, it is clear that English is not only influencing written and spoken Israeli Hebrew but that it is doing so with respect to the very nomenclatures prepared by that bastion of pure Hebrew—the Academy of the Hebrew Language itself.

NOTE

1.   According to a 1963 publication of the Academy of the Hebrew Language there were 25 dictionaries published by the Academy and its predecessor, the Hebrew Language Council. Of these, 16 were published before the establishment of the State. Later publications of the Academy in 1970 and 1975 enumerate 38 dictionaries altogether and note three more which were in press. Thus the sample of five dictionaries represents approximately 13% of all the dictionaries published at the time this study was conducted (1975).

REFERENCES

Allony-Fainberg, Yaffa. 1973. To what extent has the nomenclature appearing in the "Dictionary of Automobile Terms" (DAT), published by the Academy of Hebrew Language, been accepted in the Hebrew written literature? The 1973 Salzman Award Paper of the Academy of the Hebrew Language.

Bar-Adon, Aaron. 1973. The rise and decline of an upper-Galilee dialect. In *Language Planning: Current Issues and Research*, edited by Joan Rubin and Roger Shuy. Washington, D.C.: Georgetown University Press. Pp. 86-101.

Rubin, Joan. 1973. Introduction to *Language Planning: Current Issues and Research*, edited by Joan Rubin and Roger Shuy. Washington, D.C.: Georgetown University. Pp. v–x.

Chapter 10

Foreign Loanwords in Hebrew Newspapers

Miriam Ronen, Fern Seckbach,
and Robert L. Cooper

In Israel, Hebrew usage is based on a great number of competing factors and one cannot always predict readily which factor or which combination of factors will emerge as the main influence on how one expresses oneself. Modern Israeli Hebrew expression potentially includes the influence of all languages that new immigrants bring along as their mother tongues. Apart from foreign mother tongues, degree of education is also a factor in that higher education exposes the individual to greater contact with major Western languages, especially English. The general reading public is in turn influenced by the international news services and other communication media (movies, radio, television).

Since the influence of communication media is massive, especially from English sources, we can ask to what extent this influence actually is integrated into everyday life. The present study examines one specific aspect of such influence, the usage of foreign terms in the Hebrew daily press. Two different types of dailies were chosen for study, one an afternoon paper written at a more popular level (*Ma'ariv*) and the other a morning paper having somewhat higher literary aspirations (*Ha-arez*).

More specifically, this study aims to determine (1) the frequency of foreign terms in the two dailies, (2) their domain, and (3) whether Hebrew equivalents are available. An attempt was also made to see whether or not one could determine the source language—the language from which Hebrew borrowed the term—for each of the items.

No similar studies about these questions in relation to Israeli Hebrew have come to the writers' attention. There is one instructive study by Abraham Demoz (1963) about Amharic. More recently a study was published dealing with English-language influence on German-language newspapers in Austria (Viereck, Viereck, and Winter 1975).

PROCEDURE

In order to answer the questions raised above, we chose twenty-five issues of both dailies in each of two years, 1950 and 1974, so that one could see whether the number of foreign lexical items used had remained stable, increased, or decreased during the first generation following the establishment of the State of Israel. In order to obtain a representative selection, twenty-five issues appearing at eight-day intervals were chosen (starting with January 1), so that the issues constituted an orderly succession of the weekdays from January 1 to July 16 for *Ha-arez* in 1950 and 1974, and for *Ma'ariv* in 1974 only. The microfilms available for *Ma'ariv* in 1950 ended with May, so nineteen of the twenty-five issues for *Ma'ariv* in 1950 were selected according to the method described above. The remaining six issues were chosen from January through May providing another "week" of issues (Jan. 3, Feb. 12, March 2 and 8, April 10, and May 14).

The first 100 words of the principal editorial and the first 100 words of the lead news story appearing in the same issue constituted the study material with one exception. In *Ma'ariv* of 1950 not every issue had an editorial. In that case the editorial appearing in the closest following issue was used. In that way altogether 10,000 words were checked for each year (100 words × 2 types of articles × 2 dailies × 25 issues = 100 × 100 = 10,000). For the purposes of this study a "word" was defined as a unit of letters with a space before it and after it. Excluded were any proper names, units of measurement, and titles (e.g., *Dr.*, *Bishop*). A "foreign term" was defined as any word that is not of Semitic origin and is known in some other language.

Next an effort was made to determine the source language of the term and an attempt was made to find out whether the term had an equivalent approved by the Academy of the Hebrew Language or a commonly used Hebrew equivalent. (The Academy of Hebrew Language provides new words for terms that do not presently exist in Hebrew, either by adapting ancient terms or by suggesting terms based, in most instances, on a commonly known root.) No note was made in the framework of this study of the various possible modifications that the foreign terms had undergone to fit them into the Hebrew sentences in which they were used.

RESULTS

There were a total of 148 foreign terms in the texts chosen from the 1950 newspapers and 151 from the 1974 papers. Thus, foreign terms accounted for 1.5% of the texts of each of the years selected for study (see Table 10.1).

Table 10.1   Number and percentage of loanwords in two Hebrew dailies

Year	Daily	Editorial No.	Editorial %	News No.	News %	Total No.	Total %
1950	Ha-arez	46	1.8	47	1.9	93	1.9
	Ma'ariv	27	1.1	28	1.1	55	1.1
	Total	73	1.5	75	1.5	148	1.5
1974	Ha-arez	58	2.3	32	1.3	90	1.8
	Ma'ariv	42	1.7	19	.8	61	1.2
	Total	100	2.0	51	1.0	151	1.5

However, there were only 66 different foreign words in 1950 and only 68 in 1974. The 5 most frequently used foreign words in 1950, each appearing from five to ten times, constituted 26% of all occurrences of foreign loanwords; in 1974 the 5 most frequently used loanwords, each found from six to fifteen times, accounted for 33% of the occurrences of foreign terms. The 15 most frequently used words were each found three or more times and accounted for 56% and 55% of all loanword usage in 1950 and 1974, respectively. Six of the 15 most frequently observed words in 1950 were among the 15 most frequently observed words in 1974. The majority of items in each year appeared only once: in 1950, 63% of the terms, according for 28% of all loanword usage, and in 1974, 57% of the words, accounting for 25% of the total loanword usage, appeared only once.

It was found that many of the foreign terms appearing in both years *do* have an equivalent in Hebrew, 40% from 1950 and 61% from 1974 (see Tables 10.2 and 10.3). Yet of the 15 most frequently used words of each year, 8 did not have a commonly known one-word equivalent (paraphrased equivalents could be found, of course).

In only a little over one-third of the articles scanned were there no foreign loanwords in the first 100 words of the text (see Table 10.4). There were seven articles in 1950 (7%) and six in 1974 (6%) which had five or more foreign terms in the text checked. Thus we see that most articles did have some foreign words and that the situation is similar for both years involved.

In 1950 there were almost twice as many loanwords in *Ha-arez* (1.9%) as in *Ma'ariv* (1.1%), as can be seen in Table 10.1. This was true for both the editorial and the news items. In 1950, within each newspaper, there was no difference in the number of loanwords used in editorial and news items. In fact, the number was almost identical for each type of item. By 1974 the picture had changed somewhat. While *Ha-arez* still used more loanwords than *Ma'ariv*, the editorials in both papers used more loanwords than did the news items. The editorials had twice as many foreign words. In 1974, the fewest foreign terms

Table 10.2   The fifteen most frequently used foreign terms in 1950

Term	Existence of common Hebrew term	Domain	No. of occurrences	No. of articles in which term found	% of total occurrences of loanwords
koalizia		politics	10	6	8
komunisti		politics	9	7	7
parlementari		politics	8	7	6
diplomatia	yes	politics	6	5	4
minister	yes	politics	5	3	4
indeks		economics	4	2	3
informazia	yes	general	4	4	3
bank		economics	4	3	3
basis[a]		gen./milit.	4	4	3
ministeriyon		politics	4	1	3
formali	yes	general	4	3	3
radiyo		general	4	2	3
bal		general	3	1	2
techni		gen./sci.	3	3	2
mandat		politics	3	2	2

[a]Basis has been used in Hebrew for hundreds of years and has even been adopted into the Hebrew verbal patterns. Yet it is still recognizable as a foreign term to readers with knowledge of English.

Table 10.3   The fifteen most frequently used foreign terms in 1974

Term	Existence of common Hebrew term	Domain	No. of occurrences	No. of articles in which term found	% of total occurrences of loanwords
koalizia		politics	15	11	10
bank		economics	13	4	9
politi	yes	politics	10	9	7
minister	yes	politics	6	5	4
mandat		politics	6	5	3
diplomati	yes	politics	5	5	3
parlementari		politics	4	2	2
ultimativi		general	3	3	2
optimi		general	3	3	2
atomi		science	3	3	2
interes	yes	general	3	3	2
teror		politics	3	2	2
techni		gen./sci.	3	2	2
tank		military	3	3	2
realisti	yes	general	3	3	2

Table 10.4   Number of articles using foreign words in two Hebrew dailies

Year	Daily	Type of article	0	1	2	3	4	5 or more
					Number of words			
1950	Ha-arez	editorial	5	4	9	5	1	1
		news	6	8	5	2	0	4
	Ma'ariv	editorial	11	8	2	1	1	2
		news	11	5	4	5	0	0
		Total	33	25	20	13	2	7
1974	Ha-arez	editorial	0	10	6	2	3	3
		news	12	4	4	1	3	1
	Ma'ariv	editorial	6	6	6	5	1	1
		news	19	2	1	1	1	1
		Total	37	22	17	9	8	6

were used by *Ma'ariv*, the more popular newspaper, in its news sections, while the most foreign terms were used by *Ha-arez*, the more sophisticated paper, in its editorials.

In most cases it proved not to be possible to determine the source language from which Hebrew borrowed the specific terms, especially the international ones, such as *radio*. Few of the words used in Hebrew are exact replicas of the English form of the words, yet readers with a good knowledge of English, French, or German will easily understand the items. For example, *artileria*, artillery, can be understood through English *artillery*, French *artillerie*, German *Artillerie*, or Italian *artigleria*. Even terms with the ending *-zia* can be understood by the English speaker; for example, consider *inflazia*, inflation.

The domain in which the foreign words were used the most is *politics*. The five most frequently occurring loanwords in 1950 and four of the five most frequently occurring words in 1974 were political terms. This may be related to the fact that the source material was daily newspapers, which devote considerable attention to political affairs. In the Viereck et al. study, which covered whole issues of three different types of newspapers, the more sophisticated paper had the most English loanwords in the categories of politics and finance, and a more popular locally oriented newspaper had large numbers of loanwords in the sports and general news sections (Viereck et al. 1975, pp. 210–211). Also, the political structure of Israel is based on ideas inherited from countries outside of the Middle East, and England itself was the ruling authority during the generation preceding the establishment of the State. The importance of English as an international vehicle of scientific and technical discourse may account for the presence of the other domains represented by the fifteen most commonly found loanwords in 1950 and 1974: science, economics, and the military (see Tables 10.2 and 10.3).

DISCUSSION

Demoz considered the frequency of loanwords which he studied to be "uncommonly heavy" (p. 117) and he attributed this to a lack of an organized effort to create the needed Amharic terms, "partly because the necessary strong aversion to borrowing has been lacking and partly because a well-trained staff to accomplish such a task has not been available." We cannot compare this frequency directly with our own because Demoz cites only the number of *different* independent loanwords and because in his count he included titles, which we excluded.[1] However, it is unlikely that the percentage of loanwords which he found was much higher than our own (1.5%), even though Israel possesses a language academy one of whose aims is to supply contemporary terminology. In fact, there has been almost no change in the amount or type of foreign words used in the Israeli papers studied for twenty-five years.

Considering the fact that a substantial proportion of the loanwords that we observed have Hebrew equivalents, how can the phenomenon of borrowing be explained? One hypothesis is that the newer Hebrew words have not yet been comfortably adopted by the newspaper writers, especially writers of editorial material. Another possible explanation pertains more to the readers than to the writers and relates to the status associated with knowledge of English and other foreign languages; it is often directly associated with education and socioeconomic status. This might explain the difference between the two dailies, inasmuch as *Ha-arez*, aiming at the more sophisticated audience, employed more foreign words; *Ma'ariv*, appealing to the more general reading public, used fewer foreign words. The same explanation might account for the differences observed between the editorial and news sections in both dailies in 1974 if it can be assumed that editorials tend to be read more frequently by more educated persons.

The evaluation of our findings involves a choice between what Rokeach (1968) called the terminal as against the instrumental value of a language. In terms of our study one approach would be descriptive only, placing no negative value on the high percentage of foreign terms. Another approach would be prescriptive, raising an alarm at the heavy intrusion of Western languages into modern Hebrew expression and demanding a change. (The latter approach can be justified by the fact that only a minority of the readers are immigrants from English-speaking countries, thus possibly adding to the difficulties in the way of the many new immigrants who, reading a Hebrew newspaper, come upon these non-Hebrew words.) A third approach, also instrumental in nature, would find satisfaction that modern Hebrew is being partially Europeanized, thus, guaranteeing its nonparochial development at a time when European languages are clearly associated with major political and economic trends all over the world, and when Israelis are seeking to participate in these trends as actively as possible.

NOTE

1.   Demoz described his frequencies as follows (p. 116): "The total number of loan-words found was 631. If we count the small variations of some words as independent loans the total comes up to 725. The frequencies of occurrence in the sample for each word ranged from 1 to 269, the highest frequency being manifested by the word / *mistär* / 'Mr.' By far the greater number of words (about 85%) had a frequency lower than 10." His count was made on the loans of about 210,000 running words of text. If his average loanword appeared three times (our average was 2.2), he would have observed about 2175 items (725 × 3), or about 1% of the running text.

REFERENCES

Demoz, A. 1963. European loanwords in an Amharic daily newspaper. In *Language in Africa*, edited by John Spencer. Cambridge: Cambridge University Press.

Rokeach, Milton. 1968. *Beliefs, Attitudes, and Values: A Theory of Organization and Change*. San Francisco: Jossey-Bass.

Viereck, K.; W. Viereck; and I. Winter. 1975. Wie Englisch ist unsere Pressesprache? *Grazer Linguistische Studien* 2 (May 1975):205-226.

PART FIVE

Attitudes Toward English

Chapter 11

A Study of Language Attitudes

Robert L. Cooper and *Joshua A. Fishman*

The Israeli educational scene provides a useful context for the study of language attitudes, particularly with respect to English. That language is a required subject for all students from the fifth grade onwards. A compulsory subject on the secondary school matriculation examination, it is an important part of the school curriculum. At university, it is the medium for a substantial portion of the students' reading lists, and knowledge of the language is set as a requirement for university graduation. Bound up with academic incentives to learn English are economic ones, both direct and indirect. Direct incentives exist where knowledge of English is an explicit job requirement, as is often the case (see Cooper and Seckbach, this vol., chap. 8). Indirect incentives exist to the extent that the training or educational

The authors acknowledge with thanks the help of Bryna Bogoch, Elizabeth Nadel, Elhanan Peleg, Phyllis Rosenbaum, Yehudit Rosenbaum, Fern Seckbach, and Jean Vermel during several stages of the research reported here. Bryna Bogoch developed the five-language questionnaire and Jean Vermel developed the means-end questionnaire. Jean Vermel also collected information about Israeli adolescents' views of American immigrants, and she obtained role-playing protocols from Israeli adolescents, both of which were employed in the construction of some of the attitude scales. Elizabeth Nadel and Yehudit Rosenbaum worked on back-translations of many of the instruments into Hebrew. They, along with Phyllis Rosenbaum and Jean Vermel, administered all of the instruments. Elhanan Peleg and Yehudit Rosenbaum scored the Hebrew cloze tests, and Phyllis Rosenbaum and Jean Vermel scored the English cloze tests. Phyllis Rosenbaum scored the respondents' taped English recordings. Fern Seckbach helped with various aspects of the scoring and coding procedures. The authors also wish to thank Norman Grover for his help in computer programming.

level required for particular jobs demands a knowledge of English. One can expect, therefore, that Israeli students will have material, or in Gardner and Lambert's (1972) terms, "instrumental" incentives for learning English.

One might also expect that Israeli students will have what Gardner and Lambert call "integrative" reasons for learning English. Many Israelis have relatives abroad and many Israelis are concerned about Israel's position in international opinion. To the extent that Israeli students want to communicate with and understand the points of view of persons from abroad, an integrative orientation toward English, an international linga franca par excellence, can be expected.

To what extent are Israeli students motivated by instrumental considerations to learn English and to what extent by integrative considerations? Do students with an integrative orientation tend to learn English better than students with an instrumental orientation? Gardner and Lambert's work suggests that second-language proficiency is more often related to an integrative orientation than to an instrumental one, although the correlations typically obtained between motivational orientation and second-language achievement are typically low. Israel, however, contrasts with most other contexts in which the relationship between second-language learning and motivation has been studied. The tiny size of its population, its ties to a diaspora, and the inutility of its principal language as a medium of international communication present a relatively strong case for the usefulness of an additional language as language of wider communication both for instrumental and for integrative purposes.

What attitudes do Israeli students have toward native speakers of English, and do these attitudes make any difference with respect to their acquisition of English? Macnamara (1973), pointing to the typically low correlations obtained between second-language achievement scores and learners' attitudes towards native speakers of the target language, argues that languages often spread among people who actively dislike its native speakers. Citing, among several examples, the spread of English in Ireland, he believes that if people need to learn a language they will do so regardless of their attitudes towards its native speakers. Is this the situation in Israel as well?

Most research on the relationship between language attitude and second-language achievement has concentrated on the motivational aspects of language attitude or on attitudes toward native speakers of the target language. Students may, however, harbor positive or negative feelings about the target language itself. To what extent do Israeli students like English? Do they evaluate it positively? Do students who give more positive evaluations with respect to the attributes of English also tend to have greater English proficiency?

Language attitude is studied sometimes in its own right and sometimes in connection with its relationship to language behavior. The language behavior which is most frequently studied in connection with language attitude is language proficiency. One can also ask, however, to what extent attitude is related to usage of the target language. Israeli students have many opportunities to use English outside the classroom. They can, for example, use it with visitors from abroad and with immigrants who speak English natively, they can read English-language publications, and they can listen to radio broadcasts in English. In addition, of course, a substantial proportion of their television viewing, movie fare, and "pop" songs are in English (see Nadel and Fishman, this vol., chap. 4). Do Israeli students with more positive feelings toward English or toward native speakers of English tend to use it more than students with less positive feelings? Do students with one type of motivational orientation tend to use English more than students with another type of motivational orientation?

The research reported in this paper was addressed both to theoretical questions about the nature of attitude and attitude measurement and to substantive questions about Israeli high school students' attitudes to English. Some of the theoretical questions which motivated the research are enumerated in Cooper and Fishman (1974). The substantive questions are as follows:

1. What reasons for learning English do students consider important?
2. To what extent do students have positive feelings about the English language?
3. For what uses and contexts do students think English is particularly well suited?
4. How do students feel about native speakers of English, in particular American immigrants to Israel?
5. Do students' feelings about English differ from their feelings toward other immigrant languages?
6. Do students' feelings about Americans differ from their feelings about other immigrant groups?
7. To what extent are students' language attitudes related to their English proficiency?
8. To what extent are students' language attitudes related to the frequency of their English usage outside the classroom?

Answers to these questions were sought in cooperation with sixty-five students enrolled in secondary schools in Jerusalem during the spring of 1973.

PROCEDURE

All of the respondents attended, over a two-week period, six sessions which lasted from one to two hours each. The respondents attended these sessions during their Passover vacation and were compensated for their participation. They were recruited at two Jerusalem high schools by distributing flyers outside the schools to students as they left classes at the end of the school day. The flyers requested the participation of eleventh and twelfth grade students in research being conducted by the Hebrew University. The nature of the research was not specified. The days and hours required for participation were noted, as was the remuneration which was offered. Students were requested to sign up at the project's office, within walking distance of the two schools, in order to receive more detailed information. This enabled the investigators to control the number of students who appeared at the initial session. Inasmuch as a bonus was offered to students who participated in all six sessions, of the sixty-eight students who came to the first session, all but three participated in all six of the sessions. (These three were excluded from the data analysis.) The sessions were held at the language laboratory of the Hebrew University's Mount Scopus campus.

Respondents

The two high schools from which respondents were recruited were the Rehavia Gymnasia and the Maale School. Both are government schools, the former following a secular curriculum and the latter a religiously-oriented curriculum. The Gymnasia is considered by many to be among the best academic high schools in the country.

Of the sixty-five students who completed all six sessions, thirty-three were enrolled at the Gymnasia and twenty were enrolled at Maale. The remaining twelve came from other secondary schools in Jerusalem, recruited by friends at the first two. The respondents were about equally divided between grades 12 (52%) and 11. A little more than half (58%) of the respondents were female. With respect to self-reported degree of religious observance, most rated themselves as either "traditional" (52%) or "secular" (32%).

Inasmuch as secondary-school attendance is not compulsory beyond the ninth grade, and inasmuch as secondary-school fees are charged beyond the ninth grade (although scholarships are available for students from poor families), the students represented in this sample were primarily a middle-class lot. The students described their fathers' occupations, which were later coded on a five-point scale (5 = professions and high managerial positions; 1 = unskilled labor). A little over half of the occupations were rated as either 5 (34%) or 4 (22%), and less than 20% were rated as either 2 (11%) or 1 (6%). Almost all the students (91%) reported that they planned to continue their formal education beyond the secondary school level.

About one-fourth of the students' parents had been born in Israel and 40% had been born in Europe or the Americas. The remaining third were born in North Africa or Asia. Of the students themselves, more than three-fourths had been born in Israel. The language spoken first by the respondents as children was reported to be Hebrew by the majority (71%). Of the non-Hebrew mother tongues mentioned, French was reported by the largest number (11%), followed by English (9%), Arabic (3%), and other (9%). (These percentages total more than 100% because two students each claimed two first languages, one claiming English and Hebrew, the second claiming English and other.) No one reported Yiddish as a mother tongue, although 11% claimed to be able to understand it. These respondents represent a good example of massive mother-tongue shift to Hebrew inasmuch as that language was claimed as the first language for only about one-quarter of the parents. Among those students who spoke languages other than Hebrew as mother tongue, the average age at which they began to speak Hebrew was 6.7, and all but four of them began speaking Hebrew before the age of eight.

All in all, these students appear reasonably representative of university-oriented eleventh and twelfth grade students, at least in an urban community such as Jerusalem. (The majority of Israelis live in urban centers.) Both sexes were represented in about equal numbers; students enrolled at both secular and religious schools were represented; and the sample included students from a wide range of family backgrounds, with respect to parents' place of birth, parents' mother tongue, and fathers' occupation, although the sample had a decidedly middle-class bias. That the sample was not representative of all secondary-school students is clear. However, it appears on its face to represent that portion of the secondary-school population that is likely to have both the greatest opportunity to learn English and the greatest need to use it.

Instruments

Respondents were asked to complete a battery of questionnaires, rating scales, and tests. All materials (except the English tests) and the entire administration of the materials were in Hebrew. The students' responses to all items were anonymous. In addition to demographic information, the following broad classes of information were obtained from each respondent: language attitude, language proficiency, and language usage.

Attitude measures

Motivation to study English was appraised in two ways. First, students were presented with twelve statements, each giving one reason for studying English as a second language. These statements were designed to reflect three types of reasons for studying English: (1) instrumental (e.g., "Knowledge of English is necessary to read textbooks assigned in universities or other institutions of higher learning"; "Knowledge of English is necessary in order to pass the English matriculation examination"); (2) integrative (e.g., "Knowledge of English makes it easier to gain friends among English-speaking people"; "Knowledge of English makes it easier to get to know English-speaking immigrants better"); and (3) what we shall call here "developmental" reasons, i.e., reasons related to personal development or personal satisfaction (e.g., "Knowledge of English makes it possible to read English-language books for pleasure"; "Knowledge of English yields personal satisfaction"). Respondents were asked to indicate the three reasons which were personally most important to them.

Second, during a subsequent session, students were presented with a list of thirty-two values, most of which were adapted from Rosenberg (1956) (e.g., having interesting work to do, making a good impression on other people), and asked to rate the personal importance of each. They were then asked to rate, on a five-point scale, the degree to which each of the following language skills facilitated the personal attainment of each value: speaking Hebrew, reading and writing Hebrew, speaking English, and reading and writing English.

Attitudes toward American immigrants to Israel were appraised by both direct and indirect techniques. The indirect measures were adaptations of the matched-guise procedure developed by Lambert (1967) and his co-workers. In the classic form of this technique, respondents hear a series of voices reading a standard passage, half the voices reading it in one language and the other half reading a translation-equivalent version in another language. The voices speak each language without an accent. Respondents are asked to rate each of the voices in terms of various characteristics of the speakers (e.g., height, good looks, leadership, sense of humor). Unknown to the respondents, each speaker heard in one language is also heard in the other. Thus differences between the average ratings of speakers in each language (guise) is presumably due to differences in stereotyped views of the groups which speak each language natively, inasmuch as the guises are matched, each speaker using each language. This technique has been widely employed and adapted. (For a collection of matched-guise studies, see Cooper 1975).

In our adaptation of this technique, two groups were represented, American immigrants to Israel and native Israelis (Sabras). Americans were represented by American-accented English and American-accented Hebrew. The Sabras were represented by Hebrew-accented English and native Hebrew. Innovations in the present adaptation are the use of conversations instead of monologues and the use of context-free as well as context-laden stimuli. The context-free stimuli consisted of speakers reciting a list of ten calendar dates (e.g., "Thursday," "March twelfth," "nineteen forty-three"). The dates were "constructed" so as to reflect pronunciation problems for nonnative speakers and thus to make the nonnative speaker's accent more pronounced. The dates were not significant ones. The contextualized stimuli consisted of two sets of conversations. One set was between a father and a son at home. The son asked permission to go on a trip with some friends during his vacation, and the father, after raising several objections, finally agreed. The other set of conversations was between a teacher and a student (both male) at school. The student complained to the teacher about having failed an examination in which his answers, but not his procedures, had been correct. The teacher, after lecturing him on the importance of method, finally agreed to give a substitute examination. The scripts for the dialogues were based on role-playing protocols obtained from Israeli high-school students.

Eight male speakers were recorded. Four were Americans and four were Sabras. The same speakers were recorded in all three sets of stimuli (dates, father-son, teacher-student), and each speaker was recorded in English and in Hebrew. From each group, the two speakers with the lighter voices were chosen to play the roles of son and student.

Respondents heard sixteen voices reciting dates (four Americans in English and in Hebrew, four Israelis in English and in Hebrew). The language of each reading alternated between English and Hebrew. Sixteen test tapes were prepared with readings of dates. On these tapes, the order of speakers was counterbalanced in order to eliminate the effect of order. Respondents listened to the tapes in individual language laboratory booths so that each test tape was heard by about four students.

Respondents heard a set of eight conversations between father and son and a set of eight conversations between teacher and student. Each set contained four conversations in English and four conversations in Hebrew, with the language alternating from conversation to conversation. The pairs of speakers represented in each set were as follows: older American with younger American, older American with younger Israeli, older Israeli with younger American, and older Israeli with younger Israeli. Eight test tapes were prepared for each set, with the order of the pairs of speakers counterbalanced. Each test tape for each set was heard by approximately eight students. Each student heard a different order for each set.

Respondents listened to the three sets of stimuli (dates, father-son, teacher-student) over a three-day period, hearing one set per day. The respondents were randomly assigned to four subgroups and each subgroup was given a different treatment with respect to the order in which the three sets were administered. The order of presentation of the sets was counterbalanced, with half the students hearing the dates first, one-quarter hearing the father-son conversations first, and one-quarter hearing the teacher-student conversations first. Of those who heard the dates first, half heard the father-son conversations second, and the other half heard the teacher-student conversations second. Those who heard one set of conversations first heard both sets of conversations before hearing the dates. Thus half the respondents heard the uncontextualized stimuli first and half heard the contextualized stimuli first, and both sets of contextualized stimuli were heard either after or before the uncontextualized stimuli, with the order in which the contextualized sets were presented being counterbalanced.

Another innovation in this adaptation is that the design made it possible to derive separate scores for attitude toward group and attitude toward language. Thus attitude toward Americans could be inferred from responses to American-accented guises (totaled across English and Hebrew), and attitudes to Sabras could be inferred from responses to Hebrew-accented guises (totaled across English and Hebrew). Attitudes to English, on the other hand, could be inferred from responses to English-language guises (both American and Sabra) and attitudes to Hebrew could be inferred from responses to Hebrew-language guises (both Americans and Sabras).

Three types of response were elicited to the aural stimuli. Respondents were asked to rate each voice with respect to each of six attributes, previously obtained from Israeli high school students as distinguishing American immigrants from Sabras (e.g., high standard of living, religiously observant). Respondents were also asked to indicate the extent to which each voice aroused each of six feelings (e.g., liking, distrust). Finally, respondents were asked to indicate the probability that they would act in a given way should they meet each speaker in each of six hypothetical situations previously described. An English translation of one situation, for example, runs as follows: "This person stops you on the street and asks you to help him find his way to a place which is nearby but not in the direction you are going. It is hard to explain how to go there without taking him there yourself. You are on your way to school and are exactly on time. You know that if you take him to where he wants to go you may be late. What is the probability that you will take him to where he wants to go?" These three types of item were designed to represent three aspects of attitude: cognitive (what a person knows or thinks he knows about the attitude object), affective (what a person feels about the attitude object), and conative (what a person is prepared to do in response to the attitude object). All eighteen items were rated on six-point scales.

Three subscores were computed for each respondent's ratings of each voice: (1) cognitive (the average rating on the six items representing stereotyped views of American immigrants; the higher the score, the closer the ratings fit an American stereotype); (2) affective (the average score on the six affective items; the higher the score, the more favorable the feelings elicited by the voice); and (3) conative (the average score on the six conative items; the higher the score, the greater the claimed willingness to go out of his way to help the speaker). Average subscores were then calculated for various language-speaker combinations (e.g., a conative score for "Americans" would be the average conative subscore for all four American voices in English and in Hebrew; an affective score for "young Americans in English" would be the average affective subscore for the two voices of the American speakers chosen to represent younger persons, when speaking in English; a cognitive score for "English" would be the average cognitive subscore for all eight voices when speaking in English, etc.). The matched-guise procedures were all administered before any of the direct language attitude questionnaires or scales were given.

Parallel to the cognitive, affective, and conative measures obtained by indirect means were cognitive, affective, and conative measures obtained by means of conventional, direct questionnaires. Respondents were asked to rate, on the same scales that had been employed for the matched-guise procedure, typical members of each of the following groups: Sabras and immigrants from America, France, Iraq, and Russia. Respondents were asked to rate each of these groups separately for males of the same age as the respondent and for males of the same age as the respondents' parents.

Another direct technique was employed to assess attitudes towards American immigrants and Sabras. Respondents were asked to indicate, on a six-point scale, the degree of their agreement or disagreement with each of sixteen statements about each group. The statements were selected and translated from two forty-six-item scales developed by Grice (1934) and reprinted in Shaw and Wright (1967, pp. 411-413). Alternate forms were prepared by matching items with equivalent Thurstone-scale values as found by Grice. In each form, half the statements were favorable and half unfavorable. The forms were counterbalanced so that half the students rated Sabras on form A and Americans on form B, and half the students rated Sabras on form B and Americans on form A.

A study of language attitudes

Respondents were asked questions about each of six languages: Arabic, English, French, Hebrew, Russian, and Yiddish. This six-language questionnaire included a set of twenty semantic-differential items (e.g., rich/poor, beautiful/ ugly, intimate/formal) on which respondents were asked to rate each language. The respondents rated each language separately, with the semantic differential items for a given language appearing together on the same page, one language per page. The order in which these pages (languages) were arranged was distributed across respondents in such a way that each language appeared in each position about the same number of times. As part of this questionnaire, respondents were presented with a list of twenty domains or functions (e.g., science, oratory, military commands, cursing) and were asked to rate the suitability of each language for each domain or function.

To summarize our attitude measurements, scores were obtained for six languages (Arabic, English, French, Hebrew, Russian, and Yiddish) and for five groups (Sabras and immigrants from America, France, Iraq, and Russia). In addition, orientations to English were assessed by means of a twelve-statement questionnaire and to English and Hebrew by a thirty-two-item means-end inventory.

Language proficiency and usage measures

Respondents were administered by a language background questionnaire on which they were asked to report the degree to which they used English for particular contexts and functions. They were also asked to rate their ability to use English for various purposes.

Respondents were administered a written cloze procedure in English and in Hebrew. This procedure requires respondents to restore words to texts from which every nth word has been deleted. For a speaker's native language, the cloze is considered a test of reading comprehension, whereas for a speaker's second language it can be viewed as a global measure of second-language proficiency (Oller et al. 1972). Two forms of the test were prepared in English and then translated, via the back-translation method, into Hebrew. Every sixth word was deleted from the English and Hebrew passages. The two English passages each had thirty-three words deleted from them; one of the Hebrew passages had twenty-five words deleted and the other twenty-four. (The Hebrew passages had fewer words deleted than the English passages because several morphemes which are separate words in English, e.g., the definite article, are part of a word in Hebrew. Thus the Hebrew passages were shorter than the English passages.) All students responded to the Hebrew cloze before being administered the English cloze. Half received the Hebrew cloze in form A and the English cloze in form B, and half received the Hebrew cloze in form B and the English cloze in form A. Various cloze scores were computed for performance in each language, including the number of identical restorations (restorations of the words that had been originally deleted), number of acceptable restorations (grammatical, sensible, and correctly spelled, but not necessarily the original word), number of sensible restorations (words which make sense in the context of the passage but not necessarily grammatically correct or correctly spelled), number of correctly spelled restorations, and the number of one-word responses. The Hebrew cloze tests were scored by two native speakers of Hebrew and the English cloze tests were scored by two native speakers of English. Scorers worked independently. Each respondent's score represented the pooled score obtained from two scorers. Between-scorer reliability was very high. The between scorer correlations for English ranged from 1.00 (number of one-word responses) to 0.95 (number of identical restorations), with the median at 0.98. The between-scorer correlations for Hebrew ranged from 0.96 (number of one-word responses) to 0.82 (number of correct spellings), with the median at 0.86. (The lower between-scorer correspondence for Hebrew can be attributed to two circumstances: the respondents' performance in Hebrew was less variable than in English, and the Hebrew versions were shorter than the English ones.)

Spoken-language proficiency scores were also obtained for each respondent. Students were asked to read aloud the lists of English and Hebrew calendar dates which they had heard during the matched-guise procedures (the noncontextualized stimuli). It will be recalled that the dates had been selected to reveal maximally an Israeli accent in English and an American accent in Hebrew. Respondents were also asked to summarize aloud each of the two dialogues they had heard during the matched-guise procedures, summarizing one in English and the other in Hebrew. Respondents read aloud the dates before they summarized the stories. Half read the dates first in English and the other half read them first in Hebrew. Half made their first summary in English and the other half made their first summary in Hebrew, with the order in which the two dialogues were sum-marized counterbalanced. Finally, after the dates had been read and the summaries made, the students were asked to read aloud sixteen unrelated English sentences, each representing an English pronunciation problem for native speakers of Hebrew. The spoken responses were tape-recorded and later scored by a native speaker of English. Among the characteristics evaluated were oral grammaticality in English and English pronunciation. The former indicated the degree to which the syntax of the English summary conformed to that of a native speaker of English. This was rated on a nine-point scale (9 = indistinguishable from that of a native speaker of English). Oral pronunciation was rated along a five-point scale (5 = indistinguishable from that of a native English speaker). English pronuncia-tion ratings were made separately for each subtest (dates, summary, unrelated sentences), all ratings being completed for one subtest before ratings were begun on the next. The three pronunciation ratings were then pooled to give each student a total pronunciation score. The total pronunciation scores were presumably quite reliable, inasmuch as the correlations among the pronunciation subscores were very high (dates and sentences, $r = 0.91$; dates and summary, $r = 0.85$; sentences and summary, $r = 0.85$).

To summarize our usage and proficiency scores, students provided self-reports of their English usage and English proficiency for various purposes, and they were tested with respect to English proficiency. English proficiency was assessed in both written and oral media, the former by means of a written cloze test, from which various scores were derived, the latter by means of tape-recorded oral responses, of which evaluations of grammaticality and pronunciation were made.

RESULTS AND DISCUSSION

The results obtained from the various questionnaires, rating scales, and tests employed fall into the following categories: English proficiency, English usage, relationships between proficiency and usage, language attitudes (including attitudes toward speakers of various languages), and variables predicting English proficiency and usage.

English Proficiency

How well were our respondents able to use English? Their self-ratings were high and, as it turned out, reasonably justified. Almost all (97%) the respondents claimed to be able to understand an ordinary conversation in English, and almost all (95%) claimed to speak English well enough to participate in one. Over 90% reported that they knew English well enough to write a personal letter and 85% said that they could read English well enough to understand a daily newspaper. Almost all (97%) claimed to be able to give directions in English to a tourist on the street. About two-thirds claimed that they had to read less than half the subtitles in an American movie in order to be able to understand the dialogue.

Compared to their performance on the Hebrew cloze, their English cloze scores were reasonably good. Whereas the average student was able to make identical restorations for 38% of the missing Hebrew words, he was able to do so for 31% of the missing English words. Whereas he was able to give acceptable (grammatical, sensible, and correctly spelled) responses for 74% of the missing Hebrew words, he was able to do so for almost 50% of the missing English words. He was able to restore sensibly about 85% of the missing Hebrew words, compared to about 60% of the English words. The scores on the English and Hebrew cloze tests are summarized in Table 11.1.

With respect to accuracy of pronunciation, about 40% of the students received an average rating, on the five-point scale, of either four (noticeable deviations from native pronunciation but the accent is slight, 11%) or three (clearly a foreign accent, enough to identify the native language, 30%), and only 6% of the students received an average rating below two (strong accent but clearly English). Their oral syntax was more variable. On the nine-point scale, close to 30% of the students received scores of six or above (7 = nearly native), but on the other hand, almost 30% received ratings of one or two (1 = a large number of deviations from native English syntax).

English Usage

Our respondents reported using a considerable degree of English. More than three-fourths reported speaking English at least occasionally to high school stu-

Table 11.1   English and Hebrew cloze scores

| | Percentage[a] | | | |
| | English | | Hebrew | |
Score	$\overline{X}$	S.D.	$\overline{X}$	S.D.
Identical restorations	31.0	17.2	37.7	9.9
Acceptable restorations	49.5	26.2	73.8	13.9
Sensible restorations	59.0	26.9	84.2	11.0
Correct spellings	73.6	24.4	95.9	5.5
One-word responses	78.4	24.9	97.6	4.9

[a]Based on 33 items on the English cloze, 24 items on one form of the Hebrew cloze, and 25 items on the other. $N = 65$.

dents whose mother tongue was English. Of the respondents who did so, more than one-third claimed that in at least half their conversations with such students they used mainly English. When asked how many conversations they had had in English outside school during the month immediately preceding, 45% reported ten or more, and another 11% reported eight or nine conversations. Only 17% reported fewer than four. About half the students named at least one English-language publication which they claimed to read at least once a month. More than half (55%) reported listening to English-language non-musical broadcasts, and of those who did, about 60% reported listening at least once a week. About three-fourths of the students claimed to have read voluntarily at least one unassigned book in English during the nine months preceding the questionnaire, and over half claimed to have read at least two. This number of English books voluntarily read is impressive, although it represents a relatively small proportion of all the books which the students claimed to have read during this period. Over half the students reported having read at least ten books all together during this period and over 40% reported having read at least fifteen. All in all, therefore, most of the students exploited to some extent the opportunities which exist in Jerusalem to use English outside the classroom, through speech, reading, and radio listening. In addition, of course, these students were also exposed to English through films and television, although here the respondents had far less opportunity to restrict themselves to Hebrew-medium fare.

Relationships between Proficiency and Usage

As might be expected, those who were more proficient in English tended to use it more than those who were less proficient. However, the relationship between proficiency and usage was relatively modest, as can be seen from the intercorrelations presented in Table 11.2 between representative usage and proficiency variables. The correlations between the usage scores on the one hand (the number

Table 11.2   Intercorrelations among English proficiency and English
usage scores

Variable[a]	1	2	3	4	5	6
1. No. of English publications read	–	.53	.40	.34	.34	.40
2. Percentage of conversations in English with English mother-tongue students		–	.54	.22	.35	.28
3. No. of English conversations outside class			–	.27	.24	.43
4. No. of acceptable responses– English cloze				–	.60	.74
5. Oral English grammar					–	.61
6. English pronunciation						–

[a]N = 65 for variables 1 through 4; N = 63 for variables 5 and 6.

of English-language publications named by students as being read at least occasion-ally, the degree to which English was used with English mother-tongue students, and the number of conversations held in English outside class during the past month) and the proficiency scores on the other (number of acceptable restora-tions to the English cloze, oral grammaticality, pronunciation) ranged from 0.22 to 0.43, with the median coefficient at 0.34. While it might be argued that the correlations between proficiency and usage may have been depressed by the fact that each usage score was a single self-report item (since single items are typically less reliable than scores based on several items and thus typically yield lower correlations), higher correlations were in fact possible, as can be seen by the somewhat higher relationships observed among the usage items themselves. We can conclude, therefore, that while usage and proficiency overlapped, the overlap was not great. This was due in part, perhaps, to the relatively high proficiency of the respondents, most of whom claimed to know enough English to use it in the contexts about which we asked.

Attitudes toward English

When asked to indicate which of twelve reasons for studying English were among the three most important to them, instrumental reasons were chosen most often and integrative reasons least often. An instrumental reason was endorsed by the largest number of students (61%) as being among the three most important reasons for studying English. This was "Knowledge of English is necessary in order to read textbooks assigned in universities or other institutions of higher learning." The percentage choosing this reason was substantially higher than the percentage choosing the next two most popular reasons, which were also

Table 11.3   Percentage of respondents endorsing each of twelve
reasons as being among the three most important
personally for studying English as a foreign language

Reason	*Percentage* [a]
1. To read textbooks assigned in univerisites or other instutitions of higher learning	61.4
2. To get along when abroad	47.4
3. To become broadly educated	47.4
4. To pass matriculation examination	42.1
5. To read English-language books for pleasure	36.8
6. To get a job which pays more	19.3
7. To gain friends among English-speaking people	14.0
8. Yields personal satisfaction	10.5
9. To begin to think and behave as Americans do	5.3
10. To learn about foreign points of view about Israel	3.5
11. To know tourists better	1.7
12. To know English-speaking immigrants better	1.7

[a] N = 57. In addition to the English mother-tongue students (N = 6), 2
students did not respond.

instrumental reasons. These, each chosen by 47% of the students, were "Knowl-edge of English makes it easier to get along when abroad" and "Knowledge of English makes it possible to become broadly educated." Of the five most frequently chosen reasons, four were instrumental ones. The five integrative reasons were chosen, on the average, by only 5% of the respondents. In contrast, the five instrumental reasons were chosen, on the average, by 43%. The two developmental reasons were chosen, on the average, by 24% of the respondents. The integrative reasons, therefore, were clearly less appealing to the respondents than the instrumental and developmental ones, and of the two latter categories, instrumental reasons were by far the more popular ones. These results are summarized in Table 11.3.

The students' average ratings of the importance of each of four language skills (speaking Hebrew, reading and writing Hebrew, speaking English, reading and writing English) for promoting or retarding the acquisition of each of thirty-two personal goals are presented in Table 11.4. It can be seen, first of all, that for each language there was little difference between the average ratings for oral and written skills. That is to say, reading and writing seemed neither more important nor less important, on the average, than speaking. The largest difference between the average ratings for spoken and written skills was only half a point (on a six-point scale), seen for "making a good impression on other people" (goal 2), for which speaking was thought to be more important than reading and writing, a difference which was seen for each language.

The second observation which can be made is that English and Hebrew received about the same average ratings. Not only were the averages about the same when totaled for all thirty-two goals, but the averages were almost identical for most of the individual goals. The largest differences observed between the averages for Hebrew and for English were for goals 3 and 6, "observing the laws of Judaism" and "having your family approve of your views," for each of which Hebrew was seen as more important than English. The average ratings for English and Hebrew were highly correlated. When calculated on the basis of the combined ratings of spoken and written skills, the correlation between English and Hebrew ratings was 0.93.

To what extent were language skills seen as important for facilitating the acquisition of important goals? There was a moderate relationship between the average rating of the importance of the goals (column 1 in Table 11.4) and the average ratings of the importance of English and Hebrew as facilitators. The correlations between the average ratings of the goals' importance and the average ratings of English and of Hebrew (when ratings for spoken and written skills were combined) were 0.50 for English and 0.48 for Hebrew. English and Hebrew, in other words, tended to be viewed as more important for facilitating more important goals than for facilitating less important goals.

That English and Hebrew were seen as roughly equal in importance for the promotion of personal goals and that they tended to be seen as more important for promoting more important goals suggests that these students strongly valued their knowledge of English.

Not only did the students appear to value knowledge of English, they displayed favorable attitudes toward English vis-à-vis other languages. When asked to rate the suitability of each of five languages for each of twenty uses, English received the highest average rating on eight uses, including science, oratory, international diplomacy, philosophical treatises, and light verse. For two additional uses, novels and poetry, English received the highest average rating along with French. Thus English was the language most commonly viewed as most suitable for contexts associated with high culture and science. It was, however, also given the highest average rating for a more popular culture item, folksongs. English was even given the highest average rating for talking to babies, perhaps on the grounds that it is never too early to begin instruction in English.

The language given the next highest number of top average ratings was Hebrew, which was seen as the most suitable language for religious ritual, personal prayer, military commands, joking, lying, and sarcasm. Arabic was seen as the most suitable language for bargaining, cursing, and swearing (a large proportion of Hebrew swearing and cursing terms come from Arabic). French was seen as the most suitable language for opera. Neither Russian nor Yiddish received the highest average rating for any of the twenty uses listed. These results are presented in Table 11.5.

With respect to stereotyped notions about languages' characteristics—expressed by adjectives or expressions such as *rich, musical, precise, pleasing to*

Table 11.4 The importance of four language skills for promoting the acquisition of personal goals

Goal	Rated value of goal[a]		Rated importance of skill for promoting goal[b]							
			Hebrew				English			
			Speak		R + W[c]		Speak		R + W[c]	
	X̄	S.D.	X̄	S.D.	X̄	S.D.	X̄	S.D.	X̄	S.D.
1. Having interesting work to do	5.7	.7	4.5	.8	4.6	.8	4.6	.8	4.5	.9
2. Making a good impression on other people	4.8	1.0	4.6	.7	4.1	1.0	4.2	1.0	3.7	1.1
3. Observing the laws of Judaism	3.1	1.5	3.5	1.0	3.6	1.1	3.0	1.1	2.9	.9
4. Dressing well	4.4	1.1	3.1	.9	3.0	.8	3.1	.9	3.0	.9
5. Having a warm relationship with your father or other older male adult	4.4	1.4	3.6	1.1	3.4	1.1	3.5	1.0	3.3	1.0
6. Having your family approve of your views	3.7	1.4	3.7	1.0	3.4	1.0	3.2	.9	3.1	.8
7. Being attractive to the opposite sex	4.8	1.0	4.2	1.0	3.9	1.0	4.1	1.0	3.9	1.0
8. Complying willingly with the wishes of your elders	3.0	1.2	3.4	.9	3.3	.8	3.3	.9	3.1	1.0
9. Sticking to a difficult task	5.1	1.0	3.7	1.0	3.6	1.1	3.5	1.1	3.6	1.1
10. Helping other people	4.9	1.1	3.9	1.1	3.6	1.1	3.9	1.1	3.5	1.1
11. Being first in whatever you do	4.0	1.3	3.7	1.1	3.7	1.1	3.8	1.1	3.8	1.0
12. Having intellectually rewarding relationships with your teachers	4.0	1.3	4.3	.9	4.0	1.0	4.0	.9	4.0	1.0
13. Being honest and fair with all people	5.0	1.1	3.4	.9	3.2	.9	3.2	.8	3.1	.8
14. Sticking to your own kinds of people	4.9	1.1	3.9	1.0	3.8	1.0	4.0	1.0	3.7	1.1
15. Appreciating works of art	4.4	1.5	3.4	1.1	3.5	1.1	3.5	1.0	3.6	1.1

Table 11.4 (continued)

Goal	Rated value of goal[a]		Rated importance of skill for promoting goal[b]							
			Hebrew				English			
			Speak		R + W[c]		Speak		R + W[c]	
	X̄	S.D.	X̄	S.D.	X̄	S.D.	X̄	S.D.	X̄	S.D.
16. Having a steady income	4.7	1.3	4.4	.8	4.3	.8	4.4	.7	4.3	.9
17. Understanding and working with mechanical appliances and apparatus	3.4	1.6	3.7	.9	3.8	1.1	3.9	1.0	4.0	1.0
18. Being good looking	3.8	1.2	2.9	.7	2.9	.7	2.9	.8	2.9	.7
19. Having new and different kinds of experiences	5.3	.9	3.8	1.1	3.6	1.1	4.1	1.0	3.9	1.1
20. Being popular	4.4	1.1	4.1	1.1	3.7	1.1	4.1	1.0	3.8	1.0
21. Having a sense of humor	4.7	1.1	4.1	1.1	3.7	1.1	3.9	1.0	3.5	1.0
22. Being good in athletics	4.0	1.4	3.0	.8	3.0	.8	2.9	.7	2.9	.7
23. Giving adequate expression to feeling and imagination through artistic creation	4.1	1.5	3.6	1.1	3.7	1.1	3.6	1.1	3.7	1.1
24. Having close friends	5.0	1.1	4.1	.9	3.9	.9	3.9	1.0	3.6	1.0
25. Being looked up to by others	3.9	1.5	3.9	1.1	3.8	1.1	4.1	1.0	4.0	1.1
26. Being well informed about current affairs	4.7	1.2	4.3	.9	4.5	.9	4.2	.9	4.3	1.1
27. Being among the better students in school	4.0	1.5	4.3	1.0	4.3	1.0	4.3	1.0	4.3	1.0
28. Being able to think abstractly	4.5	1.2	3.7	1.0	3.5	1.0	3.6	1.1	3.4	1.1
29. Being cultured and sophisticated	5.3	1.1	4.5	.7	4.6	.7	4.5	.8	4.4	1.0
30. Being exceptional and unique	3.8	1.5	3.6	1.1	3.6	1.1	3.5	1.2	3.6	1.1
31. Serving the interests of the group to which you belong	3.8	1.4	3.9	.9	3.8	.9	3.7	.9	3.5	1.0
32. Having a good standard of living	4.8	1.1	4.5	.7	4.5	.7	4.5	.7	4.5	.7
Total	4.4	.6	3.9	.4	3.7	.4	3.8	.5	3.7	.5

[a]Rated on a six-point scale: 6 = extremely important to you; 1 = of no importance at all to you. N = 65.

[b]Rated on a five-point scale: 5 = skill makes it very easy for you to attain goal; 1 = skill makes it very difficult for you to attain goal. N = 63.

[c]Read and write.

Table 11.5 Ratings of the suitability of five languages for twenty uses

| | Rating [a] | | | | | | | | | | | |
| | Arabic | | English | | French | | Hebrew | | Russian | | Yiddish | |
Use	X̄	S.D.	X̄	S.D.	X̄	S.D.	X̄	S.D.	X̄	S.D.	X̄	S.D.
Science	1.5	.7	3.9	.4	3.0	.7	2.5	.7	2.7	1.0	1.2	.5
Oratory	2.3	1.2	3.8	.4	3.4	.8	3.1	.9	2.5	1.1	1.7	1.0
Military commands	2.5	1.1	3.3	.8	2.6	1.0	3.5	.7	3.0	1.0	1.4	.8
Religious ritual	2.7	1.1	2.6	1.0	2.5	1.1	3.1	1.0	2.1	1.0	2.6	1.1
Personal prayer	2.7	1.2	3.1	.9	3.1	1.0	3.3	.9	2.6	1.1	3.2	1.0
International diplomacy	1.6	.9	3.9	.8	3.4	.8	1.8	.9	2.2	1.0	1.2	.5
Novels	1.9	1.0	3.6	.7	3.6	.8	2.9	.9	2.4	1.2	1.7	.9
Poetry	2.3	1.2	3.6	.7	3.6	.7	3.3	.8	2.4	1.2	2.5	1.1
Light verse	2.3	1.2	3.5	.7	3.3	.9	3.3	.9	2.5	1.1	2.5	1.0
Opera	1.2	.6	2.3	1.1	2.6	1.1	1.5	.7	2.3	1.2	2.4	1.2
Folksongs	2.1	1.1	3.6	.7	3.0	1.0	3.4	.8	2.7	1.1	2.3	1.1
Philosophical treatises	2.1	1.1	3.2	.9	2.9	1.0	2.7	.9	2.7	1.0	2.0	1.1
Bargaining	3.4	.9	2.6	1.1	2.5	1.0	3.3	.9	2.3	1.1	2.7	1.1
Joking	2.5	1.1	3.2	1.0	2.9	1.0	3.4	.8	2.3	1.1	2.9	1.2
Cursing	3.7	.6	3.1	1.0	2.5	1.1	3.3	.9	2.6	1.0	2.5	1.2
Speaking to babies	1.7	.9	3.4	.8	3.2	.9	3.2	.8	2.3	1.1	2.4	1.2
Lying	3.1	1.1	3.1	.9	2.8	.9	3.2	.9	2.6	1.1	2.5	1.1
Persuasion	2.3	1.2	3.5	.7	2.9	1.0	3.2	.8	2.5	1.1	2.4	1.1
Sarcasm	2.4	1.1	3.0	1.0	3.0	1.2	3.4	.8	2.5	1.0	2.5	1.1
Swearing	3.4	1.0	2.8	1.1	2.3	1.1	3.1	.8	2.3	1.2	2.1	1.1
Total	2.4	.5	3.3	.4	3.0	.5	3.0	.4	2.5	.6	2.3	.5

[a] Ratings were made on a four-point scale: 4 = especially suitable; 1 = very unsuitable. N = 65.

the ear—English again received very high ratings in comparison with other
languages. Here, however, English shared top honors with French, whose average
rating on twenty semantic differential items (scored so that a higher rating reflects
the more favorable characteristic in a pair) was slightly higher than that of English.
These two languages received the highest average ratings, calculated on the basis
of all twenty items, and Yiddish and Arabic received the lowest average ratings.
Hebrew's average ratings were closer to those of English and French than to those
of the other three. These results are summarized in Table 11.6.

Attitudes toward American Immigrants

Just as our respondents displayed favorable attitudes to English, they showed
favorable attitudes to American immigrants to Israel. Their attitudes to Americans
were consistently favorable on all of the different direct and indirect attitude
measures employed.

Matched-guise procedures

For the most part, on the indirect, matched-guise procedures, the American voices
received average ratings which were either higher than or about the same as the
average ratings received by the Israeli voices, and this was true in response to the
contextualized stimuli (father-son and teacher-student conversations) as well as in
response to the noncontextualized stimuli (recitation of calendar dates). There
was only one exception to this generalization, and this was for the voices selected
to represent older persons, for whom the Hebrew guises received slightly more
favorable average ratings when spoken by Israelis than when spoken by Americans.
For any of the three subscores (cognitive, affective, conative) for any
given guise (e.g., young Americans in Hebrew) the average ratings were remarkably
alike for all three sets of stimuli (father-son, teacher-student, dates). Thus, for
example, the three cognitive subscores, averaged for each of the two voices
representing young Americans, differed by no more than one-tenth of a point (on
a six-point scale) for their English guise, and this was also true for their Hebrew
guise. Their three average affective subscores differed by no more than four-tenths
of a point for their English guise and by no more than one-tenth of a point for
their Hebrew guise. Their three average conative subscores differed by no more
than three-tenths of a point for their English guise and by no more than one-tenth
of a point for their Hebrew guise. The average subscores for each guise (e.g., young
American in English, young Israeli in English) and for the various combinations of
guises (young Americans, Americans, etc.) are presented for each of the three sets
of stimuli in Appendix A. Evidently, the contextualization of the stimuli (and the
lack of contextualization) had little effect on the average response. These results
can be contrasted with those obtained by Carranza and Ryan (1975), who found
that the manipulation of contexts in which taped monologues were presented (a
teacher giving a history lesson to her class, a mother preparing dinner) elicited
different evaluative reactions. Spanish speakers received higher average ratings

Table 11.6   Semantic differential ratings of six languages

Rating [a]

Characteristic	Arabic		English		French		Hebrew		Russian		Yiddish	
	X̄	S.D.	X̄	S.D.	X̄	S.D.	X̄	S.D.	X̄	S.D.	X̄	S.D.
Beautiful	2.5	1.4	5.3	.8	5.4	1.1	4.9	1.1	3.1	1.7	2.7	1.5
Rich	3.9	1.5	5.5	.8	5.3	1.0	3.8	1.5	4.4	1.4	3.7	1.5
Musical	3.1	1.8	4.8	1.0	5.4	1.1	3.7	1.4	3.7	1.5	3.3	1.5
Precise	3.7	1.6	4.9	1.3	4.8	1.4	4.2	1.2	4.1	1.3	3.3	1.4
Logical	3.8	1.5	5.1	1.1	4.5	1.4	4.8	1.1	4.0	1.4	3.6	1.5
Pleasing to the ear	2.7	1.4	5.1	1.1	5.3	1.3	4.5	1.2	3.1	1.7	2.8	1.5
Sophisticated	2.9	1.2	4.9	1.0	4.9	1.1	4.2	1.2	3.9	1.0	3.5	1.3
Rhythmical	3.2	1.6	4.5	1.3	5.1	1.2	3.7	1.3	3.5	1.4	3.1	1.4
Refined	2.1	1.2	4.6	1.1	5.3	.9	3.8	1.2	3.2	1.5	3.0	1.2
Colorful	3.5	1.5	4.7	1.2	4.7	1.5	4.1	1.2	3.5	1.5	3.4	1.4
Intimate	3.1	1.3	3.9	1.5	4.5	1.6	3.7	1.3	3.3	1.4	3.6	1.4
Superior	2.7	1.1	4.7	1.1	4.7	1.2	4.4	1.2	3.5	1.3	3.5	1.2
Pure	3.5	1.3	4.1	1.3	4.3	1.3	3.5	1.5	3.7	1.4	2.7	1.4
Soothing	2.4	1.3	4.5	1.1	4.7	1.3	4.2	1.0	2.7	1.4	2.6	1.3
Graceful	2.6	1.3	4.5	1.2	4.9	1.2	4.0	1.1	3.1	1.6	2.9	1.5
Sacred	3.1	1.1	3.7	1.1	3.7	1.2	4.6	1.2	3.4	1.0	3.6	1.4
Total	3.1	.8	4.7	.6	4.9	.7	4.2	.7	3.5	.9	3.1	.7

[a]Ratings were made on a six-point scale. Responses were rescored so that 6 = most favorable and 1 = least favorable rating. Only the positive characteristic for each dimension is shown here. (On the original questionnaire, half of the favorable characteristics were placed at the "6" end of the scale and half at the "1" end.) $N = 65$.

than English speakers when presented in the home monologue, whereas English speakers received higher average ratings than Spanish speakers when presented in the school monologue. That we found no effect associated with contextualization may have been an artifact of the repeated testing imposed by the experimental situation. Respondents heard the three sets of stimuli over a three-day period, one set per day. Responses to subsequent administrations may have been affected by exposure to the first administration, and contextualization effects which might have emerged from a single administration only (comparing the responses of subgroups each exposed to a different set of stimuli) may have been masked by the counterbalancing procedure. On the other hand, lack of a contextualization effect may have been real. Both contexts may have been seen as equally appropriate for the use of each language. In Israel, both English and Hebrew have important educational uses, whereas in the setting studied by Carranza and Ryan (Chicago), only one of the languages has an important educational function.

Because few differences were found in response to the three sets of stimuli, the discussion which follows is based on subscores which were averaged across all three sets of stimuli. These are presented in Table 11.7. With respect to the cognitive subscore (which represents the extent to which speakers were seen as possessing stereotyped American characteristics), the American voices were, of course, seen as fitting the stereotype better than the Israeli voices, and this was true whether the voices were young or older or speaking in Hebrew or in English. Thus, for example, the average cognitive subscores for young American and young Israeli voices, on a six-point scale, were 3.7 and 2.7 respectively when speaking in English and 3.7 and 2.8 respectively when speaking in Hebrew. For all American voices combined (in both English and Hebrew) and for all Israeli voices combined (in both English and Hebrew), the average cognitive scores were 3.7 and 3.0 respectively.

The younger American voices were seen as considerably more attractive than the younger Israeli voices, according to the affective and conative subscores. The average affective subscore (which assessed the respondents' emotional reaction to the speakers) for younger Americans, averaged across languages, was 3.8 compared to 2.6 for the younger Israelis, and similar differences were seen whether the speakers used English or Hebrew. Similarly, on the conative items (which assessed the degree to which respondents were willing to help the speakers), the younger Americans received higher average ratings (4.4) than did the younger Israelis (3.5), and comparable differences were found whether the speakers used English or Hebrew. Thus, our respondents appeared to react more favorably to the younger American voices than to the younger Israeli voices and they appeared more ready to go out of their way to help persons represented by the younger American voices than those represented by the younger Israeli voices.

The overall differences between older American and older Israeli voices on the affective and conative subscores, when combined across languages, was slight. A difference of only one-tenth of a point was seen on their average affective

Table 11.7   Average matched-guise ratings for various guises,
averaged over three sets of stimuli

Guise	Average rating [a]		
	Cognitive	Affective	Conative
Young Americans in English	3.7	3.9	4.4
Young Americans in Hebrew	3.7	3.6	4.4
Young Israelis in English	2.7	2.5	3.4
Young Israelis in Hebrew	2.8	2.6	3.5
Older Americans in English	3.7	3.6	4.3
Older Americans in Hebrew	3.6	3.3	4.2
Older Israelis in English	3.2	3.3	4.0
Older Israelis in Hebrew	3.3	3.6	4.3
Americans in English	3.7	3.8	4.4
Americans in Hebrew	3.7	3.5	4.3
Israelis in English	2.9	2.9	3.7
Israelis in Hebrew	3.1	3.1	3.9
Young speakers in English	3.2	3.2	4.0
Young speakers in Hebrew	3.3	3.2	4.0
Older speakers in English	3.4	3.4	4.2
Older speakers in Hebrew	3.5	3.4	4.3
Young speakers	3.2	3.2	3.9
Older speakers	3.4	3.5	4.2
Young Americans	3.7	3.8	4.4
Young Israelis	2.8	2.6	3.5
Older Americans	3.6	3.5	4.3
Older Israelis	3.2	3.4	4.1
Americans	3.7	3.6	4.3
Israelis	3.0	3.0	3.8
English	3.3	3.3	4.1
Hebrew	3.4	3.3	4.1

[a]Cognitive score represents degree to which speakers were rated as possessing stereotyped American characteristics. Affective score represents degree to which speakers aroused positive feelings on part of respondents. Conative score represents degree to which respondents claimed willingness to help speakers in specified situations. Each score is the mean of six items averaged for three sets of stimuli (calendar dates, father-son, teacher-student). Each item was rated on a six-point scale, with 6 = high. $N = 65$. For each set of stimuli, the number of *voices* (speakers using a given language) rated for each guise is as follows: group $\times$ age $\times$ language (e.g., young Americans in English) = 2; group $\times$ age = 4; age $\times$ language = 4; group $\times$ language = 4; group = 8; age = 8; language = 8.

subscores and a difference of only two-tenths of a point was seen on their average conative subscores.

When ratings for older and younger speakers were averaged together, across languages, the American voices earned more favorable affective and conative ratings than did the Israeli voices, but this was mainly due to the large difference between the ratings obtained for the younger American and the younger Israeli voices. To what extent was this difference real? Did our respondents really have a less favorable opinion of younger Israelis—their own peer group, in effect? It seems more likely that the difference was caused by some unsympathetic feature in the two voices that were chosen to represent young Sabras. These speakers received average ratings which were substantially lower than the ratings of all the other groups of voices (younger Americans, older Americans, and older Israelis), and these differences were seen even in the uncontextualized versions. Thus it seems safer to conclude that, all in all, American immigrants and native Israelis were viewed equally favorably on the matched-guise procedures.

There was no overall difference between the average ratings of English and Hebrew guises when averaged over all speakers. There was, however, an interaction between group and language. Speakers tended to receive higher affective and conative scores when speaking their native language. Thus Americans were viewed more favorably when speaking English than when speaking Hebrew, and Israelis were viewed more favorably when speaking Hebrew than when speaking English. These differences (which may have come about if speakers felt less comfortable using their second language, although all were quite fluent in it) were slight, however.

Direct procedures

Our conclusion that the matched-guise responses reflected affective and conative views which were about as favorable to American immigrants as to Sabras, seems borne out by the results obtained by means of more direct procedures. On the five-group questionnaire, which asked respondents to rate typical older and younger members of each of five groups on the same items employed by the matched-guise procedure (eighteen items divided equally among cognitive, affective, and conative types), the Americans, of course, received higher average ratings than the Israelis or any of the other immigrant groups on the cognitive subscore, which reflected stereotyped American characteristics. On the affective subscore, Sabras received slightly higher average ratings than did Americans, but on the conative subscore, Americans received slightly higher average ratings than did the Sabras. On the affective subscore, Sabras and American immigrants received substantially higher average scores than did immigrants from Iraq, France, and Russia. On the conative subscore, however, between-group differences were quite slight. Apparently, these respondents had more favorable emotional reactions to Sabras and American immigrants than to the other three immigrant groups but were prepared to help them all about equally, at least in the hypothetical situations about which we asked. These results are displayed in Table 11.8.

Table 11.8   Attitudes toward five groups as determined by direct questionnaire

Score [a]	Age	Sabras		American		Immigrants French		Iraqui		Russian	
		X̄	S.D.	X̄	S.D.	X̄	S.D.	X̄	S.D.	X̄	S.D.
Cognitive	Young	3.4	.5	4.1	.5	3.6	.5	2.9	.5	3.2	.6
	Older	3.3	.6	3.8	.5	3.3	.5	2.9	.5	3.1	.5
	Total	6.7	1.0	7.9	.9	6.9	.9	5.8	.9	6.4	1.1
Affective	Young	4.4	.9	4.1	.9	3.7	.9	3.4	.9	3.5	1.0
	Older	4.1	1.0	3.9	.9	3.5	.8	3.2	.9	3.4	1.0
	Total	8.5	1.8	8.0	1.6	7.3	1.6	6.6	1.6	6.9	1.9
Conative	Young	4.5	1.1	4.6	.9	4.4	1.1	4.3	1.1	4.3	1.2
	Older	4.6	.9	4.8	.9	4.7	1.0	4.5	1.1	4.5	1.1
	Total	9.1	1.9	9.4	1.6	9.1	1.9	8.8	2.1	8.9	2.3

[a]Cognitive score represents degree to which typical group members were rated as possessing stereotyped American characteristics. Affective score represents degree to which typical group members aroused positive feelings on the part of respondents. Conative score represents degree to which respondents claimed willingness to help typical group members in specified situations. Each score is the mean of six items. Each item is rated on a six-point scale, with 6 = high. $N = 65$.

A study of language attitudes

Table 11.9   Attitudes to Sabras and American
immigrants as determined by degree
of agreement with statements about
each group

Group	Rating [a]			
	Pro		Con	
	$\bar{X}$	S.D.	$\bar{X}$	S.D.
American immigrants	3.3	.7	2.6	.8
Sabras	3.9	.8	2.7	.8

[a]Respondents rated the degree of their agreement with each
of eight statements about each group. Half the statements
were positive (pro) and half negative (con). Ratings were
made on a six-point scale: 6 = fully agree; 1 = disagree
completely. $N = 65$.

In the questionnaires which asked respondents to indicate the degree of
their agreement or disagreement with statements about American immigrants and
Sabras, our respondents showed a moderate degree of agreement with the favorable statements for each group, with somewhat more agreement with the statements favorable to Sabras than to the statements favorable to American
immigrants. They showed a moderate degree of disagreement with the unfavorable
statements to each group, disagreeing about as much with the unfavorable
statements about Americans as with those about Sabras. These results are
summarized in Table 11.9.

All in all, these results suggest that our respondents did hold stereotyped
views about American immigrants with respect to characteristics such as income
and degree of religious observance but that they also held favorable affective and
conative views toward them. The affective and conative aspects of their attitude
were about as favorable toward Americans as toward Sabras, and their affective
reactions were more favorable to Americans and Sabras than to the other immigrant groups included on our questionnaire.

Attitudes as Predictors of Proficiency and Usage

Granted that the average respondent was favorably disposed toward the English
language and toward American immigrants to Israel, did respondents with
relatively more favorable attitudes know English better and use it more frequently
than respondents with relatively less favorable attitudes? It turned out that the
respondents' views of Americans, favorable or unfavorable, made little difference
with respect to English achievement or usage. Much the same can be said about

their attitudes toward the English language, with one notable exception. Students who viewed English as facilitating their attainment of valued goals tended to be more proficient in English and to use it more frequently than students who viewed English as less useful in this regard.

Table 11.10 presents the correlations between each of six criterion variables (the three usage and three proficiency variables whose intercorrelations were described above) and thirty-two means-end ratings for each of four language skills. It will be recalled that each means-end rating expresses the degree to which the students viewed a particular language skill—English speaking, English reading and writing, Hebrew speaking, or Hebrew reading and writing—as contributing to the acquisition of a given goal. It can be seen at once that a substantial number of the English language means-end items were correlated with the English criterion variables whereas relatively few of the Hebrew language means-end items were so correlated. Over 45% of the 384 English means-end coefficients (6 criteria × 32 means-end items × 2 English skills) were greater than +0.20, over 15% were greater than +0.30, and 3% were greater than +0.40. These correlations, which are not low in terms of the coefficients typically obtained between attitude scores and nonattitudinal behavior, can be compared to the median coefficient of 0.34 obtained between the three usage variables and the three proficiency variables. In contrast, only 10% of the Hebrew means-end coefficients were greater than +0.20. The English means-end items predicted the usage criteria about as well as the proficiency criteria, and the means-end items for English speaking predicted the criteria about as well as the means-end items for English reading and writing.

It will be recalled that when the students were presented with a list of twelve reasons for learning English, the students most frequently chose instrumental reasons as being among the three most important ones for them. Unlike the means-end responses, endorsements of the instrumental reasons were largely uncorrelated to proficiency and usage. Similarly, endorsements of the integrative and developmental reasons were unrelated to proficiency and usage. Inasmuch as the means-end items reflected an instrumental orientation, one might have expected that endorsements of the instrumental reasons might have been similarly related to proficiency and usage. That they typically were not may be due to the nature of the reasons which we supplied. If we compare the most highly valued of the thirty-two goals (Table 11.4) with the reasons for studying English which were supplied to the respondents (Table 11.3), we can see only a little overlap. Unlike the goals listed in the means-end questionnaire, most of the instrumental reasons for studying English that were supplied appear, on an ex post facto basis at any rate, to have been short-range ones—reasons which were more means than ends in themselves. One can argue that the means-end responses were related to proficiency and usage because the goals were of fundamental importance to the students and because English was considered more important for the more important goals. Similarly, one can argue that endorsement of the instrumental (or other) reasons for studying English were not related to proficiency and usage because these reasons did not reflect goals of such basic personal importance.

Table 11.10 Correlations between means-end ratings and English proficiency and usage

Means and goal [a]	No. of Eng. publications read	Use of Eng. with Eng.-speaking students	No. of Eng. conversations outside class	English cloze (no. acceptable restorations)	Oral English grammar	English pronunciation
English-speaking						
1	.24	.29	.39	.30	.18	.29
2	.31	.41	.31	.31	.28	.22
3	.06	-.05	.02	.05	.19	-.12
4	.10	.04	-.04	.03	-.02	-.22
5	.35	.24	.06	.12	.17	.01
6	.36	.29	.16	.32	.34	.24
7	.30	.40	.28	.10	.11	.06
8	.16	.06	-.04	.23	.27	.16
9	.24	.16	.10	.19	.28	.07
10	.13	.12	-.15	.03	.12	-.05
11	.38	.32	.26	.41	.38	.36
12	.28	.00	-.08	.20	.17	.19
13	.23	.17	.19	.03	.16	-.05
14	.28	.35	.21	.19	.13	.13
15	.46	.27	.06	.14	.11	.10
16	.16	.10	.13	.32	.25	.41
17	.22	.13	-.09	.01	-.03	-.01
18	.16	.16	.03	.17	.17	.07
19	.27	.33	.05	.27	.20	.23
20	.08	.26	.23	.23	.13	.24
21	.08	.27	.25	.11	.31	.25
22	.11	.15	.11	.17	.28	.04

[a] See Table 11.4 for names of goals.

[b] $N = 63$ for all variables except oral grammar and pronunciation, for which $N = 61$.

Table 11.10 (continued)

Means and goal[a]	No. of Eng. publications read	Use of Eng. with Eng.-speaking students	No. of Eng. conversations outside class	English cloze (no. acceptable restorations)	Oral English grammar	English pronunciation
			Coefficient[b]			
English–speaking (continued)						
23	.49	.29	.15	.40	.21	.32
24	.25	.22	.13	.07	.07	.12
25	.30	.35	.04	.18	.18	.10
26	.05	.21	.30	.21	.12	.27
27	-.08	-.11	-.07	.22	-.11	.08
28	.38	.30	.27	.26	.28	.29
29	.16	.22	.19	.41	.17	.39
30	.33	.40	.13	.25	.28	.21
31	.37	.18	.04	.03	.03	.06
32	.04	.00	-.01	.34	.23	.36
English–reading and writing						
1	.22	.18	.32	.31	.17	.31
2	.32	.49	.39	.22	.30	.16
3	.03	-.02	.03	.01	.21	-.13
4	.06	-.04	-.10	.02	.07	-.20
5	.25	.20	.02	.08	.18	-.10
6	.27	.30	.16	.21	.39	.17
7	.25	.33	.25	.07	.16	.03
8	.22	.31	.15	.18	.34	.22
9	.20	.12	.14	.13	.23	.10
10	.08	.18	.01	-.01	.17	-.07
11	.36	.30	.28	.35	.29	.29

[a]See Table 11.4 for names of goals.   [b]$N = 63$ for all variables except oral grammar and pronunciation, for which $N = 61$.

Table 11.10 (continued)

Means and goal [a]	No. of Eng. publications read	Use of Eng. with Eng.-speaking students	No. of Eng. conversations outside class	English cloze (no. acceptable) restorations)	Oral English grammar	English pronunciation
			Coefficient [b]			
English—reading and writing (continued)						
12	.27	.04	.01	.28	.11	.20
13	.04	.11	.22	-.11	.10	-.15
14	.30	.40	.23	.27	.19	.22
15	.50	.22	.11	.26	.19	.20
16	.19	.22	.22	.35	.21	.36
17	.26	.21	.02	.15	-.02	.13
18	.16	.15	.03	.19	.20	.08
19	.26	.21	.09	.34	.20	.23
20	.13	.39	.31	.26	.22	.23
21	.10	.24	.28	.08	.20	.21
22	.13	.18	.12	.18	.29	.05
23	.49	.25	.07	.39	.23	.37
24	.28	.30	.17	.15	.13	.07
25	.29	.39	.16	.16	.19	.11
26	.15	.30	.33	.27	.18	.27
27	-.06	-.12	-.07	.29	.00	.15
28	.29	.20	.19	.32	.28	.28
29	.18	.23	.22	.43	.28	.41
30	.27	.32	.11	.18	.22	.18
31	.38	.19	.15	.07	.10	.05
32	.07	.07	.04	.31	.12	.34

[a] See Table 11.4 for names of goals.

[b] $N = 63$ for all variables except oral grammar and pronunciation, for which $N = 61$.

Table 11.10 (continued)

Means and goal[a]	Coefficient[b]					
	No. of Eng. publications read	Use of Eng. with Eng.-speaking students	No. of Eng. conversations outside class	English cloze (no. acceptable restorations)	Oral English grammar	English pronunciation
Hebrew–speaking						
1	-.11	-.24	-.05	-.15	.04	-.05
2	-.12	-.09	.04	-.04	-.02	-.13
3	.02	.09	.08	.19	.11	-.04
4	.06	-.01	-.01	.00	-.01	-.25
5	.16	.20	-.04	.08	.14	-.06
6	.04	.09	-.21	-.03	-.06	-.10
7	.14	.27	.08	.04	.14	-.01
8	.11	-.02	-.18	.14	.17	.00
9	.16	.07	.03	.09	.10	.01
10	.15	.03	-.07	.13	.09	-.02
11	.21	.28	.27	.23	.13	.14
12	.04	.16	.08	-.01	-.03	.06
13	.15	.10	.15	.04	.11	-.01
14	.01	.12	.03	.04	-.06	-.09
15	.28	.17	.03	.04	.13	-.07
16	.03	.00	.04	.17	.07	.16
17	-.06	-.16	-.27	-.16	-.09	-.25
18	.13	.10	-.04	.19	.17	.04
19	.07	.26	.09	.11	.11	.03
20	-.15	.03	-.03	.11	.05	.06
21	-.13	.02	.00	.05	.05	.10
22	.17	.19	.15	.13	.24	.06
23	.16	-.03	-.06	.33	.00	.09

[a]See Table 11.4 for names of goals. [b]N = 63 for all variables except oral grammar and pronunciation, for which N = 61.

Table 11.10 (continued)

Means and goal [a]	Coefficient [b]					
	No. of Eng. publications read	Use of Eng. with Eng.-speaking students	No. of Eng. conversations outside class	English cloze (no. acceptable restorations)	Oral English grammar	English pronunciation
Hebrew—speaking (continued)						
24	.08	.17	.05	.04	-.09	.00
25	.16	.19	.02	.11	.09	.03
26	-.02	.12	.22	.12	.14	.13
27	-.09	-.07	-.05	.15	-.05	-.04
28	.22	.15	.20	.17	.17	.13
29	-.02	.05	.06	.05	-.06	.02
30	.07	.21	.05	.04	.17	-.07
31	.21	.10	.09	.09	.07	.03
32	-.11	-.10	-.02	-.11	-.02	-.03
Hebrew—reading and writing						
1	-.09	-.20	-.08	-.09	-.01	.00
2	.05	.14	.13	.04	-.03	-.13
3	.05	.02	-.02	.19	.03	-.02
4	.07	.01	.02	-.03	.03	-.24
5	.17	.23	.03	.13	.15	-.09
6	.01	.12	-.18	.01	-.03	-.16
7	.09	.25	.09	.05	.07	-.08
8	.01	.06	-.15	.00	.15	-.09
9	.19	.14	.19	.13	.17	.07
10	.14	.10	-.05	.01	.08	-.15

[a]See Table 11.4 for names of goals.   [b]N = 63 for all variables except oral grammar and pronunciation, for which N = 61.

Table 11.10 (continued)

Means and goal[a]	Coefficient[b]					
	No. of Eng. publications read	Use of Eng. with Eng.-speaking students	No. of Eng. conversations outside class	English cloze (no. acceptable restorations)	Oral English grammar	English pronunciation
Hebrew—reading and writing (continued)						
11	.30	.38	.29	.24	.22	.18
12	.05	.15	.01	.07	-.02	.05
13	-.06	-.06	.02	-.15	-.07	-.27
14	-.02	.08	-.06	-.09	-.08	-.20
15	.31	.16	.13	.08	.18	.05
16	.03	-.02	.05	.15	.14	.15
17	.07	.04	-.10	-.07	-.03	-.11
18	.15	.11	.02	.17	.25	.05
19	.04	.17	.07	.07	.10	-.02
20	-.05	.18	.14	.21	.17	.12
21	.06	.21	.17	.09	.22	.17
22	.22	.29	.22	.14	.29	.09
23	.25	.04	-.03	.33	.08	.15
24	.03	.07	.03	.01	-.11	-.07
25	.16	.19	.05	.17	.11	-.01
26	.09	.13	.19	.28	.13	.21
27	.00	.01	.03	.18	-.05	.03
28	.20	.14	.13	.25	.27	.16
29	-.08	.10	.05	.08	.01	.06
30	.19	.29	.07	.10	.20	.03
31	.26	.08	.07	.06	.03	-.03
32	-.20	-.17	-.13	-.13	-.08	-.09

[a]See Table 11.4 for names of goals. [b]$N = 63$ for all variables except oral grammar and pronunciation, for which $N = 61$.

Table 11.11   Correlations of grade point average and father's occupation with English proficiency and usage

Criterion	Coefficient [a]	
	Grade point average [b]	Father's occupation [c]
Number of English publications	.22	.18
Use of English with English-speaking students	.18	.12
Number of English conversations	.15	.32
English cloze (no. of acceptable restorations)	.58	.44
Oral English grammar	.35	.31
English pronunciation	.52	.33

[a]N's vary from 60 to 64.

[b]Self-reported grade point average for current and previous year.

[c]Respondents' descriptions of the occupation of the head of household was coded on a five-point scale: 5 = professional and high managerial positions; 1 = unskilled labor.

Other Variables as Predictors of Proficiency and Usage

Of the many language attitude scales employed, only the means-end responses were consistently related to English proficiency and usage. What other variables were related to proficiency and usage? The two most important variables were father's occupation (rated on a scale of socioeconomic status) and overall grade-point average (a self-rating of the past two years' overall average). Whereas the means-end responses were related to proficiency and usage equally, father's occupation and grade-point average were related more to proficiency (with correlations ranging from 0.31 to 0.58) than to usage (with correlations ranging from 0.12 to 0.32). The relationship between English achievement, on the one hand, and grade-point average and father's occupation, on the other, suggests that the variables which are related to success in school subjects more generally are also related to English achievement. Father's occupation was about as highly related to overall grade-point average ($r = 0.41$) as to the English proficiency scores (r's between 0.31 and 0.44). English achievement, then, seems to have acted like other school subjects for this group of respondents. The relationships of grade-point average and father's occupation with the criterion variables are shown in Table 11.11.

SUMMARY AND CONCLUSIONS

Sixty-five high school students from Jerusalem participated in an intensive survey of language attitude, usage, and proficiency, particularly with respect to English. Primarily a university-oriented, middle-class group, their English proficiency was quite good, on the whole, and most of the respondents exploited to some extent the opportunities which exist to use English outside of class.

The students' attitudes toward English were very favorable. They thought it suitable for more uses than any of the other languages they were asked about, including Hebrew. Their subjective evaluations of English—in terms of adjectives such as *beautiful, musical,* and *rich*—were higher than those for Hebrew and second only to those for French, from which they differed only slightly. Furthermore, they considered English as important as Hebrew as a means toward valued goals. The students exhibited very positive attitudes toward American immigrants, whom they evaluated about as highly as native-born Israelis and considerably more highly than the other immigrant groups they were asked to evaluate.

Students most frequently chose instrumental reasons as being among the most important ones for learning English. While endorsements of such reasons were not associated with proficiency and usage, a basically instrumental view of English proved to be correlated to English proficiency and usage, as seen in the correlations of means-end responses to usage and proficiency scores. In fact, the means-end responses were the only language attitude items to show a consistent relationship to English proficiency and usage.

The positive relationships which were seen between overall grade-point average and socioeconomic status, on the one hand, and English proficiency, on the other, suggests that English operates like any other academic school subject. The factors which promoted general academic success also promoted success in English. Those students who were relatively more successful in English (and who tended to use it more outside class) tended to view English as valuable for more important personal goals. Whether this view was an outcome or a determinant of their success in English cannot be answered from correlational data. It is plausible, however, that their view of English as valuable for personal ends was both a result of and a contributor to English proficiency—that this view and proficiency reinforced each other.

It should be stressed, when evaluating these results, that our respondents were not typical of all Israeli adolescents. Inasmuch as English is learned primarily at school, however, and inasmuch as these respondents are likely to need English, for academic reasons if for no other, their responses are instructive. They suggest that favorable attitudes toward English and toward native speakers of English are largely irrelevant with respect to Israelis learning and using English. Among Israelis who have an opportunity to learn English, those who see a knowledge of English as contributing to important personal goals are likely to learn it best and to use it most.

Average Matched-Guise Ratings for Various Guises
Presented in Each of Three Sets of Stimuli:
Calendar Dates (D), Father-Son (F), and Teacher-Student (T)

Stimulus	Guise	Mean rating [a]		
		Cognitive	Affective	Conative
D	Young Americans	3.7	3.7	4.4
F		3.8	3.9	4.5
T		3.7	3.7	4.4
D	Young Israelis	2.9	2.7	3.6
F		2.7	2.5	3.4
T		2.7	2.5	3.5
D	Young Americans in English	3.7	3.7	4.3
F		3.8	4.1	4.6
T		3.7	3.9	4.4
D	Young Israelis in English	2.8	2.5	3.4
F		2.7	2.5	3.4
T		2.7	2.4	3.5
D	Young Americans in Hebrew	3.7	3.6	4.4
F		3.8	3.7	4.4
T		3.7	3.6	4.3
D	Young Israelis in Hebrew	3.0	2.9	3.8
F		2.7	2.5	3.3
T		2.8	2.5	3.4
D	Older Americans	3.7	3.5	4.3
F		3.6	3.3	4.2
T		3.6	3.5	4.3
D	Older Israelis	3.4	3.6	4.3
F		3.1	3.3	4.0
T		3.2	3.4	4.1
D	Older Americans in English	3.7	3.7	4.3
F		3.7	3.5	4.3
T		3.6	3.7	4.3
D	Older Israelis in English	3.2	3.4	4.1
F		3.1	3.2	3.9
T		3.2	3.3	4.1
D	Older Americans in Hebrew	3.7	3.3	4.3
F		3.5	3.1	4.1
T		3.6	3.4	4.3
D	Older Israelis in Hebrew	3.5	3.9	4.4
F		3.2	3.4	4.2
T		3.3	3.5	4.2
D	Americans in English	3.7	3.7	4.3
F		3.7	3.8	4.5
T		3.7	3.8	4.4

[a]Cognitive score represents degree to which speakers were rated as possessing stereotyped American characteristics. Affective score represents degree to which speakers aroused positive feelings on the part of respondents. Conative score represents degree to which respondents claimed willingness to help speakers in specified situations. Each score is the mean of six items. Each item is rated in a six-point scale (6 = high). N = 65. The number

Stimulus	Guise	Mean rating [a] Cognitive	Affective	Conative
D	Israelis in English	3.0	2.9	3.7
F		2.9	2.8	3.7
T		2.9	2.9	3.8
D	Americans in Hebrew	3.7	3.5	4.3
F		3.7	3.4	4.3
T		3.7	3.5	4.3
D	Israelis in Hebrew	3.2	3.4	4.1
F		3.0	3.0	3.8
T		3.0	3.0	3.8
D	Young speakers in English	3.2	3.1	3.9
F		3.2	3.3	4.0
T		3.2	3.2	4.0
D	Young speakers in Hebrew	3.3	3.3	4.1
F		3.3	3.1	3.9
T		3.3	3.1	3.9
D	Older speakers in English	3.5	3.5	4.2
F		3.4	3.3	4.1
T		3.4	3.5	4.2
D	Older speakers in Hebrew	3.6	3.6	4.3
F		3.4	3.3	4.2
T		3.4	3.4	4.3
D	Older	3.5	3.6	4.3
F		3.4	3.3	4.1
T		3.4	3.5	4.2
D	Young	3.3	3.2	4.0
F		3.2	3.2	3.9
T		3.2	3.1	3.9
D	English	3.3	3.3	4.0
F		3.3	3.3	4.1
T		3.3	3.3	4.1
D	Hebrew	3.5	3.4	4.2
F		3.3	3.2	4.0
T		3.3	3.3	4.1
D	Americans	3.7	3.6	4.3
F		3.7	3.6	4.4
T		3.7	3.6	4.3
D	Israelis	3.1	3.1	3.9
F		2.9	2.9	3.7
T		3.0	2.9	3.8

of voices (speakers using a given language) rated for each guise is as follows: group × age × language (e.g., young Americans speaking English) = 2; group × age (.e.g, young Americans) = 4; age × language (e.g., young voices speaking English) = 4; group × language (e.g., Americans speaking English) = 4; group (e.g., American speakers) = 8; age (e.g., younger speakers) = 8; language (e.g., all speakers using English) = 8.

REFERENCES

Carranza, Michael A., and Ellen Bouchard Ryan. 1975. Evaluative reactions of bilingual Anglo and Mexican American adolescents toward speakers of English and Spanish. *International Journal of the Sociology of Language* 6:82–104.

Cooper, Robert L., ed. 1975. Language attitudes II. *International Journal of the Sociology of Language* 6:entire issue.

Cooper, Robert L., and Joshua A. Fishman. 1974. The study of language attitudes. *International Journal of the Sociology of Language* 3:5–19.

Cooper, Robert L., and Fern Seckbach. 1977. Economic incentives for the learning of a language of wider communication: A case study. This vol., chap. 8.

Gardner, R.C., and W.E. Lambert. 1972. *Attitudes and Motivation in Second-Language Learning.* Rowley, Mass.: Newbury House.

Grice, H.H. 1934. The construction and validation of a generalized scale designed to measure attitudes toward defined groups. *Bulletin of Purdue University* 25:37–46.

Lambert, Wallace E. 1967. A social psychology of bilingualism. *Journal of Social Issues* 23:91–109.

Macnamara, John. 1973. Attitudes and learning a second language. In *Language Attitudes: Current Trends and Prospects,* edited by Roger W. Shuy and Ralph W. Fasold. Washington, D.C.: Georgetown University Press. Pp. 36–40.

Nadel, Elizabeth, and Joshua A. Fishman. 1977. English in Israel: A sociolinguistic study. This vol., chap. 4.

Oller, John W. Jr.; J. Donald Bowen; Ton That Dien; and Victor W. Mason. 1972. Cloze tests in English, Thai, and Vietnamese: Native and non-native performance. *Language Learning* 22:1–15.

Rosenberg, M.J. 1956. Cognitive structure and attitudinal effect. *Journal of Abnormal and Social Psychology* 53:367–372.

Shaw, Marvin E., and Jack M. Wright. 1967. *Scales for the Measurement of Attitudes.* New York: McGraw-Hill.

Chapter 12

Language Attitudes in Rhodesia

John E. Hofman

*Language makes a people, and a people without pride in its language is
dispossessed of its national pride. Preserving one's language is preserving
one's culture.*

(Shona-speaking teacher trainee)

When we try to think of features that distinguish humans from other animals we
often cite language as particularly characteristic of such a distinction. Although
we no longer believe that animals make no use of language at all, humans are
surely unique in the extent to which language enables them to link the past with
the future, the present to the absent, the concrete and the abstract.

Yet, language is a surprisingly nonconscious activity. It is taken for
granted almost as much as breathing and eye-blinking. When speakers of a well-
established and widely circulating language are asked how they feel about it, they
often look astonished and reply quite frankly that they have never given the
matter a thought. Much like breathing and eye-blinking, language becomes an
object of reflection only when one's attention is directed toward it.

If language is, in fact, such a nonconscious activity, can one properly
speak of attitudes toward it? Does it make sense to ask people how they feel
about something they have never thought of? Well, it depends. In the first place,

The author greatly appreciates the help of Mr. T. Mashita, who conducted the interviews
with great skill and assisted in other significant ways as well. Many thanks are also due to
Mr. J. Haasbroek for the essays and to Mr. K.G. Mkanganwi for his translation from the
Shona.

some people do think about language—in particular when its free use, purity, or development are in some way threatened. Secondly, attitudes are rather subtle dispositions and rarely well formulated until one is challenged to verbalize them. Finally, the very fact that some people have rather strong attitudes about language and others seem to have none at all is interesting in and of itself.

Being such a spontaneous and low-profile activity, language, and in particular speech, may not merely be the object of attitudes, but point to attitudes beyond itself. When a Rusape farmer of the Shona people complains that "educated people show disrespect for parents and ancestral spirits by their use of English at home," he expresses rather strong attitudes towards both language and educated people. Moreover, he seems to feel that merely by speaking English, or perhaps some adulterated form of the native tongue, those educated people are telling him something about their attitudes toward parents and ancestral spirits. Thus, attitudes toward language can serve as indicators of attitudes toward further elements of one's culture.

Gardner and Lambert (1972) have made a case for the importance of attitudes in the learning of a second language. They have shown that interest in a people and the culture of a people speaking a certain language is an effective addition to aptitude for learning it. Other things being equal, the French-Canadian child who admires English-speaking people and their culture will acquire their language more easily than his Anglophobic peer. Possibly, also, the Salisbury (Rhodesia) child of European ancestry will be doing better with his Shona lessons if he is genuinely interested in his African fellow countrymen and their way of life.

A related line of research has also shown that a person with clear-cut attitudes toward his own language will mix fewer foreign odds and ends into his lexicon than someone who is unconcerned about such matters. Briefly, this is what was found to be the case with Israeli chemists (Hofman 1974a) and psychologists (Hofman 1974b).

In this chapter an attempt will be made to categorize language attitudes in a preliminary way in order to develop measures of these categories with respect to English and the main vernaculars in Rhodesia. As a result, some impression may be gained on how Africans and Europeans feel about their respective languages and, by implication, certain other features of their society.

The research for dimensions of attitudes follows a distinction by Kelman (1969) and previous work by the present writer (Hofman 1974b). A first and basic dimension varies between an intrinsic and extrinsic pole depending on whether a person views language as an object of value in and of itself or as useful for the attainment of ends beyond itself. A second dimension moves between a private and a public mode according to its context of relevance.

An intrinsic view takes the form of *sentimentalism* when it has to do with the private enjoyment of language; it becomes a *value* when the language appears to represent interpersonal or public symbols. An extrinsic view becomes *instrumentalism* in the private mode and *communication* in the public one,

Table 12.1   Dimensions of attitudes

	View	
Mode	*Intrinsic*	*Extrinsic*
Private	Sentimental orientation	Instrumental orientation
Public	Value orientation	Communication orientation

depending on whether a language is considered in terms of private or public advantages, respectively. The two dimensions, then, roughly define four attitude types, as shown in Table 12.1.

In Rhodesia, English is the language of wider communication and a key to upward mobility. It can therefore be expected to be useful to all (extrinsic view), but may in addition be valued and enjoyed by native speakers of English (intrinsic view). It is more difficult to anticipate attitudes toward the vernaculars. Europeans are likely to regard them of little use, while Africans may be moved to enjoyment (sentimentalism), pride (value), or both. It is the purpose of this chapter to come up with some first answers to these questions.

PROCEDURE

Samples

A brief questionnaire—containing the language scale to be described below and an open question on feelings toward the mother tongue—was sent to 800 students registered at the University of Rhodesia in 1973 and for whom addressograph plates were available. Of these, 261 students (32.7%) returned usable questionnaires in the self-addressed envelopes provided for them. Returns from students in residence constituted 44% of those canvassed, while only 26% of those not in residence responded. One reason for the low return from outside students may be that African students do not always live at the address of permanent residence during the school term, but rather in the Salisbury area. Thus mail addressed to their homes does not reach them until the end of the school term.

The same questionnaire was also administered to second-year students at two teacher training institutes, one for Africans and one for non-Africans, during regular class periods. Of the 211 responses, 100 were from the African college, and 111 from the non-African (mostly European) one. The teacher college returns should be more representative of its type of population than the University returns, in view of the bias due to partial returns likely to have affected the latter.

Also, twenty-eight interviews were conducted with twelve students from the University, nine individuals employed by various public and social agencies, and seven village parents in the Manicaland area. All of the interviewees were Africans. These subjects were not in any sense a representative or random sample, but there is no reason to suppose that another group of similar individuals would have responded differently.

Finally, an instructor at an African teacher training college—different from the one used in the questionnaire study—kindly made available thirty-one essays written in one of his classes on the topic: "Why I want (don't want) to do Shona as a teaching subject."

Questionnaire

The questionnaire, called Sociolinguistic Inquiry, has been reproduced in Appendix A. In the main, it is composed of six items, each of which calls for the ranking of completions to a problem in the vernaculars (items 1, 3, and 6) or in languages of wider circulation (items 2, 4, and 5). The questionnaire was adopted from a ten-item instrument used in a prior study (Hofman 1974b). Responses were analyzed by items, since scores summed over items showed low reliability (for reasons to be suggested later).

The questionnaire also contained a question in which the respondent was asked to state what language he had spoken at the time of entry to primary school and how he now felt about that language. A sample of verbatim replies is reproduced in Appendix B to provide some of the "flavor" of students' responses.

Interview

Interviewees were encouraged to discuss their own use of languages and the language situation in general. For this purpose the interviewer attempted to cover a set of ten questions, as follows:

1. Which languages do you read, write, and speak?
2. How do you feel about these languages?
3. On what occasions do you use them?
4. What purpose do they fill in your life?
5. To whom do you speak each of these languages?
6. Which of these language habits would you like to change?
7. Try to describe the language situation in the country.
8. What changes in the situation do you anticipate?
9. Are you hopeful that these changes will come about?
10. What languages should be used and taught in school? At what level?

The flow of questions moved from the respondent's habits to his predictions and hopes. Of special interest was the change anticipated.

Essays

African teacher trainees (in Mashonaland) have a choice of choosing Shona as a teaching subject or of not doing so. Mr. J. Haasbroek, an instructor of Shona at one of the colleges, assigned a topic to his African students in which he asked them to give reasons for either choosing or not choosing Shona. Statements that appeared to epitomize the content of students' essays were categorized and will be presented and discussed in the next section.

FINDINGS

Questionnaire Results

Results obtained with the Sociolinguistic Inquiry's questionnaire items are presented in Tables 12.2 and 12.3. Questions are grouped according to whether they deal with the vernaculars (Table 12.2) or with languages of wider circulation (Table 12.3). In interpreting means and standard deviations correctly, it must be clearly understood that students were asked to *rank* the arguments in order of preference. Therefore, the lower the reported means, the stronger the preference. In the tables (but not on the questionnaire) arguments for each item are listed in the same order (by type of orientation).

Attitudes toward the vernaculars

The first question calls on respondents to rank four arguments that might explain why "independent countries in Africa have seen fit to develop national tongues." All groups of students preferred the reply, on the average, that the national tongue is needed to permit Africans self-expression. This reflects sentimental orientation. The similarity in standard deviations shows that the range of agreement is about the same in the four groups.

On the question of the use of Shona and Ndebele as official languages in Rhodesia, all groups again tended to support one and the same argument—namely, that this would promote better communication between the major racial groups. But non-Africans opted for this argument more strongly than Africans. The latter tended to gravitate toward the sentimentalist choice of literary enjoyment.

On the third question, too, agreement is general. This time a value argument obtained first choice—that it is the main task of the vernacular tongues to "provide Africans with a focus for national identity." By rather slim margins, this was the first choice for non-Africans, too.

One notes that different attitude types dominate in different items. This accounts for the low internal consistency (reliability) of ranks summed over items, which was mentioned earlier. Responses are situation-specific. Subjects preferred a sentimentalist argument in the context of language development, a communications argument on the question of official languages, and a value argument on the issue of the broader scope of the vernaculars.

Attitudes toward languages of wider communication

On the question of why such languages as English and French achieved their present status, Africans and non-Africans are sharply divided. The reason preferred by Africans is that natives were forced to use those languages (communication

Table 12.2   Attitudes toward vernaculars

Questionnaire items [a]; options, by orientation [b]	University				Teacher college			
	Africans (N = 110)		Non-Africans (N = 151)		Africans (N = 100)		Non-Africans (N = 111)	
	M^c	S.D.	M^c	S.D.	M^c	S.D.	M^c	S.D.
1. Reason independent countries in Africa develop national tongue:								
Desire for self-expression (S)	1.75	.847	1.83	.965	1.79	.926	1.99	.991
Wish to forget colonialism (V)	2.00	.944	2.20	1.052	2.32	1.097	2.73	1.192
Easier to make living (I)	3.09	.944	3.05	.988	2.85	1.029	2.34	1.104
Try to overcome language minorities (C)	3.17	.947	2.93	.984	3.05	.971	2.94	.973
3. Arguments for Shona and Ndebele as official languages in Rhodesia:								
Further literary enjoyment (S)	2.01	1.227	2.99	.969	2.27	1.111	3.12	.961
Help Africans feel equal (V)	2.75	1.070	2.53	1.015	2.72	1.046	2.73	1.011
Make it easier for Africans (I)	3.08	.940	2.72	1.004	2.82	1.063	2.67	.891
Promote communication (C)	2.15	1.097	1.77	1.108	2.18	1.130	1.49	.898
6. Main task of vernacular tongues in Rhodesia:								
Let Africans express feelings (S)	2.32	.945	2.33	.872	2.26	1.059	2.23	.968
Provide Africans focus of identity (V)	1.71	.928	2.16	1.093	1.91	.890	2.06	1.044
Make English choice subject (I)	3.25	.999	3.33	.946	3.35	.997	3.22	1.022
Help Africans communicate (C)	2.72	1.033	2.18	1.112	2.47	.998	2.52	1.102

[a] See Appendix A for exact wording.

[b] For each item, options are listed in the same order, by orientation. S = sentimentalism; V = value; I = instrumentalism; C = communication.

[c] Mean rank. Preferred arguments, i.e., those ranked highest, have *lowest* mean rank and have been underlined for each item and each group.

Table 12.3 Attitudes toward languages of wider communication

Questionnaire items [a]; options, by orientation [b]	University				Teacher college			
	Africans (N = 110)		Non-Africans (N = 151)		Africans (N = 100)		Non-Africans (N = 111)	
	M^c	S.D.	M^c	S.D.	M^c	S.D.	M^c	S.D.
2. Reason English and French achieved special status:								
A flourishing literature (S)	2.17	.893	2.24	.994	2.07	.960	1.69	.932
Countries enjoy prestige (V)	2.58	.990	2.15	.915	2.85	.965	2.53	.864
Easy to learn (I)	3.38	.919	3.45	.774	3.03	1.004	3.35	.931
Everyone forced to speak (C)	1.86	1.052	2.16	1.176	2.05	1.174	2.43	1.081
4. Why English required in Rhodesian schools:								
Contact with culture (S)	2.85	1.033	3.10	1.002	3.01	1.014	3.12	1.090
Language of culture and science (V)	2.38	1.088	2.43	1.089	2.44	1.118	2.67	.887
Get better job (I)	2.13	.978	2.16	.927	2.14	.977	2.00	.969
Language of governing group (C)	2.63	1.240	2.31	1.209	2.41	1.187	2.20	1.169
5. If no unified language:								
Literature may suffer (S)	2.74	1.098	3.45	.909	2.32	1.152	3.59	.812
National unity suffers (V)	1.77	1.033	1.91	1.036	2.25	1.099	1.99	1.018
Misunderstanding between individuals (I)	3.02	.938	2.29	.973	3.11	.918	2.54	.900
Misunderstanding between classes (C)	2.44	1.018	2.35	.935	2.32	1.080	1.88	.829

[a] See Appendix A for exact wording.

[b] For each item, options are listed in the same order, by orientation. S = sentimentalism; V = value; I = instrumentalism; C = communication.

[c] Mean rank. Preferred arguments, i.e., those ranked highest, have *lowest* mean rank and have been underlined for each item and each group.

Table 12.4 Feelings about mother-tongue

	English speakers	Speakers of other non-African languages	Shona speakers	Speakers of other African languages
University of Rhodesia (N = 261)[a]				
Sentimentalism	16	5	31	3
Value	18	7	27	4
Subtotal (intrinsic)	(34)	(12)	(58)	(7)
Instrumentalism	48	4	22	1
Communication	32	0	4	0
Subtotal (extrinsic)	(80)	(4)	(26)	(1)
Indifference	9	0	1	0
Negativism	9	1	6	1
No answer	0	1	8	3
Subtotal	(18)	(2)	(15)	(4)
Total	132	18	99	12
Teacher training colleges (N = 211)				
Sentimentalism	11	3	19	5
Value	7	1	28	12
Subtotal (intrinsic)	(18)	(4)	(47)	(17)
Instrumentalism	47	2	13	8
Communication	10	0	3	3
Subtotal (extrinsic)	(57)	(2)	(16)	(11)
Indifference	17	0	0	0
Negativism	1	1	7	0
No answer	11	0	2	0
Subtotal	(29)	(1)	(9)	(0)
Total	104	7	72	28

[a]See Appendix B for randomly selected verbatim statements.

argument). Non-Africans preferred the intrinsic type of argument—value-oriented at the University, sentimentalist at the Teacher College. This is the one question on which there are clear differences of opinion along racial lines. Africans will not quickly forget the colonial past.

The main argument for the English language requirement in Rhodesian schools endorsed by all groups is an intrumental one—namely, that it is difficult to get a job without knowing English. Second preference, for most groups, was the communications argument, really a political one, that English is the language of the governing group. The exception to this is interesting. African students from the University of Rhodesia assigned second choice to the argument that English is becoming the language of culture and science. First-hand experience at the University had its effect.

The third item, one that treats the more general issue of language unity, again elicited fair agreement among the groups. Most assigned first rank to the argument that national unity is tied up with language unity, the Swiss experience notwithstanding. Here, non-African teacher trainees dissent. They gave their preference to the argument that misunderstanding might arise between social classes in the absence of a unified language. This is a social, rather than a political, argument.

Feelings about mother tongue

The free-response question on how students feel about their mother tongue aroused considerable intergroup variability. The framework of predetermined responses was not there to restrain impulses. The anonymity of the questionnaire often encouraged students to wax lyrical, and sometimes, rude. On the whole, African students seemed to take this question more seriously and to express stronger sentiments than their mostly European peers. Expressions of surprise at this question were much more frequent among the latter. What does he want from us? We use our language. We don't think about it. Few Africans took that view. Almost all seemed concerned—often deeply so.

In Table 12.4 responses have been classified into the four categories of the two-dimensional scheme. Those that did not fit the scheme could almost always be classified as "indifference" or "negativism." Clearly, English speakers tend to express feelings classifiable as instrumentalist or communications-oriented more often than do speakers of the African vernaculars. The latter, in turn, more often express sentimentalist or value-oriented feelings. Indifference and negativism toward the mother tongue are most frequent among English speakers. Speakers of non-African languages other than English appear to be more like vernacular speakers than like English ones. Differences are both substantively and statistically significant.

One way of illustrating the statistical summary reported in Table 12.4 is to record subjects' statements verbatim. This has been done for a small sample of randomly selected statements by the University's Shona and English speakers (Appendix B). Students' spontaneous remarks provide the reader with some of the "flavor" of language attitudes. The poetic quality of the African languages comes through in the comments made by Africans, though the comments were written in English. Speakers of Shona clearly like their language, but many English speakers, too, make it clear that they enjoy their language. We note that Shona is "soul lingo—real cool stuff" and that "English is a joy to hear spoken correctly." But it is suggested that the reader refer to the entire colorful list.

Language Interview

Attitudes, as assessed by the forced-choice items on the Sociolinguistic Inventory, do not show up as very different in the four samples of students. The interviews,

Table 12.5   Language interview summary (Africans)

	Students	Professionals	Village parents	All
Languages claimed				
Five languages, including English	1	0	0	1
Four languages, including English	1	2	1	4
Three languages, including English	5	1	1	7
Two languages, including English	5	6	3	14
One language, excluding English	0	0	2	2
Purpose of English				
Contact with English literature and culture	0	2	1	3
Helps obtain job and in commerce	4	4	0	8
Helps communicate	7	3	3	13
No response	1	0	1	2
Don't know English	0	0	2	2
Purpose of vernacular				
Pleasure of expression	2	1	2	5
Identify with culture	5	4	3	12
Communicate with friends and family	4	3	1	8
No response	1	1	1	3
Language situation in Rhodesia				
Linguistic tribalism deplored	4	0	0	4
Asymmetric relations resented	3	3	1	7
Alienation from vernacular speech decried	1	1	4	6
Modernization of Shona encouraged	0	3	0	3
Forced standardization resented	1	0	0	1
Other and No response	2	2	2	6
Anticipated changes in language situation				
More mutual learning of languages	6	3	1	10
Mixtures of language advocated	3	0	0	3
Vernaculars must be protected and developed	2	3	4	9
English teaching must be improved	0	1	1	2
Other and No response	1	2	1	4

conducted with twenty-eight Africans of different walks of life, do not bear on differences between racial groups, but strongly support the impressions gathered from Africans' feelings analyzed in Table 12.4 and illustrated in Appendix B.

Table 12.5 lists certain classifiable themes extracted from interview protocols: the number of languages claimed, and views on the purpose of English and the vernaculars in Rhodesia, on the language situation, and on anticipated changes. References to Table 12.5 will be interspersed with quotes from the interviews.

Most of the interviewees claimed at least two languages, including English, and quite a few claimed more. Language proficiency was usually limited to the spoken variety and might not pass rigorous inspection. Yet, in a world which has a high respect for oral communication, the ability to make oneself understood in several languages—or dialects of the same language—is no mean achievement. Even village parents, having wandered to southern regions in their early years, often lay claim to more than their mother tongue. As one student explains:

> *Shona is a beautiful language in its cultural expression and poems. English is*
> *a remote language because its literature brings me to many lands. I am*
> *Ndebele by tribe and must know that language. I speak and write in Shona*
> *to my friends on campus, and to people at home. I use English when I attend*
> *lectures and seminars, and Sindebele, when I speak to my girl friend.*

Students at the University converse almost exclusively in the vernacular, which was not always the case in the past. The change in public habits is usually explained as a sign of growing national pride, but no direct evidence on this was gathered in the present study. In lecture halls and laboratories, English predominates, but as soon as the student leaves the instructional setting, he switches to the vernacular—unless he happens to be talking to a non-African student.

Different purposes are mentioned for language use. English is said to meet the practical exigencies of work, commerce, and communication with members of the non-African community. The vernacular is used for pleasure and identification with tribal and national culture. The unification and modernization of official Shona is a development encouraged by the Ministry of Education, fostered by the Department of African Languages at the University, and welcomed by certain groups such as writers and publishers, but popular sentiment appears to be still mixed. A more detailed investigation of this issue is certainly indicated.

Nothing seems to be right about the language situation. Some don't like the prevailing diversity of dialects ("Each of the ethnic linguistic groups in Rhodesia tends to despise and provoke the person who does not speak their particular dialect"), and some don't like the unification of dialects ("The unification of Shona dialects is a farce, because something strange and unfamiliar is imposed on you, when you are used to a certain tongue since birth").

Village parents are particularly disturbed by what appears to them to be alienation among the young people. While anxious for a balanced education in English and the vernacular for their sons, they don't like the "mixture of English and Shona, the result of which is a fall in each and disrespect for elders." In the words of one peasant farmer from the Nyanga area: "The young people should stop using a peer group language at home and at school because then they lose manners." Another parent from Rusape insists that "apart from the learning of English at school, children must be taught customs in Shona so that they will not assimilate English customs." There are even a few proposals for involving knowledgeable village elders in the teaching of traditions and the traditional (rather than standardized) language.

Students, though accused of laxity in their own use of the vernacular and often guiltily aware of this, usually advocate the use and development of the vernaculars. Ndebele speakers are somewhat resentful of Shona ascendance and accuse speakers of Shona of not coming to meet them half way in a spirit of linguistic mutuality. They generally acknowledge the majority status of Shona and think of their own language as in a state of humiliating retreat.

One Shona speaker explains: "I am proud of the Shona language, and I shall always want to speak it. It is very unfortunate that at school and University I learn in English and not in Shona." He is, to be precise, opposed not to learning English, but to learning everything *in* English. Few actually want less English, but many would have more vernacular—Shona, Sindebele, and others. The student just quoted goes on to say: "Sindebele and English should be compulsory at the primary school level in Mashonaland; Shona and English in Matabeleland; and Shona and Sindebele in European schools." He expresses a widely held feeling that full language symmetry should obtain between all population groups (see last section of Table 12.5). Says another student: "Shona is just as important as English and should be made compulsory in European schools." Echoes still another, with even greater emphasis:

> *Europeans should learn and be taught Shona and Sindebele in schools before coming to settle in Rhodesia. Europeans who speak Shona are secure for a future under an African government.*

A further common argument for the vernaculars in European schools is to improve "human relations." But always there is the insistence on symmetry in language instruction. Proposes a Public Relations Officer from the Nyanga district, using the broadest terms of language policy:

> *I would like the Ministry of Education to regard Shona as no less important than any other foreign languages that are taught in European schools. I would like Shona to be regarded as a Rhodesian language and not as a dialect.*

The mixing of dialects if often deplored, but there are some who would have this achieved deliberately to create a new national language. This line of thought goes even beyond dialects to the mixture of vernacular languages: "I foresee the development of a neutral language borrowing words from Shona and

Sindebele. This new language will achieve national unity amongst the Africans of this country."

There is considerable awareness that language has an important role to play in whatever national dreams are being dreamt. A national language will help to overcome tribal diversity, or institutionalize it, and create greater equality with non-African partners to nationhood. A precondition to the realization of such ambitions is the development of the vernaculars to "express technical and scientific concepts," as a writer of Shona poetry puts it. A librarian from the Mrewa district feels that

> Shona and Sindebele are speedily developing and expanding in vocabulary, literature, and use. However, these developments are still inadequate to give definitions and meanings to modern technical terms.

Members of the Department of African Languages at the University feel certain that, while the vernaculars have a long way to go, there is nothing in these languages or in any others, for that matter, that precludes their eventual adapta-

Table 12.6   Classification of essay responses to "Why I *want* to do Shona as a teaching subject"

Sentimentalism
  1. "Shona gives me delight"
  2. "School children can express what is deep down in their hearts."
  3. "Young children should not grow up thinking their language to be inferior"
  4. "It is a living language which is growing"
  5. "I love it"
  6. "Nothing helps people more than building up and sustaining their language"

Value
  7. "To be human you must have tribe. To have tribe [race?] you must have mother tongue"
  8. "Shona should be encouraged by Africans. They should be proud"
  9. "This language is our inheritance"
  10. "Proud that God created me a Karanga person"
  11. "Shona is equally as valuable as English"
  12. "Our Shona language is dying slowly"
  13. "If the attitude of the younger generation continues, . . . Shona will be dead"

Instrumentalism
  14. "Pupils taught by a teacher who has not learnt Shona cannot learn properly"
  15. "To be a Shona teacher is a blessing because one knows exactly what [the child] thinks"
  16. "A child taught in English without knowing his mother tongue first can never get adequate wisdom"
  17. "Teachers and pupils have no interest. Our writers are too few"

Note: Essay responses were translated from the Shona. A statement that appeared to epitomize the contents was chosen from each essay.

Table 12.7   Classification of essay responses to "Why I am *not* doing Shona as a teaching subject"

Circumstances
1. "The times are against my wish"
2. "Where will I get security when government is minimizing vernacular studies?"
3. "I am in conflict when I see suppression of Shona and its pitiful consequences"

Poor teaching
4. "I have latent pride in Shona, but no one ever instructed me"
5. "The teacher always claimed that there was nothing to be taught in Shona, and no one would even get a job in it"

Poor achievement
6. "I am not ready to have three quarters of my class failures in Shona"
7. "The marks prove that I do not know Shona"
8. "Tell all some things a person likes but cannot do"
9. "My meagre knowledge of our blessed mother tongue"

Dialect problems
10. "My dialect hinders learning of so-called standard Shona"
11. "No doubt here people could write better Shona than me"

Regret
12. "By dropping Shona I feel guilty"
13. "Actually I enjoy Shona very much"
14. "People regard Shona as useless"

Note: Essay responses were translated from the Shona. A statement that appeared to epitomize the contents was chosen from each essay.

---

tion to any use whatsoever. Intuitively, the great majority of interview and questionnaire respondents seem to be saying the same thing.

Essay Responses

Of the thirty-one students who wrote essays, seventeen wrote about why they chose to do Shona as a subject, and fourteen wrote about why they did not choose it, or why they chose another subject. Thus, a content analysis of key sentences, one per student, yielded seventeen statements for choosing Shona and fourteen for not choosing it.

The two-dimensional scheme of language attitudes fits the classification of statements in the case of students who had chosen Shona (Table 12.6), but not in the case of those who had chosen another subject (Table 12.7). Negative action appears better explained in terms of "excuses" rather than "orientations."

Table 12.6 leaves little doubt that most key sentences favoring the choice of Shona can be classified as sentimental or value-oriented. Even the instrumental thinking has a strong value flavor. It is a "blessing" to be a Shona teacher because he is privileged to bring Shona to the child who will make use of it.

Among the "excuses" for not doing Shona (Table 12.7) there are many that reflect latent sentiment or value. Students consider themselves deprived when they see circumstances as denying them a future of teaching the vernacular. The poor teaching attributed to Shona teachers or their own failure in vernacular studies does not fill them with joy. There is no relief at not having to do Shona, but rather regret and sometimes a sense of guilt. Essay data strongly reinforce impressions gained from other material: The vernacular is serious business to the African.

DISCUSSION

Attitudes toward the main languages of Rhodesia were categorized into four types—sentimentalism, value, instrumentalism, and communication—following a scheme used elsewhere in prior research (Hofman 1974*b*) and shown in Table 12.1. To review, sentimentalism and value are intrinsic views of language as either personally enjoyable or interpersonally symbolic, it will be remembered. Instrumentalism and communication are extrinsic views of language, as either serving private or public ends. This dimensional scheme received support in an analysis of open-ended statements and essay responses about the mother tongue, but proved of limited generality in responses to a forced-choice questionnaire.

Once the scheme has been at least provisionally adopted, the general drift of differences between speakers of English and African languages makes sense. Shona, the stronger Rhodesian vernacular, is generally enjoyed by its speakers (sentimentalism) and associated with lofty hopes of nation building (value). English is far more often just taken for granted as a useful tool. "If I'd been born a Hun," says one young European, "I'd be speaking German."

Why is this difference of attitude between racial groups so readily apparent in free responses, but so completely obscured in the forced-choice questionnaire results? One way to resolve the contradiction is to resort to the well-known distinction between the cognitive, affective, and conative components of attitudes. The language attitudes scale, with its prejudged forced-choice alternatives, calls for a cognitive evaluation of rational alternatives. The open-ended question about mother-tongue feelings elicits affect. Significant portions of the interview tap the conative component, in that they ask the respondent to make recommendations of what to do next. Essay replies cover both affective and conative components.

In this perspective, language scale results can be interpreted as rather general agreement among groups on reasonable and moderately stated alternatives. Cognitively speaking, attitudes are pretty much alike. Members of different groups, on the average, judge the original need for vernacular development to have been one of self-expression, the current advocacy of Shona and Sindebele as official languages to be motivated by communication needs, and the broader task to be one of providing a focus for national identity. Similarly, the present advantages of English in the schools are viewed in terms of expediency, and the overall task of a language of wider communication is seen as the achievement of national unity. It is only on the question of how the languages of wider circulation achieved their status in the first place that a strong division of opinion sets in: Africans are haunted by the colonial past, while Europeans prefer to consider the intrinsic merits of their language.

A much sharper division of attitudes arises in the affective-conative context. Here, Africans voice more concern for their mother tongues than do Europeans for theirs and use much more impassioned language to do it with. This may be in part because there really is more room for concern in the case of the African languages—threatened as they are today by the dominance of English— and in part because Shona and Sindebele (Ndebele) are increasingly viewed as bound up with a nascent nationalism.

In addition to reflecting the same sentiments and values expressed by Africans in open-ended statements and essays, interviews allowed some glimpse into the language policy advocated. Both modernizing and traditionalist elements demand at least full equality of the vernaculars with English, but for different reasons. Peasant farmers are concerned with tribal authenticity and would prefer the preservation of dialects. The more educated wish to transcend tribalism in order to cope with national unification, thus favoring the standardization and modernization of Shona, the leading vernacular. Speakers of Sindebele, caught between giants, are sulking in the wings.

There is an ambivalence toward English among Africans. The language of the dominant groups remains the key to better jobs and wider communication, thus having great extrinsic merit. Village parents may resent its inroads into local culture, but woe to those who would have it removed from the primary school curriculum! Students and professionals, though enthusiastic about the vernacular as a focus of national hopes, realize well the importance of commanding a language of such impeccable international credentials as English.

Whereas the response of most Europeans to questions of language remains well within the issue of usefulness, especially where English is concerned, the most general expression among Africans is one of pleasure, pride, and enchantment with familiar sounds. Yet Africans are also becoming aware of language as a symbol, a potential lever to raise them from tribalism into nationhood, to permit them to deal on equal terms with speakers of English. A people, having shaped a language, is now being shaped by that language—into nationhood.

The rich data of this study have shown that language as an object of attitudes can point beyond itself towards a range of concerns as varied as individual enhancement, esthetic enjoyment, intergroup communication, and national pride. The very fact that language is so low on a scale of conscious awareness means that it can be a valuable indicator of such concerns. It would appear, in conclusion, that the issue of what language serves whom and for what purpose deserves a much more central place in public and academic planning than it has hitherto been accorded.

To each of the following items there are four responses. You are asked to rank the four responses to each item in the order of most to least acceptable. Write a *1* on the line in front of the response most to your liking, a *2* in front of the response you like next, and so on. Please rank all four choices of each item, even if you feel that more appropriate responses are available.

1. Independent countries in Africa try to develop their *national* tongue because
   _____ the foreign tongue reminds them of colonialism and dependence.
   _____ it will be easier for the African to make a living and get ahead.
   _____ they often try to overcome minorities speaking local tongues.
   _____ Africans like to express themselves in their own tongue.

2. Languages such as English and French achieved their special status because
   _____ speakers of these languages subjugated other people and forced them to use their languages.
   _____ a varied and flourishing literature developed in them.
   _____ they are relatively easy to learn.
   _____ countries like the U.S.A., England and France enjoy great prestige.

3. Advocates of Shona and Ndebele as official languages in Rhodesia will argue that this would
   _____ further the teaching and enjoyment of African literature.
   _____ help speakers of African languages feel equal to speakers of English.
   _____ make it possible for the two major races in Rhodesia to communicate effectively.
   _____ make it easier for speakers of African languages to conduct their business.

4. English is a required subject in Rhodesia's African schools because
_____ it is becoming the language of culture and science.
_____ it is difficult to find a good job without it.
_____ it places the pupil in contact with a great cultural heritage.
_____ it is the language of the governing group.

5. In countries that do not insist on a unified language
_____ national unity is adversely affected.
_____ misunderstanding arises between social classes.
_____ misunderstanding arises between individuals.
_____ literature may suffer and decline.

6. The main task of vernacular tongues in Rhodesia is to
_____ help Africans communicate with one another.
_____ give Africans a chance to express their feelings.
_____ provide Africans with a focus for national identity.
_____ make the learning of English a matter of choice rather than of necessity.

What language did you usually speak with your family when you entered primary school? _____

How do you feel about that language, briefly?

_____

_____

The following statements are a randomly selected sample of verbatim replies made by University of Rhodesia students to the free-response item on the questionnaire (see Appendix A).

Native Shona Speakers—about Shona

Sentimental orientation

Too many dialects and corruption by urbaners have disappointed me.

I like Shona, and, no matter how sophisticated my children and grandchildren become I shall try my best to encourage them to speak Shona wherever practicable.

It is very rich in vocabulary—it is very polite for example calling somebody elder to you by name is not permissible.

It's soul lingo—real cool stuff.

I love it and don't want it adulterated by other languages.

I like it and am proud of it.

I like them, but of course I like Shona more, that is because it is my mother tongue and I hardly use it elsewhere outside my own family.

I love it because it is my mother tongue and I can express myself best in it.

I love it very much because it is my mother tongue and I can be able to express myself fully.

It's super, it's nice.

There might be prejudices for it, but it certainly is very expressive, a language to
be proud and not ashamed of.

I understand it perfectly and enjoy speaking it. It is full of good humor and
interesting idioms.

I feel good.

It is rich, expressive [the language of my fathers, the soil].

It's beautiful, only now I can't effectively express myself, conditioned by circumstances like: we were not allowed to speak Shona at Boarding School.

Value orientation

Dignified.

I feel I am a true African who hasn't lost his identity if I speak Shona.

I feel proud to speak and learn more of my mother language.

It is the language of my fore-fathers but it is a bit unfortunate that due to
urbanization I can no longer speak it in its purity and fluently.

As it is my mother tongue, I don't entertain having a better substitute.
It is my heritage.

Wonderful. The language that can secure Africans like independence.

The only media through which I can have a chance to trace our history and
customs.

Gives me sense of identity and belonging.

I now regard the language as part of myself, but I used to doubt its value. I like it
now.

I like it because it is my language. I feel proud of it.

Better than English in any way.

It is just as good as any other language and I am proud of it.

Its greatest value is for learning rich moral values of African culture.

People must be encouraged to continue speaking their language—being the basis
of cultural tradition.

Embroils national pride and preservation of one's own identity. Indeed a heritage.

Instrumental orientation

It usually has a limited scope, but by being corrupted its scope is widening and
can be widened.

Gives confidence when speaking.

It is easier to communicate in it though its vocabulary is limited.

Both languages are quite rich and it is very much easy to communicate in either.

Being a mother tongue it is convenient but has many vocabulary deficiencies,
especially in technical sphere.

It is a fabulous way of communication.

I feel I can express myself powerfully and meaningfully in that language.

I express myself more explicitly, in spite of the apparent short of vocabulary that
it has, compared to the richness in English.

It has adequate vocabulary then but now its vocabulary is not enough. I speak
more freely in Shona.

I feel more at home when speaking in Shona.

Quite at home can express myself easily.

I feel it is the best language for me for it allows me to think and express myself about everything within my environment.

I like the language because it is my language and no-one resents my using it, no-one gets mad if I make grammatical mistakes, no-one gives me dirty looks if I use the language badly.

It is the language I can use freely and can understand easier than any other language. But it is not yet developed satisfactorily.

Communication orientation

It is a widely used language in this country and I like it and use it everyday.

I feel it could provide, complementary with Ndebele, a basis of national unity and easier understanding between the two major African races in Rhodesia.

Language is an essential media of communication so the more it satisfies this condition the better.

I feel that among my people it is the best language to communicate with.

Indifference

I have no feelings attached to any language so don't ask me.

Negativism

I can no longer speak it well I mean without putting in English words. I also feel that it has become inferior to English.

I feel that it is being undermined by English which in Rhodesia has a status since the more of it you know the higher the chances of getting a job.

I feel it's deteriorating. Very difficult to speak pure Shona without inserting an English word here and there to make myself understood.

I feel I am using it less and less often when I am not at home and that I am losing my command in it.

I think its scope is so limited that it can't have: (1) no scientific language significance outside Rhodesia (2) no vocabulary relevant to industrial society.

Shona taught in schools and universities is not the Shona we speak at home.

Native English Speakers—about English

Sentimental orientation

A very subtle and expressive language, the language of international communication and diplomacy, has a large and important literature.

It is an inexhaustible source of pleasure, pride, interest, but not to the exclusion of other languages.

A joy to hear spoken properly. A useful but beautiful language in theatre and literature, especially poetry.

Highly developed and expressive and able to cope with any situation.

Voluminous, expressive, because of its power of borrowing and assimilating from
all other languages.

A very expressive language, lending itself to communication in all fields, artistic
and scientific.

It's the greatest—flexible, subtle, capable of fine lucidity, widely spoken.

When spoken properly it is beautiful. It is a language of increasing importance. It
is a good thing to educate as many as possible to speak it.

I enjoy using it, find it very expressive (naturally) but French is more beautiful
and I'd like to know Shona better.

Necessary for communication, must be beautiful through communication of as
many thoughts and feelings as possible.

It can be a beautiful language if well spoken. Has a vast vocabulary and is interesting—if not merely taken at the colloquial level.

Very flexible, but lacks precision: aurally pleasing, with an exciting literature. I
am very fond of it.

Rich, expressive, the world's chief tongue. Easy to pick up.

It is quite expressive, but not as beautiful as French, and not as expressive as
Afrikaans.

A concise and colourful vehicle of communication, that has great beauty, though
it may lack fluidity.

I feel that it is an enjoyable language and I love speaking it. It is however
sometimes difficult to express myself in it.

Value orientation

I feel that all nationalities should be able to speak one language in common and
that English, with its heritage of literature, and considering that the
majority of the western world speaks it, should be encouraged.

All foreigners should learn, or be encouraged to learn, English. I feel that its use
should be made universal.

A good national language, but not to be the only one, i.e., either Shona or Ndebele
or both should be major auxillary languages spoken by *all* Rhodesians.

To be able to speak and write English really fluently is an art, but once the art is
mastered it is the key to almost the whole world.

All should learn English for a world-wide, cultural value and Shona/Ndebele for
local Rhodesian value.

Most of the greatest things that have ever been thought, said and done, have been
translated into it; it suffices, even if it is not enough.

It is one of the greatest languages, both modern and ancient, and I was fortunate
to have been born into it. It does, however, because of its spread encourage
a paternalistic attitude to other races.

It is the modern language—most expresses progress. Probably a symbol of
domination but need not be so.

It is the greatest living language in the world.

It has developed a greater wealth of heritage than *all* others. It is irreplaceable.

It is better than any Munt language.

I feel it is the greatest. I find it difficult to learn others. I realise the need to know Shona.

I feel that it is a language which embraces a great heritage, capable of expressing prosaic thought as well as the loftiest poetic inspiration.

Very proud of it but find it inadequate in many ways and would like to learn others.

Proud of it, must be bloody difficult to learn, wonderful literature, neither ugly nor terribly beautiful-sounding, other languages ought to be learnt by English-speaking people besides it.

A beauty of this world to be perpetuated in the hearts and minds of our children.

The best!

Mother tongue—exciting literary heritage. Wide affective and cognitive vocabulary.

Instrumental orientation

Generally adequately comprehensive but too full of potential ambiguities unless used with exacting precision.

O.K.

Excellent.

It is the language of my birth—I feel very highly of it.

Useful because it is international.

Glad that I speak it because at the present it is a universal one.

Unadulterated it is unbeatable as a means of communication and expression.

It is a rich and fertile, constantly growing means of communicating with my fellow man.

A language which is spoken in many countries and therefore useful.

Quite satisfactory.

A precise, and excellent language for communication for people who have mastered it. For those to whom it is a second language it may lose its benefits because it is so difficult to master.

As it is used in a great many countries I think it is a very useful language to speak.

It is what I have grown up with. It is an international language.

It is the only language I know well, and it is all right for me.

Useful.

The most useful, arrogant, selfish language in use today.

Very useful and adequate. Not a very beautiful language though.

This is the most dominantly used language in the world. Thus it is necessary for persons to understand this language in order to facilitate study and advancement.

Communication orientation

In Rhodesia it is essential to have a unified language. English is my primary choice because it is a world language for diplomacy, science and technology.

This, however, should not preclude the teaching of the vernacular to all
peoples in Rhodesia in the interests of greater understanding and heritage.

It is the language I was brought up on and it is pretty well universal.

Fast becoming "universal language." Other European languages are using English
words for new innovations (e.g. television, radio in French). Seems easy
to master basic words but grammar, context, etc. difficult, especially for
Africans and foreigners.

Efficient medium for the expression of thought both inter-racially and inter-
nationally, on a cultural and diplomatic plane.

It is very useful, and should at least be one of Rhodesia's official languages.

Extremely useful as it is so widely spoken but does nothing to help towards
establishing a national identity.

Indifference

No strong feelings that I am aware of—just chance that it happens to be my first
language.

It is no better than any other language but is simply the language that I have
been brought up speaking.

Yes.

Accept it without thinking about it.

Nothing. If I'd been born a Hun my accident of birth would have made me German
speaking.

I don't even think about it.

That an effort should be made to learn other languages as well, e.g. Shona and/or
Ndebele in Rhodesia.

English being second nature, I've never considered it (my feelings, that is) and find
it hard to do so now.

No particular feelings; I would as readily speak Arabic if I could.

Negativism

It is unfortunate in Rhodesia that English is politically and economically necessary
for self advancement. For greater racial understanding, Shona and
Sindebele should be made official languages, and should be taught at
school instead of European languages. These latter tongues should be
left as high school options.

Just as rotten as the English!

Nothing.

REFERENCES

Gardner, R.C., and W.E. Lambert. 1972. *Attitudes and Motivation in Second Language
Learning.* Rowley, Mass.: Newbury House.

Hofman, J.E. 1974a. The prediction of success in language planning. *International Journal of
the Sociology of Language* 1:39-65.

———. 1974b. The use of Hebrew terms among Israeli psychologists. *International Journal of the Sociology of Language* 3:53–65.

Kelman, H.C. 1969. Patterns of personal involvement in the national systems: A social-psychological analysis of political legitimacy. In *International Policies and Foreign Policy*, edited by J.N. Rosenau. 2d ed. New York: Free Press.

Chapter 13

Knowing, Using and Liking English as an Additional Language

Joshua A. Fishman

Three questions commonly come to the fore when the role of English as an additional language in developing countries is discussed:

1. Is English known?
2. Is English used?
3. Is English liked?

The purpose of this chapter is to explore some of the relationships between these three dimensions.

Obviously, English cannot be used by those who do not know it; however, does knowing English always lead to its being used? As for the relationship between either knowing or using English and liking it, it is even more problematic. When we examine knowing and using, only one direction of *initial* causality is possible—namely, from knowing to using. However, when we add liking to the above duo, we often cannot be sure which came first, the competence (knowing), the performance (using), or the attitude (liking). Moreover, even the degree of relationship of either knowing or using English and liking English has been little explored, setting aside all questions of causal directionality.

We will explore these relational questions via secondary analyses of data on (a) high school and university teachers and (b) high school and university students in three countries: India, Indonesia, and Israel. The data appear in Appendix A. The comparative nature (cross-generational and cross-polity) of our data thus provides another dimension to our analysis.[1]

COMPETENCE, PERFORMANCE, AND ATTITUDE AS A SYSTEM

Competence and Use

The two English-language competencies for which we have self-report data are *speaking* and *reading*. These two competencies are found to be highly interrelated in both generations (teachers and students) and in all three countries, the median correlation between them being in the mid-fifties. This is not surprising for school-connected populations, such as those we are studying, among whom second-language acquisition and use are likely to be closely linked and to proceed via oral/aural and written/printed channels simultaneously. Similarly unsurprising is the fact that teachers usually claim a higher level of competence, both in speaking and in reading English, than do students, with Israeli respondents in each generation generally claiming most competence and Indonesian respondents generally claiming least.

More surprising, perhaps, is the fact that, on the whole, the relationship between English competence claims and English performance claims is negligible (median correlation approximately 0.06). Obviously, many teachers and students acquired English in the past and have no current need or opportunity for using it. This is particularly true for teachers. Indeed, this may be generally true, as an intergenerational phenomenon; i.e., adults may be more constrained from calling into use all of the skills they have acquired than are the young. Another way of looking at this finding is that schools require students more frequently than teachers to put to use what they have learned; i.e., schools are institutions in which adults say to the young, "Do as I say, not as I do" in connection with many things, English among them. It will take more than schools to foster English use among those who have acquired it. This point is further emphasized by the cross-polity progression for English use in both generations: India (highest) > Indonesia > Israel. Since the rank order of two of these countries was reversed when we considered English competence claims, we can conclude that India tends to be a setting where far more of those who acquire English put it to use than in Israel (where many still suppress or have no use for English which they acquired natively or via education).

The Attitudinal Factor

The two attitudinal dimensions for which we have data are both school-related; namely, (a) attitude toward learning English technical vocabulary (in addition to indigenous terms) in school and (b) attitude toward using English as the language of technical instruction (instead of national language). Unfortunately, student data is available only for the first of these two dimensions since in some countries it was not felt to be possible or politic to ask the latter question of students.

With respect to attitudes toward English technical vocabulary (Att/V), these are more positive among teachers than among students. This may be a reflection of the greater English competence and use claimed by teachers. In general, however, Att/V is more related to use than to competence, particularly among students. On the whole, the relationship is a very weak one (median correlation of 0.07 among teachers and 0.18 among students).

With respect to attitudes toward English as language of instruction (Att/In), these are also very meagerly related to English competence (median correlation 0.07) and only slightly more related to use (median correlation 0.15). Thus, all in all, we can conclude that the dependence of English attitudes upon English competence and performance, or the dependence of English competence and performance upon English attitudes, is negligible—particularly among older subjects who are now further away from the period in which either constellation of factors was initially formed.

The overall attitudinal progression is India (more favorable than) > Indonesia > Israel, the same as the progression of claimed use. The overall intergenerational progression is teachers > students, regardless of attitudinal criterion examined.

The System-Economy of English as an Additional Language

The foregoing data may say something about the economy of the English-language system among academically related populations in many non-English mother-tongue countries. If the three components we have looked at are conceived of as a "natural" system, they must be considered a very imperfect system. There is great leakage or wastage in this system—from the very outset, but increasingly in the course of time—between the acquisition of English and its use. There is similar leakage or wastage when English language attitudes are viewed, either as causal (independent, predictor) or as consequential (dependent, criterion) factors in conjunction with English acquisition or use. These findings are not necessarily shocking nor even disappointing. They merely indicate that we must look outside of this system per se if we are concerned to fully and effectively explain or predict any one of the three system components.

Thus, if competence, performance, and attitude with respect to English as an additional language do not form an economical or effective system for understanding or predicting one another, there is all the more reason why a much more inclusive approach to predicting any of these components must be sought. Perhaps a more sociolinguistically oriented approach—one that calls upon various demographic, language repertoire, and attitudinal characteristics of respondents—may yet constitute an effective and meaningful system. It is to such an approach (a somewhat more complex one) that we now turn.[2]

THE ADDITION OF SOCIOLINGUISTIC FACTORS

A More Inclusive Approach to Competence

Several important considerations are clarified when we adopt an approach to explaining English competence that involves predictors other than using or liking

English. One of these is that the broader approach (via cumulative multiple correlation) is a much more powerful one, since cumulative correlations in the sixties, seventies and even eighties are commonly obtained thereby. Obviously, the additional variables are of great value. Another important finding is that non-attitudinal factors (whether demographic or language repertoire) are almost always more powerful than are attitudinal ones in predicting competence, this being so both across countries as well as across generations. (The only exception to the last finding is in connection with the acquisition of English reading among Indian teachers. Here the attitudinal factors are very slightly stronger than the nonattitudinal ones, probably a reflection of historical circumstances that obtained a generation ago.) Finally, it is also instructive to note that, secondary though they may be, attitudinal factors nevertheless still make a worthwhile independent contribution to our explanatory goal, since our multiple correlations are invariably lower without them than with them.

There are few surprises with respect to the best nonattitudinal predictors in relation to English competence: either total *language repertoire* size (LR, i.e., the number of languages claimed in addition to English) or the *complementary* competence (i.e., reading if we are examining speaking, and speaking if we are examining reading) are recurringly the best nonattitudinal predictors of competence. The two exceptions to this pattern ("highest school level" among teachers in India and "father's occupation" among teachers in Israel) have social class or social advantage overtones which may even be somewhat instructive as to the interpretation to place upon the recurring importance of repertoire size itself. Thus, it seems quite likely that an important determinant of English acquisition among teachers (and perhaps among other adults as well) was advantaged social position. Such implications are not as significant for students, probably because of the somewhat greater availability/accessability of schooling for the younger generation than it had been for the older.

Similarly, the best attitudinal predictors of English competence are easily characterizable and frequently recurring. Most common of all is the contribution of modernization attitudes (i.e., points of view related to nontraditional, nonlocal involvements). Also quite important are strongly positive views related to the national language or to nationalism more generally—these being negatively related to the acquisition of English. All in all, therefore, the combination of social advantage (or of parallel acquisition of other English competencies) and of more modern (but nonnationalist) attitudes is recurringly the constellation which is most predictive of English competence. Note that although we have examined the attitudinal factors here as antecedents, and although they seem to have a function as such, it is not unlikely that they are also subsequently strengthened by English acquisition—perhaps as much as they initially contribute to it.

A More Inclusive Approach to Usage

In many ways the broader approach to predicting English usage results in findings similar to those just reported for English proficiency. Once again, the broader approach is significantly better than the narrower approach, if measured in terms of the magnitude of the correlations obtained (high fifties to low eighties). Once again, the nonattitudinal predictors are more powerful than the attitudinal ones. Once again, both sets of predictors are required for best results.

However, in many ways English usage and English acquisition present somewhat different predictive constellations. To begin with, usage is very often less predictable than is acquisition (and this is *not* due to differences in their variability), an indication that it requires a somewhat different or, perhaps an even broader, system than the one we have attempted. In addition, the prediction of acquisition regularly reveals a generational progression quite different than that revealed by the predication of usage. In the case of acquisition, student performance is generally *more* predictable than teacher performance. In the case of use, the opposite is true: student performance is less predictable than is teacher performance. Seemingly, if we seek an even broader system to account for usage, we would do well to give greater consideration particularly to those variables that pertain to students—vocational goals, concepts of the future, and others.

The *substance* of the most predictive items is also different for usage than it is for acquisition. For usage, this substance pertains either to involvement in chemistry instruction (among both teachers and students in Indonesia and Israel) or to having had the benefit of being educated (at least in part) via English (both groups in India), insofar as nonattitudinal factors are concerned. The best attitudinal predictors, on the other hand, are more similar to those we have encountered before. As in the case of English acquisition, those who are most concerned and informed with respect to the national language are more negative with respect to the use of English in instruction.

The major new consideration introduced in conjunction with English usage is that which pertains to chemistry. This subject may be viewed as representative of the physical sciences generally—or, indeed, of the world of technology and, even more broadly, of an important aspect of the modernization syndrome previously encountered as an attitudinal component in English acquisition. Technology interests and instruction—as distinguished from the traditional humanities, which in each country are oriented and related to its respective national language, and as distinguished from the social sciences, which can also more easily be pursued via the national languages—seem to be more directly conducive to and responsive to English usage—at least until local technological instruction (and, perhaps production as well) is fully indigenized. The domain of English as an additional language, particularly insofar as usage among school-related personnel is concerned, seems more often to be the technical rather than the poetic, the philosophical, or the political. In this sense, the overall "image of English" is also likely to be different from that of French, Arabic, or other languages of wider communication.

A More Inclusive Approach to Attitudes

Only one of our basic recurring patterns in the areas of acquisition and usage is reversed in the area of English attitudes. Instead of nonattitudinal factors being more predictive, as they were before, we now find that attitudinal factors capture the honors (particularly where Att/V is concerned). However, again the total cumulative multiple correlations are quite large (and include a few of the very largest obtained in this entire study); and again both clusters of predictors are obviously needed for optimal results. Indeed, on the whole, nonattitudinal predictors are needed just as strongly in helping to predict attitudinal criteria as attitudinal predictors were needed in helping to predict nonattitudinal criteria, if not more so.

There is an invariable superiority in our prediction of Att/V over Att/In, and a rather consistent superiority in our prediction of Att/V among students relative to its prediction among teachers. As with other such findings, these two are probably explainable in our research on the basis of the relative appropriateness and exhaustiveness of the particular variables that happen to be included in the predictive systems employed, rather than attributable in any more basic sense to the criteria or populations studied.

The substantive picture with respect to predicting our two attitudinal criteria is a very homogeneous one. The primary nonattitudinal predictors are largely those we have encountered before—parental advantage, chemistry involvement, language repertoire size, English in education—plus regional (rather than national) self-description—i.e., "Javanese" rather than Indonesian, "Uttar Pradeshi" rather than Indian, "Jerusalemite" rather than Israeli. Puristic and ideological views toward the national languages are the primary attitudinal predictors and, as expected, these are consistently negatively related to English attitudes, across countries as well as across populations. Since attitudes toward the national languages are normally acquired earlier than are attitudes toward English (if only because the two languages are normally acquired at different educational-development stages) there is a possible causal sequence here that may deserve to be recognized.[3] It would seem that those adults and youngsters who acquire strong puristic and ideologically encumbered views of their respective national language are less likely, therefore, to acquire positive attitudes toward English. Admittedly, the attitudes toward English that we have examined here are rather specific ones, but they are not unimportant ones for school populations and for the spread of English in educational contexts, and our attitudinal findings may well be valid and have implications for much broader aspects of attitudes toward English as an additional language. Finally, in view of the IRPLPP findings that ideologized and purist views toward the national language regularly show a decrease between the generation of teachers (or adults), who struggled on behalf of the national language, and the generation of students, who encountered it already safely established, the long-term prospects for improved attitudes toward English would seem to be favorable, particularly if broader political and economic links with the English-speaking world remain facilitative and if the power of the United States remains relatively stable.

As for similarly fundamental directional conclusions pertaining to English attitudes in relation to English acquisition and English usage, these cannot be stated with any great certainty on the basis of our current data. It would not be inappropriate, however, to suggest that, since English *instruction* (and therefore, both English acquisition and English use) begins in the later elementary-school years in each of the countries we have studied, certain attitudes toward English have already been acquired—e.g., from exposure to the media and from interaction with the world of English-related technological "know how." Thus attitudes toward English are probably already helping to determine English acquisition and English use from the very outset, rather than merely being determined by them.

CONCLUSIONS

Our data clearly indicated that acquiring, using, and liking English as an additional language cannot productively be viewed as strictly psychoeducational considerations which can be fathomed in isolation from major societal factors. Indeed, acquiring, using, and liking English are very imperfectly (if at all) related to each other; and if they are to be appreciably understood, we must turn to more sociolinguistic considerations, attitudinal as well as nonattitudinal. Both types of considerations are always in order, although nonattitudinal factors are of greatest moment in predicting English acquisition and use, while attidunal factors are primary in predicting English attitudes.

In accounting for English acquisition, social class considerations and the interlocking nature of acquiring speaking and reading are the primary nonattitudinal predictors. In accounting for English use, chemistry involvement and English in one's education are the primary nonattitudinal predictors. In accounting for pro-English attitudes, a combination of all of the foregoing constitutes the primary nonattitudinal predictive constellation, plus an intimation of regional rather than national self-description. The primary attitudinal contributions to predicting English acquisition, use, and attitude are an equally parsimonious and interpretable set of variables: high modernization orientation, low national consciousness and low language consciousness orientations, and little concern for language purism or language planning as a whole.

It may be possible to sketch certain long-term trends with respect to both types of predictors and in relation to all three types of criteria. English may be expected to continue as the language of technology in Third World settings for as long as politically low-keyed Anglo-American domination in this domain continues. Attitudinal resistance to English in this respect can be expected to weaken as younger generations successively shed more and more of the puristic and exclusivistic ideologies that their parents and teachers formulated and espoused during the formative struggles for political and cultural independence. Acquisition and use of English should increase as educational opportunity becomes decreasingly dependent on social advantage and as modernization orientations reach successively larger population segments in the Third World. On the whole, there is no likelihood of mother tongue replacement by English. Rather, increased acquisition and use of and improved attitudes toward English as an additional language are likely, particularly in technological contexts. Other languages of wider communication (e.g., Russian, French, Arabic, Swahili) may also continue to spread outside of their political heartlands, and to do so simultaneously with the spread of English, but their primary functions are less likely to be technological and more likely to be political, philosophical, or poetic. As a result of all of these processes, the spread of English is likely to establish stable diglossia or even triglossia patterns rather than to intensify linguistic antagonisms such as those that marked the end of the nineteenth and the beginning of the twentieth centuries.

NOTES

1.   The *International Research Project on Language Planning Processes* (IRPLPP) was conducted from 1969 to 1973, with Ford Foundation support, in order to provide an empirical base for the comparative investigation of the processes, personnel, and products involved in language planning. The full technical report (Das Gupta et al. 1972, mimeographed) and the published report (Rubin et al. 1977) provide detailed information concerning many of the measures, analytic techniques, and populations mentioned in this chapter.
        The IRPLPP data was not collected, processed, or scored in a fashion designed to answer questions pertaining to the precise *level* of English acquisition, use, or attitude. Such questions, therefore, cannot be explored via this report.

2.   The broader (or more inclusive) system regularly includes the following variables which were either previously utilized in the IRPLPP research or generated from the data collected by that project: Parental acquisition and use of English (Par/Eng), English mother tongue (EMT), English in respondent's education (either as medium or as subject) (Eng/Ed), modernization score (Mod), language consciousness score (LC), national consciousness score (NC), foreign synonyms named in the field of grammar (FS/Gr), foreign synonyms named in the field of civics (FS/C), foreign synonyms named in the field of chemistry (FS/Ch), and, finally, whether respondent teaches chemistry (Chem T). Several of these variables have been discussed or utilized by Fishman 1973 and 1974 and Hofman 1973 and 1974.

3.   Only "possible," although "probable" might also be defended, since difficulties encountered in learning English may conceivably lead to more puristic and conscious attitudes toward the national language.

REFERENCES

Das Gupta, J.; C.A. Ferguson; J.A. Fishman; B. Jernudd; and Joan Rubin. 1972. *Language Planning Processes.* (Draft) Stanford: Stanford University. Mimeographed.
Fishman, J.A. 1974. The comparative dimensionality and predictability of attitudinal and usage responses to selected centralized language planning activities. Summarized in

Proceedings (of the Association Internationale de Linguistique Appliquee, Third Congress, Copenhagen 1972), Vol. II, (A. Verdoodt, ed.). Heidelberg: Julius Gross. Pp. 71–80. For additional information concerning research design: J.A. Fishman. The international research project on language planning processes (IRPLPP). In *Language Planning: Current Issues and Research,* edited by J. Rubin and R. Shuy. Washington, D.C.: Georgetown University Press, 1973. Pp. 83–85.

Hofman, John E. 1974. Predicting the use of Hebrew terms among Israeli psychologists. *International Journal of the Sociology of Language* 3:53–66.

———. 1973. The prediction of success in language planning: The case of chemists in Israel. *International Journal of the Sociology of Language* 1:39–66.

Rubin, Joan; B. Jernudd; J. Das Gupta; J.A. Fishman; and C.A. Ferguson. 1977. *Language Planning Processes.* The Hague: Mouton.

APPENDIX A

Table 13.1 English acquisition, use, and attitudes: Means, standard deviations, and correlations

	Can speak	Can read	Use	Att/V	Att/In
India [a]					
Teachers (N = 113)					
Can speak	—				
Can read	.47	—			
Use	.02	.05	—		
Att/V	.08	.04	.07	—	
Att/In	.04	.05	.28	.50	—
$\bar{X}$	5.25	3.84	1.98	42.76	8.00
s	3.83	1.80	2.60	20.70	7.94
Students (N = 245)					
Can speak	—				
Can read	.32	—			
Use	.15	.04	—		
Att/V	.30	.12	.18	—	
Att/In	—	—	—	—	—
$\bar{X}$	3.37	3.92	.51	19.70	—
s	4.17	1.66	.90	12.77	
Indonesia [b]					
Teachers (N = 288)					
Can speak	—				
Can read	.63	—			
Use	.09	.15	—		
Att/V	.09	.04	.04	—	
Att/In	.07	.03	.15	.18	—
$\bar{X}$	5.41	3.26	1.15	37.94	3.63
s	4.52	2.65	1.56	15.70	5.58
Students (N = 2212)					
Can speak	—				
Can read	.58	—			
Use	.04	.04	—		
Att/V	.01	.01	.03	—	
Att/In	—	—	—	—	—
$\bar{X}$	3.23	1.98	.43	34.36	—
s	4.02	2.90	.77	6.83	

Table 13.1 (continued)

	Can speak	Can read	Use	Att/V	Att/In
Israel [c]					
Teachers (N = 232)					
Can speak	–				
Can read	.45	–			
Use	.01	.07	–		
Att/V	.10	.05	.32	–	
Att/In	.11	.20	.11	.19	–
$\bar{X}$	8.13	4.86	.47	22.83	5.29
s	3.47	2.65	1.04	15.19	6.56
Students (N = 1982)					
Can speak	–				
Can read	.67				
Use	.18	.20	–		
Att/V	.30	.26	.47	–	
Att/In	–	–	–	–	–
$\bar{X}$	5.88	2.77	.41	11.13	–
s	4.41	2.52	.84	11.90	

Key: Att/V = attitude toward English technical vocabulary; Att/In = attitude toward using English as the language of technical instruction; $\bar{X}$ = mean; s = standard deviation.

[a]Values required for statistical significance (India): Teachers: p:01 = .23; p:05 = .17. Students: p:01 = .15; p:05 = .11.

[b]Values required for statistical significance (Indonesia): Teachers: p:01 = .15; p:05 = .11. Students: p:01 = .07; p:05 = .05.

[c]Values required for statistical significance (Israel): Teachers: p:01 = .18; p:05 = .14. Students: p:01 = .07; p:05 = .05.

Table 13.2 The prediction of English acquisition, use, and attitude in India

	Can speak	Can read	Use	Att/V	Att/In
Teachers					
Tot CR^2	.76	.76	.81	.84	.75
LR CR^2	.40	.44	.73	.58	.49
Att CR^2	.34	.46	.51	.65	.51
Students					
Tot CR^2	.80	.84	.79	.74	—
LR CR^2	.67	.76	.69	.52	—
Att CR^2	.56	.58	.54	.66	—
Teachers					
Best LR predictor	30 Total langs. reads (.21)	2 Highest school level attended (.19)	45 Eng. in educ. (.58)	7 Age at which first learned region. langs. (.29) 31 Total langs. father knows (.29)	18 Teacher of chemistry (.31)
Best attitude predictor	14 Att. to lang. plan. agency III (−.19)	55 National consciousness (−.27)	33 Att. to lang. plan. agencies (−.42)	32 Att. to indig. of vocab. in nation. lang. (−.53)	32 Att. to indig. of vocab. in nation. lang. (−.34)
Students					
Best LR predictor	35 Total langs. speaks (.54)	36 Total langs. reads (.64)	52 Eng. in educ. (.54)	[47 Cr I: Can speak (.27)] 58 Foreign synonyms in civics (.26)	—
Best attitude predictor	15 Cannot be good Xman without speak nation. lang: Disagree (.29)	54 Total modernization score (.27)	42 Att. and info. re opposing agencies (−.29)	39 Attit. to indig. of vocab. in nation. lang. (−.41)	—

Key: Tot CR^2 = total cumulative multiple correlations; LR CR^2 = cumulative multiple correlations based only on *language repertoire* predictors; Att CR^2 = cumulative multiple correlations based only on attitudinal predictors.
Note: The item numbers (e.g., 30) refer to particular designations in IRLPP research.

Table 13.3 The broader system among Indian teachers: intercorrelations, means, and standard deviations

	1	2	3	4	5	6	7	8	9	10	11	12	13	14	15	$\bar{X}$	s	
1	–															5.25	3.83	1
2	.47	–														3.84	1.50	2
3	.02	.05	–													1.98	2.60	3
4	.08	.04	.07	–												42.76	20.70	4
5	.04	.05	.28	.50	–											8.00	7.94	5
6	.04	.12	.14	.04	.21	–										3.70	1.72	6
7	–	–	–	–	–	–	–									–		7
8	.15	.06	.58	.03	.25	.34	–	–								.84	.79	8

Key:
1. Can speak English
2. Can read English
3. Uses English
4. Attitude to English in vocabulary
5. Attitude to English in instruction
6. Parental acquisition and use of English
7. English mother tongue
8. English in own education

(continued on next page)

Table 13.3 (continued)

	1	2	3	4	5	6	7	8	9	10	11	12	13	14	15	$\bar{X}$	s
9	.10	.01	.01	.10	.17	.15	—	.04	—							15.87	1.02
10	−.02	.08	−.17	−.10	−.04	.00	—	−.10	−.02	—						3.97	.16
11	.06	−.27	.07	−.09	−.07	.15	—	.10	−.10	−.02	—					4.90	.09
12	.11	.07	.02	.06	.00	.14	—	.22	.05	−.14	.06	—				.29	.46
13	—	—	—	—	—	—	—	—	—	—	—	—	—			—	
14	.12	.07	.24	.08	.02	.12	—	.20	.02	−.15	.06	.98	—	—		.55	.88
15	.03	.12	.51	.12	.31	.17	—	.54	.07	.12	.07	−.46	—	.45	—	.34	.47
	1	2	3	4	5	6	7	8	9	10	11	12	13	14	15		

Key:
9. Modernization score
10. Language consciousness score
11. National consciousness score
12. Foreign synonyms: Grammar
13. Foreign synonyms: Civics
14. Foreign synonyms: Chemistry score
15. Respondent: Chemistry teacher score

Table 13.4 The broader system among Indian students: Intercorrelations, means, and standard deviations

	1	2	3	4	5	6	7	8	9	10	11	12	13	14	$\bar{X}$	s
1	—														3.33	4.17
2	.32	—													3.92	1.66
3	.15	.04	—												.51	.90
4	.30	.12	.15	—											19.70	12.27
5	—	—	—	—	—										—	
6	.36	.22	.13	.19	—	—									4.61	2.93
7	−.02	.41	.10	−.00	—	.15	—								5.83	1.00
8	.28	.16	.54	.22	—	.28	.07	—							.22	.50
9	.15	.27	.05	.05	—	.09	.03	.12	—						4.35	1.78
10	−.05	.10	.05	−.12	—	−.01	−.40	−.14	.02	—					2.33	.99
11	.03	.23	.15	−.01	—	.05	.55	.02	.02	.33	—				4.14	1.29
12	.14	.13	−.18	.05	—	.05	.05	−.05	.07	.13	.00	—			1.44	4.64
13	.36	.15	.12	.26	—	.33	.07	.12	.06	.01	.09	−.13	—		4.51	10.89
14	−.03	.03	.07	.09	—	.03	.02	−.06	.01	.05	.01	−.04	−.06	—	1.47	10.27
	1	2	3	4	5	6	7	8	9	10	11	12	13	14		

Key: As in Table 13.3

Table 13.5 The prediction of English acquisition, use, and attitude in Indonesia

	Can speak	Can read	Use	Att/V	Att/In
Teachers					
Tot CR^2	.79	.79	.64	.65	.41
LR CR^2	.62	.63	.56	.25	.27
Att CR^2	.32	.24	.37	.59	.18
Students					
Tot CR^2	.77	.73	.58	.80	—
LR CR^2	.69	.63	.48	.30	—
Att CR^2	.22	.22	.17	.79	—
Teachers					
Best LR predictor	27 Total langs. speaks (.57)	28 Total langs. reads (.52)	1 Teaches chemistry (.41)	11 Foreign synonyms: Gram. (.11)	24 Self-descrip: Regional (.17)
Best attitude predictor	22 Discusses usefulness of new terminol. in class (.22)	13 Cannot be good Xman without speak nation. language. disagree (.15)	9 Replies to who uses best nat. lang. among writers (−.26)	38 Att. to indig. of vocab. in nation. lang. (−.59)	54 Lang. consciousness: Total score (−.14)

Table 13.5 (continued)

	Can speak	Can read	Use	Att/V	Att/In
Students					
Best LR predictor	33 Total langs. speaks (.58) [50 Cr II (.58)]	[49 Cr I (.58)] 34 Total langs. reads (.56)	30 Teacher paraphrases new chem terms in nat. lang. (−.35) 31 Teacher paraphrases new civic terms in nat. lang. (−.35)	30 Teacher paraphrases new chem terms in nat. lang. (21)	—
Best attitude predictor	56 Total modernization score (.17)	56 Total modernization score (.18)	Region of best spoken nat. lang: Java (06)	37 Att. to. indig. of vocab. in nat. lang. (−.78)	—

Key: As in Table 13.2.

Table 13.6 The broader system among Indonesian teachers: Intercorrelations, means, and standard deviations

	1	2	3	4	5	6	7	8	9	10	11	12	13	14	15	$\bar{X}$ / s	
1	–															5.41 / 4.52	1
2	.63	–														3.26 / 2.65	2
3	.09	.15	–													1.15 / 1.56	3
4	.09	.04	.04	–												37.94 / 15.70	4
5	.07	.03	.15	.18	–											3.03 / 5.55	5
6	.24	.16	.24	.06	.05	–										12.28 / 4.15	6
7	.13	.06	.12	.05	.07	.21	–									6.09 / 1.04	7
8	.16	.04	.16	.07	.03	.01	.07	–								.47 / 1.04	8

Table 13.6 (continued)

	1	2	3	4	5	6	7	8	9	10	11	12	13	14	15	$\bar{X}$	s
9	.09	.04	.12	.02	.03	.07	.07	.09	—							4.17	1.32
10	.05	−.06	.01	−.10	−.14	.09	−.02	−.00	.13	—						2.51	.95
11	.01	−.03	.02	−.07	−.04	.04	−.10	−.20	−.02	.33	—					4.80	1.52
12	.11	.14	.03	.09	−.09	.06	.00	.09	.08	.01	−.06	—				5.57	5.63
13	.20	.05	.02	.04	.01	.20	.05	.22	.14	.03	−.01	.17	—			4.45	4.60
14	.06	.08	.40	.02	.07	.12	.18	.20	.11	−.10	−.02	−.07	−.06	—		7.64	8.67
15	.03	.02	.41	.02	.04	.06	.08	.13	.12	−.05	.00	−.26	.23	.74	—	.34	.47
	1	2	3	4	5	6	7	8	9	10	11	12	13	14	15		

Key: As in Table 13.3.

Table 13.7 The broader system among Indonesian students: Intercorrelations, means, and standard deviations

	1	2	3	4	5	6	7	8	9	10	11	12	13	14	$\bar{X}$	s
1	—														3.23	4.00
2	.58	—													1.48	2.90
3	.04	.04	—												.43	.77
4	.01	.01	.03	—											34.36	6.83
5	—	—	—	—	—										—	
6	.21	.18	-.01	.10	—	—									12.85	4.35
7	.07	.04	-.01	.05	—	.10	—								5.97	.78
8	.02	.04	.02	.05	—	-.01	.02	—							.08	.42
9	.17	.18	-.03	.05	—	.24	.03	.01	—						9.00	2.24
10	-.02	-.02	-.02	.07	—	.04	-.01	-.01	.14	—					2.40	1.00
11	.01	-.01	-.03	.08	—	.10	.03	-.02	.16	.32	—				4.85	1.55
12	.13	.16	.03	.01	—	.04	.07	.02	.03	-.02	-.04	—			2.62	3.42
13	.17	.15	.04	.02	—	.08	.05	.04	.11	-.05	-.04	.31	—		1.30	3.60
14	.11	.11	.24	-.01	—	.11	.02	.06	.07	-.03	.00	.16	.28	—	3.64	6.04
	1	2	3	4	5	6	7	8	9	10	11	12	13	14		

Key: As in Table 13.3.

Table 13.8   The prediction of English acquisition, use and attitude in Israel

	Can speak	Can read	Use	Att/V	Att/Im
Teachers					
Tot CR^2	.59	.72	.63	.68	.63
LR CR^2	.43	.52	.49	.43	.53
Att CR^2	.26	.29	.31	.57	.33
Students					
Tot CR^2	.80	.76	.59	.81	—
LR CR^2	.75	.70	.44	.50	—
Att CR^2	.48	.47	.39	.77	—
Teachers					
Best LR predictor	24 Total langs. speaks (.29)	3 Fath. occup.: skilled (.30)	48 Foreign syns: chem. (.34) 17 Teaches chem. (.33)	45 Total chem. vocab. (.29)	42 English in education (.39)
Best attitude predictor	50 Total modernization score (.18) 51 Language consciousness (−.18)	14 Regional origin of public speaker using best nation. lang. (abroad) (.14)	28 Attitude to to indigenousness of vocabulary in national language (−.17)	28 Attitude to indigeneousness of vocabulary in national language (−.45)	28 Attitude to indigeneousness of vocabulary in national language (−.22)
Students					
Best LR predictor	[51 CR II: Can read (.67)] 32 Total langs. speaks (.64)	[50 CR I Can speak (.67)] 22 Total langs. reads (.61)	59 Foreign syns: chem. (.38) 29 No. of years ago last studied civics (.38)	[56 CR III Use (.47)] 53 Parental knowledge of English (.43)	—

(continued on next page)

Table 13.8 (continued)

Best attitude predictor	Can speak	Can read	Use	Att/V	Att/In
	43 Total modernization score (.45)	43 Total modernization score (.45)	[49 CR IV: att/V (.47)] 36 Attitude to indigenousness of vocabulary in national language (−.33)	36 Attitude to indigenousness of vocabulary in national language (−.76)	—

Table 13.9 The broader system among Israeli teachers: Intercorrelations, means, and standard deviations

	1	2	3	4	5	6	7	8	9	10	11	12	13	14	15*	$\bar{X}$ / s	
1	—															8.13 / 3.47	1
2	.45	—														4.86 / 2.65	2
3	.01	.07	—													.47 / 1.04	3
4	.10	.05	.32	—												22.83 / 15.19	4
5	.11	.20	.11	.19	—											5.09 / 6.56	5
6	.21	.05	.15	.24	.33	—										11.89 / 7.07	6
7	.06	.10	.17	.18	.18	.50	—									6.74 / 3.50	7

Table 13.9 (continued)

	1	2	3	4	5	6	7	8	9	10	11	12	13	14	15*	$\bar{X}$	s
8	.02	.19	.21	.06	.39	.20	.19	—								1.18	1.78
9	.18	-.01	.15	.27	-.16	.73	.49	-.07	—							8.44	3.99
10	.18	-.01	.11	.24	-.08	.55	.38	-.09	.86	—						2.88	1.31
11	.18	-.02	.11	.25	-.10	.63	.43	-.09	.90	.92	—					5.72	2.69
12	.35	.04	.18	.23	.06	.34	.31	.02	.22	.20	.22	—				5.24	8.07
13	.25	.09	.20	.20	.18	.39	.35	.05	.31	.22	.24	.36	—			6.23	8.31
14	.27	.09	.34	.28	.05	.27	.15	.02	.12	.05	.07	.35	.34	—		7.04	9.56
15*	.25	.20	.32	.29	.09	.37	.19	.04	.37	.32	.33	.40	.35	.48	—	11.75	11.32
	1	2	3	4	5	6	7	8	9	10	11	12	13	14	15*		

Key: As in Table 13.3
*Chemistry word naming: 38% of the Israeli teacher sample taught chemistry or another natural science (items 17 and 18).

Table 13.10   The broader system among Israeli students: Intercorrelations, means, and standard deviations

	1	2	3	4	5	6	7	8	9	10	11	12	13	14	$\bar{X}$ / s
1	—														5.88 / 4.41
2	.67	—													2.72 / 2.52
3	.18	.20	—												.41 / .84
4	.30	.26	.47	—											11.13 / 11.91
5	—	—	—	—	—										—
6	.55	.47	.25	.43	—	—									12.29 / 8.01
7	.35	.33	.18	.21	—	.43	—								6.12 / 3.75
8	.05	.04	.04	.01	—	.05	.11	—							.23 / .79
9	.45	.45	.28	.60	—	.33	.05	.05	—						6.88 / 4.15
10	.22	.22	.13	.31	—	.18	-.06	.06	.41	—					1.00 / 1.02
11	.33	.32	.21	.45	—	.27	-.05	.05	.62	.54	—				3.03 / 2.17
12	.25	.25	.20	.21	—	.27	.21	.04	.24	.11	.18	—			4.21 / 5.64
13	.23	.20	.20	.21	—	.22	.22	.13	.22	.07	.14	.41	—		3.13 / 5.29
14	.25	.22	.38	.27	—	.27	.22	.08	.24	.09	.15	.40	.44	—	3.54 / 6.69
	1	2	3	4	5	6	7	8	9	10	11	12	13	14	

Key: As in Table 13.3.

Concluding Sentiments

Chapter 14

English in the Context
of International Societal Bilingualism

If the frequency of an event can be cited as an indication of its normalcy (as is commonly assumed), then the incidence of societal bilingualism is obviously such as to fully normalize it. This can be readily recognized both at the level of country-by-country data (wherein it becomes clear that societal bilingualism is *present* in almost all countries and is modal in a goodly number) and at the level of tracing the spread of particular lingua francas into regions and countries throughout the world. In this volume we have followed both courses in connection with English and have found them to reinforce each other.

ENGLISH AND INTERNATIONAL BILINGUALISM

In previous centuries, linga francas spread "without the benefit of clergy," so to speak; that is, without official record keeping, data collecting, and professional analysis. Not so today. Today the spread of English (and, to a lesser degree, also the spread of French, Russian, Chinese, and even Arabic) is increasingly accompanied by the search for "hard data" as to its *differential* and *relative* penetration into various countries and segments of society. The volumes being prepared by the International Center for Research on Bilingualism on *The Linguistic Composition of the Nations of the World* (see Kloss and McConnell 1975 for the volume on Central and Western South Asia) will be replete with detailed information on the worldwide spread of a relatively few languages of wider communication— English in particular—during the post–World War II years. My own *Bilingual Education: An International Sociological Perspective* (1976) not only documents the occurrence of bilingual education in some 110 countries (with approximately 5,000 secondary education units and 100,000 elementary education units being involved) but also reflects the magnitude of the co-occurrence of English-plus-a-local-language as the predominant pattern of bilingual education in the world today. This is expressly the message conveyed by Gage and Ohannessian (1974) in their very useful recent summary of ESOL enrollments throughout the world. Finally, the present volume assembles and systematizes thousands of fragmented bits of information (chaps. 1, 2, and 3) that add up to the fact that the governmental, quasi-governmental, and non-governmental use of English in non-English mother-tongue countries today is very great and still growing (particularly in the areas of higher education, technology, business, and mass media), but that the forces and factors leading to increased *knowledge* of English, *use* of English, and *liking* for English are, nevertheless, usually quite different and unrelated to each other (chap. 13).

A host of factors have come together to foster the spread of English as a lingua franca in this very day and age when the number of independent countries is larger than it has ever been before in recorded history. However, notwithstanding the proliferation of polities—each gravitating toward one or more indigenous official/national languages—the number of "international" people has also kept growing, as a result of growth in the number of foreign technological experts, more cosmopolitan local indigenous elites, business representatives of Anglophone commercial enterprises, and expatriate students and residents, as well as because of the vastly increased tide of tourism. In city after city throughout the world these internationals constitute a speech community (superimposed upon innumerable smaller networks that are often based on divergent mother tongues) precisely because English is their lingua franca—as revealed in shops, clubs, restaurants, theaters, and concerts and by parties, publications, and mass media preferences the world over, far above and beyond the requirements of industry, technology, and (inter)governmental relations from which the international use of English initially stems (chaps. 7 and 8). Indeed, probably never before has so much of the world been so accessible via a single language, as well as via one whose volume and value at a reasonable "standardized" level is sufficiently great and sufficiently monitored to obviate any danger of its fragmentation into a variety of new languages.

ENGLISH, INTRANATIONAL BILINGUALISM, AND LANGUAGE PLANNING

The spread of English as a lingua franca is not always viewed with unmitigated pleasure. *Inter*national bilingualism may be well and good in its place, but it can have rather unexpected and undesired *intra*national consequences as well—or so it is believed. Since, for most of mankind, nations are currently the largest units of effectively organized sociopolitical consciousness, it should come as no surprise that many nations have responded at a policy level to the spread of English, to define its desired as well as its undesired functions and domains (chaps. 1, 2, and 3). Indeed, both status planning and corpus planning throughout the world today are very commonly conducted in the context of centrally "controlled" bilingualism involving an imported language of wider communication. Furthermore, both types of language planning are conducted in the context of a double approach/ avoidance conflict, with most authorities realizing at least some of the undesirable consequences of either too much stress on English, on the one hand, or too much stress on the local/national language (or languages), on the other. It is precisely because of this dilemma that some kind of planned combination of both is pursued by most authorities, with the question normally being: Which language for which purpose and for which social networks? Certainly, this recurring "mangagement" of English is another factor which counteracts its vernacularization (and fragmentation) at the very time that it is being fostered for selected uses and users (chap. 3).

We already have several fine studies of such managed or controlled or planned intranational bilingualism. Glyn Lewis' volume on multilingualism in the Soviet Union (1972), Carol Scotton's on choosing a lingua franca in an African capital (1972), the various reports of the Survey of Language Teaching and Language Usage in East Africa (Ladefoged et al. 1968; Whiteley 1975; Bender et al. 1976), and Harrison et al.'s Jordanian study (1975), all constitute examples of research on the national level with respect to policy and practice vis-à-vis controlled bilingualism. In this volume we have added several new studies of this kind (e.g., chap. 4). The concern for safeguarding one or more regional/national languages while fostering a powerful lingua franca is everywhere patently clear, even if final consensus has not yet always been reached (or imposed) concerning the societal allocation of languages-to-functions that is to be pursued (e.g., chap. 12). The resolutions that are sought are increasingly nonsimplistic and nontotalistic. The functions of the lingua francas, vital though they may be, are recurringly restricted so as not to erode the status of local official/national languages for most speech networks in their most basic and integrative functions. Certainly no massive language shifts are being avowedly engineered with respect to non(im)migrant populations, although such may nevertheless occur where officially sponsored lingua francas spill over the rhetorical dikes and dams with which they are sometimes surrounded (e.g., in the USSR, China, Latin America). It is certainly clear that a functional allocation such as that currently envisaged by the new Philippine bilingual education policy (with Pilipino for ethnically more-encumbered fields such as national literature, history, and civics, and with English for ethnically less-encumbered subjects such as mathematics and the sciences) is an expression of the all too human quest for the best of all possible worlds. Obviously one (or more) regional/national language is highly valued and felt to be needed for purposes of national *integration* and for mass *mobilization* along the road to modernity. The fact that the decision has not as yet always been made as to *which* internal language(s) should discharge this necessary function merely adds poignancy to the issue that *such are greatly valued.*

As de-ethnicized "moderns," and as purportedly national and objective scholars, many specialists in "the world of English" cannot help expressing some impatience (if not outright opposition) in connection with the recurring need of an endless array of nationalities to protect their mother tongues. I have defended and studied this need many times over the past score of years (see particularly Fishman 1968, 1973, and 1976) and, therefore, merely want to point out here that a much needed area of further study with respect to planned intranational bilingualism is that which pertains to the sociology of language-and-ethnicity. Only recently our ignorance of ethnicity was at least matched by our disinterest in it. Today, however, an obvious imbalance exists between the two. We are obviously more interested in ethnicity today but we are almost as ignorant about it as heretofore. This ignorance is not really primarily an American disease, although it does have some rather peculiarly American provincialisms-masquerading-as-sophistication associated with it as secondary symptoms. The truth is that in 3,000 years of social theory—spanning the period from the ancient Hebrew, Greek, and Roman thinkers, through the Church fathers, to the modern sociological schools—no full-fledged sociological theory of ethnicity has been elaborated, either with respect to ethnicity as a recurring basis of human organization or with respect to its own developmental transformations at the same time that other societal development has been ongoing. We are desperately in need of an unhurried and unharried review of ethnicity as a societal parameter, and of why it has so consistently received such brief and such negative attention from the great social theoreticians (Nahirny and Fishman 1977). All of the social sciences would gain thereby—not least of all, the study of planned intranational bilingualism, with its recurring struggle to protect ethnicity and mold local integrative sentiments at the same time that the benefits of English or other lingua francas accrue in conjunction with well-defined uses and users (Fishman 1977).

THE BILINGUAL COMMUNITY AND ITS NETWORKS

Intranational bilingual policy is often a very serious and very conscious (even self-conscious) affair. Operating at a far less conscious level, we find the sociolinguistic heartland of societal bilingualism: the community and its social networks. It is in this connection that the lion's share of empirical and theoretical progress has been made, particularly during the last decade, bringing us to a stage of sophistication far beyond that available when Weinreich (1953) and Haugen (1956) were reviewing and conceptualizing the field nearly a quarter-century ago. The studies of bilingualism in the New York Puerto Rican barrio (Fishman, Cooper, and Ma 1971), of Guaraní-Spanish alternation in the Paraguayan countryside (Rubin 1968), of diglossia in Francophone Montreal (Lieberson 1970), and of diglossia as well as its dissolution in various regions of France (Tabouret-Keller 1972) have all provided ample evidence of the sociodynamics and sociostasis of bilingual communities and networks. We now have rather refined accounts (and rather powerful statistical treatments yielding multiple correlations in the nineties!) of the often unconscious but nonetheless normative societal allocations of language functions which define and predict communicative competence with respect to a bilingual repertoire. Certainly the relatively uniform and consistent individual interpretations and realizations of community norms— as well as of when and to what degree it is permitted to depart from the societal allocation of functions for metaphorical purposes—has, in recent years, been rather well documented.

Unfortunately, rather few studies have existed of English abroad at this level, i.e., of the "sometimes" use (but nevertheless of the patterned use) of English for either situational or metaphorical purposes between individuals who can and do more normally interact with each other in local languages. Our findings in this volume (particularly chaps. 5 and 6) provide data precisely along these lines, as do our studies of the cumulative impact of such usage on local nomenclatures, even when the latter are themselves closely monitored (chaps. 9 and 10). Further such studies are needed, perhaps in contrast with French, Russian, or other lingua francas, in order to solidify our current impressions of what it means (connotes, implies, suggests) to speak English "with one's own" in various non-English mother tongue settings.

THE BILINGUAL INDIVIDUAL IN SOCIETAL PERSPECTIVE

Since all societal research must ultimately be pursued via measures or observations with respect to individuals, the phenomenon of societal bilingualism cannot be endlessly pursued without attending to the phenomenon of individual bilingualism. What is more, there is good reason not to try to do so. Not only is our recognition of societal bilingualism a consolidation or compositing of individual data, but individual bilingualism itself must also be viewed as a reflection of societal norms. The fact that bilinguals who are essentially fully fluent in both languages (as measured by their facility and correctness overall) are still almost never *equally fluent in both languages about all possible topics* is invariably a reflection of the fact that the societal allocation of functions is normally imbalanced and in complementary distribution rather than redundant. If we find an unbalanced but fluent bilingual, we can be sure that this is a result of his or her "real life" social experiences. If we find a fluent *balanced* bilingual we can be equally sure that the balancing act is due to special schooling and studied practice (such as that obtained by professional translators), rather than to the variety of linguistically unbalanced social institutions (home, friendship, cliques, school, church, work-sphere, government) upon which normal (and, therefore, similarly unbalanced) societal bilingualism depends (Fishman, Cooper, and Ma 1971; and this vol., chap. 3).

Because of the fact that societal multilingualism is reflected in individual behavior, sociolinguistic researchers must carefully monitor the psycholinguistic research on bilingualism as well. Every new psycholinguistic theory or measure pertaining to individual bilingualism needs to be examined for its societal implications. All motive states, personality patterns, and cognitive styles that are related to individual bilingualism must be examined for possible translatability into societal dimensions. Psychological research on bilingualism continues to be a fertile field for stimulating the sociolinguistic imagination and for further advancing the state of refinement of theory, methods, and empirical data insofar as societal bilingualism is concerned. Our multiple correlations are already encouragingly high, but there is still sufficient unexplained variance in societally-based bilingual behavior, and a sufficient number of alternative (perhaps more manipulable) variables to be sought, to make all of us extremely attentive to the bilingualism research and theory that colleagues are hammering out in departments of psychology and/or in institutes of psychoeducational orientation. In this volume we have tried to do exactly this in Chapters 11, 12, and 13—and with very promising results indeed. The position of English abroad cannot be fathomed if this topic is treated as a sociological preserve.

THE INTELLECTUAL FUTURE OF WORK ON SOCIETAL MULTILINGUALISM

I have tried to imply that the intellectual future of work on societal bilingualism is rather good because the field is coherent, important, and challenging. It only remains to be said that the future also seems bright for a less thrilling but equally vital reason, namely, that many other basic issues in the sociology of language (and even in the language sciences more broadly) are best and most easily handled (studied, conceptualized) in societal bilingualism settings. The study of language planning is one such topic. The study of language and ethnicity is another. This is no little thing. In this volume, we have, for the first time, approached language maintenance—language shift and the study of language attitudes—two topics of extraordinary theoretical centrality to the language sciences—from the vantage point of English abroad (see chaps. 3, 11, and 13). Our findings are certainly such as to be encouraging for all serious students of these particular theoretical topics, as well as for students of English as an additional language per se.

THE PAROCHIALISM OF WORLD LANGUAGES

"Small" languages and weak polities in the modern world quickly realize that they require strong partners to protect and complement them. "Large" languages and strong polities lack this realization and, therefore, run a particular risk of parochialism, provincialism, and philistinism—a risk that is all the more terrifying because miscalculations derived therefrom can have truly calamitous results. The very factors that we have found to foster the international and intranational use and spread of English—economic relations with the Anglophone world, social status (whether reflected via income or education), and interaction with modern technology and mass-media—also tend to insulate most Anglophones from learning the languages and cultures of other peoples of the world, precisely because of

Anglophone predominance in these crucial respects. The parochialism engendered by such insulation is ultimately deleterious in technology, science, and industry per se and may well erode the very supriority that leads the world to English today, thereby leading it to turn to other superior languages tomorrow. Only if the massive worldwide efforts to learn more English are increasingly matched by Anglophone efforts to learn a good bit more of the languages (and values, traditions, purposes, etc.) of the rest of the world, might the current extraordinary position of English as an additional language be any more firmly established than were those of the previous lingua francas of world history. In an increasingly interacting world, the acceptance *of* English may be increasingly related to the acceptance of others by native speakers of English. Unfortunately, we know far more about how to help the world learn English (little though that may be), than we do about how to help native speakers of English learn about the world. Perhaps further progress in the sociology of English would be helpful here as well.

THE INTERNATIONAL SOCIOLINGUISTIC BALANCE OF POWER

Throughout the world we have found an amazing capacity to accommodate to English as well as a capacity of English to accommodate to the sharing of those functions to which it has attained. On the one hand, English is still spreading, in the sense that more and more people are learning and using it. Its utility for *local* social advancement and its impact on *local* languages are everywhere undeniable. Nevertheless, English is becoming more and more sociofunctionally controlled. More and more it is a co-language of government rather than the sole such, even in the non-English mother-tongue countries in which it enjoys one official status or another. More and more it is a co-language—rather than the sole language—of education in such countries. More and more it is a co-language even of commerce, industry, and finance—the domains in which Anglophonedom reigns supreme— since increasingly the lower and middle levels of such activity are conducted predominantly in protected vernaculars. Thus the continued growth of English in the non-English mother-tongue world is primarily in a complementary or partner- ship role. The prior Western language to play a major world role was French, but it remained primarily elitist and esthetic in functional orientation in a century in which the world turned increasingly toward massification and technological modernization—two processes in which Francophonie was hardly outstanding. Thus, while English spreads as a controlled partner, no other lingua franca is as obviously doing even that, and more local vernaculars are the recipients of local official recognition or protection than was ever the case before. The international sociolinguistic balance thus rests on three phenomena of seemingly moderate stability: the spread of English, the control of English, and the fostering of local/ regional/national vernaculars. Of these three, the one that is currently most dynamic is that relating to the vernaculars, many of which are straining for further recognition. Thus it becomes all the more crucial not only whether native speakers of English can hold on to their technological superiority but also whether they can really meet the "others" halfway in the crucial sociopsychological arena of mutual acceptance.

Joshua A. Fishman

Institute for Advanced Study
Princeton, New Jersey
June 1976

REFERENCES

Bender, M.L.; J.D. Bowen; R.L. Cooper; and C.A. Ferguson. 1976. *Language in Ethiopia*. London: Oxford University Press.

Fishman, Joshua A. 1977. Language and ethnicity. In *Language and Ethnicity in Intergroup Relations*, edited by H. Giles. New York: Academic Press.

———. 1976. *Bilingual Education: An International Sociological Perspective*. Rowley, Mass.: Newbury House.

———. 1973. *Language and Nationalism*. Rowley, Mass.: Newbury House.

———. 1968. *Language Loyalty in the United States*. The Hague: Mouton.

Fishman, Joshua A.; R.L. Cooper; and R. Ma. 1971. *Bilingualism in the Barrio*. Bloomington: Language Sciences.

Gage, William, and Sirarpi Ohannessian. 1974. ESOL enrollments throughout the world. *Linguistic Reporter* 16(No. 9):13–16.

Harrison, William; Clifford Prator; and G. Richard Tucker. 1975. *English Language Policy Survey of Jordan: A Case Study in Language Planning*. Arlington, Virginia: Center for Applied Linguistics.

Haugen, Einar. 1956. *Bilingualism in the Americas; Bibliography and Research Guide*. University (Alabama), American Dialect Society.

Kloss, Heinz, and G.D. McConnell. 1975. *The Linguistic Composition of the Nations of the World*. Vol. 1, *Western, Central and South Asia*. Quebec City: International Research Center on Bilingualism.

Ladefoged, Peter; Ruth Glick; and Clive Criper. 1968. *Language in Uganda*. Nairobi: Oxford University Press.

Lewis, E. Glyn. 1972. *Multilingualism in the Soviet Union*. The Hague: Mouton.

Lieberson, Stanley. 1970. *Language and Ethnic Relations in Canada*. New York: Wiley.

Nahirny, Vladimir, and Joshua A. Fishman. *The Role of Ethnicity in Social Theory*. Ms.

Rubin, Joan. 1968. *Choosing a Lingua Franca in An African Capital*. Edmonton and Champaign: Linguistic Research.

Tabouret-Keller, Andrée. 1972. A contribution to the sociological study of language maintenance and language shift. In *Advances in the Sociology of Language*, edited by J.A. Fishman. Vol. 2. The Hague: Mouton. Pp. 365–376.

Weinreich, Uriel. 1953. *Languages in Contact, Findings and Problems*. New York: Linguistic Circle of New York.

Whiteley, W.H. 1975. *Language in Kenya*. London: Oxford University Press.